MW00982317

RAY GUY: The Smallwood Years

Introduction by John C. Crosbie
Edited by Kathryn Welbourn

Published by

BOULDER
PUBLICATIONS

Library and Archives Canada Cataloguing in Publication

Guy, Ray
Ray Guy: The Smallwood Years / Ray Guy

ISBN 978-0-9783381-2-1

1. Newfoundland and Labrador--Politics and government--1949-1972.
2. Newfoundland and Labrador--History--1949-. I. Title.

FC2175.2.G89 2008   971.8'04   C2007-905572-9

 We acknowledge the financial support of the Government of
Newfoundland and Labrador through the Department of Tourism,
Culture and Recreation for our publishing program.

Published by Boulder Publications

www.boulderpublications.ca

11 Boulder Lane, Portugal Cove-St. Philip's, NL Canada   A1M 2K1

Cover image courtesy of Living Planet

Back cover photo by Sheilagh O'Leary

Cover and book layout: GraniteStudios.ca

Printed in Canada

Contents

RAY GUY: The Smallwood Years

Introduction by John C. Crosbie
Edited by Kathryn Welbourn

Introduction
by John C. Crosbie

    This book consists of the writings of Ray Guy between 1963 and 1970, principally during the latter years of the premiership of Joseph R. (Joey) Smallwood who was the first premier of Newfoundland following Confederation on April 1, 1949.

    Throughout the 1950s and 1960s Smallwood was at the peak of his awesome political powers in Newfoundland. He exerted complete control and authority over his cabinet, the Liberal party caucus, and Liberal party members generally in Newfoundland – to such an extent that he appointed all candidates who ran for the Liberals in all elections, federal and provincial, and even decided who should be officers of the Liberal party.

    From 1949 until 1971, the main opposition to the authoritarian one-man rule of the Smallwood administration came primarily from outside the ranks of elected politicians. The most effective opposition to Smallwood's authoritarianism was led by several journalists and newspaper columnists in the person, first, of Harold Horwood, who had been elected in 1949 as a Liberal MHA, but left politics after a falling-out with Smallwood. When Horwood retired from journalism and political column writing, his place was taken by Ray Guy who, in the early 1960s, became a political columnist for the St. John's *Evening Telegram*. Guy proved to be an acerbic, harsh, satirical and humorous critic of Joey – that tyrannical premier of the province and lord of all he surveyed.

    As I was actively involved through all 23 years of Mr. Smallwood's dominance of the Newfoundland political scene, I became a devoted reader of Guy's columns in *The Telegram*. Guy still writes for other publications, including *The Northeast Avalon Times* and *The Independent*.

    To write as he did during those years Guy had to have great courage, a strong independent streak, and a great gift for satirical writing – holding up folly to ridicule and lampooning individuals who have great power but come to misuse it and to get carried away by it.

    A critic is one who pronounces judgment, and Guy is such a critic. He was often censorious and fault-finding with respect to Smallwood, with his oratorical and political excesses, his bullying tactics, and the many abuses of power and patronage that eventually became predominant in his exercise of power through his control over the House of Assembly, his caucus, the cabinet, and the Government of Newfoundland and Labrador.

    To write this foreword, I read the 400 or so pages of Guy's commentary over the 1960s and 1970s. I remember vividly and can testify that the events and incidents he wrote about in fact occurred.

    A great deal of the unsparing criticism of his columns is certainly due to what he described on September 24, 1970, as "The bottomless gullibility of the Newfoundland people." In that particular column, Guy deals with many of the events that centered around the promises and activities concerning the many announcements made repeatedly of great new industries for Come By Chance in the 1950s and 1960s, including oil refineries, petro-chemical industries, third or fourth newsprint mills – or linerboard mills that were to be built in that area or elsewhere in the province. He describes some of these oft-repeated announcements and the numerous trips made by Smallwood and his ministers during those years, as well as the many and various "final" agreements announced. Guy writes of ministers who cropped up in "mad giddy whirls through international airports," as well as "the exhilarating life it must be for those jolly jet-setters popping back and forth across the Atlantic like a bunch of yo-yos," and that "within 10 years Come By Chance would employ at least 30,000 persons," etc., etc.

In column after column Guy gives Rabelaisian descriptions of the outrageous and astounding political pantomimes put on by Joey during his many years of power.

He describes such great events as the official opening of the Trans-Canada Highway during "Come Home Year" and many other extraordinary events that many people have long since forgotten about or, if they are under the age of 50, may well not remember or have experienced. His description of the celebration of great new industries for Come By Chance on April 28, 1966, is a classic, including celebrations for the $57 million pulp and paper mill which was to produce 600 tons of paper a day and use 330,000 cords of pulpwood a year. It would be adjacent to a $29 million petro-chemical plant that was to turn out 350,000 tons of a fertilizer ingredient from Venezuelan crude oil annually. There were many hundreds of such John Shaheen or John C. Doyle fantasies announced – projects that never materialized during those mauzy, mirage-like years.

This book is much more, however, than just Guy's biting criticisms of excesses of oratory and political circuses of those years. It contains such classics as Guy's Encyclopedia of Juvenile Outharbor Delights, including such delights as "Rounders," "Winter Games," "The Aviator Cap," "Tying Cans onto Sheep's Tails," "Footwear," "The Fine Art of Doing Nothing," and "Getting the Outharbour Juvenile Rigged for Winter Months".

Along with fun-filled descriptions, Guy had many reminiscences about the character of Aunt Cissy Roach, such as "The devil has come for me at last!", "Hello Mawmouth," "A horrified chill crept up my spine," and "A House is a House and a Pimp is a Pimp." He also passes on views and advice through Uncle Crabby.

In addition to deploring and revealing political excesses – particularly of government – and exposing them to ridicule, irony, and sarcasm, this book is full of delightful descriptions of such events as the Annual Caplin Supper and Fecundity Dance, one of the social events of the season held at Bung Hole Tickle. It is replete with humorous descriptions of every type of event, political or otherwise, including shifting the chip mill to be built by John C. Doyle from Goose Bay to Stephenville, Joey writing the Throne Speech, and Guy's own aversion to the policy of resettlement.

Guy also wrote about the 1969 leadership convention when Joey ran to succeed himself to prevent the party from "falling into the wrong hands," but was challenged by other leadership contenders such as Alex Hickman and myself – I was said to be "A political sex symbol with sideburns." Guy's suggested theme song for me, sung to the tune of "Twinkle, Twinkle, Little Star," was:

> Dimple, Dimple, Happy John,
> You can really turn 'em on.
> With your wavy hair and dimple,
> You can charm both sash and wimple.

Included in this funny but well-aimed collection of wit and wisdom are Guy's definite views on public policy; his aversion to the denominational education system, the relationship between Farley Mowatt and Harold Horwood, the events surrounding the tragic story of the trapping of the whale "Moby Joe" at Burgeo, his aversion to the Smallwood government's *Newfoundland Bulletin* (which the Smallwood administration sent out free to every Newfoundland household), the suggestion made years ago by Jay Parker on the severe population reduction needed if Newfoundland was to become viable, events in St. Pierre causing the Gardes Mobiles to be sent there from France, the government's 386 great new industries, all you wanted to know about Newfoundland's highway spending at election time, and many other diverting topics.

Anyone interested seriously in our political history since 1949, or events in Newfoundland since 1949, described as they were seen by a fearless, independent, and talented writer would be well advised to read this book and enjoy themselves by dipping into it from time to time to get the flavor of how life was in Newfoundland during the Smallwood era.

To read this compendium of Ray Guy's pungent, courageous, biting, hilarious articles – published during a time when too much power was concentrated in the hands of one man, with its inevitable corrupting effect – is to be reminded once again that, as Lord Acton wrote accurately in 1887, "Power tends to corrupt; absolute power corrupts absolutely." Or in the words of poet Shelley: "Power, like a desolating pestilence, pollutes whate'er it touches." Or to remind ourselves of what Edmund Burke wrote "Power gradually extirpates from the mind every humane and gentle virtue."

We were lucky in our province to have an observer and writer of discernment and talent and with such a wicked sense of humour as Ray Guy. Boulder Publications is to be congratulated for gathering together and reprinting in a more permanent form. In particular, I congratulate Ray Guy for his fine writing and his independent spirit, for which our province owes him a great deal.

This is a must-read if we are to understand politics and the pitfalls of untrammeled power.

Foreword
by Ray Guy

Many years ago when my first book of newspaper columns was published I was a trifle disappointed with the result. I had thought the editor would have made a heavier selection of what I considered my more serious stuff. Instead the emphasis was on what I called Outharbor Juvenile Delights … chucking rocks at seabirds ("leaving no tern unstoned") or catching conners and sculpins.

His explanation was a good one. In short, that there's nothing more dead than yesterday's news … or yesterday's newspaper. My comment on the news of even a few years back would have required a heavy addition of footnotes and explanations.

Now, here's a collection of newspaper columns and articles I did 40 or more years ago. What will a large proportion of readers make of that? I hope those who were around at the time will say, "Yes, I was there, too. This really happened." But what of the growing majority?

For example: There's a piece in this book titled "This is a column." Younger readers might well ask how far down the vodka bottle I was at the time or how infused with the whacky baccy. What the hell, they might well ask, was the point of this?

The explanation to that one alone is long and convoluted. It is a take-off on, a satire of, indeed, a slap-up-the-side-of-the-head to the late writer, Harold Horwood.

Harold was many things in his time. He was a buddy of Joey Smallwood's in the fight for Confederation. When victory came, he fully expected to be made Commissar for Labrador … that didn't happen so Harold went off in a fit of pique and for years wrote an anti-Joey column in *The Evening Telegram.*

He became a czar, instead, of "the counter-culture," a guru to the local flower children, the Sage of Beachy Cove, the psychedelic king of Newfoundland. He took to Nature and to Nature's Ways and wrote about foxes and birdies and stuff for *The Telegram.*

Then once when the regular editorial writer, Mike Harrington, went on holidays Harold replaced him for the duration. His first editorial was a gob-slapper to the rest of us in the newsroom. It was titled, in child's crayon, "This Is An Editorial."

More than that, we saw signs among the psychedelic entrails that Horwood may be once again sucking up to his former pal, Smallwood, for some sort of government job.

So you can see how, after four or more decades, a book like this could sink under its own footnotes. Yet once again I trust the judgment of those excellent editors. It was written mostly in the 1960s; so to those who are still puzzled I can only say: "Ask your parents … or your grandparents!"

Some broader sketch of the times may be possible. There's no escaping Joey Smallwood. By then, he'd been rock-solid King of the Rock for over a decade with no more than three or four huddled members in Opposition and, despite little pin-pricks from some sections of the press, floated higher than ever on a cloud of triumphalism.

Smallwood first dazed and dazzled the voters with novelties like the $8.50-per-month "baby bonus" and the old age pension. Before those marvelous innovations started to wear thin, there came roads and electricity … a piece of road for one election, pavement to win the next and a string of power poles to secure another.

Smallwood was caught up on what one editorial writer called "a tide of rising expectations." Here's where his phrase "Great New Industries" cut in. At first they were merely bizarre, like the proposed orange juice factory, the herd of 20 buffalo on Brunette Island, or the 1,000 head of cattle imported to the Burin Peninsula … heralded by the immortal words: "The cowboy looms larger in Newfoundland's future than the fisherman!"

You really had to be there. But time passed and rising expectations called for ever stronger meat. Oil refineries that went bust ($500 million bust), Churchill Falls which still follows us toward the grave and an almost malignant neglect and disdain for the fishery.

"But at least he tried!" say some of Smallwood's apologists to this day. What did he try, must be our reply. He tried with every megalomaniacal fiber of his being to hold on to power is my own answer.

They were interesting times, but frustrating, too. Especially for a journalist. All public records were either destroyed or under lock and key. Somewhere early on I decided that the only course was to, perhaps, giggle the bastards to death.

That, I soon found, was slow and steady work … like the tomcat eating the grindstone. In the end Joey and the Boys collapsed under their own weight and because, for the first time in Smallwood's more-than-20-year reign, Frank Moores appeared with some actual knowledge of political organization.

Looking back from 40 years on I'm astonished by what riotous, incredible, disastrous, pell-mell, interesting times those were. False modesty to one side, I'm also amazed at how savage I was … and how funny.

Two lieutenant governors, at least one chief justice, and other current mucky mucks all benefited from my gentle chastisements of so long ago. But what of some lesser fry? I worried for about five seconds that my sucker punches of 40 years past should come back to bite them in peaceful retirement now. Was this fair?

They said and did it then. I wrote about it then. Let it stand now.

Our roads: such fun!

August 22, 1963 *Roads, Rails and Water*

Many Newfoundlanders, I daresay, are happy to hear the Trans-Canada Highway is in the home stretch.

News that the longest gap between Whitbourne and Port Blandford is now under construction came this week.

But I can't rejoice wholeheartedly. My feelings, like a meal eaten prior to departure over the old road, are mixed.

True, the TCH is fast and efficient, but when it is finally completed much will be lost.

Take the present road between Whitbourne and Arnold's Cove, for example; it's Le Mans, the Gran Turisimo and Barter's Hill rolled into one; a supreme test of men and metal; an excursion worthy of a rugged isle that breeds lady bullfighters.

Note the subtle yet definite change that comes over drivers at the end of the pavement in Whitbourne. From out of the east they come in a cloud of dust, a screech of brakes and a hearty cry of (censored). Eyes narrow, palms perspire and even the little old lady in the Mini Minor thinks nothing of taking a Grand Bank taxi on a turn.

And apart from Jayne Mansfield, this piece of road has the most dangerous curves in the world. These are due to the unique way the route was laid out. According to popular belief, a minor highways official stood back five paces and flung a fistful of boiled spaghetti at a wall map.

The spectacular results could not have been duplicated by years of intensive survey.

Consider Smith's Corner in Norman's Cove. Here, through a modern miracle of engineering, your car describes a perfect U around three sides of a local dwelling. At this particular point, you can also describe most of the other letters of the alphabet. It all depends on how hard the oncoming car hits you.

But it isn't all one mad, thrilling, headlong rush at 25 and 30 miles an hour.

Signs, wisely placed at intervals along the way, check the breakneck dash of traffic, allowing the driver to see more of the communities through which he passes.

He comes to know the people intimately, passing as he does mere feet from their windows. Picturesque glimpses of people shaving, babies being bathed and the whole family sitting down to morning oatmeal pass in review before his windshield.

Now that the TCH is soon to become a reality, it will not be necessary for drivers to take a special pledge patterned after the Hippocratic oath. Designed to protect the privacy of roadside residents, the proposed pledge was along the lines of: "And whatsoever community I shall enter ..."

On the old road even potholes can be fun. They enliven the travel-weary by giving rise to such witticisms as "Prepare to submerge," "Down periscope," "Damn the torpedoes!" etc.

However, some of the larger ones are a bit tricky and care must be taken to allow water pressure to equalize inside the car before opening doors and kicking up toward the surface.

Drivers will also miss the extra bonus of freshly killed livestock along the route. There were accepted rules. For instance, nothing heavier than a Volkswagen could be used on fowl or spring lambs, while cars of Buick caliber were good for anything up to a fair-sized heifer.

But all that will soon be behind us now. The thrills, suspense and adventure will soon be gone as cars glide monotonously over smooth, broad pavement.

Most Newfoundlanders will, after second thoughts, be saddened to see a part of our great heritage disappearing and look reproachfully at the indecent haste with which the TCH is being forged ahead.

Mr. Pearson may have good intentions in trying to finish the drive by '65, but we must reflect sadly that he sometimes just doesn't understand us.

By jove, it's a peasant!

September 4, 1963   *Culture and History*

Newfoundland is world-famous as a hunters' paradise and the opening of each season brings a host of visiting sportsmen to our shores.

Among our visitors this year is Sir Roger Fitzsimmons Fotherington-Fyfe, Knight of the Bath, Order of the Garter, Bunny Club key holder and international sport.

Sir Roger arrived here yesterday aboard his new motor yacht, the *Queen Mary II.*

An imposing five-foot-five, 230 pounds, Sir Roger is a broadly known figure on the international hunting scene. He has stalked grouse with Sir Harold, deer with Sir Winston, tiger with the Ali Khan and blondes with ex-King Farouk.

His peaceful country retreat at Oyle-upon-Sea is a haven for the devotees of the chase from many parts of the world.

We interviewed Sir Roger about his trip to Newfoundland.

"Deuced glad to be back again in the colonies," said Sir Roger. "Bracing change of climate from what we've been having in the Indies, don't y'know."

"East or West, Sir Roger?" we asked.

"Definitely East, old chap. Borneo, in point of fact. Hunted the lesser-maned pigmy kinkajou. Formidable adversary. Area east of Ketapang just south of Sukadana simply teeming with 'em, don't y'know."

"Yes, of course. Did you have any extraordinary experiences in Borneo, Sir Roger?"

"Matter of fact, yes, old chap. Head porter got into a bit of a stew with the natives. Cannibals, y'know. Dashed jolly trip, though. Have one of the blighters stuffed and hung in the Great Hall at Oyle-upon-Sea. Smashing specimen."

"One of the natives, Sir Roger?"

"Rather not. Lesser-maned pigmy kinkajou. Bit sticky getting a stuffed native through customs, don't y'know."

"Certainly," we agreed. "Now what of plans for your caribou hunt in Newfoundland this season? Is this your first visit here, sir?"

"No. Came here for a spot of shooting in '48 immediately before we annexed you to our mainland colonies. Splendid trip. Ran a bit afoul of the authorities, though."

"Really? Would you care to tell us about it, Sir Roger?"

"Egad, yes. Frightfully embarrassing. Hunting ptarmigan at the time. Took a toddy of scotch that morning to steady the trigger finger, don't y'know.

"Then out on the moors. Delightful day, plenty of covies. Bagged several brace in the forenoon. Had another nip and about to take luncheon.

"Suddenly spied what appeared to be a full-grown American elk messing about in the brush. There I was. Alone with nothing but a fowling piece.

"Stuck in m'monocle and near as I could judge the blighter was about to charge. Nothing to do but up gun and have at him. Direct hit. Appeared to be stunned momentarily but then let out a fearful roar and resumed charge, swinging galvanized pail of some sort.

"Turned out to be one of the local peasants gathering lingonberries. Rather careless of me. But still in danger. She weighed a good 16 stone, don't y'know, and extremely aroused.

"No time to reload and get another shot. I say, chaps, what a spot. Every second brought her closer. Nothing for it but to retreat. Took another nip, recorked flask and proceeded toward camp at top speed.

"By Gad, next thing I remember, there I was. Encrouched at camp, pail wrapped around m'head and the Viscountess Keeler endeavoring to restore m'circulation. A frightfully keen sport, the Viscountess.

"And by jove, had to spend the rest of the trip at camp playing bridge and that sort of thing, don't y'know."

We expressed our sympathies and wished Sir Roger every success on his present expedition to our island. ▪

How to keep 'em ... down on the still!

September 20, 1963

Resettlement and Rural Life

The mail this week brought a letter from an outport mother with problems of a personal nature. Although advice in such matters is not in my line I was so touched by her plight I could not help but repay as best I can. Here is her letter:

Dear sir,

I am writing about my boy James who will 18 next Micklemus and is got out of hand. He is got a notion to go to forein lands and talks about nothing but some place call Warbush in Labrador. Now I dont want my boy beatin about Warbush or any other bush but there is no sense talkin to him.

James is smart I know. He is already threw his Dick and Jane book and is started to make fun of my English which is perfeck as you can see. My English I lern at my poor mothers hardworkin knee. (She scrubbed, sir, for Merchant Towlow and Parson Phelps.)

Lately he is also been dwellin too much on passages in the Good Book and Eatons catalogue which was not ment for younger eyes. I chastize and clout him whenever I feels up to it but since he got his growth it dont seem to have much affeck.

His pore father crossed over in 45 when his liver give out. He was in Sin Johns shortly after our marriage and had our likeness taken which hangs in the parlor to this day.

Poor John was allways a hard worker and we was never stuck for a dollar. But James is lost interes in the fambly business and haint gone near the still in a twelve-month.

They is no reesin for James to leave home. He can make a decent livin if he took a interes in our moon shine concern or even if he fished a bit or took his orse and slide in the woods a bit wintertime.

But no. He wants a new suit, he wants a spring matres and he said if they was roads in these parts hed be getting a motor car.

Lord help us, sir, what kind of talk is that. I wants to know, sir, what the government is doin to stop this sort of thing. We cant have people runnin off to other countries or they wont be no one lef to carry on. We been carryin on here in *** since they killed off the last of the heathens in my pore granfathers day. I dont expeck they is any one been carryin on longerm our fambly has.

This country is gone mad sir. Hit aint never been the same since the old queen died.

Please give me yore thouts on this as I am seriesly thinkin of contacking the athorities and havin James put in charge.

Yores truely,

A Trubbled Mother

Dear Troubled Mother,

First let me say there are many mothers throughout the island with a problem similar to yours. Indeed, it is a problem which concerns the country as a whole. Daily, our youth is being lured away from family fire-sides with problems of such trivialities as money, clothes and cars.

The seeds of dissatisfaction are being sown in the form of blatant propaganda which leads the young and innocent to believe they can make a better living elsewhere.

A healthy, active, useful life in the fishing boat with plenty of fresh air and the substantial sum of $900 or even $1,000 a year in gross earnings is now disparaged by some so-called "angry young men" of today.

It is little wonder, madam, that many people like yourself sometimes wonder if "the whole country has gone mad" and long for the sensible, sane and tranquil days of our late and beloved Victoria.

With regards to your boy James it would seem that the main thing is to discourage him as much as possible from emigrating and open his eyes to the marvelous opportunities available to him in his own community.

Education, while it does have its drawbacks, is important. Every growing lad in Newfoundland should at least have enough education to enable him to fill out an unemployment insurance form. See that your James learns how to read and write well enough to handle the most complicated welfare application and be able to write his MHA whenever the occasion warrants.

As to your family business I suggest you consider some alternative occupation for James since the government has largely taken over control in this field.

The manufacture of toy dories and fancy beadwork for the tourist trade looks hopeful and you might try to get him established early in this booming industry.

Chastise him by all means but not, of course, at the expense of your own health. Electric cattle prods, available at small cost, have been tested extensively in the southern US and have proven effective in the matter of discipline with little or no wear and tear on the user.

Remove all offending sections from mail-order catalogues as they enter your household and confine his Biblical studies for the present to the New Testament.

Approach community leaders with the proposition that road projects can only lead to undesirable outside influences on youths such as your James and lay your community wide open to the blight of motor cars, soft drinks and baker's bread.

Have patience, Troubled Mother, and with determination you should be able to see your offspring James settle permanently and contentedly on the soil of his forefathers and, as your family has done for generations, Carry On! 🆁🅶

Boon or boom?

October 18, 1963   *Great New Industries*

Newfoundland's inferiority complex was exploded forever this week with the news that nuclear weapons would be stored on our soil.

No longer is Newfie not worth a bomb, but like New York, London and Tokyo now stands an excellent chance of absorbing at least a couple of megatons should World War III shape up as advertised.

The carping voices of dissension seem to have been at a minimum, and for the most part we are prepared to advance confidently into the nuclear future, heads held high, chests out, and survival kits at the ready.

None of this Bertie Russell nonsense about banning the bomb or nuclear disarmament, but an enlightened and realistic attitude which absolutely precludes trampling US consulate petunias or sticking pins into Lester Pearson dolls.

As has been pointed out by older and wiser men, this is our heaven-sent opportunity to repay our country (Canada) and our great neighbor (the US of A) for past kindnesses.

What finer gesture could have been thought of short of sending each of the Kennedys a genuine Gold Sail football or dispatching a year's supply of seal flippers to Rideau Hall?

One outport mother with whom I conversed immediately following the announcement was of a similar opinion.

"Two years ago," she said, "the Americans took our little girl to hospital in a helicopter after she was burned when our house caught fire.

"Letting them store those new thingamagigs here, whatever they are, is the least we can do. I'm sure those new, clear things will help them save other children like they sove our little maid."

Such trusting naiveté is both typical and touching, and of course there is no need to dispel or disillusion it with bothersome facts. What we must do is forge ahead with confidence, determined, as always, to make the most of a windfall from whatever source.

The anniversary of this momentous event will no doubt be cause for yearly celebration, which we could mark in the traditional Newfoundland manner with large bonfires.

It will also be a boon to the tourist industry and steps should be taken to exploit this angle fully. The province may now be billed in promotion literature as one of the hottest spots in Canada.

Attractive mushroom cloud lapel buttons could be distributed at Port aux Basques and Gander to put visitors in the picture at once, and radiation detection kits could be made available at these centers at reasonable rental costs.

(Actually, radiation detectors serve no useful purpose in this situation, but would enhance the "devil-may-care" atmosphere of a Newfoundland holiday heretofore supplied mainly by the unfinished Trans-Canada Highway.)

Appropriate additions will have to be made to restaurant menus. How about such specialties as Hiroshima Hamburgers and Nagasaki Hot Dogs for a start? The possibilities are limitless.

On the other hand, there is a slight possibility that peace may break out and nuclear weapons banned. This gruesome realization has caused cold shivers from Placentia East to Labrador South, but must be faced up to.

In such an eventuality, steps must be taken to hang on to "our" warheads at all costs, since a large part of the economy would depend on them. By 1965, if they're still around, they could perhaps be claimed as an historical heritage like Signal Hill, L'Anse aux Meadows and Beothuk skeletons.

In the meantime, let us look on the bright side. The arrival of nuclear weapons will probably cause a great upsurge in the building trades with fallout shelters being in prime demand, thus putting bread in the mouths of the province's needy.

Of course, with a smidgen more fallout some of the future needy may have two mouths each, thus tempering the new source of prosperity, but that is at least one generation into the future and need not bother us at this stage. 🆁🅶

Cabot made a boo-boo

November 8, 1963   *Culture and History*

It is a distressing fact that many Newfoundlanders know so little about the island's colorful past … 1497 and all that.

Actually, history CAN be fun if you take a few minutes to read up on the subject. I did and found the whole business tremendously enlightening.

You may be as disappointed, as I was, to learn that Newfoundland was not discovered by a Newfoundlander. It was discovered, like everything else, by a Russian … Eric the Red in 1000 A.D. Eric the Red and Lief the Lucky ran afoul of the law back in Greenland when they were squealed on by Sven the Stoolie.

They took it on the lam in Lief's paddle-powered yacht and sought political asylum here. Finding nothing but flat stones they called it the Land of the Flat Stones and naturally enough established headquarters at Curling from which we get the name of the game.

The light-headed Vikings (they also called it Vineland the Good) fraternized with the natives, which produced light-headed Beothuks among the best known of whom are Shawnandithit, Anita Ekberg and Mary March, all ravishing blondes.

Some say John Cabot discovered the island in 1497 but most historians hold it was the Vikings in 1000 mainly because it's a nice round number.

Cabot made a boo-boo. He thought it was Japan and called it O Happy Sight, which means Bonavista in Japanese. His roly-poly son, Sebastian, was an ambitious lad and later emigrated to the States to become a famous star of stage, screen and television.

St. John's was a prosperous port when New York City was a swamp. After what bog land reclamation did for New York the same thing is now being tried here on an experimental basis.

Sir Humphrey Gilbert, after whom the building is named, was also an important figure in Newfoundland history. He came here in 1560 or something and claimed the whole island for Queen Elizabeth I.

He called his ship the *Golden Hind* because she always came in last in the Long Island to Bermuda 40-meter races. Sir Humphrey was lost on his way back to England. He took it well: "Cheer up my lads," he said. "Lloyd's coverage is as good by sea as by land."

The French, too, played an important part. Early on in the 1600s they established a navel base at Argentia, which is in Placentia Bay. They had lots of time on their hands and their favorite sport was burning St. John's.

"Have you any plans for ze Labor Day weekend, Mon Capitaine?"

"I was just theenking of that, Pierre. Zut alors! I have eet!! Let's get the boys togethaire and burn St. Jean."

The French introduced Newfoundlanders to Canadians and started a long relationship between the two, which has continued to this day, when a chap named D'Iberville took a bunch of Canadian Indians on a guided scalping tour of the Avalon.

John Guy (not to be confused with the ferry of the same name) tried to establish a colony at Cupids but ran into trouble with the pirates, reports of which have been exaggerated. Actually, he was quite fond of Captain Morgan and Coke, which is what really led to his downfall.

Around 1850, give or take a few decades, Newfoundland's first prime minister began a curious custom among the island's political leaders by donating his head to the Confederation Building. These may be seen today gracing the main lobby like gilded baby shoes.

***

Cormack made his famous trip across the island about this time. He set out on foot equipped with only a compass, his faithful dog, Rover, and a collection of Harold Horwood columns and walked clear across the island.

***

The Second World War was fun while it lasted. American troops married 25,000 Newfoundland girls and took them back home. They found the girls attractive because of their deep-south accents, those from Burin and the Southern Shore being most popular.

Then came the great Civil War in which Union and anti-Confederate troops fought a great battle to decide whether or not customs duty on mail order goods should perish from the earth.

The Union won and welfare payments of the people, for the people and by the people were firmly established for all time. ▩

They went thataway? Newsmen find trail too late

August 12, 1964   *Great New Industries*

"Come along boys and listen to my tale,
I'll tell you of our troubles on the Marystown trail;
Come a ti yi yippee yippee ay."

It's a mighty long road from Kisbey to Goobies but Newfoundlanders have come to know almost every mile of the way.

A few weeks ago we proudly read reports of "our" 900 head of Hereford heifers being loaded on CNR cars at Kisbey, Saskatchewan, for the eastward journey.

Destined for the Flying-L Ranch near Marystown, on the Burin Peninsula, they would multiply and wax fat on the lush marsh grasses, soon providing the province with plenty of progeny for rump roasts and rodeos.

We watched with interest as they were watered at the Lakehead, transferred in Toronto, pastured at Moncton and shipped from Sydney.

Rarely has the medium of the press been so lauded for a job well done, and yesterday the story was pursued to its logical climax when a representative of *The Evening Telegram* and of Canadian Press (staff correspondent in Newfoundland, Dave Butler) traveled to Goobies to witness the actual unloading.

From our man in Goobies comes this account of the historic event:

The small rail-side community of Goobies was agog today with the long-awaited arrival of 157 head of cattle from Saskatchewan, the first of five such consignments which will be unloaded here at regular intervals during the next week.

The excitement was most evident in the restaurant where we took lunch prior to touring the stockyards.

Two cowboys attached to the Flying-L Ranch were the center of attraction as they entered the establishment in full costume – large hats, calfskin vests and cowboy boots.

Canadian Press, assuming the two cattlemen had arrived via horse and sensing an eye-catching picture, rushed outside with cocked camera but found they had driven up in a half-ton pickup.

Your correspondent noted that our two friends from the West displayed, by their selection of jukebox tunes, a strong and understandable affinity for Western music, leaning toward Johnny Cash and Kitty Wells.

Anxious to get our first glimpse of the herd, we did not dally over lunch but left the restaurant for the railroad station, while, appropriately enough, Miss Wells yodeled at the top of her lungs.

Here, we were disappointed to learn from CNR agent Dominic Lynch that the animals had arrived the night before and were already being driven down the Burin Highway.

This route branches off from the Trans-Canada Highway at Goobies and leads eventually to Marystown, Burin, Grand Bank and Fortune. On the way it passes through Swift Current, about 18 miles from Goobies.

It was near Swift Current, we were informed, that the first shipment would be pastured until the entire consignment of 800 head arrived, and the drive to Marystown would begin.

Eagerly we pressed toward Swift Current, surveying the roadside and surrounding hills for likely looking pasture sites, but as we drew nearer the community and the lowing herd still not sighted, we had a vague feeling something was not right.

Canadian Press was the first to observe that the road was not in a condition which would indicate that 157 cows had not long passed.

However, we reasoned that heavy rain showers that morning may have washed out any sign, and continued on to Swift Current where we inquired of a local resident.

He replied to the effect that he had not seen any cattle in the area lately "except Crocker's bullock halfway up Mile Hill."

Heading back toward Goobies, we were determined to leave no stone unturned to solve the mystery of the vanished herd.

"Ah figger they been rustled by a bunch of Beothics some forgot to wipe out," volunteered Canadian Press, himself a westerner hailing from New Brunswick.

This time we explored carefully the branch roads leading to the communities of Garden Cove and North Harbour, without success.

Twice, your correspondent scouting ahead on foot, came upon a promising spoor but which when followed to its conclusion led only to flocks of grazing sheep.

Several theories were advanced, one of them being that some terrifying phenomena such as a sudden and severe thunderstorm or an approaching Burin Peninsula taxi had caused a stampede, in which case the entire herd would by now be approaching Baie d'Espoir.

Another conjecture, brought on by hours of driving up and down branch roads, plunging off the trail into the sagebrush, lack of food, hordes of mosquitos, loss of blood, was that there never had been any cattle, that both correspondents had been under a delusion and suffering from hallucinations from the start.

Despondent, we headed east, even a coincidental chorus of "The Cowboy's Last Ride" on the car radio failed to lift our spirits.

It was sheer luck that one final inquiry of some highway workers near Goobies allows readers across the province and, indeed, the nation, to share the excitement of glimpsing that famous group of animals in its new environment for the first time.

Our informants told us the herd had indeed left Goobies, but instead of being driven down the Burin Highway toward Swift Current they were being pastured on bogland off the Trans-Canada about a mile west.

The spot being reached and the sun slowly sinking behind the purple hills, we could have imagined ourselves in the Old West if the Old West had had bakeapple bogs.

It was a stirring moment even though only three of the 157 head were to be seen. The rest had disappeared over the horizon some 10 miles distant, whether by design or accident it could not be learned.

One of those remaining was floundering in bog up to its T-bones a short distance from the road, obviously too weak to escape unassisted.

The concerted efforts by both Canadian Press, several passersby and your correspondent failed to free the unfortunate beast, but we were assured the cowhands back at Goobies would be notified of its plight.

The second animal was in more fortunate circumstance, having just produced a wobbly-legged offspring which seemed amazed at finding itself so far from Kisbey.

Later, as we headed back east, we observed that it had indeed been a momentous occasion.

Canadian Press concurred but was heard to lament the fact that Newfoundland's potential beef supply should have such big, brown eyes. ◼

Dildo Run: $3 million causeway opened

August 20, 1964   *Roads, Rails and Water*

Boyd's Cove, N.D.B. – For two miles the cars parked bumper to bumper, light aircraft bobbed on the rippling surface of Notre Dame Bay, motor boats loaded to the gunwales with excited passengers hove to in Dildo Run, and more than 3,000 people watched under sunny skies as Premier J.R. Smallwood snipped a symbolic white ribbon.

New World Island was an island no more, and for its 5,000 residents centuries of comparative isolation had come to an end.

Such official duties are nothing new to Premier Smallwood ("I'm sick of cutting ribbons," he joked later), but the ceremonies yesterday marking the formal opening of the new $3 million causeway to New World Island were a bit above the ordinary.

This was indicated by the fact that the largest number of House of Assembly Members ever to meet outside St. John's were in attendance: 14 of them, including seven cabinet ministers.

A 40-car cavalcade preceded by an RCMP escort arrived at the mainland end of the causeway, near Boyd's Cove, at 2:30 p.m., then traveled along the new route to the bridge and causeway across Dildo Run, said to be the greatest engineering feat ever undertaken in Newfoundland.

A crowd, estimated at more than 3,000, waited on the flag-bedecked bridge as the premier and party assembled on a platform.

Premier J.R. Smallwood; Attorney General L.R. Curtis; Finance Minister E.S. Spencer; Municipal Affairs Minister B.J. Abbott; Public Works Minister J.R. Chalker; Highways Minister Dr. F.W. Rowe; Speaker George Clarke, MHA Carbonear; Gerald Hill, MHA Labrador South; William Smallwood, MHA Green Bay; Harold Starkes, MHA Lewisporte; Ross Barbour, MHA Bonavista South; Eric Dawe, MHA Port de Grave; Steve Neary, MHA Bell Island; and Val Earle, MHA Fortune.

Transport Minister J.W. Pickersgill (L-Bonavista-Twillingate) flew down from Ottawa especially for the occasion and rejoiced that with the exception of Fogo Island he was now able to cover all of his district by car.

Federal MP Charles Granger (L-Grand Falls-White Bay-Labrador) also attended.

The mayors of surrounding towns, representatives of the clergy and officials of contracting and construction firms were among those who rounded out the impressive gathering.

The main speaker was Premier Smallwood, whose hour-long address was an elaboration of the theme that "Newfoundland is the one place in the world where miracles still happen."

He listed these "modern miracles," all of which have occurred within the past 15 years, reaching from the wilderness of Labrador even unto the wave-lashed shores of Baie d'Espoir.

The premier stressed that unless these developments and improvements are continued, the youth of the province will seek greener fields: "Fish have tails and can swim away; our young people will swim away too if we don't give them good reason to stay."

Better communications, an end to isolation, easy travel, modern conveniences, such as electricity, must be carried throughout the province if Newfoundland is to continue as such, he said.

Mr. Smallwood made two announcements in this connection; he renewed his government's promise to have the Trans-Canada Highway across Newfoundland completed by 1965, and he revealed that hydro electricity from the Baie d'Espoir construction will sell for the surprisingly low cost of one cent per kilowatt hour.

Following his address the premier announced that the 20-mile highway from Boyd's Cove to the ferry terminal on New World Island would henceforth be known as "The Road to the Isles." (The phrase was first used in this connection by former *Telegram* columnist Don Morris in a special article on the causeway project last summer.)

Signs along the highway from Lewisporte to Boyd's Cove all bear the new name of the island-hopping road.

The bridge over Dildo Run, the most strategic span in the island link, has been named the Curtis Causeway after Attorney General L.R. Curtis, in whose district it is located.

Premier Smallwood said the name would not only honor Mr. Curtis, who has served as Attorney General for a longer term than anyone else in Newfoundland's history, but would also commemorate Mr. Curtis's father who served for many years as a Wesleyan minister in Twillingate.

He then called on all the children present to assist him in the ribbon cutting, and as an old sealing gun boomed out from one of the motor boats moored alongside the bridge, the premier, swamped in a sea of children, declared the Road to the Isles and the Curtis Causeway officially open.

The cavalcade then proceeded across New World Island to the ferry terminal and Twillingate.

The new road is narrow and winding over haystack-shaped hills and through tall stands of black spruce and aspen, through the small communities of Summerford, Carter's Cove, Virgin Arm, Hillgrade, and connects with most of the other villages on the island.

New service stations and gas pumps are going up, many houses already have a car parked in front of them, but the blight of the mainland, the automobile graveyard, has not appeared.

The settlements still have the tranquil look of a small island, which will soon give way to a faster, four-wheeled tempo.

A number of cars have been operated on the island for years, but the crossing to the mainland was possible only across sea ice in winter and was often dangerous. The latest such fatality occurred last winter when a car broke through the ice and its driver drowned.

Small groups of residents greeted the official party along the way as it passed under lines of flags and evergreen arches.

Some of the children waved hand-lettered signs: "Thank you Mr. Smallwood for all you have done for us" and "New World Island liberated by the Liberals."

At the ferry dock the party boarded the ferry *Ambrose Shea* for the ten-minute trip across to Twillingate Island, where another brief ceremony was held inaugurating the new ferry service.

Here, and at a dinner concluding the day's activities in the Twillingate High School, both Premier Smallwood and Mr. Curtis emphasized that they considered the ferry service far from satisfactory.

Mr. Curtis asked the people of Twillingate Island to be patient while the new ferry service went through what he termed "a period of experimentation."

He said that many complaints had been received regarding the ferry service since it had been put into effect, but pointed out that "considerably more money is to be spent before we are satisfied with the ferry and the road."

"If the *Ambrose Shea* can't handle the traffic, then a second boat will be put on the run," said the Attorney General, reiterating a promise made earlier in the day.

The premier suggested that the second boat be named the *Frederick Carter*; both Ambrose Shea and Mr. Carter were two Newfoundland delegates who went to Ottawa 100 years ago this year to look into the possibilities of confederation.

"We jumped at the chance of getting the *Shea* because we knew if we didn't we may not get a ferry for the service here at all. Many complaints have come in, some of them more than reasonable and they will all be considered," Mr. Curtis continued.

The Attorney General said that some of the fares may need re-adjustment as they apply to vehicle weights, but this will be determined over a trial period.

The *Shea* can carry 32 passengers and six cars per trip. Rates were slashed recently from $2.50 per car to 75 cents as the result of protests.

However, he said there was no chance that a suggestion to put a toll on the causeway and the elimination of the charge on the ferry would be put into effect.

Some residents of Twillingate Island have complained that it costs them 75 cents or more to leave or get back to the island while the residents of New World Island can do so for free by means of the causeway.

Mr. Curtis explained that the causeway had been built under the federal roads to resources program with Ottawa sharing 50 per cent of the cost, and said that federal regulation did not allow for collection of tolls over such routes.

He pointed out that it would take more than 70 per cent of the tolls collected to maintain a toll station on the causeway, which would make it impractical.

Premier Smallwood left Twillingate by helicopter at 7:30 p.m. yesterday, while the rest of the party left for Gander by car. ■

Cowhand Joe leads biggest drive down last trail

August 26, 1964

Great New Industries

It was 5 a.m. and, as one resident described it, "black as the devil's Sunday shirt."

A cold Grand Banks fog swept up Placentia Bay and wrapped the marshes and low hills east of Swift Current in steady drizzle.

An unsuspecting motorist speeding past in the hours before dawn would not have realized the fantastic scene in the darkness outside the narrow range of his headlights.

If he had caught a glimpse of some of the activity he might have dismissed it as some sort of mirage, provided he didn't know the strangest procession in Newfoundland's history was being organized just off the roadside.

Two hours before, just as the fishermen of nearby North Harbour and Garden Cove were arising to go to their nets and trawls, the cowhands of the Flying-L Ranch began to round up more than 900 head of cattle to begin a 90-mile drive down the Burin Highway.

Earlier in the night, in pouring rain, the several nightriders kept watch on the herd, making sure none of the animals wandered too far from the general area.

By the time the rain had been replaced by a monotonous drizzle, all the hands involved in the drive were having last cups of campfire coffee and the roundup began in earnest.

Through the fog came the strange and awesome sounds of encouragement – "hiyah, git out, you swaybacked critter! Yiihaaa, c'mon you ornery brutes; yahooo" – the constant bellowing of contrary cows and distant crashing through the underbrush.

On horseback and on foot the 12 cowboys flushed strays out of the dripping, scrubby spruce and off the soggy marshes.

By the time it was light enough to see, an ocean of white-faced Herefords flooded the assembly area and spilled across the road, their red hides steaming after the rain.

The strange cavalcade got underway by 7 a.m., led by an RCMP car with its red light flashing.

Behind came about 150 purebred cattle and behind that the main body of the herd, a mass of milling animals stretching out for more than a mile.

At a fast walk the drive headed toward Swift Current and by 8 a.m. was pouring across the narrow, double-arched Black River Bridge.

In the community nearly everyone turned out to see east meet west – a cattle drive along the shores of the Atlantic where at times the sea lapped the edge of the road and the drivers' shrill cries were answered by the sea gulls.

Three miles west of Swift Current another old cowhand rode out to join the drive.

Premier J.R. Smallwood, dressed for the occasion in high-heeled boots, black socks, black shirt with a jaunty dash of crimson at the throat and a black Stetson, rode a chestnut horse with English riding saddle.

He followed behind the vanguard of purebreds and talked cattle with Flying-L owner Harold Lees, until the drive reached a point about eight miles from Swift Current where the cattle were turned off the road to pasture for the remainder of the day.

This morning the whole roundup procedure was repeated so that the Flying-L crew could get the herd on the road and as far along as possible before vehicular traffic became too heavy.

It is expected the trek to the Flying-L south of Marystown will take at least another five or six days.

Among those taking part yesterday were Joseph Goodyear of Gander, who brought in his riding horse by trailer especially for the event, and Walt Diamond of Glovertown as well as several men from the Marystown area.

The littlest cowboys were Mr. Lees's sons, Glenn, 7, and Grant, 10, who both rode man-sized horses and seemed as at home on them as local youngsters would be in a dory.

The Flying-L herd, which was brought in from Saskatchewan to form a basic breeding stock for this province, has already displayed its ready adaptation to the Newfoundland climate.

More than 100 animals wintered on the shores of Mortier Bay since late December without ill effects and the latest herd of 900 cattle have already produced at least half a dozen healthy calves. ▊

Residents watched in horror as young Mountie gunned down

December 18, 1964   *Policing*

The sun came up at 7:42 on a bright winter morning and from the houses, one by one, smoke rose steadily from chimneys on still, frosty air.

But it was going to be a bad day for the small, quiet town of Whitbourne.

Bob Amey, the 24-year-old RCMP constable everybody liked, was soon to be shot and killed in front of a Whitbourne store by a young man he had never seen before.

Seven hours earlier and 50 miles away in St. John's four small-time crooks serving time in Her Majesty's Penitentiary for break, entry and theft, hacked feverishly in the darkness at the wooden floor of their dungeon cell.

They squirmed out though half-frozen earth, smashed a lock on a prison door and scuttled over the walls, beginning a flight which ended in a tragic gun-battle in the streets of Whitbourne.

How they managed to escape – for the second time in less than a month – must be left for another story.

Prison information on the break, apart from a brief initial statement by Superintendent Otto Kelland has been cut off pending an investigation.

The four – convicts James Thorne, 17, Fortune; Melvin Young, 19, St. George's; John Snow, 19, St. John's; Winston Noseworthy, 21, Bell Island – had bolted in two separate breaks from Salmonier prison camp November 30 and December 3.

Why, on recapture, were all four put together in one cell? Why were they confined to a cell in the prison's abandoned dungeon? Is a wooden-floored room to be considered a maximum security cell?

How did the four cut their way out and, if with a knife, how did they manage to smuggle it into their cell?

These are some of the questions which may be answered after the investigation but which now remain a mystery.

According to Staff Sgt. Vincent Noonan of the St. John's RCMP detachment, the four stole a car from a driveway near the penitentiary and abandoned it later on Topsail Road.

Here they hijacked another car, a black 1964 sedan, and fled west over the Trans-Canada Highway.

Three miles east of Whitbourne Constable Amey and Constable D.C. Keith of the RCMP had set up a road block.

The fleeing convicts crashed through and sped on over the icy highway turning off at the Whitbourne intersection and into the community where they were to turn the quiet morning into a nightmare.

Whether or not they arrived in Whitbourne before daylight is not known. One report says they did and waited out the hours of darkness in an abandoned house.

In any case, one resident waiting at a stop for the early bus to St. John's was confronted by the four who asked where they could get something to eat.

They kept looking behind them. "Are you following us," one of the convicts snarled, brandishing an empty soft drink bottle by the neck. "If you are, we'll scuttle you in a hurry."

At about 8:30 a.m. Constables Amey and Keith found them in the stolen car on a side street about 500 feet from Barrett's store in front of which Amey was to be shot.

The two RCMP officers, revolvers drawn, ordered the four convicts out of the car and attempted to put them under arrest. None of the four were armed.

But they made a break for it. On a half-run they backed up the street shouting insults and threats at Amey and Keith, who kept ordering them to give themselves up.

Barrett's store, owned by 43-year-old Fred Barrett, is separated by only a lane from a smaller shop owned by William Drover.

The two-story Drover house is attached to the store and from an upstairs window Mrs. Drover and her two daughters watched in horror the scene below in their driveway.

They watched as Constable Amey and Keith backed the four convicts off the road and up against the front of Barrett's store.

Here, Constable Keith attempted to keep them covered with his revolver while Amey ran back down the road to the police car to radio for help from the two other officers of the Whitbourne detachment.

Then the four jumped Keith. "They knocked him down and started pounding him," says Mrs. Drover. "They grabbed him by the hair and banged his head again and again on the ground ... then they took his gun." Young, the smallest of the four, had the gun. There are houses on either side of the two stores and others facing them across the road.

On the still morning air the shouts of the four convicts could be heard throughout the neighborhood. There were savage threats, curses, and obscene warnings directed at anyone who would try to stop them.

Constable Amey rushed back from the car. In her terror, Mrs. Drover does not remember if he had his gun drawn nor did she see the convict shoot.

But she saw him stagger when the bullet hit him in the left side of the chest. He fell against a car parked in the lane and crumpled slowly to the ground.

"He seemed to reach out his gun to Constable Keith, who took it from his hand. My husband saw he was wounded from a downstairs window and went out a side door into the lane to try and help him."

Constable Keith shouted, "Get back in the house, Bill. You may get shot." Mr. Drover dashed back inside. Young sent a bullet crashing into the side of the store as Drover slammed the door behind him.

The Barrett house is located behind and is separated from the store. Mr. Barrett had just come out to open his store for the morning, entering by the back door.

He heard some shouting out front and walked over to lift the window blinds to see what was going on.

At that time Mr. Barrett was unaware of the scuffle in front and had heard neither of the two shots that were fired.

"I was looking out the front windows of the shop when I heard some footsteps behind me, looked back and saw this guy with a gun in his hand. He came in through the back door.

"I thought about ducking down behind the counter but he came over to me. 'I don't want to have to shoot you', he said, and I won't unless I got to'.

"There's the cash register," I said. "Take the money if you back in the house and I have to get back out and take care of them.

"Then he got up longside of me and pointed the gun at my chest. He motioned me out to the back door. Perhaps I could have grabbed the gun but I'm not used to these kind of things."

Young stood in the doorway with Mr. Barrett, the gun held against his chest. Meanwhile, Constable Keith had come around behind the store through the back yard and taken cover behind a small shed next to the Barrett house.

"Keith shouted to Young to give himself up. Then he started talking to him. He said 'We'll do the best we can to help you. That's the only chance you've got. Give the gun to Mr. Barrett and let him go'.

"Who is Mr. Barrett?" shouted Young. 'He's the man you're pointing the gun at', said Keith. 'Let him go and give yourself up'."

Mr. Barrett thinks it lucky none of the neighbors who were watching through windows or from around corners made any sudden moves but especially that his wife was not at home.

Mrs. Barrett had gone to St. John's the day before to visit her ailing mother in hospital.

"If she had been here," he says, "I daresay she would have tried to do something to help me and that would have done it.

"Constable Keith probably saved my life. He kept talking to Young and finally Young agreed to pass the gun over to me.

"But first you have to take the six bullets out of your gun and let me see you drop them on the ground and put your gun back in that holster," he said to Keith.

"'There's only five bullets in it,' said Keith, and he took them out and put his gun away. Then Young gave me the gun he had and I walked out in the yard."

Young stepped down out of the doorway and as he did two other RCMP officers who had arrived by this time jumped out from behind the house and covered him.

The convict made a lunge for the gun in Mr. Barrett's hand. "'Watch out for the gun', shouted Keith, and I held on to it for dear life. And kept it pointed at him."

Then Keith went out to round up the three other convicts who had jumped over back fences when Young first entered the store.

When all four had been subdued, Mr. Barrett went around to the front of the store and saw Constable Amey lying dead on the snow.

"I got a sheet from the house and put over him. The doctor was there and said he was dead. He probably died right away."

Why hadn't the RCMP constables used their guns when the three convicts resisted arrest and why didn't Constable Keith shoot Young after the convict had his revolver, some were asking.

RCMP inspector Russell said in a statement later the RCMP wanted to make the arrest without violence and would refrain from shooting unless absolutely necessary.

"I thought they could have shot to wound them when they got out of the car and were backing away down the road," said Mrs. Drover.

"I suppose they didn't want to hurt them. They took an awful lot of abuse from them … but even when they had them rounded up the Mounties didn't lay a hand on them."

By 2 p.m. yesterday all Whitbourne was talking in hushed tones about the spectacular incident which had shocked the province.

RCMP officers swarmed around the two stores where the shooting took place, measuring distances, examining the two bullet holes (one in the side of the Drover store, another in the Barrett house probably fired by Keith), taking fingerprints and looking over the getaway car.

In the lane between the two stores an elderly gentleman with hammer and saw was replacing a piece of clapboard where one of the bullets struck.

The piece of wood had been removed for study by the RCMP. Nearby, a small patch of red stains the snow.

The old man continues his work, oblivious to the comings and goings of the Mounties, as if this sort of thing happened every day.

He pauses long enough to ask "How come that bullet in your house, Fred?" as Mr. Barrett reenacts the scene once more for the police.

Although Constable Amey had been stationed in Whitbourne only a short time, he was regarded by those who knew him as a friendly, likeable young man.

"Ours was the first house he was in when he came here," said Mrs. Drover, whose husband takes care of the RCMP lockup in Whitbourne whenever there are prisoners in residence.

"He was full of jokes, always laughing. He would be down here often. I'll never forget what happened to him. Every time we go out of the house we'll have to walk over the spot where they killed him.

Rev. Bennett, Anglican Minister at Whitbourne, says Constable Amey took an outstanding part in church work even during the short time he was there.

"We heard the same thing about him from Harbour Breton where he served before coming to Whitbourne," Rev. Bennett said. "He was a good church-man and a fine young man."

A memorial service will be held in the Anglican Church at Whitbourne at the same time Constable Amey's burial takes place in his Nova Scotia hometown.

For Mrs. Drover, who watched with unbelief the incredible scene below her window, memories of the bad day at Whitbourne will remain a long time.

I hope they'll let me have his mother's address," she said. "I got to write to her. She'd want to know how it was and that her son had friends here." ⬛

The Third Mill could come at last ... IF ...

January 15, 1965   *Great New Industries*

Premier J.R. Smallwood Thursday declared Newfoundland's "one chance in life" to be at hand, chastised *The Evening Telegram* for omitting an "IF" and kept the beauteous Miss Canada cooling her heels for nearly an hour.

Newly landed in St. John's by way of New York, Ottawa, Montreal and Corner Brook after a winter holiday in The Bahamas, the premier spoke for 72 minutes after luncheon before the St. John's Rotary Club.

His countenance rosy from 10 days in the Caribbean sun and full of ginger ("I spent a lot of time sleeping, feel extremely fit"), he launched with vigor into two well-known topics, the Third Mill and Hamilton Falls.

By way of introductory levity he commended the "positive genius of Rotary officers" whom he said had arranged it so that his address would not go over the 30-minute time limit.

Miss Dominion of Canada, Mary Lou Farrell, was waiting in his office for some photographs to be taken with the premier and he held it was a devilishly clever ploy by Rotarians to shorten his speech.

The "Rotarian Plot," Miss Farrell notwithstanding, was shot down in flames. As the 30-minute time limit neared, the premier had barely hit full stride. He sat down 40 minutes later.

Part one of Premier Smallwood's duplex address dealt with the Third Mill. But before getting down to cases he allowed an apology might be in order.

During his absence from the province, an article had appeared "in a local newspaper" (*The Evening Telegram*, January 11, Page 4) in which the writer found "great hilarity ... in poking fun at the number of times I have dared mention the Third Mill."

"The author was beside himself, convulsed in laughter ... he thought it was screamingly funny, his hilarity was unrestrained to find the premier so silly, so stupid, so ridiculous as to try to get a Third Mill."

The premier was not amused. He scathed the writer for his irreverence but admitted he hadn't actually read the article.

"He's absolutely right, you know," Mr. Smallwood continued. "I have talked about it too many times for too many years."

About 11 years, all told, but he submitted that where new paper mills are concerned this is no more than par for the course.

It was also 11 years, he noted, that Newfoundland's second mill – Bowater's at Corner Brook – was talked about before it became a reality.

Admittedly, the Third Mill was still below the horizon "but not for lack of trying." Despite the scoffers, "I am unrepentant."

Every Newfoundlander who has seen Grand Falls, Corner Brook and environs and "knows of the amount of indescribable good done by Mill No. 1 or Mill No. 2 will not need any apology."

For the 11 years of Third Mill negotiations he placed the number of tries at 18, equalled by a like number of failures.

In Europe there had been negotiations with 11 companies – "Result, zero; no mill." There were seven other attempts in North America also without success.

About 1961 it seemed almost within reach but along came the I.W.A. strike.

"When we signed an option for timber rights with the second largest paper company in the world, Crown Zellerbach, it looked most hopeful."

But during the life of the option, "Newfoundland had the worst industrial warfare we have ever experienced," he said, referring to the I.W.A. business.

The premier didn't know for sure how the woods dispute affected any decision by the company, but in any case they dropped the project.

Promoting the 1963 Third Mill announcement on New Year's Eve was a decision by the Newfoundland Pulp and Chemical Company (an organization headed by US financier John Shaheen) to build the mill IF the Newfoundland government agreed to finance a $25 million bond issue.

"They said that IF the government was willing to guarantee half of the $50 million cost we would have the mill."

Harking back to *The Telegram* story of January 11, he said "the IF is lost, forgotten, conveniently overlooked" and gave some Kipling-esque advice to all concerned: "Take note of that IF today."

(Several times during his Rotary address the premier candidly reminded his audience that his predictions for both the Third Mill and Hamilton Falls were suspended by a series of IFs.)

Apologies out of the way, the premier pressed on unabashedly with the latest Third Mill announcement.

On January 8 in New York he had meet with John Shaheen ("he's done big things because he's a man who does big things") and the top man of the White-Weld group of financiers.

Stressing that he was quoting these two investors and making no predictions of his own, he brought Third Mill transactions up to date.

"They are ready to go ahead with the building of a $50 million mill at Come By Chance," dependant on an "IF" which the premier went on to explain.

"A large paper-making concern from Finland would come to supervise the building and manage the mill. They want an option to purchase the mill after so many years."

While US companies tend to regard Labrador as being part of the polar ice cap, the Scandinavians, being in much the same latitudes, know this is not the case.

Unbeknown to the press, representatives of the Finnish company in question made several visits to Labrador during 1963 to look over the black spruce stands which would supply the Third Mill. "Their eyes glistened," the premier observed.

They are scheduled to return in the next few weeks for another look at Labrador under winter conditions there.

Of the $50 million cost, Mr. Shaheen's organization would raise $10 million and White-Weld the remainder IF the Newfoundland government will guarantee $15 million of this amount.

"This will mean a nice little new town at Come By Chance, construction of which will begin as soon as the snow flies (disappears) IF the government decides to take them up on their offer ... don't forget the IF."

The premier said there was not enough timber outside Bowater's and A.N.D. holdings on the island to support a Third Mill. The wood must come from Labrador.

In the previous 18 tries one of the snags had been that no one had proven it was possible to log Labrador's forests.

However, in 1964 Bowater's had shown conclusively this was economical when they took 25,000 tons of pulpwood from Sandwich Bay, he said.

This demonstration the premier termed the key to success of the Third "and the fourth" mill.

In the light of these developments "at the risk of being ridiculed, laughed at or sneered at," he ventured to say "it looks as though we might get it at last."

From Come By Chance Premier Smallwood shifted his attention to Hamilton Falls and its 9,000,000 horsepower.

He retraced events leading up to the present situation regarding the hydro development, including Newfoundland's altercation with Quebec.

The Hamilton project would equal six Boulder Dams, produce as much power as is now used by Ontario, was the cheapest power on earth to produce, but there were a few transmission difficulties.

The first power would start flowing out of Labrador in 1970 and by 1976 some 9,000,000 horsepower would be crackling under the Strait of Belle Isle.

After some "intolerable, unendurable tactics from Quebec," he had decided the transmission lines to New England would go by way of Newfoundland and the Maritimes.

The premier held aloft the two-volume Preece, Cardew and Rider report, which he said showed without a doubt Hamilton development and undersea transmission was feasible.

Under water at the nine-mile Strait of Belle Isle and the 60-mile Cabot Strait the cables, nine of them, one for each million horsepower, would be six inches thick with insulation.

Across Cabot Strait they would weigh 8,000 tons each; for any unwary dragger hooking on to one of them, the effects would be electrifying.

"The vessel would be destroyed, it would kill all the crew – draggers would be commiting suicide," he said, but suggested in jest "it might be a good way to keep them off."

To prevent such mishaps the cable route from Port aux Basques to Cape Breton would be lined with warning buoys emitting electronic danger signals.

Warning ships would patrol the 60-mile Strait, planes and helicopters would be on constant watch overhead. The premier figured it may take $1 million a year to keep the area clear.

With doubts about engineering the feasibility of the $1,300,000,000 project dispelled, the question on which the very fate of Newfoundland now depends is whether or not it can be financed, he said.

Robert Winters, chairman of BRINCO (British Newfoundland Corporation), is now in New York looking into the possibility of selling $250,000,000-worth of shares.

If BRINCO could not do it, no other private corporation in the world would be equal to the task, Mr. Smallwood continued.

He suggested that BRINCO had every reason to make the project a success, having spent $12 or $15 million on it already.

The corporation had good backing: "I don't suppose there's one great family in Britain that has not got shares in BRINCO … the greatest name alive in the world today is a shareholder," he said, but did not name Sir Winston Churchill.

Since construction headquarters had been set up at the Hamilton Falls site, when negotiations broke down it would take six weeks for engineers and workers to move back and contracts called.

"If BRINCO finds in a week or two that the money can be raised sometime in April or May – don't pin me down to this – contracts should be let."

Atomic power is coming up fast "although not as fast as they say" as a competitor to hydro power.

"We've got to get it soon. I would venture to say we've got to get it this year," he said of the Hamilton project.

"If the lines went though Quebec we'd get some cash in return, but money is not enough. I doubt that God intended that when he put that power on our soil.

"Is there any other chance in this life for Newfoundland to have an economic breakthrough? This is our one chance in life and the next few weeks are going to be momentous ones."

Without Hamilton Falls, Newfoundland will be only a nice comfortable province among the three or four poorest in Canada, he said.

"Hamilton power can put us among the top three or four great provinces in Canada.

"We must keep up our courage and optimism, remember that we have great people, not sell Newfoundland short, realize our stock of people is as good as you can get anywhere in the world, and together with our resources will win us the greatness we deserve," he concluded. ◼

Quebec may get Churchill Falls power

March 11, 1965   *Great New Industries*

The House of Assembly learned yesterday, in a round-about manner, that Churchill Falls power is likely to go though Quebec.

BRINCO will start searching immediately for "the most economic way" to transmit Labrador hydro to the five eastern provinces, including Quebec.

Newfoundland's needs will be supplied though transmission lines under the Strait of Belle Isle, the House was told.

But, significantly, there was no mention of an important part of the famed Preece, Cardew and Rider report – the submarine cables under the Cabot Strait.

Premier J.R. Smallwood presented a ministerial statement on the project, then invited Robert Winters, chairman of BRINCO, to address the Assembly.

Neither Premier Smallwood nor Mr. Winters directly stated the Quebec bypass route was off.

However, clues to this possibility were scattered amid the convolutions of both statements.

The premier said a discussion "in the frankest and friendliest terms" was held between Mr. Winters and the Cabinet yesterday morning.

"Speaking for my colleagues, I emphasized the complete confidence of the government and people of Newfoundland in the British Newfoundland Corporation under the leadership of Mr. Winters."

Premier Smallwood told Mr. Winters how much Newfoundland wanted BRINCO to develop Labrador power and Mr. Winters told Premier Smallwood how much BRINCO wanted to do just that.

"The government and BRINCO are in perfect agreement on this point," said the premier.

"We see no reason whatever why the development should not be carried out by BRINCO and commenced in the coming spring."

According to the premier's statement he and Mr. Winters now know where they stand in relation to each other.

"The government impressed upon Mr. Winters, and he agreed thoroughly with us, that Newfoundland, as the prime owner of the power, must now and always have first claim on it and that Newfoundland's interest is and must always be paramount.

"The government is delighted with the sincerity and strength of Mr. Winters's feelings in this regard.

"For his part, Mr. Winters may have experienced delight with our expression of confidence in BRINCO itself."

At the meeting it was agreed that BRINCO will produce nine million horsepower on the upper and lower cataracts of the Churchill River.

Earlier, it was planned to get ahead with the harnessing of Churchill Falls (six million) first and tackle Muskrat (three million) later on.

"It was agreed between us today that the Preece, Cardew and Rider report on transmission of power to the island of Newfoundland via an overhead transmission line and a short submarine line across the Strait of Belle Isle would be proceeded with as part of the whole project."

Thus, Churchill River power would flow into the Newfoundland island power grid (planned as part of the Baie d'Espoir project) at Deer Lake "by 1969 or 1970."

As the premier put it, "BRINCO shares the Newfoundland government's strong desire" that Labrador power be made available to "sister provinces of Canada."

Sisterly relations between the Quebec and Newfoundland governments have been ruptured for some time.

This was the first indication by the premier since the sisterly slug-fest commenced that Quebec would get even enough Labrador electricity to pop a slice of toast.

Before yesterday's statement the premier had vigorously maintained that any transmissions route other than his "Anglo-Saxon" line was unthinkable.

Now, BRINCO will "commence immediate investigations of the most economic way to transmit Labrador power to those five provinces."

Provided Newfoundland gets all the power it needs, "we are happy to have the power that is surplus to us delivered to our sister provinces by whatever route may prove to be the most efficient and economical and consequently most profitable to Newfoundland."

When sisterly thirsts have been thoroughly quenched with Labrador juice, "we would be most happy to see the surplus power go toward satisfying the needs of our friends in the United States."

Several more million horsepower could be developed from other Labrador rivers.

So "side by side with the anticipated commencement of construction this summer" BRINCO will start a survey on the amount and cost of development of this power.

"Mr. Winters told us of conversations he has had in recent days in Ontario, New York and New England, in which he learned of the very great desire that exists for all of the power that Newfoundland can produce."

"Indeed," said the premier, "one great organization wants to buy the entire six-million-horsepower output of the Upper Churchill."

He said there appears to be no doubt whatsoever that all the water power in Labrador can be produced and sold at a profit for a lower price than any other power in North America.

"In conclusion, BRINCO and Newfoundland government are in complete agreement and see eye to eye as to the procedure to be followed.

"Mr. Winters returns to the mainland today to commence at once the implementation of understandings reached by us this morning."

The premier's announcement was greeted with loud desk-thumping applause from all government members present.

Opposition members, however, did not join in the demonstration, and failed to produce a single thump between them.

Before he headed back to the mainland and buckled down to implementing understandings reached, Mr. Winters was invited by Premier Smallwood to address the House.

It was the first time an "outsider" had been asked to do since the national president of the Imperial Order Daughters of the Empire visited last spring.

Mr. Winters said he regarded the opportunity as a high honor indeed and an experience he would always cherish.

He thanked the premier for the invitation to do so and praised the "serious manner [in which] he approached" the Churchill discussions.

The BRINCO chairman said he knew the project was the dream of the people of Newfoundland for a great many years and that, in this regard, BRINCO thought of itself as trustees of the people of Newfoundland.

"We will seek every reasonable means by which to carry out this development," he continued.

"Sometimes we may have been overly reliant on one particular means or avenue of doing it ... but it has been demonstrated that there is more than one way."

The Preece, Cardew and Rider report would be a help to BRINCO.

Its advanced technology will "put BRINCO in a position to handle other such developments all over the world."

Mr. Winters said after yesterday's discussions the Corporation would seek to make Churchill power available, first to Newfoundland, then to neighboring provinces and "subject to approval of the National Energy Board" to the United States.

An imaginative scheme it was, he continued.

It would involve the cooperation of government and private enterprise and "at least two provinces working together."

Mr. Winters did not name the two provinces.

Success could be achieved "if we work in the same spirit of harmony as prevailed in the past," he said, presumably referring to other than the immediate past.

"We must be willing to submerge our interests at a time when perhaps this is not easy."

Mr. Winters said the Churchill project is one of the greatest projects now being undertaken in the world and all Canadians should be proud of it.

Both Opposition and Government members applauded Mr. Winters, who shook hands with W.J. Browne (PC-St. John's East Extern), Opposition Leader

James J. Greene and Premier Smallwood before leaving the chamber.

The House was left to ponder on the fact that whatever interests are submerged it seems less likely that Churchill Falls power lines will be. ▪

More special police rushed to St. Pierre – Islanders shocked by treatment

April 30, 1965 *Policing*

St. Pierre – The 5,200 Frenchmen living on a barren island 15 miles off the Burin Peninsula may today be the loneliest people in the world.

Separated by nearly 3,000 miles of ocean from France, surrounded by the chilling fogs of the Grand Banks and overwhelming numbers of English-speaking peoples to the west, they have for three centuries stoutly maintained that they are more French than the people of Paris.

"France is not far away; France is here," they exclaim, placing an expressive hand over the heart.

But in the past six days the invisible ties linking France's last vestige of a once-great North American empire have suffered a greater wrench than they have had in the past 300 years.

A French warship, the *Dupetit Thouart*, was anchored off Gallantry Head earlier this week, and the 63 members of the Gardes Mobiles, who were landed under cover of darkness April 24, patrol the narrow streets in battle dress and jackboots.

Telegrams of protest and indignation have been fired off to Paris; the St. Pierre representative in the French Chamber of Deputies, Albert Briand, returned to the colony yesterday after an emergency visit to the French capital.

St. Pierrais are shocked and hurt, refusing to believe their beloved France is responsible for this "incredible" treatment.

But the surly guards are a constant reminder. These tough, efficient special police – the elite corps assigned to guard the life of Charles de Gaulle – make the insult visible.

The members of the guard find few people with whom to exchange a friendly word except some of the government officials and the children on the street corners.

Late yesterday came the final humiliation when the French frigate *Commandant Bordais* put ashore another 63 of the Gardes Mobiles to reinforce the garrison.

Briand was grim in an interview at Sydney, NS, where his plane touched down yesterday on the return trip from Paris.

"Something is very wrong," he said, "when you have 150 police for 5,000 people." The normal police force on St. Pierre is 25 gendarmes.

Despite the volatile Gallic temperament, Newfoundland's neighbors are much like Newfoundlanders themselves – a quiet, peaceable people, most of whom make their living from the sea.

"Do they think we are bandits," cried a shopkeeper on Rue Merchal Foch, "that they have to send in the army!"

Unable to believe the mother country would treat them this way, the residents are blaming Governor Jacques Herry for sending false alarms to Paris.

This view is held by the local government, including Mayor Joseph Lehuenen and Albert Pen, a spokesman for a joint committee of elected representatives and union officers.

"Colonialism should be done away with," Mayor Lehuenen said in an interview with *The Evening Telegram* Tuesday. "We are not colonials; we are all French people."

He agreed with Pen that the only people on the island refusing to support a general protest strike were some civil servants who were afraid of losing their jobs, and a few friends of the governor.

In brief, the political setup in the colony is a three-level affair: the governor is appointed by Paris; the General Council is elected and corresponds roughly to a provincial government.

The president of the General Council (Briand) also sits in the Chamber of Deputies in the French capital.

The municipal council is elected and has been headed for the past 10 years by Mayor Lehuenen.

Regular municipal elections will be held May 2 and Lehuenen is expected to be returned for another term, partly because of his stand on the present issue.

Adding spice to the rich political pudding is Albert Pen, described by the man in the street as having strong Communist tendencies.

Although a secretary of the General Council, Pen has been little known in politics on the island until the present disturbance, when he emerged as a spokesman of the people.

Sporting a well-trimmed beard, the 42-year-old St. Pierre native has studied in France, where some Communist deputies sit in the Chamber of Deputies.

The labor unions – notably the longshoremen – are at the center of events, since it was the dispute over wages on the docks which led to the abrupt expulsion from the island of the Public Works officer last year.

An enraged crowd dragged the official out of his office, and placed him on a boat leaving St. Pierre when money sent from France to increase longshore wages was not paid.

Since then, trouble has been brewing under the surface and reached the point last week where Governor Herry thought it necessary to call in the Gardes Mobiles because of "threatenings, direct and indirect" against him.

Governor Herry has not made himself available to the press. Reporters are greeted in the outer office of the Governor's Mansion by a shapely, red-haired secretary, who curtly informs them the governor is not seeing anyone.

To protest the arrival of the riot troops, which they say was absolutely uncalled for, Mayor Lehuenen, the municipal council, Albert Pen, and labor leaders called a general strike April 24.

The strike was lifted temporarily Wednesday when Governor Herry promised to do what he could to have the special police removed and to stop reinforcements being flown in from Paris.

Deputy Briand flew to Paris to make the same request in person, but yesterday the *Commandant Bordais* entered the harbor and more special police came ashore.

It is expected the general strike will be resumed, but St. Pierrais – benumbed by the treatment by France – are uncertain of the next step.

This time it will not be a matter of dumping the Public Works officer aboard an outbound boat.

The *Dupetit Thouart* arrived in St. John's around 9 a.m. this morning. The reason for her visit here is not yet known.

The citizens' committee is determined to show that the riot troops are not needed and is making strenuous efforts to prevent violence.

A telegram sent by the committee to Premier Georges Pompidou, Premier of France, reads in part:

"Perfect calm has prevailed since the beginning of the strike because (we) are determined to prove to the watching eyes of Canada the dignity of the French people."

More eyes were turning toward the tiny island yesterday as reports arrived hourly by plane.

Among those represented are Canadian Press, the *Toronto Star*, the *London Daily Express* and the Quebec *Petit Journal*.

Late yesterday reporters and photographers from three other papers and news services arrived in the small outpost which was virtually unheard of in most areas a week ago.

With the influx of reporters, the Gardes Mobiles may be cracking down on publicity.

As we drove toward the St. Pierre airport yesterday to take a small plane back to St. John's, a small group of troops stood on the corner of November Eleventh Street chatting with a group of youngsters.

We stopped and the interpreter walked up and asked if we could take pictures. The soldiers were agreeable, but said we would have to get permission from the commanding officer.

Inside the Hotel Robert, which the Gardes have commandeered, the commander – a six-and-a-half-foot individual – vetoed the idea in no uncertain terms.

As we headed back to the car we turned the camera toward the group, but the shutter had hardly snapped when a lieutenant headed toward us with a hand on his holstered pistol, shouting angrily.

The interpreter said he demanded we turn over the camera and film immediately.

We piled into the car and took off at a fast clip to the airport. Some 10 minutes later we were flying north toward the Burin Peninsula.

"They don't come any tougher," the St. Pierrais interpreter had said. "What chance have we got against them?"

A crowd of about 200 watched in silence in the Place General de Gaulle as the new contingent of troops landed.

The troops climbed quickly into army trucks and roared off. The crowd dispersed to their homes or to the small bars and restaurants for the evening brandy.

But this is one sorrow all the cognac on the lonely, windswept island cannot drown. ▓

Rockbound south coast – brave past – bright future

July 2, 1965   *Resettlement and Rural Life*

Head down and elbows pumping, the EPA plane rushed full tilt along Octagon Pond into the early morning headwind.

With a determined snarl it heaved itself from the water, skimmed the pond-side tree tops, rose over the highway and the summer cottages, and drip-dried its floats high above Topsail Head.

Some 5,000 feet above Kelly's Island the small aircraft banked in mid-air and headed west above one of the most isolated areas – the rugged south coast.

There's more to Newfoundland than can be seen from the Trans-Canada Highway. A boat would do the trick along the coast, but a small plane is 100 times quicker.

Remnants of the country's past and some of the new developments that will shape the future are tucked away in remote corners where a gull would be hard-pressed to pitch.

EPA pilot Ted Pearcey makes landings that gulls find difficult seem almost easy.

Aboard the five-passenger seaplane as it took off from Octagon Pond one day last week were St. John's businessman Gus Winter and myself and several packages of drugs and equipment for a hospital ship and clinics on the south coast.

Before the day was out we had visited an abandoned chapel in a deserted community, followed part of the course of the North East Nonsuch River, buzzed the Brunette Island buffalo herd, broke-up a 40-ton romance and spotted a forest fire at Baie d'Espoir.

All in a day's work for bush pilot Pearcey, but a unique experience for us earth-bound mortals.

Halfway across the Avalon Peninsula on a clear day (the long sheds below are the Dildo mink ranches) you can see Bell Island on the eastern horizon and the outline of 1,130-foot Centre Hill near Come By Chance to the west.

Two highways run up the chicken-neck of the isthmus. Compared with the broad, straight and business-like Trans-Canada, the old road looks from the air like an eel with convulsions.

Placentia Bay, at its northern end, is measled with islands, a few of which are still populated.

The largest of the islands is Merasheen, 22 miles long and tapering from a three-mile-wide southern end to an islet connected to its northern tip by a sandbar.

The population of the islands has been drained away because of what people who don't have it call solitude, and what people who do, call isolation.

At the northern tip of Merasheen the exodus started in 1949 when most of the people of Great Brule (pronounced BREW-ly) upped stakes and moved to greener pastures.

From the air, all that remains to be seen of Great Brule is a grassy clearing near the shore and a small weather-bleached chapel.

Pearcey circled the physical remains of the deserted community and brought us down in the small cove by the sandbar.

In 16 years, the rugged spruce have grown up around the small church to bury it almost from sight.

In the midst of its little forest the chapel is slowly going to ruin, but the inside is much the same as the people left it. Most of them were named Traverse, according to a fading list of names near the door.

The people of Great Brule, isolated though they were, did their best to make the chapel a more inspiring place of worship. Mainland collectors would probably enthuse over the results as unique examples of "folk-art."

They painted the ceiling blue with streaks of white to look like heaven. A garland of holly copied from a Christmas card encircles the walls. Curious, winged heads representing angels are painted over the altar.

"Praise God with beauty," says the Bible, and what better sight to a seafaring people than a vessel under full sail. So over the chapel door they painted directly on the whitewashed walls a square-rigger tossed on a fearsome sea.

Underneath is the prayer: "All the Saints and Saints of God Intercede For Us."

Albert Warren of Tack's Beach, on King's Island across the reach, was hauling his lobster pots off Merasheen, saw the plane and came ashore.

Mr. Warren says most of the people of Tack's Beach (population 450) are talking of moving to the mainland when the fishing season is over this fall.

Rose au Rue was deserted long ago, nobody lives in Haystack, Indian Harbour is abandoned and Spencer's Cove is left to the fog and wind.

We hoped the Saints of God saw them all safely out of their quiet harbors on the voyage to new and strange ports. Then we, too, left the island of Merasheen.

That unshapely leg called the Burin Peninsula looks unattractive on a map, but up close the veins and arteries are a lot more alluring.

Paradise River is one of them – wide and dotted with salmon holes, flowing down to Paradise Sound, at the end of which is Little Paradise, not to be confused with Great Paradise nearby.

Another is the North East Nonsuch River, no less scenic, but Lord knows where the name came from. The rivers of this leggy peninsula prove that water on the knee is not all bad.

We alighted in Baine Harbour to deliver a package to the hospital ship *Lady*

Anderson and were invited in for a second breakfast.

Once a luxury yacht based on the Hudson River, NY, the *Lady Anderson* was bought by the Newfoundland government about 30 years ago, is still going strong and, according to her present captain, good for another 75 years or so.

An uncounted number of Newfoundlanders have been born on the *Lady Anderson* and an even larger number have had appendixes, tonsils and other spare parts removed in her small surgery.

From Baine Harbour we hopped down the coast a few miles to Mortier Bay and Marystown, dropped off another package of medicine for the clinic there.

It was still only a little after noon when we took off again from Marystown, just three hours after leaving Octagon Pond. Actual flying time was about 45 minutes.

Over the Burin boot and across a short stretch of ocean to Brunette Island, that sea-girt menagerie where the Wildlife Division has installed a herd of bison from the Canadian prairies.

A bunch of potheads sporting themselves in the Saskatchewan River would be a no less likely sight.

Brunette is several miles square, flat and barren with a few tumble-down summer fishing shacks on the eastern shore but rising to 300-foot hills on the west which drop sharply in sheer cliffs to the sea.

Pearcey took us in low over Brunette, roared up through a small valley and keeled the craft over on one side to give a better view of the fauna below.

The caribou were easy to spot, showing up white amidst the dark scrub spruce. There were 12 in one group that scattered at the sound of the plane – nine adults and three calves.

Further up the hillside, munching away on marsh grass on the edge of the Grand Banks with never a thought of the lone prairie, were the immigrants from Alberta.

About two dozen of the critters were landed there last year, but an undetermined number have fallen over the cliff or have been killed by intestinal parasites.

For the benefit of buffalo fans everywhere, we can report having seen at least nine of them, apparently healthy and in good spirits. They seem to have at least doubled in size since landing on these shores – judging from their passport pictures.

Pressing on toward the community of Hermitage on the south coast we had no sooner left the bison than we came across a pair of 60-foot whales whooping it up just west of Sagona Island.

Zooming in for a closer inspection we disturbed the couple; the two spouted indignantly and sounded, heading off in the direction of the Continental Shelf, to continue the courtship on that oceanic park bench.

Open house at the zoo wasn't over yet. Nearing Hermitage, we were intercepted by two bald eagles closing fast at 2,000 feet from nine o'clock.

Superior airspeed enabled us to outdistance the feathered interceptors who turned tail and winged back to base to sit on the eggs.

The south coast must be one of the least known areas of the province since the geography which makes it spectacular prevents access by land.

Here, the interior plateau comes down to the sea, ending in towering cliffs broken by long bays and steep-sided islands.

Any difference in the way of life caused by semi-isolation can't be seen in a 30-minute visit – south coast communities have much the same outward appearance of Conception Bay villages and towns.

The absence of motor vehicles stands out, although there is the odd pickup truck plying short local roads in the Hermitage area.

In lieu of cars, south coast youths put their money into boats; 12- and 16-foot runabouts with outboard engines take the place of hot rods.

After delivering a package to the Hermitage clinic we nipped across to Baie d'Espoir and St. Alban's for a look at the hydro development which, by 1967, will have doubled Newfoundland's supply of electricity.

Trucks, bulldozers, dynamite and steamshovels are creating new lakes, diverting rivers, digging canals while government planners prepare St. Alban's and environs for the building of a new town on the power site.

Before it was selected as a townsite, St. Alban's was a typical south coast community but with more level land and surrounding forest than most.

Now construction on the power plant buildings, and other work connected with the development, is in full swing a few miles to the north.

Dump trucks, jeeps and heavy equipment rumble though St. Alban's. Three or four float planes from Gander land on the broad harbor each day, bringing in more engineers, construction workers, company officials and their wives.

All the land is "frozen" because of the development. As things stand, a father can't pass over a piece of land to his son and no one can establish a new business unless its type and location are approved by the government.

St. Alban's has hardly had time yet to realize what's hit it. But one thing is for sure, things are not what they used to be.

Mr. Winter, whose firm rents vending machines, had come to St. Alban's to see first-hand how his five pool tables were making out. A local restaurant owner has rented them, and business is booming.

One of the first features of a growing town the community acquired was a civil defence air raid siren and it was going full blast for most of the hour or so we were there.

The cause of the wail was a small forest fire in the heavy timber behind the community. Pilot Pearcey circled the growing blaze before we landed and notified Gander airport.

Construction crews pitched in to fight it, a water bomber flew down from Gander and it was out before it did too much damage.

On the way from St. Alban's to Belleoram, our last stop, we looked down on a dozen or more small communities, cut off from the rest of the country by towering hills on one side and the ocean on the other.

Belleoram is probably one of the most scenic towns in the province, ringed by 600-foot cliffs and with an island the size and height of Signal Hill standing on one side of the harbor.

From here we made a beeline back toward St. John's; Pearcey moored the aircraft at its buoy in Octagon Pond and we were home in plenty of time for supper – all in less than nine hours. ᴿᴳ

Something for everyone at "the Races"

August 6, 1965   *Culture and History*

Seated on the grass mere inches from the waters' edge the infant played quietly with his red balloon.

The judge's boat chugged around the lower end of Quidi Vidi. Its small wake rolled toward shore and washed up on the grass.

Submerged to the waist, the infant showed mild astonishment, then smiled blissfully as the cool waters again receded.

On the hill above the pond a dozen prisoners filed out of a building in the penitentiary yard, lined up on the wooden steps leading from the second story and watched.

No cheering from these spectators, not even when a jubilant blast of car horns below frightened the pigeons in the yard and sent them fluttering over the walls.

A four-year-old wearing a feathered straw hat ambled down to the shoreline with a half-empty bottle of soft drink.

Stepping gingerly in to her ankles she filled the bottle to the top with Quidi Vidi water, held it off in both hands to admire the mixture, then took a long and thirsty draught.

"Sharlene!" her mother screeched, hustling her off in the general direction of the St. John Ambulance tent.

From a distance the crowd, more than 30,000 strong, looked like "hundreds and thousands" cake decorations, multi-colored specks sprinkled thickly along the lake.

A breeze wafted the smells of warm popcorn, fish and chips, and freshly oiled parking lots among them and the youngsters roved endlessly with monkeys on sticks, kewpie dolls on sticks, whistling birds on sticks, and balloons on string.

Here, at the largest sporting event in Newfoundland, the favorite headdress is straw hats of the West Indies or cowboy hats of the American west, all made in Japan.

Nobody seems to pay much attention to the races. There is a brief flurry of interest as the starter's gun barks, but in a few minutes the boats are indistinguishable up the pond.

Back to the games of chance, the hot dogs and the novelty stands until five minutes later the shells heave into sight again.

Another murmur of applause as the leading boat slips between the buoys. The exhausted crew splash water on their bare arms; one oarsman is bent double, coughing, gasping and sick.

As the sun begins to set the enthusiasm rises. The ladies' race always gets a good hand and the old-timers watch the juvenile race closely "to see what them young fellers can do."

The climax of the day is the championship race when the reason a regatta, rather than baseball or cricket, draws 30,000 spectators in Newfoundland becomes more apparent.

It involves yellow dories pitching on the foggy Grand Banks, Churchill saying Newfoundlanders are the best small boatmen in the world, clichés about fishermen being the backbone of the country – patriotism somehow enters into it.

True, the outlandish racing shells would frighten a tomcod out of the water, but with a little imagination they became whaleboats rowed by fishermen – sailors landing His Majesty's Royal Marines in the dead of night on the coast of Italy.

Or small punts rowing though wild seas toward a foundering vessel, or a dory out in wind it shouldn't face because its owner fears the dole more than an August gale.

Yesterday's win by Jerseyside gave this year's Regatta something extra.

The fact that an out-of-town crew won brought imagination and reality a little closer together even though in Jerseyside, as in the rest of Newfoundland, rowing a boat has become a pastime rather than a way of life.

Percy Pursuivant predicts:
"Let nothing you dismay"

December 31, 1965   *News and Propaganda*

With amazing accuracy that has dumbfounded the experts, Percival Pursuivant, 123-year-old resident of the capital city, has been predicting the future for as long as he can remember.

"Forecasting the year's weather is small stuff, although I must say Mr. Drodge does a good job of it," said the venerable old gentleman interviewed recently in his modest but comfortable home at 38 Bumpkin Street.

"I don't dabble with the weather, but through a special gift inherited from my late mother who came over from the old country I can foretell all the year's events a twelve-month in advance."

How does he do it? Pursuivant is not giving away any trade secrets.

He reveals only that he climbs to the top of a 1,822-foot tolt on the Gaff Topsails on the second Sunday in Advent and precisely at 11:55 p.m. gauges atmospheric rumblings, consults the innards of a 1956 Hansard and carefully observes the way the mop flops.

At the end of an old year and the start of a new, Newfoundland's second best-known prophet consented to give readers his predictions for 1966.

"A hard year comin' up," he warns. "I'll tell ye only the bright spots. The rest would be too much for flesh and blood to bear."

We have taken the liberty of rewriting Pursuivant's predictions slightly for the sake of grammar and coherence, but the facts as he foretells them have not been altered one jot. Here are tomorrow's headlines today:

January 5: Historic first public meeting of the new St. John's city council. (Secret meetings cannot be included in this forecast.) Many bold and momentous decisions are reached, chief of which is an agreement to move a bus stop on Duckpuddle Street East 30 feet to the west.

January 12: House re-opens. Special award and memorial trophy presented to the Honorable Member for Pudops-Annieopsquotch Extern for drinking the most glasses of water (657) during the last session, surpassing the previous record set in 1869.

January 13: A 12-man Royal Commission is appointed to look into progress made by the five Royal Commissions appointed a year ago. Terms of reference of the new commission are to inquire after the five to discover "where they are and whither tending." The general public is invited to submit any clues or information.

February 28: Rain, drizzle and fog, clearing slightly in the afternoon.

March 8: Transport minister declares stiffer action by Canada in the enforcement of the 12-mile limit. The minister says that the Swiss fishing fleet is hereby barred from fishing in these waters. Fisheries patrol vessels put on a 24-hour alert.

March 21: Small tribe of Beothuk Indians, long believed extinct, is discovered on the upper reaches of the Turn Over River, placed under government protection, but wiped out by poachers in a fortnight. "Stiffer regulations may be needed," resources minister says.

April 22: Premier calls a special press conference to announce that construction of the third pulp mill at Come By Chance will begin immediately IF the wind is east-north-east when the sun crosses the line, dogberries are plentiful this year and Boston wins the Stanley Cup. Bulldozers are standing by.

May 1: The 150-odd residents of Kumquat Quay declare a state of revolt following attempts to relocate the community under the centralization scheme. Residents of this fishing community protest plans to relocate them on the shores of Octagon Pond to prosecute the ouananiche fishery. The revolt is subdued in three months with the aid of the army, navy, US Marines and the 2nd St. David's Boy Scout troop. The rebels are allowed to remain on the island but are barred from building a house with a chimney within five miles of the coast. Breaches of these regulations are punishable by 30 lashes at the public whipping post.

May 4: Premier returns from combined vacation-business trip to Bago, Bago. Reports to the House on negotiations for a kittiwake guano processing plant for the Funk Islands. Prospects are said to be encouraging and a government-guaranteed bond issue is approved.

May 17: West coast man committed for observation to the Hospital for Mental and Nervous Diseases after returning his Unemployment Insurance cheque saying he really didn't need it.

June 1: The Trans-Canada Highway in Newfoundland is officially opened with the entire British House of Lords, half the US Senate, and the Rolling Stones in attendance. The premier selects a little Deer Lake girl, five-year-old Vanessa McAsphalt, to help cut the ribbon. The opening is picketed by some service station and garage operators carrying protest signs but who remain non-violent. Site of the last shovelful of pavement to be laid is marked by a stone cairn containing the remains of one of the many motor vehicles attempting to make the trans-island trip during the 16 years the highway was under construction. During the afternoon the official party attends memorial services at the tomb of the Unknown Driver.

June 15: Premier reports to the House on combined business-vacation trip to Dar es Salaam; says prospects of a powdered rhinocerous horn industry for the south coast are extremely bright.

July 1: The first Come Home Year tourist arrives to be met at Port aux Basques by an official delegation of the Come Home Year committee. The lucky visitor is presented with a caribou statuette, a specially made pup tent bearing the Come Home Year insignia and a survival kit. Leaders of the various denominations are on hand to wish Godspeed and "Lead Kindly Light" is sung.

July 16: Premier returns from combined business-vacation trip to Ulan Bator, reports to the House on prospects for yak ranching on the Southside Hills. The attorney general and the tourist director have been mislaid on the Mongolian steppes, but are expected to turn up sooner or later.

July 29: Summer comes on a Saturday this year. Temperature at Torbay airport is said to be 54 degrees in the shade. Thousands prostrate in the heat.

August 7: Come Home Year tourist attacked by giant squid while bathing off Topsail Beach, threatens to sue government, is whisked off for a mad, gay, all-expenses-paid whirl at Makkovik, Labrador, fun capital of northern Newfoundland.

August 23: Christmas lighting is turned on on Water Street.

August 30: Come Home Year visitor is tarred, feathered and ridden along the Trans-Canada Highway on a rail by torch-bearing local residents after observing that the weather was inclement and complaining of a tail feather in his hot turkey sandwich. Come Home Year committee issues plea for more tolerance.

September 5: Premier officially opens a new $103,000 amalgamated privy at the south coast community of Gung Ho Haven. Constructed of Italian marble with rosewood paneling, the magnificent edifice was built after prolonged negotiations between the five school boards in the area. It will serve all pupils of the five one-room tarpapered schools in the small community. "A step toward an amalgamated privy is a step in the right direction," says the minister of education, who explains that with limited funds available and an eye to denominational rights the government must follow a policy of "first things first." The premier donates his entire collection of *Reader's Digest*s, dating back to February 1946, to the new building.

September 26: Fifth-year university students go on strike for higher wages.

October 17: A national referendum is held on whether or not to hold another federal election. The results being 50 per cent in favor and 50 per cent against, the entire Parliament votes itself a 12-month vacation in the Lesser Antilles.

November 5: Labrador secedes from the province and sets up its own provincial capital at Churchill Falls. The move is seen as a godsend in government circles since, as one spokesman put it, "the whole thing was getting to be a ruddy bore, anyway."

December 31: No public occurrences or alarms. Rain, drizzle and fog clearing slightly in the afternoon. All quiet on the eastern front.

"And there ye have it," creaked Uncle Percy, raising aloft his fifth glass of screech, calabogus and cod liver oil, to which he attributes his longevity and fine spirits.

We asked the aged prophet if he had any particular word of greeting or advice for our readers and the province generally.

"God rest ye merry, gentlemen, let nothing you dismay," he quavered, nodding happily over his toddy. 🔳

The new Rangers: "difficult to describe"

March 3, 1966   *Policing*

A scout is trustworthy, loyal, helpful, friendly, courteous, kind, obedient, cheerful, thrifty, brave, clean and reverent – but wait till you've seen a new Newfoundland Ranger.

Premier J.R. Smallwood nearly ran out of adjectives yesterday when he tried to describe these proposed paragons of law enforcement to the House of Assembly.

So great, diverse, important, complex, delicate, inspiring and momentous will be the duties of this singular body that the premier was compelled to admit they were "a little difficult to describe."

However, so far as the human voice and the English language were equal to it, the premier succeeded in giving Honorable Members some idea of what he had in mind.

"The Newfoundland Company of Rangers will be much more than a police force, but in some aspects it will be something less," he said, striving to bring this remarkable corps to life for the Honorable House.

It will take on both provincial and some federal law and regulation enforcement duties. Some federal responsibilities, such as those of river wardens, will be assumed if suitable arrangements can be made with Ottawa.

The Rangers will take over the duties of the highway patrol, including small repairs, and "do many things the old Rangers used to do." But their basic function will be so much more than mere law enforcement.

The premier harked back to the genius of the British Empire builders who realized that in colonial lands some liaison was needed between the scattered natives and the government. To this end, unique police forces were formed.

"Acting as liaison between the government and the people was a part of the job of the old Ranger force," he said. "They represented the government in the outback as they call it in Australia or the outports as we say here.

"There was a need for the Rangers because there was not much of an intimate contact between the people and the government."

Each Ranger was nothing less than a "mobile government office." But after Confederation, the House of Assembly became a "substitute" for the Rangers and the force was retired.

Mr. Smallwood explained to a fascinated House that members of the Assembly now perform the same function as the Rangers once did by listening to the people's troubles and making their wants and wishes known to the seat of government.

But something is still lacking, he continued, and the need is still there for a company of Rangers.

The re-formed force will be a "flexible, versatile arm of the government," reaching out into every part of the province. Stretching the anatomical analogy still further, the premier said that members of the force will act as "the eyes and ears of the government."

It will curb tree-cutting along the highway, stamp out garbage dumping near roads, wipe out summer cottage building too near rivers and ponds, halt the pollution of public waters, and do "100 other things."

The force would restore public respect for the law by being responsible for "the enforcement of a raft ... a large number of simple but important laws and regulations" which have come into "contempt" for lack of enforcement.

"If properly selected and trained, the force can become famous across Canada, and not only across Canada but throughout the US," the premier went so far as to say.

"Its members will be a visible, physical embodiment of Newfoundland hospitality," he said, and such examples of courtesy and helpfulness that visitors would go back home raving about them.

The premier stressed the value of the Rangers to the tourist industry and predicted that visitors would crowd around for snapshots just as they do with the "Mounties" on Parliament Hill.

It will take several years to build up the force, since "quality is better than quantity," and the Rangers may eventually number 400 or 500. It has not yet been decided whether or not to send them out of the province for training.

At this point a recess was called and further debate on the Rangers bill was adjourned.

***

If the premier found it difficult to describe in more detail the workings of this singular corps, he succeeded in painting such a vivid outline that Honorable Members may have found their imaginations taking over where mere words failed.

In their mind's eye they may have seen a picturesque and striking figure windblown on the summit of a tolt in central Newfoundland – none other than Sgt. Trueheart Strong of the new Newfoundland Company of Rangers.

And what a figure the intrepid Sgt. Strong cuts, clad in the proud uniform of the force which at the premier's instigation has been designed by the great Paris fashion house of Balmain.

The distinct Newfoundland regalia is topped by a white pith helmet, encircled by a three-inch band of sealskin fixed in place by a cunning badge of labradorite bearing the Ranger cipher "J.R.S." – Justice Repairs Snapshots.

Then the military tunic in dory yellow, the breeches in medium Atlantic blue stuffed into tall leather boots (made for walkin'), and over all the flowing cape of Newfoundland tartan worn this year just two inches above the kneecap.

Sgt. Strong is justly proud of the uniform and has learned to ignore the more youthful tourists who frequently mistake him for a sort of Scottish Batman.

It's been a hard day and the lone Ranger takes a brief rest from one of his main duties – courteously striking fear into the hearts of Newfoundland scofflaws.

Already today he has apprehended, smilingly chastised and/or good-naturedly arrested two roadside woodcutters, one garbage dumper, two speed limit exceeders and three public water polluters.

From 10:30 a.m. to noon he has posed for tourist cameras in front of the public building at Grand Falls, performing the same vital function abreast of the Gander air museum for two hours in the afternoon.

Before lunch, he replaced 16 sparkplugs, put on seven hot patches, repaired three mufflers, removed bumblebees from inside four separate vehicles, and performed one emergency brain operation.

At 2:24 p.m. Sgt. Strong was called on to gallantly rescue a lady butterfly collector from Boston from the clutches of a berserk black bear near the western outskirts of Terra Nova National Park.

Immediately following this, he dutifully recorded in a notebook the sighting, near the same spot, of a lesser-breasted tom tit, as is his responsibility to the Department of Natural Resources.

Later in the afternoon, Sgt. Trueheart Strong performed what is perhaps his most important duty of all, that of acting as arm, eyes and ears of Her Majesty's provincial government.

The dashing Ranger made the rounds of all the outports in his area, collecting the tapes from the concealed tape recorders in all the general stores, making casual but pointed inquiries and generally attempting to spot any signs of restlessness among the natives.

Generally, the natives were a simple lot and there had been few signs of subversive activity – more the petty infringements such as moonshine making, turr shooting, and love-making without a permit.

Shortly after 5:15 p.m., Sgt. Strong had completed his rounds and forwarded his daily report, in secret code, to headquarters.

Sgt. Trueheart Strong of the new Newfoundland Company of Rangers prides himself in the work he had accomplished so far among the rural populace, but yet he harbors a twinge of disappointment.

Despite courteous suggestions, good-natured requests and mannerly threats, he has not succeeded in getting more than a handful of the natives to call him "Bwana Trueheart" or "Sahib Strong."

Now, as an early evening breeze ruffles his Newfoundland tartan cape, Sgt. Strong looks down from his tolt observation post on the broad Trans-Canada Highway and the many little outports under his care.

"Ah well," he sighs, wearily, looking back on a typical day in the life of a new Newfoundland Ranger. "Tomorrow will be Sunday." RG

They "sinned" against Confederation – Smallwood doles out the penances

March 9, 1966   *Joey*

The miserable wretches (some of them on government benches) who voted against Confederation in 1949 should carry their shame to their graves, says Premier J.R. Smallwood.

Hauling out all the stops during the budget speech debate yesterday, the premier laid down the penance he felt those who voted against Confederation should do to help ease the mortal "sin."

At least once a year they should do public penance, confess their "sin" on the public street, wrap themselves in brin bags, in sackcloth and ashes, "and ask forgiveness of the little children" for what they had done.

They should wail and lament on the street corner, make an annual open confession and pray in public for forgiveness.

The premier said some of his best friends, even some of the present members of the government, through "chuckleheadedness and muddleheadedness" voted against Confederation.

They might have done it in sincerity but nevertheless they will carry the shame and disgrace of it to their graves, he said.

The premier said it was silly and senseless for the Opposition to be "continually harping" on the faults of the government, since the government itself admits its faults.

It would be different and there would be some excuse for this continued criticism if the government professed to be perfect.

He said the Opposition persisted in an "intolerable chorus" of listing the government's failures: "Why do they talk about the rubber plant? Why don't they talk about the cement mill?"

Ambrose Peddle (PC-Grand Falls) interjected that the government had nearly 40 members who did very well at hymning their own praises.

The premier retorted that the proper place for a government member to criticize the government was in private, and the proper place for cabinet members to fight was in caucus.

"I tell them they have fine, fat jobs, good pay, swell offices, with hard but interesting work," he said, and further instructed his colleagues not to forget who to thank for their "fine, fat jobs" – the voters and the members of the House.

"I tell them not to get too big for their boots, not to get swell-headed because they can go down a lot faster than they came up."

The premier said government members were on constant guard against becoming "conceited stuffed shirts," and, although they had extreme pride in the government's accomplishments, they were never conceited about it.

Touching briefly on economics just before closing time last night, he said Newfoundland has received about $1 billion from the federal government and there is much more to come.

However, he looked forward to the day when the province would be producing more money itself – "more honest money, the best kind of money" – and would not have to rely on the rest of Canada to the extent it does at present. RG

"What's the matter with everyone's memory?"

March 24, 1966   *Joey*

Even his best friends won't tell him.

It apparently takes more gall than the House of Assembly can collectively muster to tell J.R. Smallwood he's wrong.

Several members on both sides of the House attempted to do so yesterday, vexed the premier, and got a good tongue-banging for their pains.

When second reading of a bill relating to the Marystown fish plant came up yesterday, the premier told the House there was no need for him to go into the details because he had described the project fully the day before.

Several Opposition members protested that the premier had not mentioned the fish plant the day before. Several cabinet members also shook their heads slightly.

The premier turned on his colleagues: "I did. I most definitely did. I remember it distinctly. I described it in great detail and at great length right here in this House last night.

"What's the matter with everyone's memory? Are you all losing your memory?" he said sternly to the offending ministers, who grew rosy about the ears and kept their eyes on low beam.

"So I have to remember everything myself? I described it fully. I remember. I'm not getting demented."

A.J. Murphy (PC-St. John's Centre) manfully took the tiger by the tail: "I may be losing my mind but I didn't hear the premier say anything about it," he said firmly.

"I see some of the honorable members over there indicating they didn't hear either," Mr. Murphy persisted. "Could we have a count of hands ...?"

"Honorable members should pay attention. They should stay awake. They should stay in their seats and listen. They should pay attention and not be getting up wandering off to the corridor for a cigarette," the premier rolled on.

"If they paid more attention they'd know what was said. I'm in my seat every minute. I don't miss a word that's spoken in this chamber," he continued.

"Even the other day when I went to sleep for two minutes I heard every word that was going on. I heard every word the honorable member for St. John's East Extern said."

Sensing an opening, the indomitable Mr. Murphy pounced again: "The premier couldn't have heard Mr. Browne speaking because he wasn't in the chamber," he said.

The premier had inadvertently – and through force of habit – referred to

W.J. Browne, the former member for St. John's East Extern, who often told the premier he was wrong.

Steve Neary (L-Bell Island) ventured to explain the premier's slip of the tongue. "The premier was having a nightmare," he said.

Later during the proceedings, when the premier threatened to have him ruled out of order, James J. Greene (PC-St. John's East) said the premier was unduly irritable.

Mr. Smallwood had announced when the morning sitting opened he was going to Panama – "Mr. Speaker, I go now to Panama … to hold talks with the president of Panama …"

Said Mr. Greene: "Sunny Central America beckons and the premier is understandably edgy to get away so we won't detain him too long." He cautioned the premier to be careful of revolutions down there.

By the afternoon sitting the premier had left for Ottawa, Panama, and other parts as yet unknown.

This, plus the fact that the end of the present session draws nigh, resulted in the most light-hearted sitting so far this term. ■

Foul weather, but fine day for Come By Chance

April 29, 1966   *Great New Industries*

The temperature hovered around 32 degrees, a piercing northwest wind gusted to 50 miles an hour and a full-scale snowstorm threatened.

But the men who plan to spend nearly $100 million near the oddly named community of Come By Chance were undaunted.

A group of US industrialists and engineers, escorted by Gordon F. Pushie, economic adviser to the Newfoundland government, and Dr. Stuart Peters, deputy minister of mines and resources, yesterday visited the site on the Isthmus of Avalon where a new pulp mill and petro-chemical plant are to be established.

Plans called for the visitors to fly by helicopter to the site about two miles from the end of the local Come By Chance road, but the inclement weather grounded everything except a few hardy Placentia Bay gulls.

The party, which included Mrs. Peters and Mrs. John Shaheen (wife of the New York financier who is one of the chief investors in the project), then elected to walk the two miles along the shoreline, through scrubby spruce and across a marsh to where the mills are to be built.

The visit convinced most of the residents of Come By Chance and surrounding communities that the long-awaited and often-postponed project was at last off the ground.

Said one awed observer as he shivered in the April gale: "Must be something to it this time if them people came all the way from the States to traipse around shore on a day like this."

The jolt, which Tuesday's announcement by Premier J.R. Smallwood sent through the area, seems to be just as great as that which hit Bell Island last week.

However, the effect on the people around Come By Chance and much of Placentia Bay must be exactly the reverse of that caused by the bad news for Bell Island.

Every scrap of news about the mills since the premier's statement two days ago is eagerly heard or listened to as people try to convince themselves the almost unbelievable will really come to pass.

Reaction runs the gamut from jubilation ("I knew Joey could do it, God bless 'en!") to skepticism ("I'll open my bottle when I see the roof going on").

Until yesterday's visit by the project's top officials there was little concrete evidence around Come By Chance that the mill would go ahead.

Last summer and fall groups of surveyors and engineers roamed the area behind the community, drove a few stakes into the harbor bottom and painted cryptic symbols in blood-red paint on the rocks along the shore.

But after 10 years of announcements and hopes deferred, it took something more than that. Residents are now eagerly looking forward to next week when workers are scheduled to start drilling down through the still-unbroken turf to establish bedrock foundations.

About 11:30 a.m. yesterday a small cavalcade of cars turned off the Trans-Canada Highway at the Come By Chance intersection, 100 miles from St. John's.

They drove along the half-mile secondary gravel road, past the cottage hospital, which is the largest building and focal point of the community, and pulled up at Drover's restaurant.

Inside, the visitors – including Mr. Shaheen, Dr. Peters, and their wives, Mr. Pushie, Arthur Lundrigan of Lundrigans Construction Ltd., and Albin Smith, president of the Newfoundland Ammonia and Refinery Ltd., and J.F.M. Taylor, president of Newfoundland Pulp and Chemical Ltd. – ordered coffee and cheese sandwiches.

Learning that it would be impossible for a helicopter to take off because of the wind, they decided to walk to the site. As fortification against the elements they first drove to Goobies, about 10 miles up the Trans-Canada, where at the forest ranger station Dr. Peters had arranged an outdoor lobster boil.

Despite the occasional flurry of driving snow and the chilly wind, Mrs. Shaheen declared the lobsters to be the best she had ever eaten. Her husband was reminded of an encounter with a lobster while swimming off the Florida Keys: "It had a 30-foot wingspan," he joked.

After lunch, the party returned to Come By Chance to find that a Department of Highways grader had leveled off the local road down to the harbor where usually it is nearly impassable.

Unlike most Newfoundland outports, Come By Chance is not located directly on the sea. Most of the men are employed with the railway so that the road to the harbor is not used too extensively.

Driving down to the beach where the whitecaps tumbled ashore, the visitors got out of their cars and started out on foot – past lobster pots stacked above the high-water mark, through tangles of driftwood and seaweed to a small cove containing a few fishermen's shacks.

Here, the federal government plans to build a $3 million wharf. Then, the intrepid group turned inland through scrub and barrens for another half-mile to where the mills will be located.

After consulting a sheaf of maps and plans (which the gale threatened to scatter across the countryside), Mr. Taylor, president of Newfoundland Pulp and Chemical Ltd., took a stick to which a small sign was attached and stuck it into the ground.

Mr. Smith, president and chief executive officer of Newfoundland Ammonia and Refinery Ltd., took a similar sign and several hundred yards away across a tiny stream pushed the sharpened end of the stick into the soil.

Both signs bore the single word – "HERE."

They marked the locations for a $57 million pulp and paper mill which will produce 600 tons of paper a day and use 330,000 cords of pulpwood a year, and an adjacent $29 million petro-chemical plant which annually will turn Venezeulan crude oil into 350,000 tons of a fertilizer ingredient.

When the group made their way back to the end of the road which they had left nearly two hours earlier, they found the beach lined with about 20 cars and trucks from Come By Chance and nearby communities – Sunnyside, Goobies, and Arnold's Cove.

The vehicles were filled with people who had come to see for themselves the latest evidence that a start on "the Mill" at last seems at hand.

The visitors then drove the three miles across the isthmus to Sunnyside, Trinity Bay, where pulpwood from Labrador would be landed and moved by conveyer belt to the mill site. After a quick tour of the harbor they returned to St. John's.

A start on construction of the project is scheduled for July and at the peak building period 1,200 men will be employed. When the plants go into operation in 1968 some 600 permanent workers will be needed in the area.

What the mills will do to Come By Chance its residents are still trying to comprehend. One hundred million dollars is enough money to make every family man now living in the community with the funny name a millionaire – with a couple of million to spare.

Spread much more thinly and together with a total payroll of about $12 million a year, the effect of the investment would be felt throughout the whole province.

The weather on April 28, 1966, was downright lousy, but if plans work out it will have been a fine day for Newfoundland.

They'll be marching on Port aux Basques

May 11, 1966   *Roads, Rails and Water*

If you've planned a leisurely drive along the Trans-Canada Highway in mid-July (around Orangeman's Day) you've got another think coming.

Not that you'll have to cancel your holiday outing, but you might as well forget the "leisurely" bit. You will run head-on – so to speak – into one of the most amazing sets of events ever to transpire on these shores.

Proceed as planned, go if you must, but brace yourself and be prepared. For what? You will now be put in the light of it.

It promises to be the march into Berlin, Chinese New Year, the cross-Canada auto rally, Barnum & Bailey circus, an East Africa safari, the last of the Crusades and a Santa Claus parade rolled into one.

Gold-painted jets of the Royal Canadian Air Force will swoosh, soar and zoom in breathtaking formation; the Royal Canadian Navy, not to be outdone, will grace the earth below with one of its biggest and best bands.

The Royal Canadian Army has been called in to provide bunks and blankets for 200 people; the Royal Canadian Mounted Police will have its hands full.

There will be a mobile calliope (a terrifically loud "musical" instrument powered by steam), amazing tableaux now being constructed behind closed doors, cunningly designed floats mounted on 20-ton trucks, fireworks, speeches, flags, decorations, and bushels of potato salad prepared by ladies' auxiliaries.

The list of notables, both native and from other parts, will outshine the mechanical wonders.

Prime Minister Pearson will forsake the glamor and excitement of Ottawa to travel to the dead heart of Newfoundland. Here, he will unveil a 60-foot-tall monument from which, on a clear day, you can see forever.

And heading a two-mile-long caravan across the island, the pièce de résistance of the whole show – Premier J.R. Smallwood ensconced behind the wheel of an aging but game Land Rover.

What? What? What?

The official opening of the Trans-Canada Highway in Newfoundland, that's what.

No simple "pass the scissors, whack off a ribbon, three cheers and a tiger" sort of deal this time. This is going to be a really big show.

Yesterday, the 50 or more key men planning (or delegated to carry out plans) for this mid-summer extravaganza were called together in the hearings room of the Department of Labour, Confederation Building.

Tourist director O.L. Vardy, appointed field marshal for the march on Port aux Basques, reviewed the troops and told them Premier Smallwood expects every man to do his duty.

Local and national police, the army and navy, the engineering profession, the Department of Highways, the press (both electronic and printed), public works, the architects, the business community and – last but not, etc. – the contractors, were represented at the briefing.

Mr. Vardy gave notice from the outset that a certain amount of secrecy must be maintained.

He explained that Premier Smallwood has directed that while reports of preparations by the spoken and written word are permitted, photographs of the work in progress are verboten.

A styrofoam curtain has descended so that the amazement and delight of the general populace may be all the greater when these creations are unveiled on TCH day.

Tentative dates, to be confirmed before the week is out, have been set: July 11 (departure from St. John's), July 12 (official opening), July13 (arrival, God willing, at Port aux Basques).

According to present plans – and they're changing slightly all the time – fever pitch in the preparations will be reached on the Sabbath of July 10 when the 30 floats and sign-bearing trucks for the giant cavalcade will assemble in the shadow of Confederation Building.

At 9 a.m. the next day, the two-mile parade will be launched westward-ho with the RCAF zipping past overhead, the RCN Band opened full throttle and the police endeavoring to keep the young members of the community from under the wheels.

Premier Smallwood will head the procession driving (if the aging vehicle can take it) the identical Land Rover in which he drove across the province in 1958.

With the calliope tootling, the entourage will first descend on the town of Whitbourne, take a turn around the community, and possibly some speeches will be delivered.

Then on to Clarenville for lunch and refreshments, onward still to Gander with stops en route at Port Blandford, Traytown and vicinity.

The army (Canadian, not Salvation) will take over at Gander to provide beds, bedding and other amenities for the estimated 200 people in the tour who will be billeted in the radar barracks.

Local festivities are planned at Gander to coincide with the arrival of the caravan.

Grand Falls is the next on the list and another gay time is planned here – speeches, fireworks, a parade through town and another bash at the old calliope.

The pinnacle of the entire proceedings will be achieved somewhere west of Grand Falls at the exact mid-point on the highway between St. John's and Port aux Basques.

Here, Prime Minister Pearson will unveil, dedicate and otherwise put into service a monument marking completion of the highway but of which only a few tantalizing details have as yet been released to the public.

According to informed sources, the structure will stand on a modified tolt from which may be had a 10-mile view in all directions, weather permitting.

It will be – so far as can be gathered – in the shape of a prism standing on end and will rise to a height of 60 feet. It will be floodlit, spotlit, backlit in parts, and decorative waters may be employed.

Sunset of the second day will bring the parade into Corner Brook, where again the participants will be placed in the hands of the army.

An army representative present at the briefing promised that veterans of the wars among those taking part would be reminded of their days of military service by the double-decker bunk beds, army blankets and other facilities to be provided at this overnight stop.

Throughout the three-day trek, Golden Eagle tank trucks will cruise along with the procession to refuel the motor vehicles en route.

So as not to have the final goal and end of the trip an anti-climax, Mr. Vardy explained that special attention will be paid to ceremonies at Port aux Basques. Details are to follow.

At Port aux Basques the premier will also officially open a public building, and various local festivities are planned at the western terminal of the highway.

Ladies' organizations along the way have agreed to feed the travelers at buffets in community buildings.

An RCMP officer present at the meeting called on all those taking part to have their vehicles in top-notch condition and to employ their best drivers.

He pointed out that a single accident could cast a loom over the whole proceedings.

Tourist director Vardy said the show would go on regardless of the weather and hastened to add there was no doubt that it would be ideal. ▰

Sunshine all the way

June 7, 1966   *News and Propaganda*

The Newfoundland film that according to Come Home Year chairman Dr. F.W. Rowe will receive the widest distribution, both locally and abroad, of any such movie yet made was shown for the first time yesterday in St. John's.

Finance Minister Rowe, referring to the film "Come Home, Newfoundlander" at the last CHY meeting, said that as many copies as possible of the film will be distributed throughout the province this summer to practically any responsible group that asks for it.

Dr. Rowe said the movie was calculated to make Newfoundlanders more aware of the glories of their own province and arouse feelings of pride in the breasts of former Newfoundlanders.

The Newfoundland and Labrador Press Club, during its monthly meeting at the Newfoundland Hotel last night, got the first look at the film, which will soon be showing at halls, meeting places and on improvised outdoor screens throughout the province.

On hand for the première was the producer, Lee Wulff, internationally known sportsman and wildlife promoter who for more than 30 years has spent much of his time hunting, fishing and working in Newfoundland. He was introduced by Press Club president E.J. Bonnell.

The 27-minute color film was commissioned by the provincial government. According to Mr. Wulff such a film costs about $1,000 a minute to produce. Each print or copy of the film will cost $200 each.

Mr. Wulff and Bill Croke, official photographer with the provincial government, shot the footage; Mr. Wulff wrote the script and the film is narrated by tourist director O.L. Vardy.

Although the film is considerably better from the technical viewpoint than previous government-sponsored films, those who expected a respite from the customary heavy-handed government propaganda are in for a disappointment.

For the first few opening minutes the viewer is led to believe that here at last is the genuine article – a production that will start nostalgic tears flowing among the Newfoundland expatriates in Toronto, and cause those still domiciled on the native rock to sing "the Ode" a few decibels higher.

There are blue-green seas washing on rocky beaches, mirror-still ponds reflecting white clouds and blue sky, neat outports set amid the intense green grass of early summer, new buildings shot from the best angle, and wildflower closeups with Newfoundland bumblebees on them.

Before the more sentimentally patriotic viewer can get out the hanky and indulge in a few preliminary sniffs, the real purpose of the film becomes obvious.

It sets in early and gradually rises to a crescendo in the final scenes with narrator Vardy launching into a full-fledged eulogy of Premier Smallwood as the sun sets in golden splendor behind Confederation Building.

By this time the viewer feels like a Tobolsk peasant paying May Day homage at the tomb of Lenin.

Mr. Wulff was constrained, in a short address before the screening started, to offer an apology of sorts for any apparent emphasis in this direction.

The stress laid on one particular person is no less than a reflection of the facts, he said. Premier Smallwood has been at the helm during all these years of progress.

"If there had been a couple of other governments during that time, of course their achievements would have been shown too – but it's been the Liberals all the way." OK? OK.

What's likely to bug Newfoundland viewers, regardless of the way they mark their X, is the grossly lopsided coverage of the province, keeping in mind that you can't get everything into 27 minutes.

St. John's gets about 75 per cent of the footage, 15 per cent is devoted to Premier Smallwood wielding shovel and scissors in the wilds of Labrador, and the remainder is made up of general scenery.

New schools have gone up all over – shots of St. John's high schools. Newfoundland's youth enjoy modern recreations – scenes around St. John's swimming pools. "Construction crews work frantically" – pictures of work in a St. John's subdivision.

After about 10 minutes of St. John's the scene changes and we see an outport with a schooner docked at the main wharf. At last, a bit of fish guts and tickleace feathers to draw a nostalgic sigh from the exiles in Boston and Toronto.

But hark! Narrator Vardy is telling us that the schooner has all but faded from the scene and more Newfoundlanders are likely to be better acquainted with vessels such as these – and the camera moves in on the pleasure craft moored in the Royal Newfoundland Yacht Club at Manuels near St. John's.

A short step from there to tuna fishing and we see on the screen tourist director Vardy, stripped to the waist, battling the elusive bluefin as on the soundtrack tourist director Vardy describes the thrills and fascination of this growing Newfoundland sport.

But enough of roughing it in the boondocks. Back to St. John's and civilization where Premier Smallwood and Louis St. Laurent dedicate Confederation Building, Premier Smallwood and Eleanor Roosevelt open Memorial University, Premier Smallwood and Queen Elizabeth survey the city from Price Philip Drive, Premier Smallwood and the Portuguese ambassador unveil a statue of Gaspar Corte Real ...

When we finally bid farewell to the capital city it is to accompany Premier Smallwood to Baie d'Espoir where he officially opens the hydro project there; to Wabush in Labrador where he officially opens the Smallwood mine; to Twin

Falls where he officially opens another power project.

Our 27 minutes will soon be up. You can tell the end is near because the sunsets get rosier and so does the narration.

How well Mr. Wulff succeeds in the task assigned to him and how well the new movie captures the real Newfoundland are both shown in one aspect of the film.

Every single foot of the 27-minute production was shot in brilliant sunshine. There's no mist, no fog, no rain, no snow, no drizzle, no overcast, even. It's sunshine all the way. ▣

Baie d'Espoir project in full stride

October 17, 1966   *Great New Industries*

A weird and wonderful place is Baie d'Espoir.

Take the name, for a start. It means exactly the opposite in French to what it sounds like in local English.

A place where mud is not just plain mud but "impervious glacial till," and a purple and green house with 20 windows is fairly commonplace.

Where you can stand and look down on the top of the tallest hydro surge tank in the world; where a hill one week is a peninsula the next, then an island and disappears before the month is out.

A place where five-pound mud trout swim through the trees.

Members of the Atlantic Development Board were taken on a whirlwind tour of the hydro development on Newfoundland's south coast yesterday and came away much impressed.

"If the ADB had done nothing else but make available a $24 million grant for the Baie d'Espoir project," said Dr. Ernest Weeks, executive director of the board, "its existence would still be justified."

A similar comment came from Ian MacKeignan, chairman of the ADB, who marveled at the scope of the project and the speed with which it is becoming a reality.

Costing $84 million in all, including a network of high voltage transmission lines connecting the island north, east and west, the project will start producing the first 100,000 of a planned 600,000 horsepower by March 1, 1967.

"Frankly, it wasn't too long ago that the March 1967 deadline seemed impossible," says George Hobbs, chairman of the Newfoundland and Labrador Power Commission. "But the people on the job pulled off a minor miracle and we're bang on schedule."

About 2,000 workers are busy at Camp Boggy at the head of Baie d'Espoir with the project now in full stride. There are several years more work ahead as other phases of the development are brought in.

By plane (which circled the area several time before landing at the new gravel-surfaced air strip), by helicopter, bus, and on foot, the ADB members were given a comprehensive look at the striking progress made so far.

The dams are all but finished. Salmon River Dam, barring off the end of Long Pond, has been readied for the three huge floodgates which will keep back the waters of the reservoir.

Long Pond is already flooding its shores and rising at the rate of two inches a day toward its ultimate increase of 60 feet.

The North Cutoff Dam contains the reservoir north of the overflow outlet and except for a few finishing touches along the top is in working order.

This is where the special Baie d'Espoir mud, otherwise know as impervious glacial till comes in. It is greenish grey, looks like wet cement, and with rock quarried on the site forms the entire 130-foot-high, 2,500-foot-long North Cutoff Dam, most of the Salmon River Dam, plus several smaller retaining walls, a natural windfall for the contractors.

When the reservoir reaches its ultimate depth it will spill over into a short canal, taking the water to the edge of a plateau and through huge pipes down a steep slope to the powerhouse 600 feet below.

The drive now is to get the pipes or penstocks with the control gates at their upper ends into position before the reservoir overflows.

Midway down the slope finishing touches are being put to a 360-foot-high surge tank, one of three in the final installation, which will be the tallest structures of their kind in the world.

At the powerhouse itself the concrete outer walls and floors have been poured, and the beddings readied for the turbines which by next March will be spinning out the first 100,000 horsepower of cheap electricity for a power-short Newfoundland.

Transmission trails branch out from the powerhouse north toward Grand Falls and east towards Come By Chance. By the end of this year the power grid should be completed to Grand Falls and Deer Lake, and to Come By Chance to connect with already completed lines to St. John's.

By March 1967, a branch line to Marystown-Burin will be finished, by May an extension to Stephenville, and by September to Port aux Basques.

Even as the first stage of the project nears completion, attention is being concentrated on rivers to the west, the watersheds of which will be ultimately diverted into the Long Pond Reservoir at Baie d'Espoir.

A project map for Baie d'Espoir shows the drainage areas of the Salmon, Grey and White Bear Rivers, covering most of the interior of the island.

The lakes formed by the dams across these rivers will rival Gander Lake in size, drowning much of the surrounding countryside as is now happening at Baie d'Espoir.

And the age-old battle between the developers and the conservationists is in full swing.

More than 300,000 cords of wood were salvaged from the advancing waters of Long Pond reservoir, but even at that the water is creeping upward through the pockets of tall spruce and birch remaining.

Trout up to five pounds are being caught in the lake but already, and despite claims that the flooded areas will become a great fishing and boating playground, the truth is obvious.

Submerged tree trunks and a tangle of underwater branches threaten to make the new lakes a nightmare for the fisherman and a disaster for operators of outboard motorboats.

There were no salmon to worry about anyway in the Salmon River, say the engineers, but the Grey River, next on the list for development, is one of the best in the province.

Wildlife officials are now pressing for some means of preserving the Grey for salmon in spite of the proposed dam across its source, and some compromise may be reached.

Attention will then be turned to the White Bear River and, before the smoke of battle between conservationists and developers dies, here the focus will shift to the Terra Nova River and its tributaries.

The Terra Nova is now being surveyed as another likely source of power with a dam that would create a huge lake near the borders of Terra Nova National Park to serve a powerhouse at Port Blandford.

If the Baie d'Espoir development is confusing to the fish, the human inhabitants of the area seem to be taking it in stride.

There are few obvious external changes in the communities of St. Alban's, St. Joseph's, St. Veronica's and Swangers Cove, although under the surface the changes are many.

New prosperity has put a television antenna on every other house and the number of motor vehicles has zoomed from a half-dozen to several hundred in little more than a year.

Large freighters call at the improved and extended government wharf at St. Alban's; a dozen new homes are going up at the officially approved townsite area.

A trailer park for 40 families of top supervisors on the project stands on a hill above St. Veronica's. Under birch trees three and four feet in diameter the trailer homes, crammed with every convenience and appliance of a Toronto suburb, command a spectacularly beautiful view of the long, calm inlet of Baie d'Espoir.

The original houses of the area are unique in two ways – by the extraordinary number of windows in each and by their vivid color schemes.

Why have the houses of Baie d'Espoir so many windows? Nobody seems to know, but some of them – two-story frame buildings in typical Newfoundland outport style – have as many as eight per side and four in each end.

Many of them, painted in strong colors of green or yellow with purple or aqua blue trim, make a striking contrast against the still waters of this picturesque indraft where the heavily forested hills roll right down to the shore.

Among the new buildings at St. Alban's is a school built to take advantage of the abundant electricity to be produced a few miles away.

It is designed to be heated entirely by electricity, but of course awaits March 1 when the first power comes on.

Meanwhile, the old school is greatly crowded with two teachers to every room. Nearly 100 first-year pupils did not go back to school in September because there was no space for them.

If the rest of Newfoundland eagerly awaits the day when cheap power from Baie d'Espoir becomes available, the residents of the area sometimes look forward to it with apprehension.

An industrial area has been set aside in the valley nearby, but so far the promise of abundant and inexpensive electricity has not drawn a factory to the site.

Some residents fear that when the hydro development project is finished and the 2,000 workmen leave the powerhouse to a maintenance staff of 30 their newfound prosperity will go with them ... unless the factories move in.

Whatever happens, this part of the south coast will never be as isolated as it has been since the first settlers landed.

A road leading north to the Trans-Canada Highway is within seven miles (and one bridge) in primary stage of completion.

In little more than a year (probably by late fall 1967) it should be possible for motorists to drive down and see for themselves the wonders, both natural and man-made, that await at the head of Baie d'Espoir. ᴿᴳ

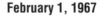 "Moby Joe" in Burgeo going on relief

February 1, 1967   *Resettlement and Rural Life*

Operation Moby Joe swings into action on the isolated south coast of Newfoundland today because Premier Smallwood has put a starving 80-ton whale on special government relief.

The first handout – live herring – was expected to be delivered today to a 60-foot mammal, trapped in Aldridge's Pond a half-mile east of Burgeo.

In response to an appeal from author Farley Mowat, who lives about a mile from the pond, Premier Smallwood told the Legislature the government had "adopted" the helpless creature and had allotted $1,000 for its care and feeding.

At the same time, he warned against any "attacks on government property" by those who had blazed away at the whale with high-powered rifles and terrified it with speed boats since it became trapped in the saltwater pond January 21.

"We may disown this whale in a few weeks," the premier said, "but we want the world to know that we don't ignore whales when they come visiting us."

It was while the premier was speaking that Public Works Minister James R. Chalker suggested calling the whale Moby Joe and the name stuck despite Mr. Smallwood's objections.

The finback whale, second only to the blue whale as the largest mammal, plunged over a submerged reef into the pond while pursuing a school of herring. It failed in several attempts to get out and was reported Tuesday to have abandoned its efforts to escape.

Both the premier and Mr. Mowat, who appointed himself the whale's protector, expressed the hope that scientists and photographers would use the rare opportunity to study one of the largest whales on earth at close range.

Meanwhile, Mr. Mowat was formulating plans to keep it alive until March, when high spring tides would make a rescue attempt feasible. The whale might be dragged and towed by the tail to deep water.

The Sou'wester's Club of Burgeo has agreed to coordinate efforts to keep Moby Joe supplied with food. A barge will be built to carry the live fish to the pond. A Memorial University professor speculated the daily food consumption of such a whale would be "several cubic yards."

Moby Joe appears to be recovering from a barrage of 500 bullets fired into his back, Mr. Mowat said. The whale was forced ashore twice during the weekend by motorboats, but now this harassment also could be halted with government authority.

Experts have said the whale probably could leave the pond but it is afraid to go near shallow water or any spot where it was grounded previously.

***

Even though the provincial government has announced it will spend up to $1,000 to feed the Burgeo whale, chances are the whale will not survive.

A Fisheries Research Board of Canada spokesman said Tuesday that to feed the whale, local fishermen will have to bring in dead caplin or dead herring. Whales, as a rule, will not feed on dead fish, the spokesman said.

He said he didn't know exactly how the fisherman planned to feed it, but he pointed out the whale would have to get all the fish before they went to the bottom. Whales won't feed off the bottom; its size makes it almost physically impossible.

He said it is probable the whale could live in the saltwater pond if the fishermen find a way to feed it properly. The best way to handle the situation would be to find some way to herd the whale out through the opening through which it entered.

Commenting on reports that another whale came close to the pond and communicated with the trapped mammal, the spokesman said it could have been the whale's mate. He said that whales do have a way of communicating to each other with sounds.

Recordings of whales communicating with each other have been made at Dildo. A group of whales communicating sounds like a group of pigs grunting and squealing, the spokesman said.

Meanwhile the federal fisheries control vessel *Badger Bay* has been sent to investigate the situation at Burgeo and report findings to St. John's. ◼

Moby Joe R.I.P.?

February 8, 1967   *Resettlement and Rural Life*

While hope springs eternal within the human breast, and the night seems darkest just before the dawn, it now appears that Moby Joe, Newfoundland's 80-ton welfare case, has gone to his reward – or at least to the bottom of Aldridge's Pond in the suburbs of Burgeo.

Premier J.R. Smallwood, manfully masking his emotions, rose in a subdued House of Assembly on Tuesday to read a distressing dispatch from Farley "Ahab" Mowat, Keeper of the Whale (Ret.).

According to Mr. Mowat, Moby Joe crossed the bar, either figuratively or actually, on the fatal night of February 6.

After an anxious vigil on the shores of Aldridge's Pond Tuesday, the Keeper concluded that the beloved behemoth had either succumbed and sunk or else (and the chance is pitifully slight) had managed to escape from the barrisway by lunging across a sandbar at the entrance.

Kindness is what killed "M.J.," Mr. Mowat concludes. Newfoundland's "hospitality" in the form of a riddling with some 500 .303 bullets and a rallying by motorboats and small aircraft.

Wounds received in this warm welcome festered and the whale became exhausted after visitors scared it by coming too close in boats and planes.

Even $1,000 worth of herring (or the promise of same) failed to compensate for this initial reception and Moby Joe is presumed to have shuffled off this mortal coil and sunk, dead as an 80-ton doornail, to Davy Jones's locker.

At Mr. Mowat's suggestion the premier expressed gratitude to all those at home and abroad who had sent good wishes and offers of help and took note of the "massive interest of the mainland press" in the whale's situation.

"All Newfoundlanders will feel a lively regret at his (or her) passing," said the premier, as eyes moistened and a slight flurry of Kleenex occurred on both sides of the honorable House.

"I am confident that in this world of strain, uncertainty and worry, millions have had just a little relief, a moment's distraction from their own troubles, as they followed the fortunes of Moby Joe."

Several members nodded gravely and those on Opposition benches appeared on the verge of delivering something suitable from Tennyson.

The premier said the fine work done by Mr. Mowat was much appreciated and that he could never erase from his mind the picture of Mr. Mowat boarding Moby Joe and rowing the stricken whale out of the shallows into deeper water.

In a poignant sequel, Mr. Mowat reported later that a search had not turned up the remains but it was presumed that the deceased lay in nine fathoms of water at the bottom of Aldridge's Pond.

"A guardian whale which had been keeping vigil near the entrance disappeared late Monday afternoon and it has not been seen since."

The keeper of the late whale said the failure to save Moby Joe was due in part to the extreme isolation of Burgeo. A team of whale experts spent the last five days trying to reach the place but even the US Navy couldn't get them there, he said.

"Had they arrived earlier it is likely that the seriousness of Moby's condition would have been recognized and treatment could have been given in time."

Aldridge's Pond is 500 yards long, 300 yards wide and about a half-mile downwind from Burgeo.

In time, Moby Joe is expected to rise again to the surface, in which case the regret of Burgeo residents at the passing of their late guest is expected to be even a little more lively than that of the general Newfoundland populace.

For this reason interment arrangements are being thought of and a cost-plus contract may be let to one of the several large Newfoundland firms well experienced in handling such delicate matters.

No herring (red or otherwise) by request. RG

No R.I.P. for Moby Joe ...
stiff problem for Burgeo

February 10, 1967   *Resettlement and Rural Life*

Moby Joe, the friendly but famished 80-ton pet of the Newfoundland government for two weeks, lay dead and dangerous today on the surface of the saltwater pond at Burgeo where he died.

Ironically, the deadly infection threatening anyone who touches the huge carcass apparently was the result of the only unkind hand raised against the whale during his imprisonment behind a reef at the mouth of the pond.

Doctors ruled Thursday the whale died of septicemia, a blood poisoning caused by massive infection of wounds suffered January 21-22 when "a handful" of the 1,600 residents of Burgeo blasted away at the helpless creature with ex-army rifles.

There are no available antibiotics capable of curing anyone who contracts the infection from the whale, doctors said, warning residents not to try cutting up the carcass for disposal even though the stench is almost unbearable.

The whale may be towed out to sea and sunk with naval gunfire.

Author Farley Mowat, who was appointed keeper of the whale by the Newfoundland government, said Thursday Moby is causing a "hellish stench."

A husband and wife doctor team at Burgeo, Doctors Michael and Ann Calder, said it's possible that anyone touching the whale could pick up the infection, which is actually blood poisoning on a massive scale. The infection is so strong, however, that antibiotics would have no effect.

"Then," asked Mr. Mowat, "how are we going to get rid of the body?"

He said the whale rose from the bottom of the pond some time Wednesday night and was discovered around 9 a.m. Thursday. It was bloated about 12 feet above the waterline and covered with snow.

"The stench from the dead whale is terrible and if there is an easterly wind the people of Burgeo will have a big problem. They have to get it out, but they are not certain how."

Health Minster James McGrath said Thursday the government will likely find some way to get rid of the body.

Mr. Mowat suggested that arrangements be made with the United States Navy for a gunboat to tow the body out to sea and sink it with gunfire. It would have to be final, he stated, because if the body ever re-floated, it could become a navigational hazard.

The whale, nicknamed Moby Joe after Premier Smallwood announced that the government would provide $1,000 to fishermen who would catch herring for the whale, entered Aldridge's Pond January 21 while chasing a school of herring.

Mr. Mowat, admittedly hurt by the mammal's death, said it could have been kept alive if residents hadn't fired at it. He explained yesterday that "the whole of Burgeo shouldn't be blamed for killing the whale as it was just a minority group."

He said his estimate of 500 bullets in the whale was "a conservative guess." There are enough brass cartridges along the shoreline to collect and sell for scrap metal, Mr. Mowat said.

"The local hardware store was selling cartridges for two days straight."

A guardian whale, which had apparently been keeping in contact with Moby Joe since he entered his saltwater prison, was off the entrance to the pond all day Wednesday, but because of stormy conditions Thursday it was not known if it was in the area.

The author said he will probably write a book about the whale and "it won't be pleasant; it will describe the conditions here at the time."

"It won't be for money, either," he said. ☒

No more 'round the mountain:
We'll be ridin' CN buses*

October 6, 1967   *Roads, Rails and Water*

"What? By train!" asked the surprised CN ticket agent when I phoned for reservations.

"Right," said I. "St. John's to Port aux Basques. And return the next day. No, I'm not traveling on a pass."

No shame to the poor man. Well he might marvel. The CN still gets some passengers undertaking the 547-mile trek but one asking for a double dose with no time off for a rest cure between must be a rarity.

Even the Royal Commission on Transportation has declined an invitation by the railway unions to try it just ONE way. *The Telegram* rushed me in where royal commissions fear to tread.

And, as I said to myself frequently between Gravol ("for the prevention of nausea and vomiting") tablets and complimentary CN meals during the course of the 1,094-mile experience: "What a hell of a way to make a living."

The railway wants to do away with the 86-year-old train passenger service and speed travelers back and forth by bus. Strenuously opposed are the railway unions and the St. John's city council which fear loss of jobs and business, and Joseph O'Keefe, MP for St. John's East.

Railway employees are circulating "save the train" petitions. Opposition Leader Gerry Ottenheimer says no changes should be made until the public has been polled.

Here is my straw vote on it for Gerry and this advice to the venerable members of the Royal Commission: Stick to your guns, chaps, and don't risk the trip.

Come on with the buses. Train travel in Newfoundland is a tedious, grueling, outmoded, slow and painful way to get about. Planes, cars, buses, motorcycles, or roller skates must be better. Crawling across on your hands and knees can't be too much worse.

Second class for Newfoundlanders

The island's railway had "second class" built into it from the start. A bill passed by the government in 1881 stated that "the railway intended to be constructed shall not be what is deemed in England or the United States, a first-class railway."

Donald Gordon, former president of the CNR, implied shortly before his resignation that Newfoundland still could not afford better than second class.

It would take at least $150,000,000, he said, to straighten out our crooked little railway and move the rails one foot, two and a half inches further apart.

Newfoundland's rails are now a substandard three feet, six inches wide –

the only narrow-gauge line of its length left in North America.

Our rail cars and diesel engines have to be especially made and are the same size as those in use in some of the small banana-belt countries of South America.

Still, says Mr. Gordon, the narrow-gauge is not to be sneezed at. With the $179 million in improvements made since Confederation there is now no reason to convert to standard gauge and "wisecracks about the Newfie Bullet are no longer warranted."

On the other hand, railway union leader Esau Thoms says CN has become sloppy about its passenger service. More people would go "the way of the worry-free" if the cars and service were spruced up.

Whatever the cause, CN's train passenger service is going downgrade with the throttle open. For the first six months of this year CN carried 43,585 people. In 1965, for the same period they had 83,744.

Gordon D. McMillan, CN's area manager, said recently: "The public is abandoning the rail passenger service – not us."

Perhaps the public shouldn't be faulted too much on this account.

Away we go on the Bullet

So away we go. If forced or, for some weird reason you must travel across the island by train, you must present yourself at the old stone terminal Water Street West not later than 11:30 p.m. on Mondays, Wednesdays, or Fridays.

The first thing that may strike you (apart from porters burdened down with baggage) is that the inside of the station has been REDONE in CN modern.

Light paneling, fluorescent lights, new drink machines, pay lockers for parcels and electric blue jackets for the lads behind the counters.

Once outside on the train platform, however, you will soon find that the railway is still attached to its traditional colors – Nazi green and chopped liver.

And there, panting to be off, stands your conveyance. Identical in size to those chugging through the Honduras jungle it consists of a 1,200-horsepower narrow-gauge diesel towing a couple of mail cars, four "day coaches," a diner and five "sleepers."

At the outset, let me admit that I cheated. I had a sleeper … $23, meals included. I chickened out of the supreme test – jogging across the island in a "day coach."

People do. Those who can't afford a sleeper or who are traveling by train for the first time and aren't aware of the terrors involved.

A stroll through a "day coach" at 2 a.m. is an unforgettable sight. The Black Death has struck. Twisted bodies sprawled in fantastic shapes. Mouths agape. Hideous snores and groans.

Bottles rolling from side to side as on a derelict vessel. Frightened children crying. Limp arms and legs flopping in the aisles as the train jiggles and jolts through the night.

A degrading experience for those forced to travel on Newfoundland's second-class transportation system designed for second-class citizens.

There are two things which prove impossible in a CN "day coach" – sleeping and raising a window.

Only twice in my life have I succeeded in wrenching open a CN window and in one of these cases it later crunched down on my elbow.

Sleeping more than 10 minutes at a stretch in the day coach is the equivalent of swimming Cabot Strait in a suit of armor. The seats are so cunningly designed that writhe and twist as you will, some part of your frame will come in contact with bare metal or wood or glass.

The Bullet averages at least one "killer lurch" every 10 minutes. You either stay alert or risk getting your face smashed against the windowsill.

Could the solution be a sleeper? Since the westbound leaves near midnight CN beds you down as soon as you step aboard.

Sleepers and day coaches alike, however, have the same type of ventilation system. Sleeper windows will rise a few inches – to reveal another sooty pane containing a small strip of dirt-clogged screen.

More air could pass through a mosquito's nostril. No. The CN method is to pump all cars full of fumes, smoke and grime in downtown St. John's and hermetically seal them.

The characteristic smell on the CN is of coal smoke and stale urine. The coal smoke is, as has been explained, pumped aboard and locked in at St. John's.

The latter fragrance is emitted mainly by the washroom. So incredible was the stench in the Bishop's Falls (sleepers are named after prominent stops along the railway) water closet I was led to investigate others. They were all alike. The men's, anyway.

Situated over the pertinent fixture in the men's convenience is a card quoting the Canada Criminal Code on spitting and gambling in public places.

I would lay a two-to-one bet that no one can take a deep breath in a CN train washroom and still remain standing. You take a deep breath outside, hold it as long as possible and when that gives out risk pinching little breaths and shallow gasps.

From time to time a porter circulated through the Bishop's Falls sleeping car dispensing a few quick squirts of Florient air deodorant, then bashfully hiding the can under his jacket.

He was like the fly spitting in the ocean.

All for the sake of a beer

And so to bed. All is quiet in the Bishop's Falls sleeper, the tranquility broken only by the rhythm of the wheels – whackety whack, whackety whack, smash, bang, lurch – and the rending screech of rusty metal rubbing together where the cars are coupled.

Soon the air is rent by an internal commotion which revolves around a flurry of enthusiastic oaths delivered with a Scottish accent.

Heads pop out, top and bottom, from behind the chopped liver curtains. The grand old Scottish curses are redoubled.

Eventually, the racket dies down, mystified faces withdraw behind the curtained walls. Peace reigns once more. Whackety whack, whackety whack, smash, bang, lurch.

Then at 2 a.m., "up she goes" again. This time the Scotsman far surpasses his previous efforts. The lights are turned on. The porter is summoned. The fragrant air turns blue. There are threats and curses and angry words which take at least 20 minutes to subside.

Only next morning are the details revealed. In every CN car there is at least one drunk.

Those who would deplore this custom have obviously never traveled across the island by train cold sober. Just as the invention of ether relieved untold suffering in the operating room so does alcohol have its place on the CN.

Our drunk had taken a case of beer into his top bunk and supped away as the Bullet jogged merrily through the night.

In the berth below lay one-half of a Scottish couple, now resident in Toronto, and returning from a holiday in quaint hospitable Newfoundland.

The first row started when the chap in the upper dozed off and spilled a bottle of beer on the tourist in the lower.

The second fracas, half-hour later, occurred when the jolly traveler in No. 3 upper became nauseous, leaned out, and spewed all over the occupant of No. 3 lower.

In came the porter, wrested the remainder of the beer away from the bad boy and threatened to heave him off. At which he began to snore. He slept peacefully until dawn.

"Oh, it's not been a bad holiday," observed the Scottish tourist next day. "Just before leaving we went to a rrrestarunt forr a bite and a fight starrted. They locked the dooors and there we were in the midst.

"Aparrut from that and you bluddy idjot lost night we hod a verra nice time. Aye, we plon tae coom back next soomer. We lairned this time how tae save a few dollarrrs along the way."

For all that, his wife looked a bit washy and made frequent trips to the brake for the only fresh air available.

"Odd," said he. "She generrruly hos a cast irron stoomik when traveling. Moost ha been thot bit of business lost night."

Later, as we neared Port aux Basques, boozy Bill, still three parts, began pestering the porter for the return of his beer. Denied, he commenced tongue-banging and insulting the Scottish couple.

"Let's gang up and heave the bastard through the porthole," suggested a Bell Islander, fed up by now with this treatment of visitors to our shores.

At that the culprit scuttled off and was not seen again in the Bishop's Falls sleeper for the duration.

It all helps pass the time. So do meals.

Action galore in the diner

There always seems to be a preponderance of elderly ladies in the dining car. They do a lot of sighing that the food and service is not what it used to be.

But the diner still seems to bring out the grande dame in them. Paper serviettes have replaced the white linen cloths, the silverware is getting a bit shabby, you still write out your own check (with a rather brusque reminder from the waiters not to put in the price) and after the grub is stowed away, an offer "would modom care for after-dinner mints?"

Most of the items on the menu now cost $1.90 with soup, tea and dessert extra.

For this price I had five sausages of four-and-one-half inches in length, a scoop of mashed potato and 23 pieces of green bean. Then 40 cents for a heaping tablespoon of rice pudding and 15 cents for a cup of tea.

If CN takes its air on at St. John's it must get its supply of water from Port aux Basques.

Our western gateway has the dirtiest looking drinking water I've ever seen. Hotel guests there sometimes complain that the toilet wasn't flushed after the last room occupant left. It was.

Fill a bathtub and you can't see the plug in the bottom. In a glass it looks only a shade lighter than Guinness Stout.

If the railway insists on serving Port aux Basques water it might consider placing a small card with each carafe: "For our patrons we have provided the celebrated Eau de Port aux Basque certified by Dr. Schlezwig-Holstein of Heidelburg to be beneficial in the case of liver, kidney, stomach and lung ailments."

And charge extra for it. That's what the Europeans do with their dirty water.

There's action galore in the diner. As the train jogs along, the dishes tend to wander around the table and with each jolt head for the edge.

I got a shot of hot tea up the nose just east of Millertown Junction while at the same time a man across the way poured Eau de Port aux Basques into the lap of a woman sitting opposite him.

Our menu covers depict scenes on mainland trains. Bright upholstery, woodgrain paneling, large windows, wide cars. They might as well sling a lead life-ring to a drowning man as circulate that on Newfoundland trains. We're second class, remember.

Back in the coach you get tired of watching the scenery joggle past. It is impossible even to read. After a few minutes one eyeball starts rolling around independently of the other.

Always someone to talk to

But one good thing about Newfoundland trains is that you need never be stuck for someone to talk to.

Black strangers come in and sit down and within five minutes have launched into the story of their lives from the cradle to the present – whether you want to hear it or not. Plus what you can gather by eavesdropping.

I soon learned that in the Bishop's Falls car there were the Scottish couple and two other mainland tourists, two sick people coming from St. John's hospitals, three welfare cases, two relatives of railway workers traveling on passes and six youths and two girls going to the mainland for work.

Sitting opposite me were an extremely distraught looking pair, mother and daughter.

"Oh, my God, my God, my God," the younger one would sigh profoundly. The mother, leafing through a *True Story* journal, also gave signs of distress.

It was soon disclosed that they were "on welfare," that the younger had spent some time in the orthopedic hospital, was now discharged and her mother had journeyed in to take her back home.

During her stay, the daughter had cultivated a boyfriend in the great city. I presumed her disconsolation was due to the parting.

There was talk of marriage at Christmas.

"I was talkin' to 'en the other night," said the mother. "'E got grade eleven, 'aven't 'e? 'E can get a job on that. What do 'e want to go back to school for? Said 'e was afraid 'e wouldn't pass. Said 'e had a lot of worry."

"'E got a lot of worry!" snorted her offspring. "What the 'ell do 'e think I got! My God, my God, my God. My dear, you'll never see me going to the h'alter by Christmas."

They had a small "picture in a minute" camera with which they would photograph each other from time to time. This diversion seemed to raise them out of the dumps a little.

Then they settled back to make rather cold-blooded plans aimed at ensuring the proposed Yuletide nuptials would come off.

"As soon as we get back you'll write 'en a letter. Next week we'll send 'en a parcel with a cake into it."

The daughter had a four-pound bag of toffees which she generously passed round in the general area. After the fourth candy I declined and, by way of a pleasantry, said I must "watch my figure."

At this, my younger neighbor launched suddenly into a flurry of wails, groans and sobs. I was dumbfounded at this outburst.

"Save your tears, my dear," said her mother over the top of *True Story*, "h'or you won't 'ave none left for later."

Upon closer scrutiny I discovered that the young one was definitely in what used to be called an "interesting condition."

They gradually calmed down and took a few more pictures, which seemed to do them a world of good. My faux pas was apparently forgiven. We finished the toffee.

As they detrained at their destination I wished them good luck.

"Same to you, sir. Sniff. Sniff," said the daughter.

"Come on. 'Urry up. My God. I'll never h'undertake another trip like this. Come on. Knock off snuffin'. I 'lows if your father 'aven't got nothin' left from supper I'll knock his 'ed off."

Bound for Toronto

Conversation drifted back through the rattles and squeaks from other parts of the car.

Two girls who had lately worked in a St. John's tavern were on their way to Toronto seeking employment. They were got up in what they figured was the height of Toronto style.

One of the tourists, a woman who hailed from Toronto, was telling them about the wonders they might see in the big city. One of the young emigrants sat there bug-eyed while the other giggled nervously.

Toronto Tourist was obviously enjoying their reaction: "What? You've never ridden the subway? Oh, you'll LIEE-k it. They go like CRAAAY-zy!" Bug eyes. Giggles.

Then in came a young man, also bound for employment in Toronto. But he had been there before and in consequence assumed no slight swagger.

The two innocents abroad then heard another account of the golden metropolis and the Toronto Tourist had a little of the wind taken out of her sails. He promised to look out for them on the journey along. Bug Eyes relaxed a bit and Giggles wasn't quite so nervous.

The trip to Port aux Basques took about 20 hours. We had left St. John's near midnight and jolted into the western terminal about 7:30 p.m. the next day. In 1898 it took 27 hours and 45 minutes.

As we staggered off the Bullet a friend of theirs, who had driven across in a car, greeted the Scottish couple brightly:

"Well, here you are at last. We slept at home in bed and still got here before you."

That was the kind of remark we could all do without. Those who took the train because they didn't know better didn't need to have it rubbed in.

Those who couldn't afford to come any other way didn't need to be reminded further that they were second-class citizens.

The long trip back

The return trip began at 10 a.m. next day. More whackety whack, whackety whack, smash, bang, lurch and the screech of rusted metal. And the porter with his ineffective little squirts of Florient.

And the joggling limbs and rolling bottles and frightened children crying in the day coaches. It will take a day and a night to reach St. John's.

Away from dreary, rocky Port aux Basques, past the wide beaches and surf and rolling sand dunes of Cape Ray, up through the portals of the Long Range Mountains into Codroy Valley.

Who's aboard this trip? A small crowd. Two elderly and former Newfoundlanders returning for a visit. A lively and silver-haired woman who soon reveals that her father was a Spanish captain.

Six lads returning to the island from Toronto "for the winter" – unable to kick the inherited habit of summer work and winter rest begun centuries ago in the fishing boats.

A young mainlander who said he was a freelance photographer with a sudden impulse to come to Newfoundland and stay for a year.

Two sick people on welfare going to the hospital. Five people traveling on a railway pass. Seven girls going back to school.

One woman who was deaf and kept telling everyone how because of her affliction she missed her train in Montreal and had to wait two days for another.

But there is a mix-up in tickets and most of the interesting passengers get moved to another car, including the daughter of a Spanish captain and the young freelance photographer.

Sitting opposite me is the deaf woman who took off her shoes, rolled down her nylons and put up her feet. She is the loudest chewer of gum I have ever heard. Even above the whackety whack, whackety whack, smash, bang, lurch you can hear her top plate clicking and scrunching.

She came from her daughter in Ohio? Poor soul, I thought. She figured her daughter would take her in and keep her. But they couldn't stand the way she chewed gum. So she was coming back to live out the rest of it alone.

Behind me are the elderly and former Newfoundlanders.

"Look mother, there they are. See them there. That's Newfoundland to me," says the man. Damned if his voice doesn't tremble a bit.

Not like on the mainland

I think he is right. You don't see them just like that on the mainland, even in Cape Breton. Scrubby, scrawny, pitiful, miserable spruce bushes growing on the cliffs by the sea.

Their roots are tangled around the rocks with a death grip. You can't pull them out. They are too tough to be broken off. They are too whippy to be sawed off. If you try to chop them with an ordinary axe, the axe will rebound and maim you. Only a razor edge will do it.

More Newfoundland than that boggy, fly-eating weirdo, the pitcher plant.

The train tows you past the untidy backsides of a string of small communities and larger towns. Past lonely shacks scattered over the barrens with moose horns over the doors and children with no school out front.

It has been a good year for juniper, if nothing else. From one end of the island to the other they are green, fluffy, luxuriant – so vigorous they look like a strange, new species.

Up the Codroy Valley and Humber Valley where you get the feeling you are trespassing on the private domain of the paper companies. Their roads and signs and tractors and men are everywhere.

Through Corner Brook and Deer Lake which are Bowater's and Lundrigan's. Over the barren Gaff Topsails which nobody wants except the people in the shacks with the moose horns.

The CN in Newfoundland has not yet got around to installing the glass-roofed scenic dome cars they picture on the diner menus. A film of St. John's soot and grime dims our windows – and you can't get them up.

At Windsor a few more people come into the half-filled car. Among them is a teenager who is going to join the air force. He'll be in for seven years.

No work in the mill, he says. There used to be a few jobs but the new machines finished that off. He hopes to play the trombone in the air force band and will miss home, especially shooting ducks in the fall.

All hands are tucked in again before we get to Gander. The deaf woman, whose daughter in Ohio wouldn't keep her, complains bitterly that the porter has put all the young girls in the lower berths while an old woman like her has to climb to an upper.

Whackety whack, whackety whack, smash, bang, lurch. The deaf woman in the top bunk is ringing for the porter. When nobody comes she tries to clamber down by herself, can't, and crawls back.

Next morning, she complains to everyone that she didn't sleep a wink because the porters were laughing and carrying on "until all hours" with the young girls in the lower berths. A lie.

Through the early morning fog we crawl into St. John's along the greasy Waterford River, past the chopped liver freight cars in the railyards and the Nazi green day coaches waiting on the siding.

Out into the familiar St. John's air which the CN has provided its passengers in stoppered cars for the whole journey.

The victims of the day coaches stumble off, numb, red-eyed and bewildered into the arms of the aggressive men calling "taxi, taxi."

Come on with the buses. It won't be the easiest way in the world to travel but compared with the trains it will be fairly comfortable and mercifully quick.

It's not all bad

Some things about trains I'll be sorry to see go. For one thing, the scenery isn't all barrens and scrubby spruce – and you have lots of time to admire it.

At both ends of the railway at Cape Ray and Holyrood there are stretches where the train all but takes to the water, traveling for miles along the beach.

Seabirds and waves create an inspiring panorama.

No more impressive entry into the island could be imagined than the gap through Table Mountain into the splendid Codroy Valley.

I like the way the railway skirts closely the rivers and lakes – Georges Lake, the Humber River, Deer Lake, the Exploits. It's murder on timetables but as a scenic route it can't be beat.

And some second thoughts on shacks. When is a shack not a shack? When it's a summer shack.

Isolation and a certain crumbling at the edges are attractive features in a summer place. In these respects many of the buildings by the railway in remote places far surpass the summer subdivision colonies by the highways with their white paling fences.

It would be comforting to think that all the remote shacks along the railway were summer places. But what of the children playing out front in late September? Still, they might commute to a regional school every day by helicopter for all I know.

Then there are the railway personnel who still manage to do their job and be courteous about it even under trying circumstances.

Sure, the water looks dirty but the way the waiters can balance three plates on each arm as the dining car all but turns end over end takes your mind off it.

The elderly ladies miss their table linen but they still feel elegant when the waiter asks, "Would madom care for after-dinner mints?"

And absolutely the best way to go home for Christmas is by train, with the university crowd going cracked, the out of town shoppers burdened down, the holidaying workers opening their bottles a bit early, a guitar in every car and everyone exceedingly warm and merry and the snowy hills rollicking past.

The thing I'll miss most about trains is the way they encourage people to talk. I'll miss the people who do you the honor of telling you all their troubles and hopes starting within five minutes after they sit down.

But these people deserve better than second class. ▉

* This column won a National Newspaper Award.

Newfie, Nigger, Frog, or Wop

February 1, 1968   *Culture and History*

Newfoundlanders, what are we?

We're slobbering idiots, slack-jawed simpletons, rustic fish-billies living in Dogpatch-on-the-rocks lower than Lower Slobovians, the laughing stock and "white trash" of the rest of Canada.

Why one province of Canada should have become the object of scorn and derision of the other nine is a mystery to us. Do we deserve it? If we do, we'd like our fellow Canadians to tell us why.

If the present fad for ridiculing all things Newfoundland continues, it could leave a scar that will take a long time to heal.

We can take a joke at our own expense – God help us if we couldn't. But most of the stuff now directed against us from the mainland is steeped in sarcasm and laced with malice. There is no honest humor or fair criticism in it.

Patrick Scott, columnist with the *Toronto Star*, is the latest to rake us with a superior eye. His account of the opening of "Spring Thaw" in St. John's is the grossest example of mainland condescension we have yet seen.

Then there are the "Newfie Jokes" that have been the mainland rage for more than a year. We have yet to see one of these "jokes" that prompted laughter rather than nausea.

Mainland newspaper editors seem unable, or unwilling, to grasp the fact that "Newfie," like "Nigger," "Frog" or "Wop" is a term of derision. The Americans, some of whom are masters at this sort of thing, pinned the title on us 20 years ago. "Goofy Newfies," remember?

Still, the mainland press delights in using the term. Last week in our country's capital the *Ottawa Citizen* had a front-page headline "Newfies save ship, claim it as prize."

Residents of PEI are called Islanders, those of Nova Scotia, Nova Scotians, but we must always be "Newfies." Headline writers might not be expected to use "Newfoundlanders" – it's too long – but what's wrong with the abbreviation "Nfldrs?" Not colorful enough?

Newspapers aren't the only media that take glee in reflecting this province in a funhouse mirror.

Local CBC people say privately they are sickened by the directives from CBC headquarters in Toronto when a television film on Newfoundland is in the works.

"Forget the facts; get us lots of color," the local cameramen and directors are told. Color? This means lots of grizzled, toothless, pipe-smoking fishermen, plenty of ragged, barefoot urchins, scads of multi-colored houses clinging to the cliffs. That's color. Boy, are we colorful.

The professors have joined the scramble to record and preserve this abundant "color" – all in the interests of science, of course.

Several years ago a sociologist came to Memorial University straight from the jungles of Borneo where he had been engaged in studying some remote tribe of cannibals.

He had scarcely landed here when he lit out for a Bonavista Bay community laden down with typewriters and tape recorders to do another study of an equally colorful tribe.

Our sociologist lived in that community a year (with pictures of bone-through-the-nose cannibals on the walls of his quarters), enlisted his children to eavesdrop on his neighbors, and came up with a scholarly treatise on the tribal mores of the locals.

This paper, riddled with inaccuracies and shallow as a pothole, has been published by the university and made available for study by mainland sociologists and students.

Now, the National Film Board, cooperating with the university, has embarked on an "experiment" which, according to initial reports, will see dozens of outports committed to film.

There's nothing fancy or artistic about them. They'll just show the "honest-to-God truth" – a sort of mini-royal-commission report in celluloid. The first one on Fogo cost $50,000. They're for "study."

If this catches on we can expect the outharbors to be swarming this summer with beard-and-beret lads stumbling over each other's tripods and telephoto lenses in the frantic search for the raw truth – and color.

Our Tourist Development Board has not been caught with its pants down when it comes to promoting the "colorful Newfie" image.

During Come Home Year, the Tourist Board commissioned one of the largest mainland advertising firms to design ads for mainland magazines, newspapers, and posters. The whole campaign cost more than $100,000 of our money.

What did we get? Newfoundlanders were portrayed as cartoon characters, dancing atop a keg of screech, pop-gutted figures in orange pants and green suspenders, snaggle-toothed caricatures boozing and reeling through the pages of every large publication in the land.

When the mainland press does such a good job of ridiculing us free of charge, why should we have to pay our own government to do the same thing?

Newfoundlanders, what are we?

We're human beings. We've had a hard existence for 400 years and some of the rough edges still show. We don't mind jokes and criticism if they are made with good will. We often laugh at ourselves.

But we'd like our fellow Canadians to laugh with us for a change – not at us. We're tired of being treated like some lost tribe with bizarre customs and ridiculous manners.

We don't like to see our outport people pinned to the wall and examined by sociologists like rare insects. There's room for science and scholarship, but also the need for a bit of respect for human dignity.

Some will say we're too sensitive about the whole thing. Why don't we dismiss it all with a laugh, a shrug or a wisecrack?

It's difficult. If the "colorful Newfie" binge was balanced by some honest and helpful reporting from the mainland, we could.

But the avalanche of abuse and ridicule from our fellow Canadians is unrelieved by any glimpse of charity or understanding.

If it continues, there's some danger that we'll become paranoid, suspicious that everyone is out to get us, fearful that everything we say or do will be the butt of a joke or the object of scorn.

Should that happen, our fellow Canadians will really have something to laugh at.

Much as we hate to deprive them of still another snicker at our expense, we'll do our best. █

Mr. Speaker. I spy strangers

February 26, 1968 *News and Propaganda*

There you sit, reading the latest news from the People's House, as reported in the People's Paper.

More House of Assembly news comes at you over the telly, and still more House news on the radio – in snatches between Top Ten ditties.

What you're hearing and reading is not, of course, what honorable members said. It's what another bunch of people thought they said.

This other bunch is referred to as (among other things) the press. Some of them are on view to the general public each day the House is in session. There's no admission charge.

You'll see them sitting in one corner of the visitors' gallery located over the heads of her Majesty's Loyal Opposition and facing Her Majesty's Government across the way.

They may strike you as a rather nervous-looking lot. Tense and worried. Other members of the press sit inside in two rooms off the gallery with earphones clamped to their little pink shells.

They're just as edgy looking as the bunch outside. Why are they all worried? Why do they look like a group of bald-headed men being circled by a flock of bloated pigeons?

It's because they can't afford to make many mistakes.

They can't often get by with what they thought the honorable member said. They can't often get by with what the honorable member thought he said.

The only thing standing between them and a fate worse than death is a fair and accurate rendition of what the honorable member did say.

Press tape recorders are not permitted in the House. Hansard, the official record of what was said, is six or seven years behind schedule and getting later every day.

The only tools they use to record what the honorable member said are lead pencils and a few sheets of paper. (Right, foolscap.) But after years of practice, day in and day out, they're pretty good at it.

This bunch sits and scribbles. Their version of what the honorable member said is the one you'll hear over 15 CBC television or radio outlets in Newfoundland.

They also make the honorable member's words known to you over CJON, CJOX, CJCN radio and television outlets.

You hear their reports on VOCM radio from St. John's, on CKCM in Grand Falls and CHCM in Marystown.

This bunch of scribblers reports the honorable member's words to you through the *Newfoundland Herald*, the *Daily News*; their version of what the honorable member said is repeated 58,000 times over (on weekends) in *The*

Evening Telegram, St. John's, and *The Western Star*, Corner Brook.

Their version of what the honorable member said is sent out through Canadian Press to every daily newspaper but one (104) in Canada. If the honorable member really said a mouthful, they'll let the Associated Press in the USA and Reuters in Great Britain and Europe in on it.

So if they make a mistake, they make it in capital letters 10 feet tall ... and they'll hear about it.

They'll probably hear about it first from Premier Smallwood. If so, they'll be honored with a blast from the loudest unamplified conch this side of the Rocky Mountains.

In the past, the premier has passed considered judgment on reporters whose reporting of the House he did not like:

"That creature, that thing, that little scoundrel ... a bitter and unscrupulous opponent, personally, of the Liberal government ... he hates me with a personal vindictive hatred ... he is either drunk, incompetent or a fool ... a mischievous-minded person with a poverty-stricken mind ... this dastardly clown ... this journalistic knave, this loathsome literary scavenger ... this insult to the great profession of journalism ... this cut-throat, this rat ... this filthy, literary rat ... a scavenger ... a scallywag ... a poor psychopath, a drug fiend ... a literary assassin ... investigated for Communism ... a contemptible cur, beneath the respect of decent men."

Naturally, this doesn't worry them at all.

Well, do they worry then because they've got no right to be in the House? It's a privilege for the press to be there. Nobody has ever gotten around to giving them the right.

The legislature, if it wanted to, could sit forever in secret behind closed doors. What reports you'd hear would be the ones they wanted you to hear.

All an honorable member has to do is come to his honorable taps and deliver the quaint phrase: "Mr. Speaker. I spy strangers."

At once, everyone in the gallery, public and press alike, can be shooed out and the doors barred against them.

No? Well do these scribblers in the press gallery worry about being "Called Before the Bar?" They used to do it in England in the days of public executions for sheep stealing.

The last time this happened in England was in 1819, but in Newfoundland the premier threatens to do it just about every session. My turn came the session before last:

"The press is not as great as Parliament. No court is. WE are the High Court of Newfoundland. We're next to the Queen. The House can order any person before the Bar of this House and deal with him as the House sees it fit," etc., etc.

But the bunch of scribblers don't lose too much sleep over that either.

If they didn't "presume to take notice of the proceedings," most honorable members would probably be much more distraught than they are when an honest mistake is made.

Have not some honorable members spoken of the fierce competition among backbenchers from outlying districts to speak on Thursday so as to take advantage of *The Telegram*'s weekend circulation?

Have not some honorable members asked reporters to make sure that instead of the picture of them *The Telegram* used last time it use a more flattering profile with this report?

Then why do the scribblers worry so much?

They worry because they realize – between bottles of sarsaparilla – they have just as important a job to do for you as do honorable members.

The members sit in the House because you put them there; the press sits in the House because you want them there.

Neither group is perfect, but nobody has yet found a better way to do it. Indeed, other ways have been tried and have led to disaster.

The scribblers snicker aloud when someone mentions that rather pompous motto of the press: "Ye shall know the truth, and the truth shall make you free."

But they continue to worry about the truth. They worry whether or not they're doing a good job of digging out the truth for you.

They'd have a lot easier job if everything was black and white ... good guys and bad guys like in the old Western movies. Trouble is, there's nobody around these days with the guts to be an out-and-out saint or devil.

And they DO worry about making mistakes in reporting what honorable members say. That's only common decency. And while it's only part of getting the truth to you, it is a part.

To deliberately twist or alter what an honorable member says so as to show him to you in his true colors is not the way to do it.

There's only one way to do that. It is to show you the difference between what an honorable member SAID and what he DID.

That's another reason why the press takes pains to see that an honorable member's remarks are recorded correctly.

So the scribblers worry. That flock of pigeons is coming around for another swoop, their heads feel very bare and there's no room to duck. RG

Take the civil service out of St. John's and what have you got?

March 1, 1968   *Resettlement and Rural Life*

Ank Murphy, the redoubtable member for Me 'n Ned country, can hardly believe his ears. Has the honorable member opposite gone light in the head?

Has the honorable member opposite stayed out too long in the sun on those west coast skiing hills he is so fond of prating about?

He said it AGAIN! God help us, sir, it is more than St. John's Centre flesh and blood can bear!

Clyde Wells, the adventurous member for Humber East (a district situated somewhere west of Donovan's Overpass), is stepping in where even one of your more intrepid angels fears to tread.

"Out there, Mr. Speaker, is where the REAL Newfoundland is!" exclaims Mr. Wells, flinging an expressive arm to the westward. "St. John's is not Newfoundland. Out there is the reason for the existence of St. John's."

The member for St. John's Centre expands with indignation. Is there such a thing as a British bulldog by the name of Murphy? Docile and amiable in time of peace, slow to anger, but in wartime a bundle of ferocity. And this is war!

Poor Mr. Wells, unmindful of his perilous situation, plunges ahead: "St. John's is a parasitical city. Take the civil service out of St. John's and what have you got? Purity crackers, bullseyes and beer!"

Other St. John's members fidget and bristle, but all eyes are on the member for St. John's Centre. Will this blasphemy go unpunished? Can St. John's Centre – the repository of the heart and soul and gizzard and other internals of this island – much longer contain itself?

A breathless hush falls over the House. An almost unbearable tension descends. But hark, the crisis seems to be passing. The eagle suffereth little birds to sing!

Mr. Wells, still innocent of the awful peril which he, through the grace of a Higher Power, has passed, prattles on undamaged.

Except for a few gasps of outrage, the member for St. John's Centre has kept himself in check. Honorable members have witnessed the incredible! The whispered question "Why?" passes through the ranks.

Once again the member for Humber East is skirting the brink of that fearsome chasm. Thousands will flock to Corner Brook for the skiing. They will enjoy that famous west coast dish, corned snow.

Tourists will come from near and far to ski and to visit that great new industry, a modern slalom cannery on the shores of Humber Arm.

Skiing in St. John's? Mr. Wells suppresses a snicker. Skiing in St. John's where you have a blinding blizzard one day and slush and mud the next?

Once again, the member for St. John's Centre shows outward sign of the titanic struggle within him and – the wonder of it! – forbearance emerges the victor.

But, lest readers assume the matter has ended there, ominous signs to the contrary have been noted on the floor of the Chamber.

Mr. Wells's colleagues have been looking at him with pitying and downcast eyes. They have been regarding him as one who is soon to face a trial from which he cannot emerge. They whisper together and nod sadly in his direction.

They know, as do we, that the awesome wrath of the member for St. John's Centre is like unto a smoldering volcano. It may erupt suddenly in the midst of the Committee of the Whole. It may explode during presenting petitions. It may rupture the Budget Debate.

Sooner or later Mr. Wells will meet his moment of truth. Mr. Murphy already struggles to control a full head of steam.

His constituents in St. John's Centre – led by the most famous of them all, Me 'n Ned – are even now manning the shovels for an assault on the coal pile.

Poor Mr. Wells. Too late will he have learned that the wrath of a St. John's Centre man is not a thing to be tampered with.

So young he was, so bright and so full of promise. It was a privilege to have known him.

* * *

As noted before, individual sets of earphones have replaced the loudspeaker in the press gallery.

Each newsman brings along his own set. The variety is wide. There are the simple, utilitarian First World War fighter pilot models used by *The Evening Telegram*; the more pretentious, space-capsule types supplied to CBC correspondents; the peanut, transistor-radio earphone used by one of the radio stations.

But the most magnificent pair of all belongs to veteran newsman Arch Sullivan who is, in consequence, the envy of all his co-workers.

This splendid instrument is a wonder to behold, a miracle of modern technology. Huge padded earpieces cradle the ears in luxurious comfort. The form-fitting headband makes it a joy to wear.

A control panel is attached whereby the user may raise or lower the volume of each individual earpiece at will. The flick of a switch transforms reception from mono to stereo at will.

But despite his obvious pride in this singular piece of machinery, Mr. Sullivan seldom wears it. Instead, he prefers to lay the set on his desk, turn up the volume and listen in as to a small radio.

His reason? With the huge, foam rubber earpieces engulfing his head, the maze of wires and control panels dangling down, the switches and dials in place ... he can't see. RG

Just call him Twinkle Toes

March 4, 1968   *In the House*

Just call him Twinkle Toes. Thomas Valentine Hickey, the PC member for St. John's East Extern, has proved himself the fastest fancy footwork artist in the House.

Trying to argue with Mr. Hickey is like trying to slam a swinging door, catch a leprechaun, or bring down a partridge with a .22 rifle.

He nimbly skips, wheels, ducks, dodges, and pops up somewhere else, leaving his opponents frustrated and exhausted. Mr. Hickey inherited more from his Irish ancestors than red hair.

And it works. At least it works better than anything the Opposition has tried in recent years.

Friday, he led government members on a merry chase with his charges of injustice in welfare. Nearly the whole government pack lit out after him in full cry – the big guns, the shotguns, the slingshots and the peashooters.

They may have cornered him a dozen times, but he didn't appear to be cornered. In a House debate, that seems to be 90 per cent of the battle.

Chief sniper for the government side turned out to be Ed Roberts, the premier's assistant.

Mr. Roberts, who can at times assume the attitude of a porcupine afflicted with ingrown quills, brought into play his sophisticated university brand of heckling and riposte.

But what works onstage at good old Hart House, University of Toronto, doesn't go over too well in these parts. Like, man, these cats are square.

"That's like asking, when did you stop beating your wife?" roared Mr. Roberts at one point. Ank Murphy retorted indignantly that Mr. Roberts was getting personal.

Mr. Hickey said Mr. Roberts had no business dragging his wife into it. Both Opposition members seemed to be quite serious. Good Lord, can they be that square?

Mr. Roberts's charge of "McCarthyism" also went over with a dull thud. That particular squelcher doesn't have the punch and significance here it would have on a US of A platform.

(*The Making of a Newfoundland Premier* would be a valuable addition to Mr. Roberts's library. His present guidebook, *The Making of a President*, loses a lot in the translation.)

And so they blasted away at the agile Mr. Hickey – Premier Smallwood with the bazooka, Dr. Rowe with the fowling piece, Mr. Roberts with the blowgun, Welfare Minister Val Earle with the slings and arrows of outrageous Fortune, and Steve Neary (the poor man's Ralph Nader) with the air rifle.

They did everything but hit him over the head with the mace, but still he rolled merrily on. Well, perhaps "merrily" is not quite the word.

On one occasion, Mr. Hickey appeared to charge the Speaker with being less than impartial and was asked by Mr. Speaker to withdraw this unworthy remark, which he did. He then continued his verbal ballet.

"He's saying nothing! He's saying nothing!" chorused government members, but when Mr. Hickey's speaking time was up they agreed to give him an extension.

Apparently, they figured if they gave him enough rope he'd hang himself – but he didn't. Instead of suicide, he chose a duel with welfare briefs at 50 paces.

High noon is 5 p.m. Saturday, March 16. Mr. Hickey has given the government 15 days to appoint a royal commission to investigate the welfare system, or else he'll "tell all."

If the St. John's East Extern member is as lively on his pins as he was in the House Friday, it should be an interesting match.

But as every western movie fan knows, the thing about these high noon duels is that you also have to watch for the glint of gun barrels in second-story windows.

❧ Most members just sat there, slack-jawed ❧

March 11, 1968   *In the House*

"I don't care if it's socialist or what it is. If it comes from the scriptures, it's good enough for me and I'll stand by it!"

So declared Uriah Strickland (L-Trinity South – barely) Friday when Ank Murphy (PC-St. John's Centre) said a text Mr. Strickland quoted from the Bible was socialistic.

Mr. Strickland told the House he had been casting about for some time for a text which would sum up the Liberal government's policy.

"As is my custom before going to bed, I turned to Holy Writ," explained Mr. Strickland, "and my eye lit upon a verse from Second Corinthians, which I think sums up this government's policy perfectly."

For I mean not that other men be eased, and ye burdened: But by an equality, that now at this time your abundance may be a supply for their want, that their abundance also may be a supply for your want: that there may be equality. (II Corinthians 8:13-14)

Most members just sat there, slack-jawed. They could not honestly share Mr. Strickland's triumph at having struck on such an apt text. It DOES take a bit of thinking out.

But Mr. Murphy caught it in a flash and declared it to be socialistic. Whereupon, Mr. Strickland produced his famous retort.

Perhaps Mr. Strickland's biblical quotation was meant to serve two purposes. Earlier in his speech, he had called for higher salaries for members of the House.

In the Bible chapter Mr. Strickland quoted, St. Paul is trying to raise donations from the Corinthians for others of the Christian sect who are in hard straits in Jerusalem.

According to the chapter summary in the St. James version of Holy Writ, "He stirreth them up to a liberal contribution for the poor saints at Jerusalem."

Mr. Strickland was looking for more money for House members. You could say, "He stirreth them up to a more liberal contribution for the poor member for Trinity South who requireth much more campaign funds if he hopeth to squeak through again in the next election."

***

Doomsday can't be far off. The big crash must be just around the corner. Hard times must be headed down the chute.

In recent weeks, our two best-known Little Mary Sunshines – Premier J.R. Smallwood and Don Jamieson – have made statements which, for them, could be considered forecasts of gloom and doom.

These two professional optimists have never been noted for slacking back on the rosy predictions or toning down their psychedelic visions of the future.

But now Mr. Jamieson tells us we may be in for a depression equal to that of the 1930s. Premier Smallwood tells us 1968 won't be the greatest year yet. Vietnam, you see. We'll have to just mark time!

If that wouldn't send a shiver down the spines of even those who dote on every word that falls from the lips of the rose-tinted duo ... what would?

Even when they were preaching their silver-lined gospels at the top of their brass-bound lungs, the times around these parts weren't all that good.

What dread calamities must we now be heading for when the "Sunshine Boys" not only turn down the volume, but switch to another record with a completely different tempo?

Shudder! Gasp!

***

Mr. Strickland did such a splendid job finding a biblical verse to suit his government's policy, we hope he doesn't stop there.

It should be easy to find verses in Holy Writ that would fit members of the House to a "T." To help Mr. Strickland out in this project, we modestly make a few suggestions.

We list the names of some of the members. Below that we list some Bible quotes. All he has to do is fit the proper quote to the appropriate name. There are several spare quotes to make his job easier. He may choose other members' names to fit the spares.

Readers may also find the exercise fitting to the season and may pass a profitable half-hour joining the quote to the right name.

B.J. Abbott, municipal affairs
Steve Neary, Bell Island
Alex Hickman, justice
Val Earle, welfare
Dr. F.W. Rowe, education
Max Lane, mines and resources
Premier J.R. Smallwood
Opposition Leader Gerald Ottenheimer
T.V. Hickey, St. John's East Extern
Uriah Strickland, Trinity South
John Crosbie, health
Ed Roberts, assistant to the premier
W.J. Keough, labor
Bill Callahan, Port au Port
A.C. Wornell, Hermitage

"It is better to dwell in a corner of the housetop than with a brawling woman in a wide house." (Proverbs 21:9)

"He cometh as a fearful noise and a mighty wind." Isaiah

"Better it is that thou shouldst not vow than that thou shouldst vow and not pay." (Ecclesiastes 5:5)

"And he wrote in the letter, saying, 'Set ye Uriah in the forefront of the hottest battle, and retire ye from him that he may be smitten'." (Samuel 11:15)

"Stand by thyself, come not near to me, for I am holier than thou." (Isaiah 65:5)

"He that earneth wages, earneth wages to put it to a bag of holes." (Haggai 1:6)

"Wheresoever the carcass is, there will the eagles be gathered together." (Matthew 24:28)

"He saith among the trumpets, ha, ha; and he smelleth the battle afar off." (Job 39:25)

"If I ascend up into heaven, thou art there; if I make my bed in hell, behold thou art there." (Psalms 139:8)

"Even a fool, when he holdeth his peace, is counted wise." (Proverbs 17:28)

"How long halt ye between two opinions?" (Kings 18:21)

"Is not the sound of his master's feet behind him?" (Kings 6:21)

"And the Lord opened the mouth of the ass and she said unto Balaam, 'What have I done unto thee, that thou has smitten me these three times?'" (Numbers 22:28)

"Thou shalt become an astonishment, a proverb and a byword among all nations." (Deuteronomy 28:37)

"A feast is made for laughter and wine maketh merry, but money answereth all things." (Ecclesiastes 10:19)

"Let him go for a scapegoat into the wilderness." (Leviticus 16:10)

"Let another man praise thee and not thine own mouth; a stranger and not thine own lips." (Proverbs 27:2)

Disgrace in Fogo a Go-Go

March 12, 1968

Culture and History

Eric Dawe (L-Port de Grave) tells us that some of the people in Hibb's Hole want the name of their place changed to something more "dignified."

Dignity is sweeping the country these days and we expect all members of the House to be swamped with petitions from voters who want the names of their communities prettied up a bit.

Some of the more forward-thinking communities have already made the change. Piper's Hole to Swift Current. Bay Bulls Arm to Sunnyside. Famish Cove to Fairhaven. Tickle Harbour to Bellevue. Blackhead to Acneville.

The field is still wide upon. Carbonear, for instance. It is a mystery to us how the residents of that place have put up with such an undignified name for so long.

Carbonear. It sounds like a disease – a fungus of the earhole. Then there's Harbour Grace. Extremely undignified. It sounds like the name of locally made, greasy salve you use when you have a bad case of Carbonear.

The name Gander is equally undignified. We expect to see a request any day from the residents of that town for a more dignified name. Gander – a flat-footed bird that drags its keel. Collinsville would be much nicer.

Fogo will have to go-go. It's as undignified as those near-nude hussies who shake their frames in front of beer parlor patrons. How the residents of Fogo have lived it down for so long we'll never know.

Bishop's Falls is scandalously undignified. It suggests a picture of an upper churchman being defrocked after disgracing himself in a Fogo a Go-Go. This name-change petition will no doubt have church support.

Hermitage is out. It sounds too much like hemorrhage. Bonavista will be scrapped. There's a Bonavista Cold Storage Company. What dignified citizen would want to live in a town that's named after a cold storage company? It's enough to give you a Hermitage.

It is amazing that Corner Brook has lasted so long. The name reeks of indignity. What kind of brooks do you find on corners? Brooks that run in gutters and breed rats and other parasites, that's what. Our west coast city deserves something better.

St. John's must also get on board the dignity express. The "saint" part is not so bad. But "John"? The vulgar name for a public convenience? Shame haunts the residents of the capital city daily on this account. The name has to go.

Residents of all these towns and cities clearly have even better reasons for wanting the names of their communities changed than do the residents of Hibb's Hole.

Still, this Conception Bay community has taken the lead. Evidently, some of its citizens have a highly developed sense of dignity. Shame, shame on the rest of us.

***

QUOTE OF THE DAY

P.J. Canning (L-Placentia West), noted critic of local education, turns his attention to the state of education abroad:

"There's not a decent family in the US today which wouldn't change their school system for ours."

May we presume from this that no more than 49 per cent of US families are decent? Otherwise, why haven't they out-voted the non-decent families and replaced their present setup with our glorious system?

We suspect that the only thing holding the US back is lack of information on the Newfoundland system. The decent thing for Newfoundland to do is to exchange Mr. Canning for the faculty of Harvard University.

It would be the least we could do.

***

Opposition Leader Gerald Ottenheimer complained because Ed Roberts, the premier's assistant, was allowed to ask a question about skiing whereas many opposition questions are disallowed because they are not "urgent."

Pat Canning (L-Placentia West) said there wasn't a decent family in the US which wouldn't change their school system for Newfoundland's.

Alex Moores (L-Harbour Grace) said Ottawa should pay trawlers a daily subsidy to help shore-up a sagging fresh fish industry.

Mr. Moores told Ank Murphy (PC-St. John's Centre) some Newfoundland blueberries had been exported to Nova Scotia for the making of blueberry wine.

Opposition Leader Ottenheimer repeated his earlier opposition to the name "J.W. Pickersgill Fellowship." He said university fellowships should not be named after living, retired politicians. Dead, retired politicians, OK.

That's it. If you heard or read no more than the above few lines about what happened in the House yesterday you wouldn't miss much.

True, much more was said. Most of the members were in their places. (They pay themselves $8,500 per session.) About half-dozen of them helped fill the three hours (3 p.m.-6 p.m.) with talk.

If you want to find out some more of the things that were said you may read the news stories for the House in today's *Telegram*.

Read them all aloud at a moderate clip and you will find that you have used up much less than three hours. Yet the members of the House spoke continuously for three solid hours.

What then, are you missing by reading reports in *The Telegram* instead of sitting in the strangers' gallery of the House for three hours?

The news reports you read here contain what *The Telegram*'s reporters and editors consider to be the most important comments made in the House for the day … blueberries and all.

Select what you think is the least important comment reported here. Ask yourself if you'd care to sit in one place from 3 p.m. to 6 p.m. to hear less important and less interesting remarks.

Then ask yourself if any 42 men could do a much better job of wasting three hours. 🆁🅶

Start crawling

March 14, 1968   *Liberals and Pea Seas*

Good afternoon, ladies and gentlemen. CJRS television is all set to bring you the sports spectacular of the season.

A vast crowd has assembled here at picturesque Goobies where the Burin Highway branches off from the Trans-Canada. An expectant hush hangs over the throng.

True to his word in the House on March 13, Justice Minister T. Alex Hickman starts at noon today to crawl the 140 miles to Grand Bank.

Viewers may remember the justice minister's stirring words on that occasion: "I have told the Minister of Highways I will crawl on my hands and knees from Goobies to Grand Bank if this will convince his officials of the desperate need to have a paving program started this year."

Viewers may also recall the equally stirring reply of the Minister of Highways: "Start crawling."

Mr. Hickman is now on all fours in the center of the highway and awaits the starting gun. He is suitably dressed in track shorts and a natty blue jersey, and wears a small sign – "No Riders."

Now, here's the gun … and he's off! A great cheer goes up from the crowd. He's holding a brisk and even clip down the middle of the road, coughing slightly at the dust, but forging ahead.

From this angle he appears to be maintaining a steady speed of from 0.3 to 0.5 miles per hour. How about that, sports fans? Now, he's fading from view around the bend, head well back, elbows slightly bent, "No Riders" sign bobbing in the breeze.

Ladies and gentlemen, we switch now to the district of Bonavista South where the member, Rossy Barbour, is crawling from Lethbridge to Bonavista proper.

Mr. Barbour was heard to remark earlier that "Alex might have something there," and embarked on his own crawlathon. The Bonavista South member ran into a bit of trouble yesterday about two miles east of Summerville.

Mr. Barbour was involved in a head-on collision with a west-bound automobile of foreign manufacture. There were no injuries, but the vehicle suffered extensive damage.

We move now to Bonavista North where the member, Municipal Affairs Minister Beaton Abbott, is on the last lap of a crawl from Gambo to Cape Freels.

Mr. Abbott was last seen doing the Australian crawl across a large pothole three miles east of Indian Bay. Fears are held for his safety. Air and Sea Search and Rescue from Greenwood, NS, have been called in. It's a really big pothole.

Wait. There's a speck in the distance way off on the horizon. I think ... yes, it is. B.J. has hove in sight. He appears to be dog paddling quite strongly now and turns over on his back occasionally for brief rests. What a fighter, ladies and gentlemen.

Now we go down to Placentia East where Provincial Affairs Minister Dr. G.A. Frecker set out some time ago to crawl from Point Verde to St. Bride's.

Dr. Frecker is the only bilingual crawler in this unique drive to soften the highways minister's heart. His fellow crawlers are claiming that Dr. Frecker has an unfair advantage.

They charge that when he gets tired of crawling on his hands and feet, he can switch over and crawl on his mains et pieds. The A.A.U. [Amateur Athletics Union] will make a decision shortly.

The provincial affairs minister had an unfortunate accident yesterday. He collided head-on with Finance Minister Dr. James McGrath, who had been crawling up from Branch to North Harbour.

Dr. McGrath, member from St. Mary's, apparently went off-course and ended up in Dr. Frecker's district. Attempts are being made to re-locate the Branch-North Harbour Road – a difficult task considering its close resemblance to the adjacent bog.

There's no action in Trinity South today, it being the Sabbath. Uriah Strickland, member for the district, says he will resume early Monday and crawl on to his heart's delight, heart's desire and heart's content.

Now, here's a late sports roundup. In White Bay South, William Rowe has advanced as far as Flatwater Pond. In St. Barbe South, Gerald Myrden has crawled to the outskirts of Spudgel's Cove. In St. Barbe North, Public Works Minister James Chaulker continues gamely past Flowers Cove.

The late word from Burin district is that Mr. Hickman has run into some trouble on the road west of Marystown, at a Flying-L cattle crossing.

Now we have an interview, ladies and gentlemen, with the man who is, in a way, responsible for it all, Highways Minister Eric Jones.

Tell us, Mr. Jones, does your department intend to pave the area of road crawled over to date or will you be waiting until all the crawlers have actually reached their destinations?

"Well, Bill, the truth is we can't afford to pave any of these roads at all. I just didn't have the heart to tell them."

Did you hear that, ladies and gentlemen! Remember, you heard it first on CJRS. Our highways minister, despite his stern exterior, has a heart of gold.

I hope our listeners will (sniff, sniff) excuse me. I'm so choked with emotion at our highways minister's disclosure of his other, tender and compassionate side. I can hardly (sniff, sniff) carry on ...

Besides, I spent my last free weekend crawling all the way from Aguathuna to Cape St. George (sniff, sniff) in the district of Port au Port. Waaaaaaa ...

***

All but members of the House have been barred from Hernando's Hideaway, otherwise known as the Liberal common room.

Time was when news reporters could pop down to the Liberal common room and question members further on the points they had brought up in the House. Now they must do so in the corridors.

The "Off Limits" notice went up early this week. Late last week, Premier J.R. Smallwood – who had been taking a nap on the common room sofa – was disturbed several times by reporters who came in to ask questions.

Now, unless you're a member you can't get in even if you knock three times and say, "Joe sent me." I tried it. ■

The solemnization of Holy Cabinetry

March 18, 1968   *Joey*

A remark in the House on Thursday brought to light a little-known sidelight of parliamentary procedure from which the workings of Newfoundland's government are derived.

Health Minister John Crosbie remarked: "The premier asked me to change portfolios. Seeing as we're in the same position our wives are, he has only to ask and we do it – because we want to do it, of course."

Thus stimulated, we decided to pursue the reference further and phoned about to all the leading churchmen.

They referred us to a quaint parliamentary ceremony of earlier times in which premier and cabinet minister were joined as one.

We discovered in the archives a yellowed and musty copy of the *Book of Uncommon Prayer* (authorized for use in all the round churches which the devil couldn't corner), and while leafing through its pages, discovered the very ceremony for which we were looking.

The brief but stirring ritual was patterned closely after the modern order of nuptials and was referred to as "The Solemnization of Holy Cabinetry."

It seems that when a premier in those times decided to take unto himself a new cabinet minister, he embarked on an ardent period of courtship culminating in what was known as the seduction.

The cabinet minister may or may not have been in what was referred to in genteel parlors as "a delicate condition" when the banns were published. The *Book of Uncommon Prayer* is not clear on this point.

However, the banns took the form of three public denunciations of the Opposition by the prospective cabinet minister. This was followed in due course by the ceremony of Holy Cabinetry.

This moving ceremony, of which every politician dreamed from puberty onward, was conducted in the Cabinet Room, which was gaily decked out for the occasion with old campaign posters and party manifestos.

The ceremony was conducted by an elder minister of the crown. Premier and cabinet minister-to-be were brought into the chamber to the organ strains of "Oh Promise Me."

The elder minister then asked the cabinet minister-to-be: "Wilt thou have this man to be thy gracious premier, to work together according to God's ordinance in the holy estate of Cabinetry? Wilt thou applaud him, parrot him, honor, obey and keep him in municipal affairs and in health and forsaking all other, so long as you both shall continue to enjoy a plurality of the electorate?"

To which came the reply: "He damn well better."

At this poignant point, there were usually a few muffled sobs from the congregation, especially from relatives of the cabinet minister, if it happened to be a politically mixed marriage.

Then the premier repeated after the elder minister of the crown: "I ..., take thee, ..., to be my humble cabinet minister to have and to hold from this day forward, for better, for better still, for richer, for even richer, in municipal affairs and in health, to love and to cherish till defeat at the polls do us part, according to God's holy ordinance; and thereto do I give thee a key to the executive elevator."

Sometimes what were known as "double key ceremonies" were performed in which the cabinet minister was given a key to the executive elevator and a key to the official lodge on the Gander River, a famous salmon stream in Middlesex.

The happy couple left the chamber to the triumphal organ strains of "Blest be the Tie that Binds." The congregation showered the pair with shredded contract tenders.

A footnote in the *Book of Uncommon Prayer* says there was a move in earlier times to have the word "obey" removed from the vows. However, this met with vehement objections from the leading prelate of the day, the Archbishop of Gambobury.

The word "obey" was not only retained, but at this point in the ceremony the cabinet minister was required to prostrate himself while the premier placed a foot on his head.

***

Premier J.R. Smallwood told the Opposition in the House, March 14, there were 56 men working at Come By Chance and that another 97 connected with the project are working "elsewhere in the province."

Reports from Come By Chance say that nearly all the workers on the site were laid off March 11. Only a handful of office workers and watchmen remain.

Since the whereabouts or identity of those other 97 is not known, it is difficult to discover if they were affected by the lay-off.

***

Uriah Strickland (L-Trinity South) called on the House last week to increase members' salaries so they could make politics "a full-time job."

Mr. Strickland was no doubt taking the Christian attitude and thinking of others, not himself, when he made the request.

As a member of the House, Mr. Strickland receives $8,500 a session for his labors as the representative of Trinity South.

He is also a director of the company which operates a ferry service between Portugal Cove and Bell Island – a company subsidized in large part by federal funds – and receives a yearly salary of $6,000 for this duty.

A combined salary of $14,500 a year presumably places the honorable member well out of the grasp of poverty.

***

It's an ill wind. Opposition Leader Gerald Ottenheimer refused to continue his speech in the House on Friday when Premier Smallwood sat him down with a technicality.

Mr. Ottenheimer says he may give the rest of his speech outside the House at a press conference on Wednesday.

Normally, the premier is the last speaker in the debate and has the last word. But the premier intends to speak Tuesday and end the debate. If Mr. Ottenheimer makes the rest of his speech public Wednesday, he'll have a rare opportunity – the chance to have the last word.

Of course, the premier's speech may spill over into Wednesday – a not unlikely event. In that case, Mr. Ottenheimer may decide to postpone his press conference until Thursday.

There is also the chance that the premier may dig up another technicality. It is not often that he forfeits the last word without a fight. ☒

The Thoughts of Chairman Joe

March 21, 1968   *Joey*

True Revolutionary thought and action is sadly lacking in the Young these days. Our Young need a fresh reminder of the glorious Words and Deeds that have made the People's Democracy great.

Youth must have constant inspiration. What better way to sow new seeds of fervent dedication to the Cause than through the Thoughts of one whom we must continually praise for all the blessings we now enjoy (excepting Life itself – that we get from our friendly neighborhood newsstand) – Our Leader, the Only Living Father, Chairman Joe.

As a humble service to our glorious Youth and to the glorious Cause, we shall present here from time to time the precious, inspirational and revolutionary "Thoughts of Chairman Joe."

Right-thinking Youths will clip the "Thoughts" as they appear here and bind them in a small, plastic-covered book and keep them ever on their persons.

Only the callous and reactionary pawns of decadent Toryism will refuse to do so. The true Revolutionary Youth will not be caught dead without his copy of the "Thoughts."

Copies of the "Thoughts" will be kept on hand for constant reference in otherwise idle moments as the right-minded Youth travels along the glorious People's Highway, sips a beverage in one of the illustrious People's Taverns, or waits between classes in the revolutionary People's Teaching Factories.

The true Revolutionary Youth will not fail to scan each day's issue of the People's Paper and particularly the reports here of the People's House so as not to miss additional "Thoughts" to add to his little Red Book.

Copies of the "Thoughts" will be waved proudly at every spontaneous rally, manifestation, demonstration or protest – all of which will take place on the 24th of each month in honor of the Only Living Father's birthdate.

The Thoughts of Chairman Joe

(How grateful we are that the Chairman still leads us along the True Path when we realize how close we have been in the past to losing his irreplaceable guidance.)

April 1964: "I'll stay in public life until (a) I drop dead (b) I'm kicked out by the voters (c) I'm so fed up with it I'll walk out or (d) I'm too tired to go on. Now (c) is most unlikely and so far I've felt no tiredness whatsoever …"

September 1960: "I feel a little tired. I have traveled 100,000 miles this year and I have had a lot of burdens and problems – very heavy problems – dumped in my lap this year."

December 1959: "I wouldn't mind getting out of politics, I am getting a little bit fed up with them."

September 1958: "I'd like to get out ... in a year. I've had my rendezvous with history. I'm not going to be one of those politicians who hangs around too long and becomes a pitiful figure."

September 1962: "If I can get a good, strong, young team of Liberals in office and get the fisheries development program working, I am gone."

October 1962: "I hope and pray I will never have to lead the government in another election."

November 1962: "I prophesy that I will be in my last days as premier, five years from now, if not before then."

February 1963: "If the Liberals win the Canadian election – and there is little doubt about their winning it – I think I will be retiring so I can attend to some other things I have in mind."

September 1967: "I'm getting off Newfoundland's back. This is my last election."

March 1963: "It's easy to talk about retiring but it's difficult to retire. When someone or something has been good to you – as the Liberal Party has been good to me – it is not easy to retire from it."

(We are truly moved when we see the Chairman's great humility by his willingness to share the glory and the praise with others.)

December 1950: "In this effort ... we have the very great benefit of the knowledge and experience of Dr. Alfred Valdmanis, who, in this drive for economic development, is worth his weight in gold to Newfoundland."

(Unlike to lesser mortals, it is given to the Chairman to see beyond the realm of the present and into the furthermost reaches of the future.)

To the Royal Commission on Economic Prospects of the Atlantic region: "The cowboy looms larger than the fisherman in Newfoundland's future. The time will come when we'll have our own Calgary Stampede ..."

(The Chairman's amazing grasp of the fishery and his realization as to where his true destiny lies is revealed to us.)

January 1962: On being asked if he would become federal Liberal leader: "I would a million times rather be a big fish in a little bowl than a little fish in a big one, so I stay right where I am now."

(We are inspired by the Chairman's love of every living thing and share his anguish at being soul-seared by well-meaning but insensitive persons.)

June 1960: On being presented with a totem pole (wooden) by the Newfoundland Forest Protection Association: "Every tree that is destroyed – not turned into paper or some other useful purpose – should represent a pain in the heart."

(We are encouraged by the Chairman's example to place our complete faith in the promises of other right-thinking persons – with some reservations.) ▨

The Coffee Break Act

T.V. Hickey complained yesterday the government wouldn't even agree to an Opposition proposal to have a coffee break.

Although this unique coffee break legislation hasn't come up in the House yet, we can just about guess how the debate will go if it does.

Mr. Speaker: "Second reading of a bill, An Act Respecting an Intermission During Daily Sittings for the Purpose of Allowing Honorable Members to Quaff a Caffeinated Beverage, Known as the Coffee Break Act."

Mr. Hickey: "I have brought in this bill, Mr. Speaker, with the welfare of all honorable members in mind. I think a great injustice is being committed here when we have to sit for three solid hours in isolation and are deprived of a cup of coffee. Let me just say this …"

Premier: "Ah ha. The honorable gentleman is losing his temper again. He's getting red in the face. He's flying off the handle again."

A.J. (Ank) Murphy: "I think the premier is the one losing his temper."

Education Minister Dr. Fred Rowe: "Shut up! Shut up!"

Mr. Hickey: "Let me just say this, Mr. Speaker. I know what I'm talking about. I have my facts. The premier can make fun of my red face all he likes, but I'll go on record here and now and I'm not afraid to come right out and say it – there are members on both sides of this House who enjoy a cup of coffee.

"Now I may be ridiculed for saying this; I may be called ignorant and a crackpot and a traitor, but I don't mind. I can take it. And I'm not afraid to state it in public."

Opposition Leader Gerry Ottenheimer: "In supporting this bill, Mr. Speaker, I would like to say that while I am 50 per cent in favor of those who would ah tell us that uuumm while there is a certain amount of ah shall we say difference of opinion among those who ah ummmm in spite of what we may have heard on both sides will ah if the conditions are favorable ummm ummm and there are no shall we say extenuating circumstances ah actually sit down and ummm more or less drink ah umm coffee. Umm?"

Labour Minister W.J. Keough: "Mr. Speaker. Four score and ten years ago every man and his dog drank bog water. When this millennia has passed into history the sons of our loins will take note and say: 'They sat about on their fat fannies and chewed the fat about a coffee break. Did not life among the galaxies mean anything to them?'"

Mr. Murphy: "May I ask the honorable gentlemen a question? What's all this talk about loins? Are we supposed to be discussing the price of pork chops here?"

Dr. Rowe: "Shut up! Shut up!"

Ed Roberts: "There's McCarthyism for you! When did you stop beating your wife?"

Premier: "Mr. Speaker. Are the honorable gentlemen opposite serious? Are they really serious? Do they actually expect anybody to take them seriously? Or is this just another display of gross, unmitigated, unforgivable, astounding, incredible ignorance?

"Do they seriously believe that the Queen's Ministers would actually ask Her Majesty the Queen, through His Honour the Lieutenant-Governor (who represents Her Majesty the Queen) for permission to drink coffee ... COFFEE ... under the Union Jack on the doorstep of the People's honorable goodness gracious House?

"What do they want? Do they want Her Majesty's Loyal Ministers to be a party to treason? Is that what they're suggesting? Is that what they're trying to get at?"

Mr. Ottenheimer: "Point of ah order Mr. ummm Speaker. I stand to be corrected on ah this and while there may be some who disagree and others who will agree, I say that is their ummm privilege. But ah I would say this, that ah ummm this reference to ah treason is not very ummm nice."

Dr. Rowe: "Shut up! Shut up!"

Premier: "Treason! Pure, unadulterated, downright treason. Treason. Yes, treason. Sheer, unmitigated treason! Treason! Treason! Coffee? That's treason! (One hour and twenty-six minutes later.) No, Mr. Speaker. The honorable gentleman will never have it to say they forced this government into a coffee break.

"I'll say right here and now that the government has planned some action on this. No, the honorable gentleman opposite cannot take one iota, not one scintilla, not one atom, not one particle of the credit.

"This was thought of long ago, Mr. Speaker, long ago. I and the Honorable Minister of Education thought of it 14 years ago while floating down the Goose River in Labrador on a log raft.

"Sometime during this session, this government will bring in legislation, not for an ignorant, picayune, treasonous coffee break, but for a glorious, loyal, noble, British tea break."

Government members: Thump, thump, thump, thump.

Mr. Hickey: "In closing the debate, Mr. Speaker ..."

Dr. Rowe: "Shut up! Shut up!" █

He has the same gift, on a smaller scale, that Adolf Hitler had

March 28, 1968   *Joey*

"I'd like to get out … in a year. I've had my rendezvous with history. I'm not going to be one of those politicians who hangs around too long and becomes a pitiful figure."

Thus spake J.R. Smallwood to John Clare, then editor of *Maclean's* magazine, in September 1958.

Mr. Smallwood is nine years older now. He's still with us. How much longer can he stay and not be a "pitiful figure"? Maybe 12 years. More likely 12 months.

Whether Mr. Smallwood leaves now or when he's 80, he'll still be a pitiful figure. There's one figure who is just as pitiful as a politician who hangs around too long. A politician out of office.

The greater the power a politician has held and the longer he has held it, the more forlorn a figure he cuts when he leaves. Mr. Diefenbaker now cuts a forlorn figure. But he did not hold power for 20 years, nor did he have one-tenth the power, relatively, that Mr. Smallwood has enjoyed.

Winston Churchill stayed too long. He became an embarrassment to the country during his latter years in office. Then he retired and became a "living legend," growing old and senile, a forlorn shadow of what he once was. De Gaulle is staying too long. Pearson almost stayed too long.

How has Mr. Smallwood planned his retirement? He cannot expect to "half retire" – to name a successor, then attempt to pull the strings from Roache's Line, to direct the show from behind the scenes.

Although the office of premier in Newfoundland has become distorted and twisted out of shape, a basic rule of politics still applies to it. Only one man can sit in the premier's chair at a time.

The premier must either hold on to the wheel with all his might or else let it go altogether. If he relaxes his grip at all, he will find his power slipping from his hands at an ever-accelerating rate.

This rule applies in all forms of politics but particularly where the power of the leader has been exceptionally strong. In Russia, for example, a leader's slide from power comes with brutal suddenness.

In politics there are always the eager young hopefuls hovering in the background – just as in the animal kingdom there are always the young bucks getting ready to challenge and depose the old bull.

From behind the cabinet room doors come the first rumblings of the challenge. Some of the younger men are claiming to have forced revisions of the budget.

Mr. Smallwood could retire if he wanted to.

But for one who has been top dog so decidedly and for so long, the mental shock of retirement would be great. He might, as he says, devote his time in retirement to the writing of books.

Older men, whether they admit it or not, begin to wonder what history will say of them. But while they make history they cannot write it.

Mr. Smallwood's books will be interesting and useful historical references, but they will not be history books. *The Story of Newfoundland* – with no Valdmanis, no Bell Island, no half-billion-dollar debt – is not a history book.

Neither will *The Life and Times of J.R. Smallwood* ghost-written by a Time Inc. hack be a history book. No one is ever privileged to know his real place in history. Others write it after they are dead.

Mr. Smallwood has obtained his place in history, whatever it turns out to be, through two factors: (a) the circumstances of Newfoundland after the Second World War and (b) a special gift he possesses.

He has the same gift, on a smaller scale, that Adolf Hitler had. Hitler had it and so did Napoleon and Churchill and Kennedy. So may Pierre Elliott Trudeau.

The fancy name for this gift is "charisma." It means the special power to sway and convince, almost mesmerize, individuals, audiences, provinces or countries. The Beatles? Their charisma is artificial – manufactured.

You may see real and dramatic evidence of Mr. Smallwood's charisma at any sod-turning or ribbon-cutting, particularly in the outports. I have seen it seven or eight times.

He stands on a rough, outdoor platform around which is gathered a crowd of from 100 to 300. Soon the familiar, grating bellow from those mighty lungs begins to envelop the crowd.

Watch closely and you will see a weird change come over 10 or a dozen people in the audience. Their gaze on the speaker is intense. They begin to breathe heavily. They sway very slightly on their feet. Their mouths hang a little open.

Look even closer and you will see that their eyes have an unnatural glaze. Small children quarrel and shout around them, but they take no notice. Only a direct bomb hit could break their trance.

No need to go to an outport sod-turning. Witness the fascinating emotional binge at St. John's Airport last fall when Mr. Smallwood came home after his operation.

He was enveloped by a sea of Liberal women. Some laughed, some shouted, some waved handkerchiefs or tried to touch him. A few burst into hysterical tears.

For the past 20 years, all of us have been affected to a greater or lesser degree by Mr. Smallwood's rare gift of charisma.

If he does not want to hang on so long as to become a "pitiful figure," there is a simple guide. All he has to do is note whether the people with the glazed eyes are as numerous as they once were. If they are not, the hour is late. ▓

Circuses in lieu of bread

In the House

Far be it for me to suggest that the premier is slowing down, but I will say he has shown a surprising lack of action lately as regards smokescreens and diversions.

In the past, whenever things looked gloomy or another policy fell flat on its face, it was the premier's practice to come up with something spectacular to take people's minds off the grim facts.

But in the midst of our present troubles, the premier has been untypically slow in providing circuses in lieu of bread.

The June 25 federal election is a godsend in this regard, we know, but it cannot be expected to divert people from nasty reality for some weeks yet. Neither can another whale be depended on to go aground, as was the case during the troublesome Grand Falls hospital dispute.

Being a patriotic Newfoundlander with the greatest respect for established traditions, I take the liberty of offering a few possible courses of action. These suggested feints and ruses would give the government a breathing spell in which to dream up some of its own.

(1) Mines and Resources Minister C. Max Lane might make a few more references to the fact that Farley Mowat says the Vikings landed at Bellevue Beach, Trinity Bay. Then, when interest has been aroused, Mr. Lane might announce the discovery of what are thought to be Viking artifacts at Bellevue Beach Provincial Park.

These need not be elaborate. An empty Norwegian sardine tin or the muffler from a Volvo automobile will serve the purpose. This would create great public interest for a day or two.

(2) When this wears off, the premier can keep the ball rolling with the announcement that Newfoundland has purchased the Isle of Wight off the south coast of England and will transport it to the middle of Conception Bay.

If someone happens to ask why (which in Newfoundland is highly unlikely), the premier can tell them the isle is to be used as a breeding ground for bushbabies.

It is even more unlikely that anyone will ask what bushbabies are, but if they do they may be told that these are appealing little animals with brown eyes the size of wooden buttons on women's winter coats.

After a few days, another announcement is made that a new industry will be set up to make women's winter coats from bushbaby pelts. This will create an extremely noisy diversion with the SPCA and the sealing interests joining forces against the plan. A complex ruse like this should be good for at least a week.

(3) Provincial Affairs Minister Dr. G.A. Frecker might announce that a

three-day reception and government banquet is to be held in honor of Benito Mussolini, who will make his first visit to Newfoundland.

This should cause a considerable stir, especially among those who thought that Italian gentlemen had long since resigned from public affairs. It need not be mentioned until after the festivities that Signor Mussolini hails from upstate New York where he has operated a restaurant for the past 47 years.

(4) The premier might announce that he will make a great announcement May 12 which will affect, directly or indirectly, some 2,183 Newfoundlanders.

This announcement will mean more work for the province's newspaper reporters, newsboys, typesetters, radio and television reporters and personnel, and will consequently affect their families as well.

Then on May 12, the premier might announce that his announcement of the May 12 announcement was so successful and provided so much additional work for newsmen that he will make another great announcement on May 26. This could be kept up indefinitely, and although some may think it a novel ploy, it has been used before with great success.

(5) Fisheries Minister Aidan Maloney might announce the launching of a great new industry in Newfoundland, to be known as "the fishery."

Mr. Maloney might disclose that the decision to start this great new industry came following the report of a special commission which studied the possibilities for more than a year.

The commission would have found that there are great numbers of edible creatures in the waters around Newfoundland which are known generally as "fish." It would have further informed the government that in other parts of the world, thousands of people make a living by extracting these creatures from their liquid habitat.

He would amaze Newfoundlanders with the news that ingenious contraptions known as "boats" are employed and the "fish" are entrapped by devices called "nets." This new intelligence would set the whole province buzzing for at least nine days. 🅡🅖

I am not a puppet

May 15, 1968   *Liberals and Pea Seas*

Goodness gracious! What a state I'm in! I can't take all this excitement like I could one time. It makes me giddy in the head and I have to go lie down with cold cloths to my poll.

A blizzard in the middle of May! It's almost more than flesh and blood can stand. Whatever in the world is the cause of this unnatural weather? Is it a sign from above?

What I fancy is that the gods are angry with Mr. Crosbie and Mr. Wells. It wouldn't surprise me one little bit, either, if we got a report that the veil of the temple has been rent in twain.

As you may or may not have heard yesterday (depending on what newspaper you read), Mr. Crosbie and Mr. Wells bolted from the government, and now sit on the opposition side of the House.

They say they quit. Premier Smallwood says he hove them out. Whatever the ins and outs of it, the premier managed to get in a few quick kicks in the shins and a knee to the groin as they scrambled out the door. He was also able to pitch some pots and pans after their heads as they skidaddled down the driveway.

Nothing would do, of course, but for the premier to get all the lads together (the ones who are left) and let them tell him they still love him. With two cabinet posts now up for grabs, the sincerity and conviction with which the backbenchers, in particular, complied, was an inspiration to behold.

One after the other, each in turn, far into the night and the wee hours of the morning, they hailed the "Only Living Father" as the "modern Moses" and the "new messiah" – among other things.

Some of the testimony resembled that of sinners saved by grace; more of it recalled the endorsements of satisfied users of Lydia Pinkham's Celebrated Elixir.

The premier said he was at times moved to tears. That's understandable. All the cabinet ministers were strenuous in their efforts to refute the charge that they were puppets. Up popped one minister: "I am not a puppet." Up popped another minister: "I am not a puppet." Up popped another: "I am not a puppet." Up popped …

Dr. Rowe said that Premier Smallwood was a strong leader and all strong leaders, at one time or another, were called dictators. He went back as far as the British Prime Minister Disraeli.

Disraeli, said Dr. Rowe, had grabbed the Suez Canal without telling anyone in the cabinet a word about it. There just wasn't time to tell them.

What surprise packages can we look forward to?

The premier grabbed a few Expo pavilions but they really don't stack up alongside the Suez Canal. However, we have every confidence. We expect to wake up any morning and find we're the proud owners of the Washington Bridge or Easter Island or Hubert Humphrey.

Nat Noel took another tack in an attempt to demonstrate the difference between puppets and Newfoundland cabinet ministers. The cabinet, said he, is rather like the army.

In the army, he said, the men must obey the officers and sometimes the officers must enforce discipline for the good of the men. In Mr. Noel's elegant phrase: "A good kick in the guts from a leader never did anybody any harm."

If that's the way Mr. Noel likes to get his kicks it's OK with us. At the same time, we hope he also maintains a broad mind toward those who like to get their kicks by pulling the wings off houseflies.

Further down the line William Callahan, MHA for Port au Port and former CJON news director, gave reasons why the government hasn't tabled that report of the Royal Commission on Economic Prospects.

As usual, Billy hit the nail on the head. "The government would be crazy to provide the Opposition with ammunition," he explained.

That's the first sensible and logical excuse we've heard. The report is extremely critical of the government. Making it public before the June 25 election would be making a switch for their own backs.

Carry on, William.

But, mercy me, Tom Burgess, aren't you the strange one? All your colleagues popped up on cue, sharp as tacks and bursting to declare their allegiance to their leader. Not one second did they hesitate.

You, on the other hand, couldn't decide one way or the other but asked for some time to think it over. Why be half sure? (As they say in the underarm deodorant ads.)

This much is sure, if you finally come to the conclusion that you do have confidence in the government you'll need every scrap of blarney you can muster to make up for the deadly hesitation.

The most comical thing of all to watch was the way most government members tried to disentangle themselves from the vicious attack the premier made on Mr. Crosbie's integrity.

This fancy bit of footwork reached its peak with P.J. Lewis, minister without portfolio, who paid glowing tribute to the two defectors. At one point it seemed that Mr. Lewis would call for a medal to be struck in their honor.

All in all, it was an extremely upsetting day. So if you'll excuse me, I'll get the cold cloths and go have another lie-down. ▨

Today is a sorry day for you

Resettlement and Rural Life

If you are a Newfoundlander, today is a sorry day for you – I don't care what your "Happy Province" licence plates say.

Because today is the day that Mrs. John Dare, a middle-aged outport housewife, prayed desperately would never come. Now it is here to bring sorrow to her and to you.

Until last fall, Mrs. Dare lived in a small community on an island in Placentia Bay. Her husband was a fisherman and made no better and no worse a living than his neighbors.

Mr. Dare and the oldest of their three sons caught enough fish even in bad years to support the family. They kept gardens and grew enough vegetables for their own use. In winter they cut and brought home wood for heat.

Their proudest boast was one that used to be almost universal in Newfoundland – that they "never owed no man nothing."

Then last summer a strange thing happened in the small island community. Almost overnight a rumor swept the harbor that the place was to be abandoned. Nobody quite knew why, just that "moving fever" was on the bay.

Some said a government feller came around and started it; others said that there'd be no clergy and no teacher next year; nobody wanted to be left behind in the winter. There were frantic preparations.

On the last day before they left, Mrs. Dare went up to the graveyard on the hill. There were several other women there. Then she went back down to finish packing all the belongings they thought would be useful in the new home.

What they could not take they piled in a heap on the beach and burned, because they knew that soon after they left gangs of young men in motorboats would arrive to smash and pillage the deserted houses.

They left on that fall day with sadness but not without hope. There was a lot of talk on the radio about a third mill at Come By Chance with plenty of jobs and money. The government-approved relocation center on the mainland to which they were going was near Come By Chance.

At the mainland relocation center, they found an earlier influx of people from the islands had taken up all the available houses and land. They were told the only place they could get was a small plot in a government-approved subdivision on the outskirts of the community.

They had about $3,000 in moving money from the government, but found this was hardly enough to cover the price of the piece of land. As the government grants had increased, so had the land prices.

They found that even a small house would cost more than $10,000. There was much confusing talk about bank loans and mortgages and financing which they only half understood. They do know they can no longer say they "owe no man nothing."

Mr. Dare worked through the winter, building a wharf and fishing stage, but the few dollars they had ran out and he cannot finish it.

There is still news on the radio about the "Come By Chance complex" nearby, but the few dozen men who were working on it were laid off a few weeks ago. Even last winter only one man from the resettlement area found work there.

They have no land to grow vegetables. They must pay for stove oil. They have a monthly electricity bill. There is a small bill for "town council services." There are people looking for school and church donations.

Early this spring Mrs. Dare could see it coming. They spent as little as they could on food. There seemed to be no one to help them. Most of their neighbors in this strange place were strangers to them.

Mrs. Dare began to get desperate. Why? No one can starve now in the Happy Province. Some clever politicians played a very cunning trick when they put that on the licence plates. Repeated 200,000 times – "Newfoundland, the Happy Province." If we see it often enough, will we begin to believe it?

She was desperate because of a silly principle that used to be one of the strongest among the Newfoundland people – that the day an able-bodied man accepts the dole, he becomes something less than a man.

Even in the bad times, thousands of Newfoundlanders fought off the dole as they fought the storms on the sea and the worst a hard land could put against them.

Last Saturday there was nothing left in the house to eat, and no money. Some neighbors gave her enough to make a dinner yesterday. Today ...

The welfare office is about a mile away from the subdivision. It was one of the first things built at the resettlement center. It has two welfare officers and a secretary. They are kept quite busy.

Mrs. Dare tried to get to the welfare office early this morning before there were many people on the road to see her go. The officers gave her a paper (no trouble at all) for $80 a month.

She went with it to the store and whispered to the woman behind the counter. She thought that all eyes in the store were on her. She passed over the paper and was glad they did not ask her to sign it because her hands trembled.

But why shall you worry? Because, when the strongest and most honest and simple among us must walk that road early in the morning, where is there hope still for any?

If you are a Newfoundlander, today is a sorry day for you. ▉

Dear Uncle Ray

June 5, 1968   *Liberals and Pea Seas*

From time to time I receive letters of a personal nature. Cries for help from folks in distress out there. People who turn to these columns in desperation – and I do mean desperation.

While advice of this nature is somewhat beyond my scope, I am so touched by these plaintive appeals that conscience will not allow me to put them aside.

To the best of my ability I shall attempt to bring some measure of comfort and consolation to these troubled souls.

Dear Uncle Ray:

I am at the end of my tether. I am a candidate in the upcoming election and early on in the campaign I struck upon the device of kissing young girls in public.

This has been used to great effect by Mr. Trudeau and at first I found it to work extremely well for me. So effective was it in keeping my name in the public prints that I did not have to trouble with such tiresome things as policy and platform.

But of late my life has been made a perfect hell by a certain sex-starved spinster who has followed me around my district for the past two weeks.

She has the habit of pouncing on me with shocking abandon at the most inopportune moments and will average three or four assaults in the run of the typical campaign day.

On Thursday last, for example, she clambered onstage in the F.U. Hall in Kumquat Quay, where I was outlining to an enthralled audience my stand regarding a revision of Canada's membership in the North Atlantic Treaty Organization.

This shameless Jezebel laid hold of my person and, with the most passionate shrieks, endeavored (to the applause of a large crowd) to tear the outer garments from my back.

What am I to do? I have tried eating garlic and wearing black woolen socks but nothing seems to work. Please help.

More Than I Can Chew

Dear Chew:

Draw the lady in question to one side and offer her $10 a day more to stay away than your rival candidate is paying her to accost you. Judging from your photographs this can be the only explanation.

Even a Kumquat Quay spinster couldn't be THAT desperate.

Dear Uncle Ray:

I am ready to throw in the towel. Please help me.

In my election campaign I have concentrated on kissing babies and I consider it a poor day indeed if I do not kiss a minimum of 25 babies in arms plus 35 ambulatory infants below the age of two years.

The trouble is that at the end of the day I find myself in a distressing condition.

Tell me, has it been scientifically proven that parents' political leanings are reflected by their offspring to this extent?

Also, what can I do about it?

Greatly Puzzled

Dear G.P.:

I fear I do not have the answer to your first question.

With regard to the second, however, you may hold out hope. The Pautch-Schlendheim method of dry baby-kissing has been tested extensively in the US and Australia with good results.

By this method the kisser simply holds the infant kissee at arm's length. This places the kisser at a safe distance from the kissee so that no embarrassment can result.

But, you may ask, how can the kiss be planted at arm's length? Have no fear. Considering the magnitude of the average politician's kisser, this distance should prove no obstacle.

Dear Uncle Ray:

I am at my wit's end. I have made a terrible mistake through mistrustfulness and can only hope my experience will prove a lesson to others.

For some time I have had the suspicion that the police are discriminating against the party of my choice. My automobile is covered fore and aft with political stickers.

Monday week I was parked on the main street with several minutes still on the meter. Yet as I advanced I perceived a figure in uniform standing near the car with a slip of paper in hand.

Enraged, I threw myself upon him and gave him a good pummeling.

Imagine my chagrin when I discovered him to be a Salvation Army officer checking his grocery list.

Embarrassed to Tears

Dear Uncle Ray:

I believe I am going mad. These past three weeks I have been employed as a full-time teabag squeezer at Mr. Cashews's political coffee parties.

My job is to get three cups of tea from a two-cup bag. Yesterday, I received firm instructions to increase the number of cups got from one bag to FOUR.

It is next to impossible to get four cups from a two-cup bag. Several ladies have already complained of lint in their beverage.

My professional pride has always been intense. I am beside myself with worry. What am I to do?

Exhausted

Dear Exhausted:

Resign immediately from your present position and run as an independent candidate. A teabag squeezer of your integrity would do much to upgrade the present sorry state of politics in this country. ▩

The harder you pinch 'em, the louder they squeal

June 10, 1968 *Resettlement and Rural Life*

Hallelujah! At long last – a nasty letter! Since I started writing these pieces I can immodestly say I've received a good bit of mail – all of it complimentary.

Grateful though I was, I still worried. No nasty letter. It just wasn't natural. At last I have one – to the editor, no less, on page 6. It comes from a certain Kevin A. Wadman of Arnold's Cove, Placentia Bay, and it's as nice a nasty letter as you can wish for.

The harder you pinch 'em, the louder they squeal. Good old Kevin let out a yelp you could hear from Come By Chance to Chapeau Rouge. Finding civilized language unequal to expressing the frustration within his bosom, Mr. Wadman has dipped his pen into rattlesnake venom.

Two things I've done lately seem to have increased the steam pressure in good old Kevin's hot little head. One was a series of articles on the Iverson-Matthews report on centralization – a report commissioned by Memorial University with the aid of a grant from federal fisheries.

The other thing that got him hot and bothered was a column last Monday about the trials of a "Mrs. John Dare," whose family was forced – through lack of planning and management of the centralization scheme – to take able-bodied relief.

Mr. Wadman took it for granted that that piece was about Arnold's Cove. Maybe it was. Maybe it wasn't. There's nobody in Arnold's Cove by the name of "Mrs. John Dare," says Kevin.

That's true, there isn't. Did he really expect me to plaster her real name in print? She has enough trouble already. I took pains to keep her identity secret. "Mrs. John Dare" was a name I made up – but I can assure Mr. Wadman her plight is all too real.

Unfortunately, I found out later there are several new families in Arnold's Cove with a name that sounds something like "Dare." I understand they've been getting embarrassing phone calls from certain parties.

I don't know these people, have never seen them, have never spoken to them. I'm sorry the fictitious name I used turned out to be so close to theirs.

However, good old Kevin will have to quote the poetry of Alexander Pope a few more times and do a bit more twisting to make the people of Arnold's Cove believe I'm making fun of them – just because I showed some pity for one poor woman who (through no fault of her own) has been forced to eat the dole.

Mr. Wadman goes on to sneer at the Iverson-Matthews report as a slap-up job by "an Ontario sociologist." It might cool his fevered brow to know that

Professor Matthews was born and brought up in Newfoundland, taught classes at Memorial University, and later was clever enough to get a job at a famous American university.

More news for Mr. Wadman. Professor Matthews told me in a letter the other day he has been invited back to Newfoundland by Memorial University to teach there and to do several more years' study on the effects of centralization.

There was one piece of GOOD news in Mr. Wadman's nice and nasty letter. I find I'm supposed to be an Arnold's Cove taxpayer and that I owe the "town council" $7!

Last year I spent part of my holidays at Arnold's Cove. When I got a "service fee" bill for $7 from Mr. Wadman I thought the poor man (having so much other business to attend to) had made a mistake.

Now I find that other people who spent only a few days at Arnold's Cove while passing through have been billed by Mr. Wadman. People who left the community 20 years ago to make their homes in Canada have been billed by Mr. Wadman.

Now that Mr. Wadman assures me there was no mistake, I'm overjoyed. I rushed out right away and mailed him $7 under cover of registered mail. I don't want to miss out on that little bargain.

One of the things a taxpayer gets for his money is the right to keep an eye on and criticize the town council. Mr. Wadman has just signed on the second biggest mouth in Placentia East. He may soon wish I was in a lot hotter place than Communist China.

But who in the world, you may well ask, is Kevin A. Wadman? Mr. Wadman comes to us from Bar Haven, an island community (now deserted) in Placentia Bay.

Unlike some other island merchants, Mr. Wadman had the great foresight to move off the island before his customers did. He set up shop on the mainland (Arnold's Cove) some years before the exodus began. When the other people on the islands got caught up in centralization, good old Kevin was ready to welcome them with open arms.

Being a modest type, Mr. Wadman aspired to no higher post on the "town council" (a body which was not elected but appointed) than town clerk. The "Mayor" is one of his employees.

Good old Kevin has been loud in his praise of the way centralization has been carried out. He says it has been of great benefit to many people. No doubt it has.

But I venture to say that few people have benefited as much from centralization as has the enterprising Kevin A. Wadman. ▨

Smeechy Pastures Refining plant
is open for business

June 12, 1968   *Great New Industries*

Good afternoon all you folks out there in radioland. We're coming to you today from a broad expanse of bogland located some three miles west of the picturesque community of Sen Sen Junction.

A vast throng is assembled here to witness the official opening of a great new industrial complex which is expected to be of inestimable benefit, as usual, to this province.

The premier is on hand with his golden tin snips and will cut the ribbon to officially open the first factory (and the finest of its kind) in the world for the manufacture of moose-dropping jewelery.

It's a glorious day, the crowd is in a holiday mood, and apart from nine elderly spectators getting bogged on the way in to the mill site, there have been no mishaps. Our latest reports are that six have been recovered.

In the background, we see this magnificent edifice soaring to a height of 20 feet above the tuckamores and stretching some 20 feet away into the distance … the Smeechy Pastures Refining Company (Canada) Ltd.

The first sod for this complex, you may remember, was turned just prior to the provincial election of 1958. The second sod, just before the federal election of 1962. The third sod … Oh, oh, ladies and gentlemen, I believe … yes, from our vantage point here atop this great pile of sods we see that the ceremonies are about to commence.

First we'll hear from His Honor, the Mayor of Sen Sen Junction:

"Mr. Premier, Honorable Minister, ladies and gentlemen. This is indeed a great day in the history of our community and indeed in the history of the whole province.

"This great new moose-dropping jewelery complex will do much to relieve unemployment in the area. I may say that no less than one-quarter of the total work force of Sen Sen Junction will be employed here – namely, myself and my brother-in-law.

"We give all the credit to the premier and the great work he has done behind the scenes to bring this industry here … not forgetting the $5 million government-guaranteed loan without which none of this would have been possible. We say a heartfelt 'Thank you, Mr. Premier'."

Ladies and gentlemen, the thunderous applause you hear in the background is for the mayor of Sen Sen Junction who has just kissed the premier's foot. Now, we have the minister of mines and resources to explain the background of this new industry.

"Ladies and gentlemen. As we all know, this great new enterprise had its origins in the mind of the premier who some years ago happened to read in a newspaper (no, not THAT newspaper) of a Mrs. Win Robertson, a Prince George, BC, housewife, who first developed moose-dropping jewelery.

"The government has brought Mrs. Robertson to Newfoundland as expert consultant on this great project and she will pilot the plant through its infancy.

"The great simplicity and possibilities of the process are what first attracted the premier. Mrs. Robertson explains that the raw materials are collected in the countryside when at a proper state of maturity, trucked to the factory and impaled on rows of toothpicks.

"Here, they are sprayed with a molten glass fiber, allowed to cool and are then mounted on cufflinks and tiepins. Brooches and bracelets bearing such sentiments as 'Sweetheart' and 'Mother' are expected to be added to the line later. Engagement rings are another possibility.

"As resources minister I foresee a great future for the moose-dropping jewelery industry in this province and forecast that before many years it will even outstrip the fishery.

"According to our figures on the rate of decline in the fishery and our predictions on the rise of the M.D.J. industry, we believe the two will be about equal by early 1970.

"Thanks to the great efforts of our leader it is not too much to expect that moose-droppings and Newfoundland will become synonymous in the eyes of the world before long."

Ladies and gentlemen, we hear another great wave of applause as the resources minister concludes his address. The great moment has arrived. A tense hush falls over the crowd. The official ribbon-cutting shears are removed from their black velvet case and presented to the premier.

We might explain at this point that the premier has elected not to give a speech at this time. We are told that he has yielded to party pressures in this regard. This may explain the strip of adhesive tape.

It may also explain the larger than usual crowds here today to witness this novel spectacle. Now the ribbon has been cut and the Smeechy Pastures Refining plant is open for business. We have seen a bit of Newfoundland history in the making. RG

Heart to heart and brain to brain

June 17, 1968   *Joey*

If we live through this we'll live forever. We're into the seven-day home stretch, the campaign lads have worked themselves up to fever pitch and seem hell-bent on driving everyone else to the brink of hysteria.

They're pulling out all the stops, shouting and ranting like souls possessed, ruining their health, whipping themselves into a lather and giving everyone within earshot the dry heaves.

But we must be charitable. Consider, for instance, our "holier than thou" attitude toward the Negro problem in the US. Who knows how we'd behave if we were in the same position as the southern whites?

By the same token, if we had a chance to hook on to an $18,000-a-year job, in which landing the job was the hardest part of it, we might be willing to make jackasses of ourselves too.

Then there's the burning passion in the bosom of each and every one of the candidates to serve their country. We mustn't forget that.

In any case we're getting a bit of entertainment out of it, even though the price we have to pay for these amusements is scandalously high.

Have the Liberals run out of teabags? They have at last unleashed their secret weapon, their Big Bertha, their 16-incher, their heavy artillery, in the shape of the Only Living Father.

(Isn't it odd, by the way, how a title will stick? Joey came to be known as the Only Living Father of Confederation during last year's Centennial wingding. He positively basked in the nickname and it was inscribed on his little book, *The Peril and the Glory*.

Ever since, we have been unable to think of him as anything but the Only Living Father.)

Anyway, the Only Living Father had a speak in Spaniard's Bay on Thursday and was entertaining as usual – if nothing else.

"Only God in heaven," he declared, "can look down on Newfoundland and describe what Confederation has done for us."

While we're waiting for this description from Higher Up, we may ponder the reasons for the delay. The contract for the construction of the world lasted only seven days. Can it be that the Supreme Contractor must take even longer to figure out the state Newfoundland is now in? We'll stay tuned.

Joey went on to express his boundless devotion to Pierre – and for once words nearly failed him. We used to think that the Only Living Father had struck it off pretty good with Mackenzie King, Louis St. Laurent and Lester Pearson, and even had a few good words for Johnny D.

Now we find that his love for these lesser lights, compared to his ardent political passion for Pierre, is as a guttering candle alongside a raging forest fire.

Only now has a true union of mind and spirit been achieved. These two supreme intellects have met and melded in a blinding flash that will no doubt illuminate the civilized world and may even throw a scare into the uncivilized parts.

"Pierre Elliott Trudeau is the first one to see it my way," declared the O.L.F. at Spaniard's Bay. "We are heart to heart and brain to brain ..." That's about as cozy as you can get, you must admit.

Joey and Pierre! What an awesome spectacle to the world these two blood brothers present! The dynamic duo unleashed, strolling through the corridors of power at Ottawa sniffing their daisies.

Trudeau and Smallwood. Smallwood and Trudeau. Already household words from sea to sea – like cabbage strainer or carpet sweeper. Made for each other; each complementing each; the two final pieces of the Great Jigsaw Puzzle fallen into place; the circle completed; the spheres in harmony.

From one end of this great nation to the other – from the sea-girt shores of Newfoundland to the majestic mountains of British Columbia – a pregnant hush has fallen. Lesser mortals gape in wonder. It's rather like the effect of an eclipse of the sun on savage tribes.

Flower power and jaw power are welded by the hand of fate into an invincible combination. What can stand before them? What need for an election at all? A mere formality.

The two colossi are as one. The trench coat and the bow tie are joined. We are reminded of Michaelangelo's mural in the Sistine Chapel in which the Creator and Adam touch fingertips.

A mighty clap of thunder echoes across the nation. Pierre and Joey! Blood brothers! Joseph R. Trudeau Smallwood. The symbolic exchange of names.

But wait.

On this great and fateful occasion has the vast network of the Canadian press – both printed and electronic – failed us? Has not the only Canadian prime minister in history to see it Joey's way signed his name (even once) as Pierre E. Smallwood Trudeau?

We have not heard so and can only conclude that the press has fallen down on the job by neglecting to record this piece of intelligence. Never mind. A small point.

Canadians! Behold the molders of your destiny! Joey and P.E.T. walking off, heart to heart and brain to brain into the sunset ... with God trudging along at a respectful distance behind them. ⬛

People deserve the kind of government they get

June 18, 1968 *Democracy*

Notice. Great political rally in the F.U. Hall at 8:30 tonight. Hear Murdock Vespucci, candidate for Boxy-Poomsocks-Phlegm, discuss the Burning Issues – Come one. Come all. Free refreshments.

Mrs. C.B. Twilly (to Mrs. B.C. Knucks): "I 'low I might go to that, Beatrice, if we can get out of it early enough to see 'Another Man's Family'. I seen buddy's likeness in the paper the other day."

Archy Smop (to Amboy Pipsqueak): "I 'low, old man, we'll get a couple of crocks on our unemployment cheques, set in the back where we can make a quick bolt, and put 'er up."

J.B. Bunion (to Mrs. J.B. Bunion): "Do you feel up to it tonight, Patience, my maid? I 'low if we can make it at all we should go along. Lord help us if he don't see us there and our pensions is cut back."

Pasmore Malinger (to Sebastapol Mope): "Don't say I'm not goin' to ask HIM a thing or two. He's goin' to get it hot and heavy, I can tell you. The doctor turned me down and I'm goin' to 'bide turned down and I don't want to hear no talk about cuttin' the welfare."

Filbert Shagoff (to Nabob Paselm): "What I wants to know and what I'm goin' to know is when they goin' to patch that pothole in breast of our door. I don't want to hear none of this stuff about what they're goin' to do down the shore or up in Ottawa. That got no interes' for me."

Are such comments still common in Newfoundland – in town and out of town and all around the town? There'll always be some but if they're too plentiful we all have cause for worry.

Let's face it. People who shouldn't be allowed a duck licence are allowed to help decide how the country (or province) should be run.

Anyone who is still outside the walls of H.M. Penitentiary or the mental hospital can mark an X. The theory is that there are enough average, ordinary, common sense voters to offset the damage the lunatic fringe and the near-morons might cause.

In the same way, it is presumed that there are enough common sense voters to weed out any lunatics or morons who might be running for public office.

Any way you look at it, the average, common sense voter has a big responsibility. His job is not an easy one. It's just as hard as ever to tell the sheep from the goats.

All candidates have one aim – to get elected. They use the most effective ways open to them to persuade voters to vote for them. A few years ago, the "Deafen and Mesmerize 'Em" tactic was most popular.

A candidate would get on a stage and rant and roar and call on the flag and his Maker and freedom and justice and motherhood, shout a lot and say little in the hope that his audience would stagger out of the hall (and to the polling booth) in a benumbed and unthinking state ... and put their Xs opposite the name still ringing in their ears.

Today, more subtle methods of persuasion are in fashion. There's not so much ranting and roaring. Everything's more quiet, played down – and sneaky.

Candidates are sold like tinned beans and washing powder. They play on deep, dark stuff in the backs of our minds that we never knew was there.

Something like that recent magazine ad for whiskey: "Buy Dad a bottle of Old Rotgut Royal for Father's Day. Sure it costs a lot. But so did you."

The real message: "After all that poor old grey-haired, God-fearing, hard-working daddy of yours did for you, you ungrateful, miserable slob, you can erase a little of these guilt feelings by giving him a bottle of our outrageously expensive fancy-package hooch."

So it is with political campaigns these days. It's all very well to say that the common sense of the average voter will prevail – but what do you do when they've found out ways to outwit your senses?

Of course, all this new-fangled, low-keyed persuasion jazz is wasted on some of the types who are going along to hear Murdock Vespucci discuss the Burning Issues in the F.U. Hall.

The old-fashioned ranting and roaring will work just as well on them. They haven't got the sense to see past their miserable little noses anyhow. If there are enough of them, they'll elect one of their own number to Ottawa or Confederation Building.

It's no easy job being an average, ordinary, common sense voter these days. It's hard work. The only consolation is that the more of them there are, the better the government will be.

One adage still stands out through the ranting and roaring and subtle persuasion – people deserve the kind of government they get.

Once we've elected our members, our best bet is never to take our eyes off them for one second. If we start believing that any of them are so honest they don't have to be constantly watched and so no word of theirs need be questioned ... we're asking for bloody trouble.

That's because they're not programmed robots but humans like the rest of us. Until the ideal state is reached and suitable robots become available, the average, ordinary, common sense voter has his work cut out. ⬛

Guy's Encyclopedia of Juvenile Outharbor Delights: Catching Tansys, Jumping in the Bog

June 28, 1968   *Outharbor Delights*

Let's take a bit of a spell.

Let us turn aside, gentle readers (and you roughnecks, too) from the hurly-burly of this wicked world and cast our thoughts on finer things.

Let us try to recover from the shock of discovering there won't be a provincial election this fall.

Let us take time out to recuperate from the good news that Chairman Joe is going to stick with us (for our own good, of course) until the Liberal tide comes in again.

Let us take our wind on the eve of glorious summer, step out of the hot air and sit awhile in the warm breezes.

Let us get plump and jolly and healthy, the better to face the winter again and whatever other battles may come.

Let us get into a blue-green summery mood by glancing through that renowned volume – *Guy's Encyclopedia of Juvenile Outharbor Delights* – a rare tome not to be found in even the O.L.F.'s library.

Turning the pages at random, we come across an item on "Catching Tansys": Directions. Perceive that the tide is out. Walk on the landwash among the wet rocks in sneaker boots and with pants legs rolled up.

Obtain a medium-sized glass crock at high-water mark and fill it one-quarter full of Placentia Bay. Lesser bays may suffice in a pinch.

Turn over a rock near the water's edge. Observe the swarms of swimps (sand fleas) and crabs underneath it. Disregard crabs unless you are "Catching Crabs" (described under the heading on Page 472).

Under every fifth rock there is a tansy. A tiny brown eel with a yellow belly. Grab for it. It will dart away under another rock. Turn that over and grab again. Inside of five or ten minutes you will have turned up half the beach and caught your tansy. Drop it into the glass crock.

In two or three hours you will have caught a dozen tansys. Sit on the grass in the sun and admire them for 20 minutes. Take one out and look at him. Take them around and show them to others. Drop one down a little girl's back – if you are a little boy.

Sling some into Aunt Martha's duck pen. Watch the ducks swallow them and jiggle their tails. At supper time, throw the rest back in the landwash for tomorrow. Throw rocks at empty bottle until smashed.

"Jumping in the Bog": Locate a rail fence on a marsh next to a bog. Take off boots and stockings and lay them to one side. Roll up pants legs. Roll up the legs of your long underwear (compulsory uniform until mid-July) and climb to top rail. Jump.

First prize to the one sinking deepest into the warm mud. Aim for quality jumps rather than quantity. Helpful hint: Jump UP rather than OUT and so gain force through altitude.

Continue for at least an hour until someone goes to his waist to establish a record that will stand for the summer. Replace boots and stockings; roll down muddy pants legs. Go home and get a good lacing.

"Heaving Rocks at Steerins" (Terns): Get some fish livers and pitch them out in the water 50 feet upwind from the spot where you will be heaving rocks at steerins.

Climb up to the top of the bank (cliff) and collect some rocks for heaving. Some say round rocks are best. George Albert, however, always preferred his rocks a bit on the flat side. Flat but not clifty. Flat and beachy.

Soon the steerins will come along diving and fluttering after the liver which is drifting into range. Ready your rocks. Heave at steerins.

Heave rocks until liver floats out of range. If still in the mood, get some more liver and some more rocks. After an hour your arm may drop off.

A word of comfort to the SPCA. It is a well-known fact that no one ever hit a steerin with a rock. I never did. They see the rock coming, wait until it's three feet away, duck, and laugh at you.

To the best of my knowledge, not even George Albert ever hit one and he could heave a rock further and straighter than anyone on our side of the bay. Which is to say he was the champion rock heaver in Newfoundland.

One chap once claimed to have hit a steerin and showed one for proof. It was later discovered that he had picked it up dead around shore.

His disgrace was complete. He was shamed to tears. For a whole month he was not allowed to join in "Playing Rollers," "Making Bone Narrs," "Foundering Cliffs," "Playing Rounders," "Flying Dust," or that supreme, absolute delight of all, "Catching Conners."

More about these later. Enough for now to say that anyone who tries to pretend ever he hit a steerin should not be trusted. A fellow like that would cheat at cards – or grow up to become a politician. ◼

Guy's Encyclopedia of Juvenile Outharbor Delights: Catching Connors

July 2, 1968   *Outharbor Delights*

Pity the poor creatures in warmer countries where the seasons never change. Where summer is eternal and they never know the pain of waiting and the joy at last when summer comes.

It's here. Hit 70 yesterday. Same today. How sweet it is.

In keeping with the grand arrival and in hopes that it will help exiled Newfoundlanders now back on vacation to remember, we offer still another selection from that rare volume *Guy's Encyclopedia of Juvenile Outharbor Delights*.

Turning to one of the main chapters we come across the supreme and classic pastime among the younger outharbor set – "Catching Connors." Absolutely nothing is half so popular.

The equipment is chastely simple. Get a flake longer off the fish flake for a pole. From the fishing stage obtain some net twine, one and a half times the length of your pole. Borrow a fish hook – the Swedish Mustard Number 15, of course.

Get some bait. Codfish hearts, naturally. If fish are scarce, you can pick some wrinkles (snails) off the rocks or the sunken wharves and crack them. But codfish hearts are best by far.

Lie flat on the wharf with the pole extended over the edge. If there is a slight lop on the water and you can't see to the bottom, get some cod oil from the blubber barrel and throw that out. The oil will make it calm.

Let your hook drift down into the green depths. You will see swarms of conners milling about, having a grand old time and nibbling on fish guts. They range from little brown ones, three inches long, to big old ones, a foot long with blue bellies.

The only object is to see how many conners you can catch. Big ones are sometimes preferred, but not necessarily. Lay them on the wharf to expire or put them in a half-puncheon of water and watch them swimming around. Some mainlanders call them perch and eat them, the dirty devils.

There are other things to be caught from wharves on summer days. But one thing not to catch is sculpins. It is more of a trick not to catch them than to catch them.

They lie on the bottom and unless one moves you can't see it. Ugliest brutes in creation, sculpins. They're a dirty green-brown and full of spines and spikes and lumps. All head and mouth.

If your bait drifts by one, he inhales it. Gulp. Glug. You have him and no doubt about it.

But now that you have him, what are you going to do with him? Your hook is way down inside that fearsome mug. He's bristling his spines and puffing himself up bigger. He's glaring at you with evil, mottled eyes.

If you have a small hatchet you can chop him up and get your hook back. The only thing that looks worse than a sculpin is a chopped-up sculpin. Eccccchhh! Which is why you will not try to catch sculpins.

However, catching flatfish is great sport. They're brown on the back and almost as hard to see as sculpins, but they won't take bait. They must be jug.

You lash four Mustard Number 15 hooks together to make a jigger, let it lie on the bottom until the flatty swims over it. That's how they're jug.

A flatty has two eyes way up forward and his mouth is on sideways. Everyone knows why the flatfish's mouth is on sideways. A long time ago it was on straight.

One day he got too big for himself and said loudly: "The salmon is king of the sea? Cripes!," twisting his mouth as he said it.

At that very moment his mouth froze in a permanent sneer. When you jig a flatty you can see for yourself and no mistake about it that this is true.

Regard the poor flatfish, little children, take heed and never pooh hoo your betters.

Then there are eels. Now we're getting into the field of the specialist. It's all very easy to catch a conner or even a flatty, but an eel is something else.

They have to be jug, too – no easy job. They either stay under the wharf with only their heads sticking out of the kelp or woggle along at a fast rate from one place to another. It isn't everyone who's clever enough to jig an eel.

There are, as you will know, two kinds of eels – Eels and Pizen Eels. Eels (American) are fairly plenty. They're brown and smooth and not as big as Pizen Eels. Three or four may be caught a month.

Pizen Eels (conger) are grey and rough and have wavy fins the whole length. They're four feet long, maybe more. They're not so plenty.

Perhaps only once a summer will a Pizen Eel be caught. A red-letter day it is for the lucky person who catches one. He is absolutely top dog for at least a week. Hemingway would have understood.

Pizen Eels are fun to catch because they're poison. If you catch one he will make a dart at you and if he bites you you will die on the spot in terrible agony. Just the tiniest nip, mind you.

Everyone knows someone who heard tell of someone who was nipped by a Pizen Eel and died on the spot.

There is tons more stuff that can be caught from a wharf on a summer day. Tomcods, maidenrays (skates), sea trout and mackerel … and the sun shining down, the sea gulls fluttering over the blue water all the while, and every day a week long. ▩

Guy's Encyclopedia of Juvenile Outharbor Delights: Walking Around Shore, Picking Up Stuff

July 4, 1968 *Outharbor Delights*

Before presenting a further installment of *Guy's Encyclopedia of Juvenile Outharbor Delights* – some of the stuff little fellers around the bay used to do for pastime – I must clear up a few points on earlier installments.

Someone (at least) was puzzled about the reference to "Making Bone Narrs." To make a Bone Narr, you cut a bendy stick about three feet long and tie string on both ends to make a bow in it.

Then you get a long thin stick with a notch in one end, fit the string in the notch and shoot the stick with the Bone Narr – like the Indians in the picture books.

Concerning sculpins: *Telegram* staff writer Wick Collins tells me that in Italy sculpins are considered a great table delicacy.

OK. Every man to his fancy, I say. But if I ever get to Italy I'll be damn cautious about what I put inside my chops. Lord save us.

Then there's the Mustard Number 15 hooks … the best gear for "Catching Conners." It came out in print "Mustard" but as every self-respecting conner catcher knows it's "Mustad."

Today's Juvenile Outharbor Delight is just as widely known as Catching Conners. It is none other than "Walking Around Shore," a noble pursuit if ever there was one.

"Walking Around Shore": (General directions and also incorporating that associated delight, "Picking Up Stuff.") You will need a shore for walking around and since you are lucky enough to be in Newfoundland, you have 6,000 miles.

An excuse to do it is not necessary, although if you are over 10 years old and below 65 an excuse will come in handy in case you are accused of wasting time.

Picking up wood is a good excuse. All you have to do is haul a few likely looking pieces of firewood above high-water mark and pile it. Or bring back a nice piece of BC var (fir) – always appreciated.

Or you can say you're going to have an eye out for the family horse put out on the country for the summer. Or you can even take a brin bag and say you are going to pick up some blue mussel shells and white rocks – greatly favored by the old folks for doing up graves.

These few little duties are quickly done and you can get down to the real business of "Walking Around Shore" and "Picking Up Stuff."

Most of the good stuff for picking up is laid along by the tide in a neat line at the high-water mark. There are always a few glass floats from nets in either clear glass, bottle green, or dark amber. Sometimes there's a big outlandish one of a different color from Other Countries.

There are rocks with queer marks on them to save. Rocks that are round as a hen's egg and not a blemish. Small rocks that are absolutely pink like frosted glass and might be worth something.

You may find, once a summer, a bottle with a note into it. That's something, I tell you. Because you can send it away and they'll send you back a fifty-cent piece. Not many can have that to say.

There are dead gannets and gulls and ducks. If you sneak around the points you might come across a fox mauling one over. Dead birds are more plentiful these days, but a lot of them are covered with black grease, so even the foxes won't eat them.

You may also pick up someone's lost boat. It might be a poor one chopped out of a fence paling or it might be a little schooner, full with flour-bag sails and coarse black thread.

There are all kinds of caps. People on vessels are always losing their caps. If you keep at it, you can make up a collection of sailors' caps from foreign lands.

Hoares egg shells (sea urchins) are good for looking at the sky through when you sit down to take a spell. They're light green on the outside and full of pin holes like lace curtains.

There is the scattered doll washed ashore. Pitiful, they are, like drowned little people and likely to give you a start if you come across one suddenly.

There are little tin cans full of emergency rations; pieces of board with foreign language on them; money purses (skate egg cases), black and hard as leather for putting coppers in; strange shaped bottles with no notes into them; small yellow wrinkle shells for saving and looking at.

One thing you must never touch if you see one is a round iron ball with spikes sticking out. A man down the bay came across one, gave it a clout with his axe and got blown up. Don't say you weren't cautioned.

The great hope of all good shore walkers (juvenile) is that they will pick up something nobody ever heard tell of. It will be the talk of the whole community and they may even send away to find out what it is. Instant glory.

Walking Around Shore, sad to say, is not what it used to be. The plastic, you see, has nearly ruined it. Before now, the wood used to rot, the bottles got smashed and ground up and the tin cans rusted away.

The landwash was always being cleared away for the next lot of good stuff to wash ashore. But plastic. It will never rot in the walls of hell.

It keeps drifting in and piling up. Plastic dish-soap bottles, plastic bleach bottles, plastic pans and buckets, sheets of plastic, in screaming scarlet, bilious yellow and morgue white.

A solid line of garish plastic trash at high-water mark everywhere. Everywhere.

Walk around shore now, excuse or no, and never mind if someone thinks you're wasting time. It may soon be too late. ◼

You'll get a copy whether you want it or not

July 10, 1968   *News and Propaganda*

Here's a little quiz for you. Answer this question correctly and win first prize of a secondhand teabag.

Name the newspaper with the largest circulation in the world.

The answer is *Pravda*, which is a newspaper printed in Russia. Millions of copies of *Pravda* are distributed throughout Russia every day.

Why is *Pravda* the biggest newspaper in the world? Because it is the only general newspaper in Russia. It is printed by the government and in Russia only government newspapers are allowed. All others are outlawed.

If this was a strict quiz perhaps you wouldn't win your secondhand teabag if you answered *Pravda*. Maybe the judges would say it was the wrong answer.

The judges might say that *Pravda* is not a newspaper at all. Most of the newspapers in the world – all the real newspapers in the free world – are not printed by governments.

Only under dictatorships do governments have complete control of newspapers. When a dictator overthrows a democracy the very first thing he does is padlock the newspaper offices and either shoot the newspaper owners or dump them in jail.

This is what any dictator does first, be it the Communist type such as we see in Russia and China or the fascist type such as reigned in Nazi Germany and in Mussolini's Italy.

The dictators know instinctively that their greatest enemies are newspapers. Free newspapers. They know they'll never be safe until the newspapers are strangled. So they do that first.

Then they start to print their own newspapers. Official government newspapers. Dictators know that free newspapers are their greatest enemies. They also know that newspapers they can control are their most valuable tools.

A government-controlled tool that can do a splendid job of brainwashing the whole population. A tool that will print only one version of the news – the dictator's version.

The only news the people will see is the news the dictator wants them to see. Only news praising the government and the dictator. No criticism of the government. No reports of government stupidity. Not a whisper against the government.

Because there are no other newspapers this is all the people can ever read about. Can you call this "news"? Or is it government propaganda? Is this a newspaper? Or is it a tool?

Most people call it government propaganda – which is why the judges may say that *Pravda*, for example, is no newspaper.

Real newspapers are not published by governments. They are published by people or groups of people who generally have no connections with governments.

Real newspapers are published by people who do not take sides in politics but who simply ask: "Is this government policy in the best interest of our readers or not?"

Thus we see that in a democracy newspapers are controlled by the people. If the people feel the newspaper is not concerned first about the people's interests, they won't read it. No readers – no advertising. No advertising – no newspaper. Did you know YOU control this newspaper?

Which brings us around to our sermon for today. (OK. I know it's summer. But we can't have fun and games every day.)

The very first thing Premier Smallwood has done in his vigorous drive to put himself back on top (or as he terms it, to put the Liberal party back on top) is to start an official government newspaper.

Are you surprised that the very first thing the premier has done is to start an official government newspaper? Like the one that was published during 25 years of the Commission of Government dictatorship?

No one knows better than he what a splendid tool a government-controlled newspaper is.

This so-called "newspaper" will be printed at an expense to you – WHETHER YOU WANT IT OR NOT – of about $7,000 a month. Printed by a government which claimed for years that Hansard (a report of what was said on both sides of the House) was too expensive.

You'll get a copy – whether you want it or not – once a month. That's fair enough. You paid for it. More than 100,000 copies will be printed, giving it the largest circulation by far in Newfoundland.

The premier says Newfoundland needed a government-controlled "newspaper" because the regular newspapers, radio and television stations weren't giving the people enough news of the right kind.

The first issue of this government-controlled "newspaper" is already out. Let's see what the premier means by the right kind of news.

Starting at the back we see that all the "news" is favorable to the government. Very favorable. "Newfoundland is fourth in Mineral Production." Good show. Quota maintained under five-year plan?

"Motor vehicle sales indication of affluence." "Soft drink and beer sales striking example of prosperity." "Increase in personal income; agreeable and encouraging."

We learn what a splendid chap John C. Doyle is as he "pioneers again in Labrador." What a splendid job the government is doing at Come By Chance, Baie d'Espoir and in centralization. Everywhere.

This splendid and apparently perfect government tells you how great it really is – gives you all the news the premier thinks you should read.

And on the front page … there's a huge picture. It takes up half the front page. And who is that picture of? Come now. Need you ask? The man himself, the Only Living Father – Premier Joseph R. Smallwood.

That was his very first step. What will be his second? ▣

You are a speck in the ocean

Democracy

Tuesday evening I saw something pretty good around 7 p.m. It isn't often that I do.

A couple of weeks ago I bought one of those what they call television sets. You may have seen one. They're about the size of a breadbox and there's a glass in the front.

You plug this machine into the electricity, stand back a bit and wait. It starts to buzz and the glass lights up and you see the likeness of people in it. The feller who thought that up had some head on his shoulders.

But the fellers who put stuff over them are not quite so bright. Most of the stuff is the same. A bunch of people sit around telling jokes. One joke. Ha ha ha ha ha. Another joke. Ha ha ha ha ha ha. Another joke. Ha ha ha ha ha ha.

You never see who it is that is doing all the laughing. They must be off to one side somewhere. They always use the same Ha ha ha ha ha ha ha, over and over again. It's always the same length and never louder one time than another.

Anyway, one good program we see on the television comes on Tuesday evening on what they call Channel 8 by the name of Summer Tempo.

They have bunches of young girls and young fellers singing on it from schools around the province. Real people. I am not much of a hand at saying whether anyone sings good or anyone sings bad.

But I do like watching this Summer Whatyacallit anyway because it would do you a world of good. What it is is that they're real people from around here. No raving beauties and no jackasses. Real people.

Tuesday evening last they had on a bunch of young fellers from St. Francis School in Harbour Grace. They were singing mostly slow stuff from a good while back.

I allow they wouldn't rip into one of those new rock and roll songs if the teacher's back was turned. No, poor hand!

One thing struck me most and a strange thing about it because it was one of those songs from the West Indian islands. The islands with the white sand beaches and the black people and the palm trees.

Not much like our own island. What a funny thing that a song from the West Indian islands should strike you here.

"O, Island in the sun
Willed to me by my father's hand
All my days I will sing in praise
Of your forests, waters, your shining sand."

I fancied it struck the young fellers from Harbour Grace the same because they opened out on it. They sung through the bits about "cutting sugar cane" and "walking to the sound of drums" and bore down when they came to this "O, Island in the sun" part.

More than half the people I went to school with have gone to Toronto. Perhaps most of the school singers from Harbour Grace will go to Toronto, too. That Royal Commission report they have out tells us that 4,000 and more leave every year.

One tows the other. If you stay in Toronto two years you'll get used to it and stay for good. Jobs of work are open to anyone, even Grade Eights, at $85 a week.

The singers from Harbour Grace who go will find Toronto a great place with lots of stuff to see and do. They'll get used to it. It's not like you were going to another country altogether. It's Canada.

But it is not Newfoundland. The thing that might strike you about Toronto is that it is so big and you are so small. There are 2½ million people there.

You can't climb up on a hill and see where the city ends and the trees begin. It is very flat and all the same.

You will ride back and forth to work every day very easily on the buses and subways because they run them very well, winter and summer. And after work you can go out to see some of the great things there are to see.

Day in and day out everything will go smoothly. It is very easy to live in Toronto because they have it all arranged. Summer and winter. It is convenient. You always get back and forth to work.

One funny thing about Toronto is that you might not feel so much like a real person as you do in Newfoundland. There are so many people, you see. You are a speck in the ocean.

Helpless to do anything. Helpless to change anything. Everything is put before you (and well laid out, it is) and you take it or leave it and you change to fit.

In Toronto, you may find out who those people who laugh off to one side on the television joke programs are. You might get to be one of them.

It is easy to live in Toronto. It is not so easy to live in Newfoundland. If you want to go to Toronto it is easy to get there, easy to get a job there and easy to stay there.

If you stayed here it would not be easy. But if you tried hard you could do something here you could not do in Toronto. You could change it. You could help make it be what you think it should be.

It would not be easy. You would have to rage. Savage. Fierce, fierce, fierce. Shout louder than the gale. Overcome the gale.

Rage to change this island to what you think it should be. You have the right and you can. Because it's yours.

Willed to you by your father's hand. ▦

Maggoty with bulldozers

Hello, hello, hello. And how have you been toughing it, my pretties? None the worse for the wear, please God.

Here's his mother's boy back from holidays. Soggy in the butt and mildewed around the gills. Waterlogged. Caught without his feathers oiled.

Three weeks in the ashes. Hardly a day fit to poke outside the door. So I scraped up precious little news to pass along. Have you heard any at this end?

One thing I did catch a sketch of is that there'll be a provincial election this fall. One day the flood let up for a few hours so I knocked off caulking the ark and ventured out. That's when I picked up the scent of it.

Yes, sir, if there's not a provincial election this fall the weather isn't the only thing out of kilter. The surest sign there will be one, of course, is that Chairman Joe says there won't.

In case you haven't noticed, some of the shakier districts are maggoty with bulldozers and highway trucks. Absolutely maggoty. They're tumbling over each other on the byroads. Going full tilt. In a perfect frenzy.

Where in the name of patience did they dig up all that machinery?

Did they hire it from the mainland or did they borrow it from Labrador?

In some places bulldozers outnumber the people. Mucking about in the ditches. Assaulting the countryside with lustful intent. Digging bog out of one spot, shifting it to another, then moving it back again. Trying to wear it out.

Tearing the cow paths asunder. Searching for more moose trails to upgrade. Taking to the very landwash in pursuit of something at which to look busy.

Now, I ask you. If there's no election in the wind isn't this a shocking waste of energy? Was there ever such a wild display of tearing up roads without an election in the background?

And the members. There's another sure and certain sign. Like the robin redbreasts in the spring. Some of them are even visiting their districts.

Would a member go so far as to visit his district if there wasn't an election coming up? Not if the past is any indication.

On top of all this we have started to get a new installment of Great Announcements.

Come By Chance. It seems now that the oil refinery is going to beat the third mill to it.

Oil tanks the size of zeppelins for Come By Chance. Oil tanks so big that some of the residents are afraid they'll block out what little sun they do get. Really big oil tanks.

Great industries here. Great industries there. Industries one on top of another. Industries sprouting like rubber plants. Studies and surveys for still more industries.

Never mind the fishery. The pulp mills – pooh hoo. Great industries are the ticket, my lad. And shut up saying you seem to have heard it all before. You'll never get a trip to Grand Falls talking like that.

While we're waiting for all those really great industries to descend on us from above, what better way to pass the time than with a provincial election?

Provincial elections? Never mind that stuff for now. It's much more profitable to talk about the weather.

Blessed gracious! The like was never known. Oh, the poor farmers with hardly a decent straw of grass to put before their cattle this winter. Oh, the poor fishermen with still another burden to bear.

Oh, the poor little children having to traipse back to school all fishbelly white for lack of sun.

And oh, those poor brutes of tourists. Dear visitors, what can we say to you? If we could afford to give you a rebate on your holiday money we would. But the way things stand we can't even afford a salt rebate – loans from Germany notwithstanding. We're sorry.

As soon as I pitched back in St. John's off my holidays I took up the telephone straight away and called Frank Rowe.

If there is anyone who can tell us what the hitch in the weather is, I said to myself, it is Mr. Rowe. He's the man in charge of the weather station at St. John's Airport.

What I was looking for, actually, was something specific to curse up in heaps. I had to set aside a whole half-hour (with a five-minute break for refreshment) for the same purpose.

It isn't much satisfaction to simply swear on the weather in general. You have to pin it down. Mr. Rowe put me in the light of what is going on.

This slush we're getting is all coming down from the Great Lakes, he said, but before I could get warmed up over the Great Lakes he hastened to add that our good weather comes from there too.

What happened is that a succession of storms have moved down on us from the Great Lakes – bang, bang, bang – but instead of passing a bit to the south and pumping warm air up over the island they've turned northward and stalled.

There they sit off the Funks, the hairy devils, dragging down rot and muck and sleet and rain and the decomposed carcasses of kangaroos and dumping it all on our long-suffering heads.

I thanked Mr. Rowe for his kind efforts to help me. But I'm still left with nothing specific at which to swear. I guess I'll have to take it out on something else.

A state of frenzied jubilation

Great New Industries

It is impossible, under the circumstances, to stay calm, cool and collected.

Your brain reels. Your pulse races. Your breath comes faster and you wonder whether your underarm deodorant can stand up under the strain.

All around, you see people at the same high pitch of excitement. Pure joy radiates from every face. There's a lighthearted skip in every step. Indeed, the whole province is in a state of frenzied jubilation.

The flags and bunting will, no doubt, be flung out today. Although the Announcement hit us like a bombshell yesterday, people were not able to control their emotions long enough for more formal celebrations. Today – the flags.

In downtown St. John's kissing in the streets reached a peak yesterday forenoon and the uninhibited display of joy continues unabated in the capital today.

While the celebrations threatened at times to get out of hand, the police took a tolerant view and few arrests were made. There was little looting of stores as occurred at the end of the Second World War.

Across the island and into the furthermost reaches of Labrador bonfires blazed on every inhabited hill. Muskets were discharged in every hamlet around the coast and church bells rang unceasingly.

A long-time observer of Newfoundland affairs says he has never seen such a display of public joy and enthusiasm on the island.

These celebrations, he says, even exceed the general jubilation when the news was flashed to Newfoundland that John C. Doyle had skipped safely across the border to escape a US jail term.

Even that memorable occasion of 15 years ago when the government predicted that Newfoundland would become the world's foremost mink breeder can't match it, he says.

In fact, he is of the opinion that it far surpasses the dancing in the streets on that fateful day when Premier Smallwood announced that the cowboy would replace the fisherman in Newfoundland.

Our observer tells us he has run down the long catalogue of Great and Momentous Announcements made by the premier but can find nothing to equal the frenzied excitement that now grips the province.

"When the premier announced that Dr. Valdmanis was worth his weight in gold to the Newfoundland people, there was a great outpouring of public joy and gratitude," he continues, "but nothing to match this.

"When the premier announced that only over his dead body would a certain iron ore plant be built outside Newfoundland in Quebec, there was bell-ringing and flag-waving," he says, "but there's just no comparison to what we are seeing today.

"When the premier announced that Newfoundland had 'escaped the clutches of Quebec' and Churchill Falls power would flow through the island on its way to the New York subways, people wept openly and perfect strangers hugged each other in the streets.

"But that was only small stuff," he says, "compared to this. As were other Great Announcements – chocolate bar factories, rubber plants, battery plants, at least five Third Mills, the great Fisheries Conference.

"No, not even the Great Announcements of recent times – the great quartzite venture at Placentia and the great goat-breeding enterprise spring to mind – can hold a candle to it.

"If I were searching for the nearest thing to it," he continues, "I would have to say that the Great Announcement on the shipment of Panama orange juice to Newfoundland aboard Golden Eagle oil tankers runs a close second.

"There were, as you may remember, incredible scenes of celebration at the time. Schools were let out. Liquor stores stayed open around the clock. People were beside themselves in ecstasy.

"But the Great Orange Juice Announcement was only a poor second. This latest Announcement tops them all. Just look out that window. Down there in the street.

"It's the Mardi Gras, a Royal Visit and quitting time at Confederation Building rolled into one. Fantastic!"

Thanking our observer for his observations I went down into the teeming streets and was swept along by the jubilant throng. Car horns blew. Women held babes in arms aloft. The air was alive with confetti and paper streamers.

"Haven't you heard the Great Announcement?" screamed one overjoyed citizen who wore a party hat and swigged from a hip flask. "Salt! Salt discovered on the west coast! Vast amounts of salt!"

"And potash," interjected his companion. "Vast, vast amounts of potash. Beautiful, wonderful potash. Just think. Until yesterday we didn't even have ash, let alone a pot to put it in."

"Oil, too!" chimed in another. "A great underground reservoir of oil. Caustic soda. Chlorine. Vinyl chloride in abundance. And they say there may be vast peanut butter deposits nearby."

"One of the greatest discoveries of minerals in the long history of this province," added still another. "No doubt about it. Have you heard that the Long Range Mountains are 86 per cent Limburger cheese?"

At last report they're still not certain about the peanut butter deposits, and the oil reserves have yet to be confirmed. Never mind.

At least we may get enough salt out of it so that everyone can take a grain with the next Great Announcement. Rebate or no rebate. ▩

They're outraged. Absolutely rory-eyed

September 3, 1968   *Roads, Rails and Water*

There's a song in my heart. These past few days I'm on top of the world. Colleagues say: "What's wrong with Guy lately? I thought I saw him smile."

There is sunshine in my mildewed soul, brothers, because some dear people on the west coast have been calling me nasty names.

They're outraged. Absolutely rory-eyed. Their blood is boiling and bubbling like the Big Falls on the Humber. They'd like to see all manner (blush) of interesting and painful things done to me.

The mayor of Channel-Port aux Basques even plans to buy a special pair of shoes with which to boot me in the quarters next time I'm out his way.

All this is extremely heartening. My beady little eyes light up to see that some hot-blooded west coasters are showing the true Newfoundland spirit.

Too often we Newfoundlanders act like sheep. We endure all sorts of outrages without a whimper. But now and then we figure we've been pushed a bit too far and the results are inspiring to behold.

What started the fuss was a couple of articles I wrote about the CN ferry service between North Sydney and Port aux Basques.

What scandalous and outrageous things did I report about Port aux Basques? I said the port was ramshackle. So it is. The port, mind you. Not a word about the houses, gardens, people, or public monuments.

I said visitors would be comforted if someone advised them that although the water was muddy brown it was perfectly safe to drink.

I said the ferry terminal was like an abandoned potato cellar or a crypt with the lid half off. It is. I said that $3.21 was an outrageous price for a scrap of defrosted grilse, sludgy french fries and green peas dimpled with age. That's about it.

Joan D. Wilson of Port aux Basques was moved to declare: "God made the earth the way it is – Port aux Basques included – but maybe Mr. Guy has a complaint there, too."

Come, come, my ducky. We mustn't try to shift all the responsibility for the way the earth is onto God's shoulders. We must accept a little of the blame ourselves.

She suggests that I was drunk (unfortunately not); that I should be ashamed to call myself a Newfoundlander (we all have those moments); that I enjoy showing off my meager supply of sarcastic adjectives (true); and that I'll "go down to the vile dust from whence he sprung, unwept, unhonored and unsung." (No danger. Any good funeral parlor will provide the tears, song and honor galore – if the price is right.)

Have I lost a "constant reader" in Fred G. Matthews Sr. of Corner Brook? Mr. Matthews says the whole thing was "a diatribe of trash," especially "his bitter outpourings against the community of Port aux Basques."

Boy! If you call THAT a "bitter outpouring" you should hear me when the people in the upstairs apartment start one of their noisy parties at 2 a.m.

Walter Simms, also of Corner Brook, accuses me of making his blood boil. He seems to agree with Joan D. Wilson that I'm getting dangerously close to blasphemy: "God created the rocks, fog and brown water and there isn't much that can be done about it."

With his blood still at a rollicking boil, Mr. Simms continues: "So come on, you little Guy, and write something nice about Port aux Basques and its people and help boost our tourist industry.

"If you cannot do this, please keep your big mouth shut and go work in the lumber woods or go to Vietnam where you can be of some use to the world ..."

Mark E. Staple, mayor of Channel-Port aux Basques, wrote conveying his disgust "and the disgust of the wonderful people of Port aux Basques ..." (I think they're wonderful too and they don't even vote for me.)

"Our hotel was unmercifully torn to virtual shreds by some of the most ridiculous and vicious remarks ever to fall from the pen of a writer," says Mayor Staple in an extravagant burst of praise.

The mayor of our rocky western gateway continues: "I do not know for sure if Guy is a Newfoundlander, but if he isn't he should be invited to leave the province via Our Rocky Western Gateway.

"I would deem it a great pleasure," he says, "to be on hand decked out in a special size shoe to wish him bon voyage ... I am sure he would need one of the cabins he couldn't get when he was here last time."

Gracious, mayor! Please make sure it's me you put the boots to and not some poor unsuspecting tourist who makes a similar complaint about the facilities.

You and your number 12s could do more to ruin the tourist trade than another bad summer, if you think that's the best way to get to the bottom of your troubles.

Bless their cotton socks, every one of 'em. They figured, at first glance, the honor of poor old Port aux Basques and its citizens was being foully besmirched. The reaction was heart-warming, rousing and unsheepish.

Now, they'll take a longer glance – realizing that criticism and hatred are two entirely different things – and they may find a few shreds of truth among the trash.

They may discover a few ideas which, if acted upon, would make our rocky western gateway an even better place. That is all the harm I wish Port aux Basques.

See all the pretty taxes

I know you've been puzzled. So have I. Mr. Wells. Mr. Crosbie. Mr. Barbour. Mr. Burgess. Mr. Smallwood. Salt mines. Conventions. Elections. It's all very complicated.

There was a time I thought I'd never figure it out. But after working on it all through the Labor Day weekend I believe I see the light.

Once you get it untangled it's all very simple. So simple, in fact, that a child in kindergarten can understand it:

Look Dick. Look Jane. Look. Look. Look. Look David. Look Ann. This is Mr. Smallwood. See Mr. Smallwood. No, Dick, no. Never mind what Daddy calls him. Naughty, naughty Daddy. This is Mr. Smallwood.

He is the premier. See. See. See. See the premier. He has been premier for 19 years. Not five years. Not 10 years. Not 12 years. Not 15 years. Not 18 years. But 19 years.

He has been premier for a long time. A long, long time. Oh. Oh. Oh. Mr. Smallwood was premier when Daddy was younger than you are. Yes. Yes. Yes.

What is the premier's job, David? What is the premier's job, Ann? What? What? What? His job is to spend money. Money. Money. Money. Isn't it fun to spend money? Fun. Fun. Fun. The premier's job is to spend money. Lucky, lucky premier.

What money does he spend, Dick? What money does he spend, Jane? Other people's money. Yes. Yes. Yes. Other people's money. Isn't it great fun to spend other people's money? Oh. Oh. Oh. Good Lord, yes!

What is this money called, David? What is this money called, Ann? What? What? What? This money is called taxes. Taxes. Taxes. Taxes. Oh. Oh. Oh. See all the pretty taxes.

Look Dick. Look Jane. Look at all the taxes. More and more taxes. More taxes for the premier to spend. Spend. Spend. Spend. Lucky, lucky premier.

People say: "Look. Look. Look. See the premier. See. See. See. See all he has done for the province." Funny, funny people. What has the premier done? He has spent their money. Oh. Oh. Oh. Funny, funny people.

Look. Look. Look. This is the House. No, Dick, no. Not that kind of House. No. No. No. Naughty, naughty Dick. How would Dick like a punch up the air hole?

See. See. See. This is the House. Look. Look. Look. See Mr. Crosbie. Look David. Look Ann. Cast your baby blues on Mr. Crosbie. What was Mr. Crosbie's job? What? What? What?

Mr. Crosbie's job was helping the premier. Mr. Crosbie's job was helping the premier spend other people's money. That was Mr. Crosbie's job. See. See. See.

The premier is cross with Mr. Crosbie. My. My. My. Why is the premier cross with Mr. Crosbie? Why? Why? Why? Why David? Why Jane?

Oh. Oh. Oh. Naughty, naughty Dick! Unhand Ann this instant, Dick. Tut. Tut. Tut. I don't care if you ARE going steady, having been inspired by recent ecumenical developments. Later. Later. Later. Pay attention. Look. Look. Look.

The premier is cross with Mr. Crosbie. Cross. Cross. Cross. Mr. Crosbie said the premier was not spending other people's money right. Mr. Crosbie said the premier was spending other people's money wrong. Wrong. Wrong. Wrong.

See Mr. Wells. He says Mr. Crosbie is right. Right. Right. Right. Mr. Wells says Mr. Crosbie can spend other people's money better than the premier. Better. Better. Better.

Look. Look. Look. See Mr. Burgess. What does Mr. Burgess say? What Dick? What Jane? No. No. No. No one can figure out what Mr. Burgess says. Only his hairdresser knows for sure.

Oh. Oh. Oh. See Mr. Barbour. Run, Rossie, run. Look. Look. Look. See Rossie run. What does Mr. Barbour say? What? What? What? Mr. Barbour says he can spend other people's money better than any of them.

See. See. See. All the other members in the House. All the other members who help the premier spend other people's money. Look. Look. Look.

What do they say, David? What do they say, Ann? No. No. No. They don't say much. They don't know if they're punched or bored. Oh. Oh. Oh.

The premier says he will have a meeting. The premier says he will have a meeting to see if his loyal friends say he can spend other people's money better than Mr. Barbour can. What do you think they'll say? What? What? What?

Mr. Crosbie says he will have a meeting, too. Mr. Crosbie says he will have a meeting to see if his friends say he can spend other people's money better than the premier or Mr. Barbour.

How many friends has Mr. Crosbie? How many? How many? How many? How many friends has the premier? How many? How many? How many? That's the $64,000 question. Whose money? Right. Right. Right.

What will the people say, Dick? What will the people say, Jane? What? What? What? Would you care to place a little bet on the side with your lunch money?

The people will have the last say. Yes. Yes. Yes. Isn't it fun to be people, David? Isn't it fun to be people, Ann? Fun. Fun. Fun. ▨

Strapped with everything but a strap

Schools

School days. How old do you have to be before you start nattering about the good old days? Apart from the first two or three years, all my school days fall inside of Confederation.

That wasn't so long ago. Or was it? Ah, those happy hours spent at good old Buchenwald Elementary – otherwise known as St. Michael's and All Angels.

Fact is, it was kindergarten, elementary, primary and high school rolled into one 30-by-50 room. One big happy family, we were, our education in the hands of one teacher who got paid $80 a month for trying to turn sows' ears into silk purses.

There were hundreds of these concentration camps all over Newfoundland and I guess there are still some left.

I hope so. Because I'm going to need someone to back me up when the Pepsi generation starts accusing me of telling lies.

Ah yes. They were a bit on the rugged side. A notch above those hard knock British schools Prince Philip favors. Something of a cross between a Georgia chain gang and the Spanish Inquisition.

A sado-masochistic setup. The object was to civilize us by whatever means possible before we were unleashed on an unsuspecting world. A charitable and Christian object if ever there was one.

But original sin being what it is we resisted to the last ounce. That's where the conflict entered into it. It was up hill and down dale all the way, and the trail lined with walking wounded.

Let me say now it wasn't all blood, toil, sweat and tears. We did have our golden moments. And a few of those $80-a-month educators deserved 10 times that amount. More about these sunnier aspects later.

As far as I'm concerned, however, these good teachers were in the minority. Most of them did it because it was the only job open to them. Until we got to Grade 11 we had never run across one who had been inside a university door.

Since they hadn't the slightest idea how to civilize us by the standard means, they set out to pound civility into us. In doing so they also got rid of a lot of the stomach knots that come from being trapped in the only job open to you.

The sounds of an average school day were the sounds of a continuous TV western fistfight. The whack and crunch of flesh and bone being assaulted. We got strapped with everything but a strap.

No. I tell a lie. I remember one humanitarian who tried to play it according to the Geneva Convention. With a small grant from the school board he purchased a quantity of tapping leather.

From it he fashioned a three-foot-long regulation strap which didn't leave any marks. But by this time we had grown proud of our scars so we stole it and shoved it down the outhouse hole. He had to go back to making do with whatever odds and ends were handy.

Throughout the years we were strapped with a kitchen chair leg, the buckle end of a belt, a piece of driftwood, a strip of wainscot ripped from the classroom wall, a piece from the top of a desk, a broom handle, a handgaff handle, a heavy wooden ruler with a strip of tin down the edge, and, for variety's sake, a half-fathom of one-inch manila rope.

They all had their different little whims and fancies. One was partial to placing straying lambs near the red-hot pot-bellied stove – just out of scorching distance – with a 12-pound volume of Bible stories held above the head. You soon longed for the snows of yesteryear.

Another was prone to creeping up behind you and judo-chopping you on the back of the neck. He was six-foot-two.

Then there was the five-day stand. He was a great advocate of the military system of discipline. You'd come in on the morning after the transgression and remain standing at attention beside your desk.

You stood there throughout the morning, through recess and until dinnertime. After dinner you remained standing again until four o'clock. Same procedure the following day and for as much as five days in a row.

One of our colleagues always used to faint off after standing for a day or two. It broke the monotony. His color started to fade. That was the first sign. He'd sway back and forth and his eyes would turn up.

Then flump-o! Sometimes he split the back of his head on the desk behind and sometimes he didn't.

The prize of the lot was imaginative if nothing else. He'd make a fist and latch only your nose between his fingers. Holding tight he'd smash down hard on his wrist with his free hand. Four or five times.

That glorious set of airholes you see in the snap above is not entirely due to heredity.

On days when he felt up to it he'd make you kneel down in front of him, put your head between his knees, then bang his fists against his knees. This brought his knees in contact with your ears with great force.

And so it went year after year. New surprises around every corner. As long as they held off with the bamboo splinters driven under the fingernails we kept in good spirits.

They didn't civilize us, thank God, and now I don't suppose anyone ever will. So it wasn't a dead loss altogether.

(Tomorrow: More Golden Moments – the Resistance.) RG

The glories of denominational education

September 11, 1968   *Schools*

Several graduates of "city schools" told me yesterday that youngsters in one-room outport schools were not the only ones to be brutalized by mad dog teachers. They got their lumps too.

Well, I sympathize but I still say – small stuff! Teachers in "city schools" at least knew their subjects. And if some of them were nasty-tempered they couldn't go too far with it.

There were other teachers and principals around who could see what went on. But consider our case. All grades from kindergarten to 11. One room. One teacher.

For at least a year this one teacher had practically absolute dominion over us. Captain Blighs they could be and Captain Blighs they most often were. Why?

There was this education mania in the air: "You can't get anywhere these days without an education. I never had the chance but, by God, I'm going to see to it that my youngsters have a chance – supposing I have to lace them to the school door every day."

Right up to school-opening date we were never sure we'd get a teacher. Who'd want to come out to a one-room school and teach all grades for the salary of $80 a month?

At the last minute someone generally turned up. It didn't matter much what the tide brought in. If he called himself a teacher, that was good enough. There was a huge parental sigh of relief. Their offspring were assured of the chance they themselves never got.

The fact that a "teacher" had been secured overwhelmed everything else. It didn't matter much if he had two heads and drank beef blood for lunch. A teacher was a teacher.

If some of the outrages he committed leaked out, the news was actually welcomed: "That's what we want – a good strict teacher. HE'S not going to let the youngsters rule him. No sir. I told mine if they come home talking about the strappings they got I'll give them another and twice as good."

Now and then an outraged mother would kick up a stink if one of her girls or smaller boys came home with cuts and bruises. But it didn't amount to much.

On top of that there was, in later years, the Baby Bonus. You were worth $8 a head while you stayed in school. Out of school – however bad it was – your value dropped to zero.

OK. So some burly six-foot "city school" teacher will occasionally go ape and smash a 12-year-old across the face. He won't do it too often and he won't get away with it for long.

What went on inside some outport schools was witnessed only by the inmates. "Tales out of school" were discouraged or disbelieved.

And what DID the tide bring in? There were exceptions, but mostly they were 18-and 20-year-olds who had barely scraped their heels through Grade 11 and a few weeks of summer school, and who couldn't teach a chimpanzee to peel a banana. Or more mature misfits who were simply desperate for the 80 bucks a month.

There they sat day after day growing more frustrated and bitter and twisted, lashing out with the strap and the smash in the face and whatever other tortures they could dream up to get the gas off their stomachs.

There they sat and even got a little bit of applause because "they weren't letting the youngsters rule them."

Now. Let me say this. And let me say it good and loud. Between kindergarten and Grade 11 I must have encountered a dozen teachers. Most of them were miserable misfits who quickly turned into classroom sadists to cover up their failings.

But ... there were three or four among them who – considering the circumstances – deserve to be numbered among the saints and the martyrs.

They didn't have university degrees and they were up against a frightful job, but they managed to show us that bashing skulls is not the only use for a book. They will have their reward.

These bright spots were far between. The misfits and the sadists far outweighed them.

What were the results? A few kids managed to squeak through to Grade 11. But there were far more who were doomed for life by these slaughterhouses just as surely as if parts of their brains had been removed by surgery.

Like the "Country Churchyard" it was. There were potential doctors, lawyers, teachers, engineers and skilled tradesmen who were cut down before they were old enough to shave.

They dropped out in Grade 8 or earlier, and whatever they've achieved since beyond the pick and shovel is to nobody's credit but their own.

It need not have been that way. Therefore the shame and the guilt must rest on somebody's head. In our case (and let me know if our case wasn't typical of much of Newfoundland) there were half a dozen other communities within a 20-mile radius.

They could have gotten together, built a half-decent school somewhere in between and attracted teachers worthy of the name. It seems so obvious. Why wasn't it done?

Well, where have you been, baby? Haven't you guessed? These half-dozen communities represented three or four different denominations. Christian denominations.

So if you please – don't talk to me about the glories of denominational education. Because I may vomit. ◼

Golden Moments in Newfoundland Education

September 12, 1968   *Schools*

More Golden Moments in Newfoundland Education. Important points either overlooked or hardly touched upon in Dr. Rowe's scholarly volume, *Education in Newfoundland.*

There was Walter, for example, who had a fashion of sticking his bare backside out the outhouse window. One day, George Albert got him fair and square with a mudball from a distance of 15 yards and that in a strong crosswind. A singular accomplishment.

Surely such a feat deserves a place in the annals of Newfoundland education, be it under the heading of recreation and athletics or perhaps Logistics and New Math.

The windows of our one-room school looked directly out onto a meadow that was generally filled with horses and sheep. Our new schoolmistress was aghast. School-opening, you see, coincided with the mating season.

So the next day we formed into ranks in the schoolyard and marched off to the blueberry hills. We picked a porkbarrel full of berries, which were sold.

Out of the proceeds, our resourceful schoolmistress purchased enough dark green window blinds to cover the bottom halves of all the windows.

The bright rays of the sun shining in through, she explained, might have seriously damaged our eyesight. So much for biology classes.

Holidays? There were holidays in abundance. When the month's allowance of coal was finished ahead of time and the pot-bellied stove lost its ruddy glow, we got a half-holiday.

Well, it was more or less a holiday. We had to spend it gathering driftwood around shore to fuel the pot belly for a few more days.

If not, the snow drifting up through the cracks in the floorboards wouldn't melt and run out again.

There was a holiday whenever the schoolmaster wanted to go turr shooting. There was a holiday of sorts when the public health nurse came round to hunt our heads for lice.

Once when an elderly resident of the community committed suicide, the whole school, from kindergarten on up, got a holiday to go help look for him. One of the Grade Eights found him at low-water mark.

If the holidays were not coming fast enough, someone stuffed brin bags down the chimney and filled the room with smoke. Classes were adjourned and it generally took the rest of the day to clear the stoppage.

The focus of the classroom was not the blackboard but the pot-bellied stove. It was always kept red-hot and the scholars who sat nearest it were parboiled on one side although those in the far corners had to keep on their wool mitts.

Oh yes. I kid you not. This wasn't back in the dark ages. It was after Confederation. For all I know there may still be some temples of learning like it in the Happy Province.

Vast clouds of steam arose from the vicinity of the red-hot stove. Steam from the students who sat nearest to it. Steam from the dozens of pairs of wet mitts under it. And steam from the cocomalt kettle on top of it.

Cocomalt. The government used to send it out to all the schools. Tins of ominous-looking brown powder. It had a unique taste that lay somewhere between chocolate and mouse droppings and was said to be good for you.

At recess we'd line up with our mugs while a senior student put two spoonfuls of the stuff into each. Another added boiling water. If the teacher wasn't looking the chef would fill your cup with powder and add a few drops of water. The result was a sickly-sweet paste guaranteed to clear every tooth out of your head.

Sharpening of pencils also took place around the stove. Everyone had a piece of razor blade for the same purpose. Pencils had to be sharpened over the coal bucket so as to keep the premises tidy.

If, while sharpening a pencil, you could manage to drop a piece of crayon on the red-hot stove lid, there was a dash of flame, and a great billow of riot control gas filled the room. That was at least a half-hour's holiday while the room was being ventilated.

Discipline, as noted before, was often varied and bizarre, but one of the most welcome punishments was to be locked out in the unheated school kitchen for half the day. You were allowed to take your mitts, parka, aviator cap and other survival gear with you.

When the sentence had been served the convict staggered out with a look of pure bliss – bloated on bully beef, moldy partridgeberry tarts, lumps of sugar and other leftovers from the last social.

Visual aids and teaching helps were not unknown. Although the Second World War had ended nearly a decade before, yellowing wall posters requested us to collect rubber and not aid the enemy by loose talk.

In one corner sat a large box of plasticine, a putty-like substance left by some previous and more progressive regime. The only use to which it was put in later years was in sculpting lewd figurines to show the girls and make them titter in geography class.

If the teacher approached to investigate all you had to do was give the piece of progressive pornography a quick bash with your fist and the evidence was reduced to an innocent blob.

And so it went. One golden moment after another. Lord! Is it any wonder that we're a bit weak in grammar and trigonometry? ▩

The Evening Telegram's
One-Man Expedition to the Bitter End

September 25, 1968   *Resettlement and Rural Life*

Corner Brook – A full schedule. A tight itinerary. A busy 24 hours during my first visit to the magnificent west coast. Not even time for that famous Corner Brook amusement center, the Ball Diversion. Work, work, work.

Today in History: *The Evening Telegram*'s single-handed attempt to scale the island's highest mountain is thwarted. But *The Telegram*'s One-Man Expedition to the Bitter End is a shining success.

The Telegram's bright hopes of placing a man (namely myself) on the top of the island of Newfoundland came within a hair's breadth of success, but our highest island mountain (Lewis Hills – 2,673 feet) remains unconquered. Labrador has hills over 5,000 feet.

When I began the assault early yesterday I was supremely fit in consequence of secret training all summer. I had walked up the Court House steps in St. John's at least twice a week and climbed Barter's Hill once every fortnight.

Because of the difficulty in securing porters here in Corner Brook (they have a great fear of the legendary "Moozunter" or abominable gunman), I decided to go it alone.

Equipped with oxygen, ice axe, crampons, survival gear, two chocolate bars and a pack of cigarettes, I made my way to Aguathuna and launched northward into the great Lewis Hills range.

I left civilization behind me in the foothills at Point au Mal and, already breathing heavily from lack of oxygen (elevation 53 feet), I followed an abandoned mining road deep into the mountains.

Rounding a bend I suddenly came face to face with a dreaded "Moozunter" who informed me that the bridge across Fox Island River was out.

Dashed were my hopes of standing on the summit, the roof of Newfoundland, and erecting a stone cairn to house a small likeness of the Sovereign and a copy of the weekend People's Paper – the whole to be topped by a Union Jack.

Sadly, I made my way back to Aguathuna, vowing to mount another expedition at the earliest opportunity. Our Rivals are said to be on the hand of launching their assault – but never fear. We now have valuable first-hand information.

The Telegram's single-handed attempt to conquer our highest peak took me well past midday. However, the flush of discovery, exploration and achievement was upon me.

I motored out onto the Port au Port Peninsula, thus commencing *The Evening Telegram*'s One-Man Expedition to the Bitter End.

As you can see by the maps, that long point sticking up from the Port au Port Peninsula is one of the most extraordinary bits of real estate in the province.

I found I was wrong in thinking it to be a glorified sand bar. It is a 15-mile ribbon of solid ground, no more than a few hundred feet wide along most of its length.

A narrow fisherman's road took me along this natural pier to within two miles of the Bitter End. Here, I disembarked from my conveyance and set out on foot.

Onward, ever onward, trudged *The Telegram*'s One-Man Expedition to the Bitter End – the sting of his recent failure in the Lewis Hills assault making him unmindful of such discomforts as a sock trod down in the heel of a shoe.

I came at last to the automatic lighthouse. Here the sod ended although another half-mile of rock stuck out further into the sea. Since there were no witnesses, I could have stopped right there and claimed to have reached my goal.

Yet, I seemed to sense the eyes of the great Editor in the sky upon me. Footsore, yet bearing ever in mind a certain obligation to *The Telegram*'s readers, I pressed on.

The rocky tip grew more narrow until it was a mere 10 feet wide – the Gulf of St. Lawrence crashing (well, lapping – it was a calm day) on one side of me and the waters of Port au Port Bay performing a similar function on the other.

A wave of patriotism swept over me as I at last gained the Bitter End and placed a rock (which I carried for the same purpose) into the shallow water off the very tip.

"The Bar" on the Port au Port Peninsula is, as of 5:43 p.m. September 24, 1968 A.D., a good six inches longer. The maps will have to be redrawn.

As I place the stone into position, the words of "Land of Hope and Glory" swept through my mind ... "wider still and wider, shall thy bounds be set."

As the mosquito said when he spat in the ocean, "'Tis all a help." In fact, I recommend this method of territorial expansion to every man, woman and child on the island in case we lose Labrador.

All this and much, much more during the first 24 hours of my first trip out this way. If I can ever get over the astonishment and wonderment and get my tongue back in gear you may never hear the last of it.

Oh, my duckies, what a country we've got hold of!

Guy's Encyclopedia of Juvenile Outharbor Delights: Rounders

September 30, 1968   *Outharbor Delights*

I don't know what you expected today but what you're going to get is "Rounders." Another chapter from that ancient volume, *Guy's Encyclopedia of Juvenile Outharbor Delights*.

It is an entirely different delight to "Conner Catching" or "Foundering Cliffs" but one that was indulged in throughout the island. The rules and customs varied, no doubt, from one locality to another.

But I believe I can offer a description of "Rounders" in its purest form since we weren't well enough off to play it with baseball bats. Nobody knew where the rules of the game came from but they seemed to be born in each generation by some strange form of inheritance.

All the equipment you needed was a ball about the same size of an orange. Many kinds of balls were used but in later years the baseball-sized sponge ball was held in great esteem.

You set out four "posts" including "home" in the manner of bases in a baseball game. Home was usually the corner of the school; first post, the other corner; second, large rock; third, the corner of the outhouse; and so back to home.

There were two sides or teams and no limit to the number of players on each. As with the ancient kings and warlords, the two biggest lunks among us got to be captains. Democracy didn't enter into it.

These two hairy brutes would announce they were going to be captains and there was never anyone else big enough to disagree. The captains picked the sides, selecting the most likely runners and ball-throwers first and working their way down to the little knock-kneed and near-sighted Grade Threes.

Now that the two sides were formed there came the ceremony of "heaving up a rock." A flat beach rock of proper size was kept on hand for the purpose.

"OK," said Captain A to Captain B. "You can have the first pick. I'll take the dry side."

"Right," said Captain B, adding rather unnecessarily, "then I'll take the wet side."

The rock was held aloft for all to see and then one side was spat upon with great vigor. It was given the proper flip into the air and everyone rushed to the spot where it fell to the ground.

"Wet side up. Wet side up. Our side in."

With their gallant captain at their head the "in" side lined up against the school near "home." The "out" side were spread around the field in no particular order except that no one could stand "in past the captain."

The captain of the "out" team stood about eight or ten feet away from and facing the home post. From here he gave "tips" (or pitched, as they say in baseball), tossing the ball underhanded.

The person receiving the "tip" (the batter) smacked the ball as hard as he could with his upraised hand. Each person was entitled to "three good tips."

The object was to knock the ball far enough away so that you could make it to the first post before the ball was returned to the captain and he touched "home" with it.

If you made your run and the ball was caught on the first bounce or rolled behind you, you were out. If someone on the other side caught the ball before it hit the ground, the whole side was out.

You could stay on a post as long as you liked and while touching it you were safe. But once you got off the post on the way to the next you were a living target.

Anyone on the other side could sling the ball at you when you were not touching a post. If they hit you with it you were out. You could dodge and run to avoid being hit. The chap trying to hit you had to stay on the spot where he received the ball.

If you managed it right you could be hit and still stay in. Those with a high pain threshold could disguise the limp caused by a compound fracture and insist that the rock-hard ball never touched them. There was a 50-50 chance of brazening it out.

Once you were declared "out" either on the first bounce or after being crippled by a hurled ball, there was only one way you could get back in again. One of your team mates had to run you in.

To do this, he had to make the rounds of the posts and back home three times – and he was only allowed to stop on a post once. During the rest of his travels he was a sitting duck, dodging those cannon balls and trying to gain a few posts when somebody else got a tip.

Day after day, week in and week out, we played rounders. Then, suddenly, we'd drop it for some other juvenile outharbor delight. We wouldn't think of it again until one day someone would be moved by some strange inner force and suggest, "Let's play rounders."

Oh, there was much, much more to playing rounders than that. It is something that can never be captured completely on paper. There were incredibly complex and unwritten rules and guidelines.

Rounders had its own mystique, its set of traditions and customs that came down to us from Lord knows where. Some say Ireland. Kids today who spend their time watching the world series on TV would never understand.

They say that Britain's wars were won on the playing fields of Eton. I wonder what it was that Rounders prepared us for? **RG**

Mr. Gwyn has sniffed the bottle but has not tasted the medicine

October 1, 1968   *Democracy*

At 3 a.m. Saturday, September 28, the Holiday Inn in Gander rocked like a Brazil Square boarding house on the night after VE Day.

Shouts and screams and wild laughter echoed down the hotel corridors. Three tipsy revelers rolled arm in arm along the hall, singing at the top of their lungs and stopping at intervals to pound on room doors.

Bangs and crashes, whistles and catcalls from some rooms assaulted the ears of other hotel patrons who were trying to sleep. Elderly and irate mainland tourists called in vain for a bit less racket.

Finally the uproar died down, only to erupt anew at 7:30 a.m. when the celebrants rolled out and piled into their cars for the drive to Grand Falls.

They were some of the "grass roots" on their way to the Liberal convention in Grand Falls – ready and raring to help shape the destiny of Newfoundland and the future of us all.

I'm sure that not all the "grass roots" were so boisterously eager to tackle the task that lay ahead of them as were some of this particular contingent. I expect the majority looked forward more soberly to their duties.

But who made up most of the 1,400 in Grand Falls? Where did they come from? Their faces seemed vaguely familiar. They appear to have cropped up at other Liberal gatherings of this sort.

Are they taken out of storage like stage scenery when needed, dusted off and arranged in rows? You get the creepy feeling they have electrodes planted deep in their brains and are wired to a master control button backstage.

When the button is pressed, does it cause their hands to rise from their laps and slap rapidly together? Is that how it's done?

All those tired old faces. And, much more depressing, some tired young faces. How fitting that the most outstanding specimen of the latter group was elected president.

Mr. Cashin may be young in years, but he has the attitude of a politician of 68. Who can talk more and say less than young-old Dickie? Who better gives the impression of having been left a political career in somebody's will with no choice but to make the best of it?

Then we heard a resonant echo of his master's voice sprinkled liberally with left-over chin-lifters. "Mistakes of the Heart." "Develop or Perish." "Gamble on the Future." "Develop or Perish."

The mighty wind from Swift Current, St. John's, and Ottawa is so close to inheriting the premier's chair he can smell it. With the prize so near, the human barrel-organ opened out full throttle.

Has anyone ever told Mr. J. that no matter how tempting the dessert, it isn't polite to salivate in public?

Is this all there is to the "grass roots" of Newfoundland? I, for one, don't dare let myself believe it. If I did, I'd pray to God that the island would sink to the bottom of the sea just after lunch tomorrow.

For the first time in a long history we have a chance to have something more than another dictatorship. Was Grand Falls all the hope we have? Is this what the new Newfoundland Liberals look and talk like?

If there is a new and more inspiring breed of Liberals around when are they going to show themselves? And – so that no hope will be overlooked – can't we try to capture at least one new PC alive to see what he looks like?

What we saw in Grand Falls was the makings of the same chilling set-up that we've known for the past 20 years. For the past 300.

Is there something in our nature that wants nothing but paternalistic government, that can't exist without a Father Figure to tell us what to do, that can't sleep nights except under the wing of a Daddy Dictator?

Last night, Richard Gwyn, the young English-Canadian author of the book on Smallwood, mentioned what he termed "the type of hysterical criticism that appears in *The Evening Telegram*."

Mr. Gwyn has made a close study of Newfoundland, but (as he chides us for saying) he is not a Newfoundlander. He has not lived under the dark shadow of fear and suppression cast by the unlimited power of his subject.

He didn't have to look on helplessly as cabinet ministers, judges, magistrates, merchants, clergy, university professors and teachers cringed behind the heels of the dictator like whipped puppies.

Mr. Gwyn has sniffed the bottle but he has not tasted the medicine.

He has not seen our jaws frozen with fear in these dark and ugly times when the merest whisper against the throne of the Only Living Father was swamped in a merciless torrent of abuse, threats and power-backed rage.

If Mr. Gwyn had been a Newfoundlander in those times (forgive us again, Richard) and was scrabbling toward a crack of light in the shroud that smothered him, even he might have shown some hysteria.

And if he let himself believe – after seeing Grand Falls – that there was something in the Newfoundland nature that would allow and even want those days to return again, he'd be more than hysterical.

Maybe, rather than face that possibility, he'd cut his throat. ■

We ate "a meal of trouts," seal, rabbits that were skinned out like a sock

October 9, 1968   *Resettlement and Rural Life*

What feeds we used to have. Not way back in the pot auger days, mind you. That was before my time. I mean not long ago, just before the tinned stuff and the packages and the baker's bread started to trickle into the outports.

Out where I come from the trickle started when I was about six or seven years old. One day I went next door to Aunt Winnie's (that's Uncle John's Aunt Winnie) and she had a package of puffed rice someone sent down from Canada.

She gave us youngsters a small handful each. We spent a long time admiring this new exotic stuff and remarking on how much it looked like emmets' eggs. We ate one grain at a time as if it was candy and, because of the novelty, didn't notice the remarkable lack of taste.

"Now, here's a five cent piece for you and don't spend it all in sweets, mind." You never got a nickel (remember those small Newfoundland nickels?) without this caution attached.

Peppermint knobs. White capsules ringed around with flannelette pink stripes. Strong! You'd think you were breathing icewater. They're not near as strong today.

Chocolate mice shaped like a crouching rat, chocolate on the outside and tough pink sponge inside. Goodbye teeth. Bullseyes made from molasses. And union squares – pastel blocks of marshmallow.

Those mysterious black balls that were harder than forged steel, had about 2,537 different layers of color and a funny tasting seed at the center of the mini-universe.

Soft drinks came packed in barrels of straw in bottles of different sizes and shapes and no labels. Birch beer, root beer, chocolate, lemonade, and orange.

Spruce beer, which I could never stomach, but the twigs boiling on the stove smelled good. Home brew made from "Blue ribbon" malt and which always exploded like hand grenades in the bottles behind the stove.

Rum puncheons. Empty barrels purchased from the liquor control in St. John's. You poured in a few gallons of water, rolled the barrels around, and the result was a stronger product than you put down $7.50 a bottle for today.

Ice cream made in a hand-cranked freezer, the milk and sugar and vanilla in the can in the middle surrounded by ice and coarse salt. I won't say it was better than the store-bought stuff today, but it tasted different and I like the difference.

Rounders (dried tom cods) for Sunday breakfast without fail. Cods heads, boiled sometimes, but mostly stewed with onions and bits of salt pork.

Fried cod tongues with pork scruncheons. Outport soul food. Salt codfish,

fish cakes, boiled codfish and drawn butter, baked cod with savoury stuffing, stewed cod, fried cod.

Lobsters. We always got the bodies and the thumbs from the canning factories. When eating lobster bodies you must be careful to stay away from the "old woman," a lump of bitter black stuff up near the head which is said to be poisonous.

I was always partial to that bit of red stuff in lobster bodies but never went much on the pea green stuff, although some did.

We ate turrs (impaled on a sharpened broomstick and held over the damper hole to singe off the fuzz): some people ate tickleaces and gulls but I never saw it done.

We ate "a meal of trouts," seal, rabbits that were skinned out like a sock, puffin' pig (a sort of porpoise that had black meat), mussels (best got on the Saturday between Good Friday and Easter when the tides are lowest) and cocks and hens, otherwise known as clams, that squirt at you through air holes in the mud flats.

Potatoes and turnips were the most commonly grown vegetables although there was some cabbage and carrot. The potatoes were kept in cellars made of mounds of earth lined with sawdust or goosegrass. With the hay growing on them, they looked like hairy green igloos.

A lot was got from a cow. Milk, certainly, and cream and butter made into pats and stamped with a wooden print of a cow or a clover leaf, and buttermilk, cream cheese. And I seem to remember a sort of jellied sour milk. I forgot the name but perhaps the stuff was equivalent to yogurt.

There was no fresh meat in summer because it wouldn't keep. If you asked for a piece of meat at the store you got salt beef. If you wanted fresh beef you had to ask for "fresh meat."

Biscuits came packed in three-foot-long wooden boxes and were weighed out by the pound in paper bags. Sultanas, dad's cookies, jam jams, lemon creams with caraway seeds and soda biscuits.

Molasses was a big thing. It was used to sweeten tea, in gingerbread, on rolled oats porridge, with sulphur in the spring to clean the blood (eeeccchhh), in bread, in baked beans, in 'lassie bread.

It came in barrels, and when the molasses was gone, there was a layer of molasses sugar at the bottom.

Glasses of lemon crystals or strawberry syrup or lime juice. Rolled oats, farina, indian meal. Homemade bread, pork buns, figgy duff, partridgeberry tarts, blancmange, ginger wine, damper cakes.

Cold mutton, salt beef, pease pudding, boiled cabbage, tinned bully beef for lunch on Sunday, tinned peaches, brown eggs, corned caplin.

And thank God I was 12 years old before a slice of baker's bread passed my lips. RG

The land Joe gave to Doyle

October 15, 1968   *Culture and History*

Happy Valley – I was up bright and early yesterday morning packing sandwiches and molasses bread and polishing up my boots – ready and raring to join in the march from Goose Bay to the Quebec border.

It struck me as odd that the civil defence sirens weren't wailing and that there were no mass movements of militia through the sandy streets of Happy Valley.

However, I surmised that military secrecy had been imposed in the light of the present emergency and went about the grim duty of preparing for battle.

The electrifying news had struck this area the night before. René Lévesque and the boys were intent on occupying Labrador by hook or by crook.

The calmness and lack of panic with which the bulletin was received by the populace in this part of Labrador amazed me. No one displayed his emotions and there was no hysterical talk.

So after a good night's rest, I assembled my kit and proceeded down to the Hudson Bay store on Hamilton River Road. I assumed that here the home defence would be issued 12 gauges, sealing guns and golf clubs from HBC.

Imagine my surprise when I arrived there and found that the only other people present were two Eskimo kids about eight years old. They were trying to knock a sparrow out of a dogberry tree with a couple of plastic store-bought slingshots.

If finally occurred to me that no one else was the slightest bit interested in marching across Labrador to head off the Quebec battalion at the border.

It just goes to show what mistaken ideas we of the "outside" have of Labrador. If no one seemed too distressed about the news from Quebec, perhaps it's because some of them are too busy making plans to separate from Newfoundland.

How much of this separatist talk is serious and how much is just a parlor game to pass the long northern nights, I can't say.

But the fact is that from the coast to the Quebec border, there is a deep and widespread resentment of the type of treatment Labrador is getting from Ottawa and in particular from St. John's.

"The government takes $60 million a year out of Labrador and we get only $5 million back," is repeated like a litany. I don't know where the figures come from, but it's the catch phrase in Labrador.

"They come in here and gang-rape Labrador," is another familiar complaint. "Everything is taken out to grease the rest of the province."

In the Goose Bay area, where a town of 6,000 hangs suspended on a whim of The Pentagon, repeated promises of alternate industry have worn thin long ago.

The idea of substituting dependence on the US war department with dependence on an American wheeler-dealer bail-jumper is not all that appetizing.

Significantly, the only permanent representative in the area of the famed chip mill enterprise is a public relations man.

The communications link between the island and mainland Newfoundland are spider-web thin. Not the least rotten are the governmental links.

There's the deputy minister who professed surprise that there was no lumber industry to make use of the splendid forests of Labrador. Apparently he has forgotten that BRINCO and Doyle own practically every tree up here.

There's the young university graduate who took over the job of Labrador commissioner (a sort of colonial office) and soon ran head-on into disillusionment over the official Confederation Building policy on Labrador.

There's his replacement, a retired police type and old Labrador hand, who boasts publicly of having tortured native prisoners.

There's a government welfare policy in Labrador that stinks so highly it'll take more than a snow job in the *Newfoundland Bulletin* to disguise the odor.

All in all it's little wonder that Lévesque's threatened "invasion" has aroused so little interest.

Those who are working to make their homes in Labrador and have come up here for something more than a fast buck may not be fooling when they talk about a takeover of their own. ◼

Newfoundland is far, far more than an island

Culture and History

Happy Valley – We're all touchy, the whole kit and caboodle of us. Touchy as a fistful of festered hangnails when "outsiders" come along and start commenting and criticizing.

In Labrador, anything beyond the Labrador borders is generally referred to as "outside." That makes anyone from the island part of Newfoundland an "outsider" in his own province when he comes up here.

Outsiders who presume to comment on Labrador affairs stand a chance of getting a swift kick in the oolituk. Too often, there's just cause.

Blame for this touchy state of affairs lies on both sides of the Strait of Belle Isle. What do 65 per cent of the residents of St. John's, for example, really know about Labrador?

I don't set myself up to be holier than thou in this matter. If my job hadn't brought me up here a couple of times I'd probably still have the same cockeyed ideas about Labrador as most of the rest of you ... not that I'm any expert yet.

On the other side of the coin, what do those Labrador residents, who get all hot under the parka when outsiders comment, actually know about Labrador themselves?

Most of those who live on the Labrador coast have never seen the western mining towns. Most Labrador City-Wabush residents know more about Montreal than they know about the coast.

Even the majority of those centrally located Goose Bay residents know little about Labrador except what they can see from their kitchen windows.

Communication is a big part of the problem and so is our short-sighted view of what Newfoundland is and who our brothers are.

Too often our view of Newfoundland is not wider than the street on which we live, and our idea of who is our neighbor and brother will stretch only to include the people next door.

Talk about us feeling like Canadians. How can a St. John's man or a Corner Brooker ever hope to look at a map of Alberta and say with conviction, "this is my country?"

How can he hope to do that when he can't even think of the mainland part of Newfoundland except as a barren snow-covered land of ice and igloos "down on the Labrador"?

Or how can residents of Labrador claim to know the province they live in when they lump the other half of it under the label of "outsider"?

(While we're on the subject, and as one festered hangnail to another: St.

John's, you really bug me when you grandly and superciliously dismiss the whole province lying beyond the Topsail overpass as "out around the bay.")

Newfoundland is far, far more than an island. But the Strait of Belle Isle may be the widest nine miles of water in the world. It'll take more to bridge the gulf caused by neglect and lack of communication than the childish trick of changing the name of the province to "Newfoundland and Labrador."

Let's make a modest start. From the center of Labrador may I ask you: Did you think, numbskulls, that the six-month-long Arctic night had already set in?

Then it will surprise you to know that today at Happy Valley, near Goose Bay, late roses and gladioli are still blooming in front of the houses.

It will shock you to know that Labrador is no further north than England and that January days in the heart of Labrador are no shorter than they are in London or Liverpool.

It will astound you to know that the winters here in the center of Labrador are far more sunny and pleasant than they are in St. John's. I have seen both.

It will amaze you to learn that the trees in the endless forests of "barren" Labrador are taller and straighter than the masts of any schooner.

It will confuse you to know that thousands of your brother Newfoundlanders are slant-eyed, brown-skinned and as fine to look at as the handsome people of the South Sea Islands.

You will be ashamed, as I am, for every moment lived in ignorance of what you call "your" Newfoundland. ▨

Pretty as a park are the
forests of Labrador

October 18, 1968   *Resettlement and Rural Life*

More on the Labrador. Yesterday, as you will remember, I had just got back from a short cruise to Goose Bay and vicinity and put you in the light of what the country looks like.

I can't go back over that again for the sake of you lot who only take the Weekend paper, except to say that the idea that Labrador is nothing but barren rocks and bog is cockeyed nonsense.

There's this big mess of pinkish sand – up to 1,000 feet deep – at the western end of Lake Melville. These huge sand flats stretching as far as you can see was brought down by the big rivers – the Kenamu, the North West, the Goose and the Churchill.

Goose Bay, Happy Valley and North West River are located here at the end of the 100-mile-long saltwater indraft known as Lake Melville.

Now this vast field of sand is by no means barren. Where the bulldozer hasn't disturbed it, it's covered by a great forest. Black spruce is the Labrador tree but it looks a lot different from the same tree that grows on the island.

All the Labrador trees are amazingly straight. Almost any one you'd pick would make a perfect flagpole or schooner mast. Straight as the teeth in a comb.

The Labrador trees are straight and inclined to be stalky much like a potted flower that didn't get enough sun. Whether this is due to the soil or to the climate, I don't know.

The black spruce, for example, is nearly all trunk growing 40 feet or more tall with tiny branches for the size of it. With its short and few branches the Labrador spruce looks like a fuzzy telephone pole.

Much of it is the size of a power pole or smaller, but I did see trees up to three feet in the butt. Wonderful stuff for lumber and a sinful waste if it is all cut for pulpwood with the bigger timber not set aside.

There are also great stands of aspen (what we call apse) and birch, straight as a whip, tall and averaging the size of a cabbage boiler or better in the stump.

Pretty as a park are the forests of Labrador. This is because the trees are so straight and taut and the trunks are bare of branches on the lower half. There is little scrub between them, and you can walk for miles.

Adding to the scene are those large carpets of what they call caribou moss. It's a pale green color – almost exactly the same color as that little bit of stuff on watches and clocks that glow in the dark.

Picture then, a typical Labrador forest of tall straight spruce with the ground below clean and uncluttered with this crunchy moss that looks like pale green snow.

Every now and then you'll see a squirrel. They are brown in color and about the size of a rat, although more like a weasel in shape. You can get up to five feet of them before they dart away.

The spruce grouse is a common bird and hard to tell apart from a partridge. We were driving up that new bit of road along the Churchill River when a car coming toward us stopped, a man got out and ran toward us with a gun.

Before we had a chance to stop we nearly ran over one of these spruce grouse quat up in the middle of the road. Stunned as hens, they are. The bird hopped off the side of the road and the man went after it.

They say you can go among a flock of them and shoot every last one if you want to. Shoot one and the rest will fly off 20 feet or so and pitch again. There's certainly not much sport to it.

This new "tote road" they talk about is a frail affair, but it opens up a lot of splendid country in the Churchill River valley. It's supposed to run from Goose Bay to Churchill Falls.

They finished about 50 miles of it from the Goose Bay end and I believe 80 or so from the other end. Late this summer the contractors, for some unexplained reason, dropped everything, leaving a gap of nearly 200 miles between. I hear Lundrigan's are supposed to take up the contract next spring.

I don't know what it is they're supposed to "tote" over this road and I can't see it as being the basis for any kind of permanent highway.

At the Goose Bay end, at least, it is simply a 20-foot-wide, three-foot-deep layer of sand laid on top of the ground. More crooks and twists and turns than a can of spaghetti.

Already the rain has washed deep gulches in it and I'd say that by next spring there won't be a mile of it that's passable. It shouldn't be confused with this "Trans-Canada Highway" across Labrador they're talking about.

But what country! Every now and then you cross a smaller river that runs into the awesome Churchill. The closest spot to the big river we came in 30 miles of driving was about two or three miles.

You come to the top of this hill and there's a lookout. Below in the valley through vast stands of spruce, aspen and birch runs the Churchill River. More like a lake – Gander Lake perhaps – than a river. Stop the car and get out and you can hear the roar of the Muskrat Falls in the distance. Only half the yellow leaves have yet fallen from the aspen.

The overall impression is of a vast, wide and rich country – a northern "Big Valley." How unlike the false picture we have of Labrador – barren, windswept, snow covered and cruel.

What a sight to make you feel there's a chance for Newfoundland. How fierce and savage would it make you fight against those who would misuse, squander, sell or give it away. ▉

How I stopped worrying and learned to love the O.L.F.

October 28, 1968   *Joey*

THIS IS A COLUMN.

It.

That's what you have to be with.

With it.

Somebody stole my crayons so I can't do much with layout. My best. That's what I'll have to do without them. Surely there's room for another thinking man's Ron Pumphrey.

Never let it be said that Guy is not with it. Like, man, flip flop. With it. The new face. The other face. Forthwith.

Corner Brook.

Conventions.

It's time to wallop the stuffing out of the idea that those Liberal conventions are rigged. This slander, this lie, this complete distortion is widely believed by many.

Not one. Not two. Not three. But many.

The simple, unadorned, statistical fact is that those thousands and thousands of Liberal delegates are not department store dummies.

Let's start at the bottom.

Legs.

They all have legs. They're self-supporting as regards legs. Oh, their knees may knock a bit at times. But they've got legs. Thousands and thousands of legs. An average of two legs per delegate.

Ankles. Thousands and thousands of ankles. Hardly one of them there without ankles.

Thumbs. Noses. Eyebrows. Navels. (Is there anyone so outdated that he doesn't understand why Liberal delegates have navels?)

Eye teeth. None. (Wouldn't you give yours, too, for one of those little cards?) Summer moles. Appendixes. TWO nostrils each. It all adds up to thousands and thousands of nostrils.

Hair. Adam's apples. Buttocks. Etc. Etc.

Etc.

Any one of these components may seem insignificant in itself. It's when you add them up that they count. Thousands of Liberal delegates.

Oh, to be among that carefree, metaphysical band. As Enkidu, according to the ancient lines from the Sumerian epic of Gilgamesh (and he, as you know, was a Chuang Tzu Taoist), said 2,300 years ago:

"The tree that stands stiff and hard is broken in the storm: the reed that bends remains entire."

Oh, to remain entire. And neo-Freudian.

Over the weekend thousands of right-thinking, forward-looking, spiritually autonomous Liberals met amid the yellow-shafted flickers and lesser-winged pine grosbeaks at Corner Brook.

THIS IS MORE OF THE SAME COLUMN.

How I envy them.

The Liberals, not the grosbeaks.

Card carriers. Invited. With it.

I could cut out my tongue. Or flip flop.

The Liberals at Corner Brook. A more inspiring sight than the birth of the universe. Or a Norway rat in heat.

Sure, they have their little drawbacks. But that doesn't mean they aren't happy. The ruin-and-doomers would have us believe that everything in the garden is not rosy. Nasty things.

They should learn. Like me. How I stopped worrying and learned to love the O.L.F. Transcendental serenity. I'm working on it.

Let's take a look at the accomplishments that support and sustain the Liberal delegates as they gathered at Corner Brook.

ARDA

ADA

FRED

BILL

JOE

ABIGAIL

ABAGAIL?

Fishermen's gas rebate.

Salt deposits. Potash. Some oil. Peanut butter, maybe.

Gill net replacement program.

Arnold's Cove – Utopia on the Rocks.

Cheaper soft drinks.

Churchill Falls – a good deal.

Ultimate defeat of the hemlock looper.

A future that "boggles the mind" (as someone once said).

New stuff everywhere.

This is not a complete list. Just jogging your memory. If you want still more facts all you have to do is read your *Newfoundland Bulletin*.

Oh, that I had not said all that ruin-and-doom stuff that I did. New cabinet posts being created left and right. Never mind. I'll make amends or I don't know a yellow-bellied sap sucker when I see one.

If they won't make a repentant sinner the minister of culture, the least I can expect is the editorship of the *Newfoundland Bulletin*.

Pretty foxy.

What?

THIS IS THE END OF THE COLUMN. 🆁🅶

Hello, fellow Smallwoodians

October 29, 1968 *Joey*

The time for sniping and picking and belittling Mr. Smallwood's government has passed. We enter a new era of re-assessment.

The non-constructive, negative and carping "gloom-and-doomers" referred to in a *Telegram* editorial on Friday (and by Liberal Association president Richard Cashin in Corner Brook on Saturday) are as dead as dodos.

Strange words indeed coming from one who has some reputation as a government critic, i.e., a "gloom-and-doomer." I blush with shame to recall the works of my deluded past.

Where, then, do I get the gall to expect forgiveness, as it were, for past folly? After all the petty insults and the half-truths twisted into so-called "witticisms."

My one and only hope lies in the generous and great-hearted statement made so often by our premier: "While the light holds out to burn, the vilest sinner may return."

I am convinced in my heart that the leader of the great Liberal party and the father of the new Newfoundland will forgive my past stupidity. But will readers? This is my real worry.

Will readers who have followed these scribblings for some little time really be convinced that I have undergone a sincere change of heart?

I must do more than solemnly declare that I have. I must try to explain the motivation for my past actions and the circumstances that have brought me at last to see the light.

It must not be thought that I was a "Joey critic" (even now I cringe at the very phrase) because I failed miserably in the past to get into some government office on Mr. Smallwood's coat tails. Not so.

Neither must it be thought I was after vengeance because my family failed to get liquor licences and government spoils. They didn't get it because (poor fools) they didn't seek.

Or it must not be presumed that I am a bitter and twisted 65-year-old who yearns for the "good old days" that the great Liberal leader has led us out of. I'm 29 years old.

But old enough to have better sense, you say. Ah, there's the key to my sudden conversion. Older and wiser.

Any of these three typical "reasons" for criticizing the Smallwood regime would at least be understandable, if not pardonable.

My case is a bit more grave than that. I had the false and outlandish notion that there is no such thing on the face of the earth as a tolerable dictatorship.

I foolishly saw it as a government that had used the great power given it by the people in the first few post-Confederation elections to secure itself in office – by spoils, graft, corruption, political bribery and other such nasties – for two decades.

I was led astray by the old saw that "absolute power corrupts absolutely" and so concluded the only thing for us to do was shovel out Confederation Building like a stable in the spring and make a new start.

What a childlike, black-and-white view of it all! What a mistaken picture of the great Liberal regime of the past 20 years!

What really opened my eyes was the Liberal convention in Corner Brook and others that went before it. And now I stand – a sinner saved by grace.

The futility of being a government critic, i.e., a "gloom-and-doomer" as revealed by the young Mr. Cashin; Mr. Jamieson's explanation of the "gamble on the future" concept of government which makes it as easy to understand as a radio quiz program; the realization that "mistakes of the heart" are not the same as plain mistakes.

We learn that one-man rule CAN be a good and great system of government if you have the right man. We have been blessed with probably the only one in existence.

Mr. Smallwood confirms for us that for 20 years he and he alone selected Liberal candidates and charted Newfoundland's course. But he really didn't want it that way. He was forced into it.

He was merely following the way set down by Newfoundland's past. He merely drifted with the tide into a regime of one-man rule that endured for 20 years. Graft? Political bribery? Spoils? Good heavens, no! There was no need. Was there?

We draw a step nearer to conversion. Who else, with no prior experience or training, could have taken on his shoulders all the top planning for every conceivable field of government – from new industries to fisheries to centralization to cost-plus contracts?

Who could have taken on such a task and made only mistakes that are so insignificant nobody but nitpicking, negative, non-constructive "gloom-and-doomers" give them a second thought?

Water under the bridge. Mistakes of the heart. What profit to dwell on them? Who can condemn a man for leading a province down dead-end streets when he does so with the best of intentions? Look instead to the optimistic future of the *Newfoundland Bulletin*.

As Mr. Cashin put it so penetratingly in Corner Brook: "Where is the alternative?" Can the "gloom-and-doomers" offer us another the equal of this human phenomenon?

There is no question that the one-man rule that has served Newfoundland so gloriously in the past is the only conceivable way for the future. But never in 1,000 years will nature bless us with another individual who can fill the role.

So we must beg Mr. Smallwood to stay with it. He may even have to be forced, but there is no other choice. The whole of his Liberal party were and are content to place themselves completely in his hands.

The majority of the Newfoundland people (without benefit of political bribery and such) were wisely content to do the same thing for 20 years. Until June of this year when something terrible happened.

Even faced with the prospect that this June madness continues to grip Newfoundland, I, for one, belatedly come to my senses and humbly beg to join the dwindling but valiant ranks.

Farewell, gloom and doom.

Goodbye, if necessary, Newfoundland.

Hello, fellow Smallwoodians. RG

The most charming and agreeable bitch

November 8, 1968   *Democracy*

The only alternative – the *Newfoundland Bulletin*? How does that grab you?

No need to worry about having to face the alternative. Not after that startling and heartening coincidence on Wednesday when both Harold [Horwood] and I (or I and Harold) wrote on home-brewing.

The heart and soul and sole repository of original thought in this country (setting aside for the moment "Open Line" and "Here and Now"), namely the People's Paper, does not let its readers down.

Here we have two of the greatest columnists the world has ever seen (or is ever likely to see, for that matter) rising above the chaff and the trivial to settle simultaneously and spontaneously on a subject that Really Counts.

Lesser journalists might have nattered away about Nixon or fourth mills or student power or space bombs, but Newfoundland is blessed with two superior intellects who went instinctively to the crux of the matter. Home-brew.

Let the readership rejoice in its good fortune. In one single and glorious day you had the sage of Beachy Cove expounding on crabapple champagne and blueberry burgundy, and Arnold's Cove's own Henny Youngman extolling the merits of cock ale.

I, for one, knew I had hit the nail on the head as usual when a letter signed "Teetotaler" poured in, castigating me for upholding demon rum, the ruination of many a happy home.

Give her prohibition and the Mafia any day, what? That's the way people are, missus. We're a rotten lot, but we're the only rot we've got. If your old man didn't drink, he'd probably chase young schoolgirls or vote for yellow dogs.

And now, today, we continue with things that Really Count.

Yesterday, I was introduced to the most charming and agreeable bitch it has ever been my privilege to meet.

All the more wonder when you consider her background. The lady is of German descent, and is of that particular class of German-bred, and is drilled in the ways of savagery and cruelty.

However, her ancestors must have lived in Newfoundland for some years, because every vestige of balled-up aggression, sadism and intolerance has been drained from her.

All the inefficiency, gentleness and short-sightedness that hangs in the Newfoundland air has seeped into her bones. If the Gestapo that trained her could see her now, they'd blow up and burst in the face of such a monumental failure.

They'd take out their steel Lugers and put steel bullets through their iron hearts. A German police dog that has forgotten how to snarl.

Instead, she passes her time pursuing with great intensity and devotion the one way she knows of communicating with the two-legged gods around her. Running after stones and bringing them back.

The lady has a problem. Her inefficiency and short-sightedness placed her in a family way. The father has cleared out and she is left with five merrybegots to brighten her days.

By invitation, I went in company with Farley Mowat yesterday to view her offspring up in under a house. They're three weeks old. As we were admiring them, two small girls came down from the house to deliver a message:

"Mom sent us down to ask you if you wants one. We got to drown them. They're getting too big. But one is spoke for."

And four not spoke for. The former Keeper of the Whale went into a rather embarrassing song and dance that placed me in the role of champion of the underdog and the only one cracked enough to risk a flood of requests from people seeking homes for unwanted goldfish.

I stood up under that blarney, but Farley knows our every weakness.

"Look at their reaction, will you, when you mention the word Smallwood," said he.

And who could deny it? You had only to say the word and the five scraps of fur turned instantly into miniscule bundles of fury. The most violent of the lot, the small one in back, worked himself up into such a sweat he nearly tumbled off the rock he stood on. Nearly.

We tried spelling it. But you could only get as far as the "w" before they would all launch into another furious expression of outrage. A pity indeed to drown such thoroughly admirable and intelligent Newfoundlanders.

Oh, it's a hopeless cause – which is the best and only kind of cause. Who can save all the pups and stranded whales in the world from the satellite H-bombs of the US and Russia that orbit constantly above our heads awaiting the radio signal to drop? (Did you read that in *The Telegram* yesterday? Page One.)

You can't do anything, really. You can only drive out through Petty Harbour and on to Maddox Cove, past the schoolhouse, and ask anybody where the Urshler house is. And speak for one.

The lady who is their mother would hate you for taking one, but she has forgotten how to hate. That's her problem. What's yours? RG

The invasion has begun in earnest

Culture and History

Have you noticed? The invasion has begun in earnest. The alien beings are everywhere. Because they look so much like us, they're hard to spot.

In fact, they'd be almost invisible if they kept their mouths shut. That's what gives them away. Those quaint mainland and British accents.

Their names, too. Look through the phone book and see how many "non-Newfoundland" names you can spot. The woods is full of 'em.

Engineers, teachers, tradesmen, doctors, nurses, university professors and presidents, sociologists, anthropologists, researchers, radio, television and newspaper people, civil servants, deputy ministers, town councilors, mayors, bishops, lord bishops, clergy, old people in retirement, artists, dramatists, students, children.

The head of the RCMP, the head of the CNR, the head of the CNT, the head of the CBC, the head of Memorial University, the head of the Anglican Church, the head of the Salvation Army, the heads of every development in Labrador, the heads of all our new industries, the heads of some of our biggest fisheries enterprises, the heads of our two military bases (naturally), the heads of national parks, the heads of many federal government departments here, the head of the Newfoundland Hotel, the head of Holiday Inn.

Water Street is one of the last holdouts, but, even so, bank managers, finance company managers, insurance company managers and a raft of others have invaded that hallowed ground.

A cheap and easy way to kick up a racket would be to point the finger at the invaders as a group and blame them for all our trials and tribulations.

But that would be a misleading and futile exercise, and it would be grossly unfair to tar them all with the same brush. All we can do is take note of the fact that there has been an invasion and give them a small piece of advice.

The invaders run the full gamut, from the lady in Farley Mowat's book who said "These people are scum and they'll always be scum" at one end of the scale, to Mowat himself at the other.

Between these two extremes are the carpetbaggers, the ones who want to do something **with** Newfoundland, the ones who want to do something **for** Newfoundland (I don't know which of these two are the worst), the ones brought here by their jobs or money, the ones who come to study us, the ones who are running away from something, the ones who want to find something, the ones determined to "become" Newfoundlanders ... and every shade between.

It would be a task for one of the invading sociologists to classify the types that make up the invaders and catalogue their reasons for coming here.

They may not be the types who flood Africa intent on either "bettering" the lot of the Africans or bettering their own lot – the missionaries, imperialists, escapists, and peace corps do-gooders.

Yet, Newfoundland is different enough to attract a broad general type of invader. It must be something more than our delightful climate that attracts them.

The very least we can say is that the type of people who come to Newfoundland are different from the type of people who do not come to Newfoundland. There must be some characteristics they share as a group.

It would be to our advantage to find out more about the invaders – their motivations, their aims, their outlook – if only because so many of them are to be found in top positions where their actions affect all of us.

There's not much point now of setting up the cry "Sweep out the invaders!" is there? Any hope of keeping Newfoundland "pure" is long gone. It's about as futile as trying to keep Canada "pure" by insisting on a certain Canadian TV content. Or keeping Quebec "pure" by making everyone there learn French.

The type of invader who calls us scum or comes here with a carpetbag or tries to "better" us will get their lumps in due course. Something dark and evil and terrible will happen to them.

To the whole lot of them we can say, "Don't be too cocksure that because this place is different to what you're used to it should be changed."

The shining examples are not what they used to be. The greatest one of all – the "American way of life" – has developed some nasty cracks.

And a thousand times better to live in some shack in a Newfoundland outport than in the midst of an endless Toronto or New York slum where even the air is against you.

We can tell the invaders – friendly and otherwise – that for the past two or three decades we've had "progress" stuffed down our throats hand over fist.

It took Toronto and New York and Chicago and London centuries to get in the mess they are now in. There are some who have tried to push us to the same exalted state in just 20 years.

Dear invaders: We are weary of being pushed. We are so stuffed with "progress" we are ready to retch or bust. If you sincerely want to become Newfoundlanders you can help us find out what there was that was good about Newfoundland.

You can help us try to salvage any of the good there is that you and we have not destroyed. It's already a lost cause, but who says wakes can't be fun? ▨

Harold and Farley used to be friends

Harold and Farley used to be the best of friends, you know. Oh, yes. Harold stood up for Farley at Farley's wedding.

Now they've fallen out. Harold gave Farley a blow below the whale and Farley gave Harold a blow below Carbonear. The fight got rather nasty – which is to say, interesting.

The funny thing about it is that they're scrapping over who has the most right to speak for the Newfoundland outport. Farley, who set up house in one for five years, and Harold, who claims that Carbonear and Beachy Cove are "outports."

Both have written books about outports and they've had hard words with each other over which book is closest to the truth.

Harold hit Farley a blow below the whale when he said that outport life was hard and lacking in warmth. He put a dent in Farley's image of the idyllic, north sea island outport by this indirect reference to the "Moby Joe Affair."

The whale is one of Farley's weak spots. He's still trying to explain it. He says the people who pumped the stranded animal full of lead were outporters who'd been corrupted by the outside.

What happened to the whale doesn't fit into Farley's view of the outports. Real outporters wouldn't be capable of doing it, he says. They would and are, of course. If he doesn't swallow the whale with the rest of it, he's admitting that his view of the outport has holes.

Harold saw Farley's weak spot and hit his view of the outports where it hurts – by reminding him there is cruelty and coldness in the outports too. But in order to deliver Farley a telling blow, Harold had to expose his own weakness as a spokesman for the outports. (Say, doesn't this shape up like one of those classic battles between the Viking gods?)

Harold went overboard when he said there was no warmth in outport life. He reveals that his view of the outports is just as full of holes as the view of outports without whale-killers.

Farley strikes back. He says that Harold's view of the hard and cold outport is colored by his own childhood experiences in "outport" Carbonear. Give me back my sou'wester. The party's getting rough.

To be sure, there's no warmth in Harold's outport book *Tomorrow Will Be Sunday*. Not even when he tries to inject it. There are no real people. Only skeletons of people, one-dimensional caricatures, frames hammered out of iron.

Harold writes better books about foxes than he does about people … but this is a subjective view. If foxes could read they might differ.

Now we have two pictures of the Newfoundland outport. Harold's cruel and iron-cold outport and Farley's idyllic north sea island outport. Will the real outport please stand up?

As far as I can see, the real outport lies somewhere between these two extremes, but I'm not brave enough to say where. Writing about outports is a tricky business.

You can come close enough to it to satisfy people who have never lived in an outport, or people who have lived in an outport some time in the past. The former group can't discriminate and the latter have their memories clouded by time.

But it is a harder job to do justice to the outport itself. The only people who can tell us what outports are really like are real outporters – and real outporters aren't in the book-writing business.

Pink people don't do a very good job of writing books about Negroes. William Styron, who is pink, wrote *The Confessions of Nat Turner* as he thought Nat Turner, who was black, would write it.

Most pink readers thought "The Confessions of Nat Turner" offered a clear insight into the mind of a black person. Most black readers thought Styron missed the boat completely.

As for former outporters writing books about outports – they don't have much chance either. You are either an outporter or you aren't. If you leave for even a year you can't become a real outporter again. You can't go home again.

Who can describe what it is like to be a four-year-old kid? The four-year-old can't because he can't write and can hardly talk. When he gets to be 30 and can talk and write, he still can't tell us what it was like to be four.

Mixed together in the same 30-year-old pot are the experiences of two years, four years, 10 years, 15 years, 20 years, and 30 years. You can't pick out the experiences of four years and examine them separately. They're colored and mixed with those of other years.

So if an outporter leaves an outport he can write books about outports but not for outports. If someone from outside goes to live in an outport he can write about, but not for, outports.

All this is a quibble, of course. If everyone got hung up on these points we'd never have any books. Our two bearded and doughty and self-appointed spokesmen for the outports don't let such trifles faze them.

In the opinion of this outporter, who left for a few years and can't go home again, Farley, in his and John de Visser's book *This Rock Within the Sea* comes as close as anyone can to speaking for the outports and against centralization, one of the most heinous crimes ever committed against the Newfoundland people.

Of which much more later. ▧

Guy's Encyclopedia of Juvenile Outharbor Delights: Winter Games

November 21, 1968   *Outharbor Delights*

Gloom and doom, my duckies. Frustration and despair wherever I look. Some people taking what I said about the invaders the wrong way, and me determined, for spite, not to try and explain what I "really meant."

And I can't put off buying snow tires much longer and she's hard to start in the mornings. And I'm running out of unshrunk socks. And I find that my brand is among the highest in nicotine and tar content.

And Wick Collins, who is a fund of miscellaneous detail, told us the fascinating origin of our most famous four-letter word and I'm frustrated because "good taste" forbids passing it on.

Ah, yes. I know something of how those US astronauts must feel. I see that one scientist tells them they're likely to get trapped in a permanent orbit around the moon and another scientist warns them their legs and arms may drop off from the force of re-entry. Reassurance from all directions.

Some are driven by gloom and doom to Scotch or hashish or politics. I seek refuge from the overbearing cares of the world in that excellent but addicting volume, *Guy's Encyclopedia of Juvenile Outharbor Delights*.

The last time, you many remember, we turned to the section on Winter Delights and dwelt at some length on that universal outharbor winter delight of "Randying."

It was by no means an exhaustive treatise on the subject and I am indebted to Lorna, a former resident of Heart's Delight (no kidding), for reminding me of another sideline of Randying, namely, "Making Trains."

With all hands lying flat on their coaster you make a train, you see, by hooking your toes into the bow of the coaster behind. You rattle down the hill in a long snake and there's the feeling of being caught up in the irresistible force of a buffalo stampede.

If one of the head coasters turns over he's got the prospect of having a dozen or more run over him and probably kill him if the hill is steep enough. Which is what made it so much fun.

Hockey is the top juvenile delight these days, of course. On every frozen bog hole between St. John's and Port aux Basques we see dozens of small youngsters bow-legged under about $100 worth of equipment each. Elbow pads, shin pads, shoulder pads, helmets, masks, pants, stockings, sweaters, sticks – the works.

I don't want to be a fuddy-duddy about this but I have my doubts when I see the little fellers rigged out in uniforms correct to the last detail with the proper number of players on each side, regulation goals and the lot.

Put a grown-up referee with a whistle in the midst of them and it's something else again. It reminds of the ad on television where this young woman says, "Please, mother! I'd rather do it myself!"

But we digress. The hockey (or "hurley") I'm talking about involved $6.95 skates they "sent away for and had come" out of the catalogue; two rocks for goals; all hands – including some of the hardier girls – in; pickets off the fence and a tin can for a puck.

Playing hurley was especially fine on moonlit nights. When you got tired of playing you could drop out without disrupting the game and engage in associated delights such as skating down to the other end of the pond with your jacket for a sail, making a fire, and much, much more.

You don't knock my kind of hockey and I won't knock yours. Except to say it seems to be a rather grim business these days. I am reminded of the Prussian nanny who says to the kiddies: "You WILL have fun."

Skating on black ice was another thing. On fine days the sky was reflected in it and it made you giddy to be skating on the clouds. You could lie on your stomach on black ice for a long time trying to see the bottom. You could sit on your coaster with a spruce bush held up for a sail. You could skate far up a brook.

"Copying Clampers" was another universal juvenile outharbor winter delight and fraught with almost as much danger as Randying. Clampers, as any clamper copier knows, are pans of saltwater ice around shore. They're five or ten feet across and from six inches to a foot or more thick and light blue in color.

The main object of copying is to get wet. To get wet you have to jump from one clamper to another until you slip in, capsize a clamper or stand still too long and sink it. Sooner or later you'll get wet, but the thing is to get wet in the most daring manner possible.

"Heaving Snowballs." It was cricket to dip them in water and let them freeze, or to make them solid by squeezing them between your knees or to leave them in the porch and let them melt a bit. But putting rocks in snowballs was something dark and ugly.

Rocks in snowballs took the fun out of Heaving Snowballs just as the introduction of gunpowder took the fun out of war. There's an evil streak in those who put rocks in snowballs.

"Digging Tunnels." You find a massive snowdrift and you see how long a tunnel you can dig before it caves in and traps you. One of the most intense bits of terror I can remember is being trapped under 10 feet of snow at the end of a 30-foot tunnel.

That's enough. The gloom and doom has dispersed, until it's time for the next fix. But I hope those poor brutes of astronauts don't get trapped in a permanent orbit around the moon.

Who will dig them out? 🆁🅶

The real story of the Burgeo whale

December 3, 1968   *Culture and History*

At last, as they say, it can be told. The real story of the Burgeo whale. The whale for which the government promised $1,000 in assistance, that a giant papermaking machine was named for, that dozens of newsmen from the eastern US and Canada flocked to see.

The whale that gave Burgeo on the south coast something of a reputation as the Dallas of Newfoundland ... if you want to get symbolic about it. Moby Joe, alias Moby Josephine. Remember?

A few weeks ago I said the whale was the weak spot in Farley Mowat's view of the Newfoundland outports ... that he couldn't believe "real" Newfoundlanders would do such a thing and tried to excuse it.

Farley replies: "Who killed the whale? About a dozen people did all the shooting. All, without exception, were NEW Newfoundlanders. Some were technicians at the fish plant. Two were merchants of the new class. Some were lads who work the lake boats, home for the winter.

"Not ONE was a working fisherman. Maybe the fishermen were just too busy for such nonsense. Maybe they didn't have the money to squander on ammo. I don't believe it.

"There were six fishermen who passed through the lagoon in which the whale was trapped, morning and night. Not one offered, or suggested, violence to the beast.

"On the contrary, these men were outraged at the shooting. One of them said: ''Tis a sin, that's what it is'. And he meant it. Outport people are cruel? Of course. Man is cruel, period.

"But the wanton cruelty displayed in the shooting of the whale was not typical of outport mentality as I know it. It was absolutely typical, however, of the actions one observes amongst the liberated urban homo saps of today for whom cruelty for its own sake has become a way of life. Whale me no whales!"

Farley says that of the 2,000 rounds of ammo fired into the whale more than 1,500 rounds were army-issue steel-jacked bullets supplied by the federal government to the Canadian Rangers detachment at Burgeo.

"Most of those who shot at the whale were members of the valorous local band of Canadian Rangers. The acting CO released a case of army-issue ammo to his brave boys for the specific purpose of shooting at the whale! Using army-issue .303 rifles into the bargain."

Continues Farley: "So I suppose you could say the whale was slaughtered in defence of this fair land of ours.

"Terrible threat it was, too. Contact with it, alive and undamaged, might, just conceivably, have moderated the rampant killer instinct which is very likely going to obliterate us all one of these fine days. And that instinct ... is NOT an outport specialty.

"This little band of gentlefolk (that killed the whale) were not, are not, of the true outport breed. They may live in an outport still, but they have become corrupted aliens in the world that gave them birth.

"Every man's opinion of a group of other human beings depends entirely on the experiences he underwent with them. My experiences with outport men, women and children have been, on balance, among the best experiences in a long and busy life. So call me a romantic.

"I remain convinced that outport Newfoudlanders are amongst the best of the human breed and I consider their destruction at the hands of the little toad-minded men in government is as evil an act as any perpetuated by any Genghis Khan."

And there you have the definitive word on the demise of the famous Burgeo whale. That settles that. Or does it? As with Dallas, the rumors are likely to continue, no matter what.

I can only add a whale experience of my own. One day when I was 16 or 17 a bunch of pothead whales appeared in the harbor. Something new. Pandemonium broke loose all at once.

Every available motorboat cast off, carrying every able-bodied man and youth in the community. For a whole afternoon in mid-September they rallied the potheads back and forth, pumping shotgun shells, bullets and slugs into everything that broke water.

They speared and hacked the potheads with every makeshift harpoon they could get their hands on, and before long there was hardly a whale that did not trail a cloud of blood.

All the while, a federal fisheries boat, which happened to be there, scurried back and forth at the mouth of the harbor to keep the potheads from escaping.

There was some talk of how much money the potheads would fetch as mink food, but although the whole lot of them were slashed and loaded down with lead not one was ever beached. It's a wonder, though, that no people were killed.

I didn't have a gun or a harpoon, but I had a ringside seat at the head of one of the motorboats and, as I recall, I had a whale of a time. I found it all tremendously exciting and can't remember having any qualms about it.

But Farley has the answer for that, too. He has said earlier there are no real outports on the Avalon Peninsula. In that case, our trouble in the Isthmus of Avalon was that we missed being a real outport by about five miles. ■

Round them up and herd
them into corrals

December 4, 1968   *Joey*

"Kiss me Kate" has nothing on it. What a show. There was Chairman Joe onstage at the Arts and Culture Centre with a chorus of reverend gentlemen as a background and those super spectacular charts nine miles long and two miles high, as a centerpiece.

And he, with a small flake longer for a pointer, skipping from stage left to stage right and back, spouting dollars like a slot machine with the hiccups.

One interesting point emerged. We heard Chairman Joe (he IS going to retire, isn't he?) take a brand new approach to the problem of raising more money. From now on it will have to come from the pockets of the people!

Do our ears deceive us? For 20 years he published and propagated and promoted the myth that every cent spent on good works in Newfoundland came either from "Uncle Ottawa" or out of his own *** pocket. What's up now?

Does he figure that the old line about his fabulous silver-lined *** pocket has worn thin? Maybe he thinks we're getting smart enough to put two and two together and realize that Joey can only give out what Joey takes in.

And is this an elaboration on the old myth? We hear from several government quarters these days: The people themselves will have to start taking a greater share in the financing of education, of this and that and the other thing.

Ah, ha! Eureka! Hot Doggy! A virgin, pristine, heretofore untapped source of revenue has been discovered! The people. It'll have to come out of the people's pockets this time. A brand new concept.

Oh, the people may complain a bit at first about this bothersome novelty of having to pay for public works and services. But not too much if you break it to them the right way.

They won't squeal too much if you make them believe that for the first time in history they're going to have to start paying the piper. If these few extra cents appear as taxes in the next spring's budget they won't mind, will they? They got off scot-free before.

If you think this theory of what goes on in the back of Chairman Joe's hot little head is too outrageous, you should restrain your hoots a moment. Until you consider what a brilliant success he had – for 20 years – with the myth of his bottomless *** pocket.

But suppose that all this talk means more local taxes. Municipal taxes. Local school taxes. More community service fees. Taxes per head. More property taxes. That kind of taxes.

Suppose the aim is to have all these little hole-in-the-rock town and community councils (not forgetting our "cities") take the dirty end of the stick.

Have them absorb the tax shock instead of the provincial government.

All the backlash would then be cushioned by the local lads – not like in the last federal election when a tax hike helped put six Liberals on the breadline, temporarily.

So was this one of the main aims of centralization? When people lived in small groups all around the coast you couldn't lasso them and milk them there. They were too scattered.

Round them up and herd them into corrals – sometimes referred to as "growth centers" – and then you can set up some little local council to milk them for you, when the time comes, and not even get your hands dirty or suffer at the polls.

It might have worked, too, if centralization had worked. But those who see centralization as a clever way to skim off more cream are in for a monumental disappointment. If we may hazard one more simile, you can't get blood from turnips.

Bob Moss says he heard one man liken the government's centralization scheme to their other scheme of transplanting caribou. I heard a man go one better than that.

"The government rounded us up and unloaded us down here (in a "growth center," the name of which you can probably guess) and we're like 1,000 sheep put in a meadow that couldn't even support 100.

"We've got the grass here chewed down to the bare rocks already; the government has fleeced us out of what bit of independence we did have; we're naked to the wind. What's the government going to do now? Make mutton out of us?"

And still we hear about dollars. What else is new? Think back. What else have we heard about for 20 years except dollars? Millions of dollars. Millions upon millions of dollars.

There's nothing wrong with dollars, but it was a total, one-minded, burning obsession with dollars. Dollars and power even before people. And where has it led us?

Retire, my laddie. Give it up. Don't be tempted to try to re-sink your hooks into the soul of Newfoundland. It's too late. You've played with Newfoundland long enough – more than anyone had a right to or will ever have the chance to again.

You've mauled Newfoundland and shaken her and given her away piecemeal, and played games with her, and had your fun. Your friends say there's no one who cares more for Newfoundland.

So what? To say that is only to say that you are a Newfoundlander. There are 500,000 others who care not one jot, not one tittle, not one iota less. They're people, now, not sheep. 🆁🅶

⸺᷎ Newfoundlanders are living on a dung hill ⸺᷎

December 6, 1968   *Democracy*

If you live on a dung hill – or if you live next door to a dung hill – you find the stench intolerable at first. But if you keep a scented hanky to your nose for the first few days, you'll get over the first revulsion.

Before long you can even take the perfumed handkerchief away at times, and still keep your stomach from heaving. You get used to the stink. You learn to live with it and it doesn't bother you.

Newfoundlanders are living on a dung hill. Newfoundlanders have been living on a dung hill for the past 20 years – and how far beyond that I'll leave to the history buffs in other columns to say.

The air we breathe is quavering with a putrid stench – but we don't mind it. We don't notice it. We've grown used to it. It's been so long since we've taken a breath of fresh air we've forgotten what fresh air smells like.

Power corrupts. "Absolute power corrupts absolutely," is an old political saw. Then what do you get when you have absolute power for 20 years? Absolute corruption.

In our case, absolute apathy must go hand in hand with absolute corruption. When some new scandal or piece of corruption or graft does leak out in all its gruesome detail, there's a nine-day wonder, a few "tut tuts," and out come the scented hankies until the stink blows away.

All of us have learned to live with the stink, to stick our noses in the stink, and tolerate, if not enjoy, it. It is only when a strong easterly wind blows a whiff of it across to the mainland that we get back some second-hand reaction.

It is left to mainland observers to be shocked, to wonder what kind of people we are to be so inured to corruption that we can grin, empty-faced, in the teeth of it. We are becoming the wonder of Canada for our gullibility and apathy. How soon before that old mockery "Newfoundlanders are too green to burn" is dragged out again?

We like to believe that we aren't really subject to dictatorship, for which we must turn for comparison to Duvalier's Haiti or Castro's Cuba. We like to think that there are at least a few strong and independent men in the cabinet. What a fallacy.

They, among all of us, have the scented handkerchiefs clamped most firmly to their noses. They, who live at the very center of the dung hill, have either learned to enjoy the stink or have sprinkled their hankies well with their own delusions and rationalizations.

The *Montreal Star* recently got another whiff of the stench that pervades Newfoundland and sent down a special correspondent, Boyce Richardson, to investigate the source. He rehashes the old corruption and turns up some new bits.

Richardson says that Greg Power, who was Smallwood's right-hand man for nearly half the 20 years, is quite willing to describe how he made large profits from knowledge gained in cabinet meetings and that Power goes on to say that "all the ministers made money in the same way."

Power told of leaving in the middle of one cabinet meeting and using the information he had gained there, gathered up $30,000 and spent it all in shares in a certain asbestos company.

He says he bought the shares at $1.70 and sold at $6.55, although "some of my colleagues were braver than me and hung on longer."

Power is quoted: "I don't see anything wrong in that so long as you are not robbing the people you represent or the country you are ruling. That money came from the financial circles."

Richardson comments: "Yet a clear profit of $145,000 made by the use of such knowledge would be sufficient in most Canadian communities to bring about the resignation of a minister."

Yes. In most Canadian communities. In most civilized communities in the world. But not in Newfoundland where still another stink rises unnoticed into the quavering air.

What's your price? How many boots would you lick in return for a profit of $145,000 for a few hours "work"? How much loot would have to be waved in front of your nose before you put your own interests ahead of the country you were sworn to serve?

Richardson reports on an interview in which Smallwood says: "Now, there is Mr. Curtis, former minister of justice and attorney general. He comes back every time; he has been elected 16 years. Maybe they just want to make sure they keep their seats in the cabinet."

"But he says to me, every time, they didn't vote for me, they voted for Joey Smallwood." Richardson notes: "The hapless Mr. Curtis reads a newspaper trying to pretend he is not hearing it."

No government ever reaches a state of absolute morality, but it is a goal to be sought. If a government basks in rottenness what hope is there for anything else?

And what of those at the very center of the dung hill? They have learned to live with themselves now, but what of the time when the winds at last blow Newfoundland clean?

The stink will rise from their very graves to tell all who pass where lie the pawns of Newfoundland's era of absolute corruption.

The sad and ugly time of apathy and scented hankies. 🄀

Joey loves me? Way to go!

It was early yesterday afternoon and I was still abed recovering from my patriotic duties of the night before – namely, helping drink Newfoundland out of the hole – when I heard my name mentioned out in the living room.

Not an unusual thing. But hark! That voice. A scythe stone trying to rape a cheese grater. There was no mistaking it! Our Only Living Millstone was making reference to my humble person.

Out I tumbled and stumbled toward the television from whence came the Master's voice. The mind could scarce conceive what the eye perceived and the ear received.

But there was the honorable gentleman, large as life and twice as saucy. Being interviewed, he was, by a group of kids on the program "We Want An Answer."

How they brought the topic around to my unworthy self I'll never know, but I was just in time to hear the Gambo pixie exclaim: "Ray Guy? I love him! He's my third greatest asset."

I had to sit down, right then and there. Every bit of strength left my legs, sir, my head started to spin and I thought I was in for another attack of the DTs.

Third greatest asset? After what? Smallpox and double hernia? I still believed the worst about the man, you see. But no. No. No. No. He continued: "Ray Guy is my greatest asset – after Confederation and the blessings it entailed."

A flood of remorse swept over me like an ocean wave. Seldom have I felt so unworthy. Tears filled the beady, bloodshot eyes of asset number three and fell with deafening spatters to the carpet.

The hard heart fluttered like a little jingle bell and the cruel face melted like an ice-cream cone (chocolate chip) spilled down the bosom of a fat lady.

The man continued, piling one endearment on top of the other until I was reduced to a quivering mass of abject remorse for past folly.

His ardor knew no bounds. He said I was dirty, filthy, below-the-belt, and a mental case – or words to that effect. A matter of true love, if ever there was one.

He said I flew into such a condition, frothing at the mouth, that he could fancy the columns to be spattered with flecks of foam. Overwhelmed with affection, I was. Killed with kindness.

Anyway, there sat asset number three for a long time, head in hands, suffused by a kind of rosy glow. Here was the O.L.F. with such a load on his overworked brain – buying up defunct fish plants, designing souvenirs for Steve Neary, shifting chip mills around to suit the wind, planning vacations with some relatives in Jamaica.

Yet here he'd found time to express such tender sentiments toward such a miserable and undeserving worm as I and on semi-prime-time television, too.

I have poured my feeble best into some sort of reply. Namely, "Sonnet to a fellow mental block" or "It takes one to know one." In keeping with the solemn circumstances, the work is set to the same tune as that of a familiar Sunday school song.

(Immoderately, with foam-flecked feeling):

Joey loves me? Way to go!
Why was I the last to know?
Emily Post, tell me one thing,
Who's supposed to buy the ring?

CHORUS
(Bear down and clap)
Yes, Joey loves me!
Cold sober, was he?
Plants kisses, does he?
On asset number three.

Joey loves me, not his horse.
Pure platonic love, of course.
Heartbroken, P.E.T. and Ed Roberts?
Put a plaster where it hurts.

Joey loves me, tenderly.
I'm filthy, dirty. "But," says he,
"His foam-flecked columns can't withstand
The stuff I dump on Newfoundland."

Joey loves me for my grit
He's got another name for it.
Unrequited love's a sin,
And so I'll pile it to his chin.

CHORUS
(All over the building)
Yes, Joey loves me!
Cold sober, was he?
Plants kisses, does he?
On asset number three. ▨

It's a bird! It's a plane!
It's the savior of his people

January 7, 1969 *Joey*

The place falls apart no doubt about it, whenever he turns his back for five minutes.

Utter chaos. We can see now that we would never do without him. Indispensable, that's what he is. There's not another who could take his place.

We're poor little lambs who go astray whenever the good shepherd takes a coffee break. We're helpless infants exposed to a cruel and confusing world whenever Daddy leaves us for an instant.

Steve Neary is right, you know. We must beseech the Only Living Father on bended knee not to leave us. The night is dark and we are far from home.

He who knows all, sees us all and has all the answers wouldn't cut us adrift on an angry, chaotic sea, would he? Whatever would become of us? Lost forever without a lamp to our feet.

The Only Living Father. He who binds up our little cuts and bruises, so to speak, and calms our foolish fears about the dark at the top of the stairs. Indispensable.

For example: The great Happy Valley Chip Mill Crisis. To be sure, it was the O.L.F. himself who set it off with the announcement that the mill ("proposed") would be transferred from the Happy Valley area to Stephenville.

Having thus declared that this imaginary mill would be built on an imaginary site near Stephenville instead of on an imaginary site near Happy Valley, he lit out for a Jamaican vacation.

Then the fun started. That imaginary chip mill was the only hope the people of the Happy Valley-Goose Bay area had as an alternative to the USAF base.

Since US bases abroad have a nasty habit of closing down even quicker than iron ore mines, they clung to the only hope in sight.

Who planted the hope in the first place? Why, the O.L.F., of course, in many a great thunder and lightning announcement. Anyway, the O.L.F. giveth and the O.L.F. taketh away.

When our little Indian-giver took wing for the warm sands of Montego Bay, he left behind a pretty chaotic mess – as if he didn't know.

Happy Valley wasn't so happy anymore. There was consternation, rumors, talk of separation, talk of a separate political party and that disturbing feeling again of being suspended from a great height by a single rope. Not even an imaginary safety line, now.

Some people decided not to build that new house. Some people started making plans to abandon the town. Across in Labrador West, the grumbling over the raw deal Labrador has got from the government in St. John's increased.

The big Quebec newspapers pressed their reporters and correspondents now stationed permanently around Labrador for more stories about the anti-Newfoundland, pro-Quebec feeling that was supposed to be sweeping Labrador.

A hard-looking situation. A grim-looking situation. But … LOOK! Up in the sky! It's a bird! It's a plane! It's … it's … the savior of his people, back in the nick of time to straighten everything out.

Yes, my duckies, our one-man traveling circus, our single-handed pacifier, the Great Puppeteer himself. He alone knows the proper strings to pull to calm us down. He alone has all the answers.

He has condescended to make a visitation to the troubled area on Friday, where he will speak to the distressed multitudes. The only living tranquilizer. He will soothe their fevered brows.

Who knows what calming medicine Dr. Smallwood will take to Happy Valley? Oh, there'll be medicine, no doubt about that. The gentleman is not used to making such visitations only to be booed and hissed. He must be sure of the medicine or he wouldn't be going.

Maybe it will be the mass hypnosis trick, the group confounding ploy, used to such great advantage in the past – although it did show some cracks at the late, great education conference.

Or maybe Happy Valley will learn that in place of that imaginary chip mill it will get a great imaginary orange juice plant or a great imaginary nutmeg factory.

He'll think of something. It's his specialty. He's been back from Jamaica for a day or so and has had time to figure something out.

Or was it all figured out long ago? Long before he made the pre-Jamaica announcement did the farseeing O.L.F. have the speech written that he will make in Happy Valley on Friday?

Is this all just another well-organized ploy to make us all realize how lost we'd be without him? Do we detect another plank in the great imaginary Indispensable Leader image?

It would be some comfort to know that in the great audience at the great meeting at Happy Valley on Friday there will be at least one person carrying a big, juicy, over-ripe tomato.

Not a real tomato, of course. Good gracious, no. Not that. But a big, juicy, over-ripe IMAGINARY tomato.

Because, as always, it's the thought that counts. ▓

Richard Nixon: A big bear hug

January 23, 1969   *Joey*

Washington, DC (Special) – Apprehension and concern over US foreign relations continues to mount here today following reports of a curious event during the recent Inauguration festivities of President Richard M. Nixon.

The capital is agog with the news that the new administration may be facing a serious crisis in foreign affairs after word leaked out that President Nixon had greeted the head of a remote and obscure Canadian province with "a big bear hug."

Rumors of the incident have spread like wildfire throughout the civilized world. They are said to have originated in the Canadian province of Newfoundland and-or Labrador.

Reports, yet to be confirmed, say that the government leader of that province, a Mr. Smallwood, claims that the president singled him out at one of the inaugural balls, rushed over to him and gave him "a big bear hug."

Other reports, equally vague yet growing rapidly in credence due to the odd silence of the White House, say that Mr. Smallwood claims the president gave him "a big bear rug."

Repercussions in both world and state capitals have been both rapid and ominous. Senator Wilberforce P. Standhoff (Dem.-Ill.) summed up typical domestic reaction.

"The Republicans socked it to Lyndon Johnson when he picked up one of his beagle dogs by the ears. He never really got the better of that early bad publicity," said Senator Standhoff.

"Now, if it is true that President Nixon gave this foreign potentate Smallwood a big bear rug you may be sure we'll make the most of it. We'll have the conservationists, the anti-vivisectionists, the SPCA and the anti-blood-sports lobby lined up before the week is out."

Senator Standhoff said that if, on the other hand, Mr. Nixon gave Smallwood "a big bear hug," he is almost certain not to get a second term in office.

"Now I ask you. Has Mr. Nixon even given the governor of New York a big bear hug? Has the president ever given the governor of California a big bear hug?"

"Why, to my certain knowledge Mr. Nixon has never even squeezed the elbow of Vice-President Spiro Agnew," the senator continued. "Is this right? Is this proper? Is this American? To give the leader of some obscure foreign territory a big bear hug when there are so many un-hugged but huggable 100 per cent, red-blooded American leaders right here at home?"

In Paris, General Charles de Gaulle has threatened to suspend diplomatic relations with the US unless President Nixon offers him two big bear hugs and a buss on each cheek.

General de Gaulle is said to have been outraged by the incident. "The only show of affection we have ever gotten from the United States," he charged, "is five Xs on a dinner invitation from Jacqueline Kennedy. This is an outrage and an insult to the honor of France."

Observers believe the general will make the most of the affair because of Newfoundland's altercation with the French-speaking province of Quebec over the territory of Labrador.

There was hostile reaction from India, which perhaps recalled the faux pas once made by Vice-President Lyndon Johnson, as he then was.

Mr. Johnson, while on a visit to the Middle East, took a fancy to a Pakistani camel driver and invited him to Washington for a special tour of the White House. India-US relations remained cool for some time as a result.

A lead editorial in *Pravda*, the official Soviet news organ, hints that the Cold War may have taken a turn for the worse. It recalled the 1965 Nixon-Smallwood visit to Moscow when Mr. Smallwood is said to have made some uncouth remarks outside Lenin's tomb. Besides, they claim that the big bear hug is a Russian invention.

Great Britain has also registered dismay. As one foreign office spokesman put it: "Damn sticky situation, don't y'know. If it is Mr. Nixon's idea of protocol to greet the heads of minor and obscure provinces with big bear hugs what will be his manner of greeting the heads of great and once-great nations?

"I think one may say," he continued, "that unless the situation is clarified, H.M. the Queen will not consider a state visit to the United States during Mr. Nixon's term of office."

Canada's Prime Minister Pierre Trudeau has refused comment except to say that he thought it was no business of the press who Mr. Nixon hugged.

The president himself has declined comment until he has conferred with the Joint Chiefs of Staff, the Justice of the Supreme Court and Mrs. Pat Nixon.

However, the White House has flatly denied another rumor also originating in Newfoundland that the president would call a special session of the US Congress to consider renaming the Lincoln Memorial in honor of Mr. Smallwood. ▨

Guy's Encyclopedia of Juvenile Outharbor Delights: The Aviator Cap

January 27, 1969 *Outharbor Delights*

It's a funny thing about *Guy's Encyclopedia of Juvenile Outharbor Delights*. Some like it and some don't. So what's so funny about that? Well, half do and half don't.

The replies that a lot of readers were good enough to return from that "questionnaire" I had in the other week were split 50-50 on it.

Roughly half said: "For pity's sake, knock off those crummy outharbor delights and stick to politics." Which left the other half to declare: "For pity's sake, knock off politics and stick to the things that really matter – outharbor delights."

What can you do? Today, I did have it in mind to knock together something on the "Pied Piper's Music." I lugged out some files and started to look up some of the original and outrageous statements of Premier Whatsisname has used in announcing "new industries."

But I couldn't really work myself up to the proper pitch on that and left it for another day. Those who favor politics will have to be content for today to let the man speak for himself.

Come to look at it, he really doesn't need any help. Might just as well waste an effort in pushing a bus that's running out of control downhill.

Liars! Liars! Filthy liars! All lies! Twisters and distorters! A damnable lie! A damnable, damnable lie! There's not a newspaper in Newfoundland that will say a decent word about Joey!

So said Joey in Corner Brook on Friday to a group of Liberal ladies. All we can hope is that there won't be too much damage when the bus finally crashes at the bottom of the hill.

And now to the things that really matter – for today. We never did get to the end of that passage in the *Encyclopedia* that dealt with Aviator Caps and other wearing apparel for the young outharbor master.

These redoubtable juvenile bonnets, constructed of the toughest pigskin the world has ever seen, were worn universally from late October to the end of May.

The earflaps were lined with an ominous-looking substance which was said to be fur but which felt more like frayed ends of manila rope.

On the brow was a crescent-shaped flap faced with the same kind of fur. This flap was generally fastened up to the main body of the headgear by means of a snap. But in inclement weather or when the wearer participated in the Major Winter Delight of "Heaving Snowballs," this brow flap was let down.

It afforded the wearer the same protection as the sniper shields on First World War German helmets.

The most stylish manner of wearing these pieces of headgear was with the nonchalant air of an RAF pilot. The sniper shield was kept snapped up in place except under the aforementioned circumstances.

The earflaps were let down around the ears but the straps that dangled there from were not fastened under the chin. It was only in weather such as prevailed the night Lucy Grey was lost that the chinstrap was fastened.

Ordinarily, the straps dangled on each side, the pale winter sun glinting from the buckle and snap fastener, a very faint jingle not unlike that produced by the spurs of a western gunfighter, and above it all the leather sheen of that noble pigskin crown.

More secure than a soldier in his pillbox was the outharbor juvenile inside his Aviator Cap – his cranium protected from all the slings and arrows and snowballs with rocks in them that the outside world could hurl against him.

The fur-lined earflaps muffling all the harsh and disagreeable sounds of his environment like the soul-deadening dingle of the schoolbell and the dispiriting cry from the porch door of "Dinnertime!"

In time, the Aviator Cap acquired its own particular smell. Rather like a sweating horse. It was a familiar smell and therefore vastly reassuring. The garment was not washable so that this comforting smell was attained after only a few years of wear.

The whole piece of gear was lined on the inside with a faded purple material of exactly the same color as that used in pauper's caskets. However, it wore just as well as the rest of the cap. Flannel in texture but tungsten steel in durability.

Disadvantages were few. There was one flaw in its design. Hail, sleet, snow, rain, every form of precipitation that fell upon the crown of the cap was funneled down the back of the neck.

And once he was ensconced inside the helmet, the wearer had to be careful of turning his head quickly. If he did so, one of the straps whipped up and the metal buckle gave him a stinging cut in the face.

But these few petty annoyances were greatly outweighed by other advantages of the Aviator Cap. The chinstraps could be chewed. Here was an excellent piece of oral gratification readily available at all times.

The outharbor juvenile could enter into a pensive mood whenever the fancy struck him and chew away on the chinstrap of his cap, deriving both solace and greater insight into the true nature of the universe. Or plan terrible revenge on the gang on the other side of the harbor.

This is but a slight and superficial survey of a few of the aspects of his remarkable headpiece. The topic is deep and space is limited.

It has always surprised me that some advanced student at the university has not written a treatise on the Aviator Cap, elaborating on the sociological, psychological, aesthetic, mercantile and political realms it entails.

If properly done, it should earn him a Ph.D., no sweat. RG

What will Premier Smallwood do when he retires?

January 30, 1969   *Joey*

The whole of Newfoundland and much of the rest of the western world has for months been pondering the BIG question:

What in the world will Premier Smallwood do when he retires?

I'm sure the same question must also have occurred to the premier himself. Perhaps it has caused him to hang on in office until he has decided on a suitable form of post-retirement employment.

But surely, given the many talents and the prodigious energy of this remarkable personage, there should be little trouble or uncertainty on this account.

As for ourselves, after he has done so much for Newfoundland, we must not be narrow and selfish about it. We should be willing now to share him with the rest of the world. How the world would receive such an offer is another matter.

It need not concern us at this time. We are sure that somewhere, either at home or abroad, there's a market for one second-hand premier, slightly dented but in perfect working order from the mouth down.

No need for despondency over how to fill those retirement years. As the nursery rhyme tells us: "The world is so full of such wonderful things, that I'm sure we should all be as happy as kings."

I sincerely trust that what follows will not be interpreted by suspicious and uncharitable persons as an overeagerness to see the day of retirement. I simply mean to be helpful to all concerned.

After some little thought and deliberation I have drawn up a short list of possibilities. It is by no means complete and I am sure that readers can think up many other suggestions of their own.

AFTER RETIREMENT, WHAT? SOME POSSIBILITIES

1. Canadian ambassador to the US. Who else in the whole of the country has been in receipt of a "big bear hug" from President Nixon, as well as being "heart to heart and brain to brain" with Prime Minister Trudeau? He could be the heretofore missing link between those two great nations.

2. Lecturer at the London School of Economics.

3. Manager of a hotel in Panama.

4. Official Entertainer for Canada. A similar function is now being performed on a small scale by an enterprising person in the city of Vancouver, BC. The idea is a good one and could be extended to

the national scene. In times of boredom and depression what better source of light entertainment (mostly unintentional) could be found?

5. Director of development and improvement at Banff National Park, Alberta.

6. Chief accountant at Fort Knox.

7. A cost-benefit deducer for Canadian universities. He could give regular speeches at these institutions. From the reaction of the students it could be determined whether or not our education dollar was being wasted.

8. Internal security adviser to Papa Doc Duvalier in Haiti.

9. Combination stableboy, groom and flag-bearer for Ian Paisley.

10. He could write a book on "Hitler Was a Great Man."

11. Or join the CIA and solve the mysterious case of which little pig went to market and which little pig stayed home.

12. Or rejoin *The Telegram* as a reporter and do a follow-up story on the Alcock and Brown flight.

13. Or give Greg a hand with the Leghorns.

14. Set up a gambling casino on Bell Island.

15. Become full-time chairman of the Doyle memorial trust fund in Liechtenstein.

16. Or director of personnel at Churchill Falls to take charge of French Canadian-Newfoundland relations between the workmen.

17. Apply as sure-fire shark repellent at Montego Bay, Jamaica, during the winter season.

18. Or as a one-man riot-control squad for the United Nations. Wherever trouble arose he could be sent to pour oil on troubled waters. Language would be no barrier. "It isn't what he says, but how he says it," according to one of his cabinet ministers.

But we need not continue. The list of possibilities is endless. Of one thing we may be sure. To whatever line of endeavor Mr. Smallwood turns his talents, he will bring to it the same success that he has brought to the economy of Newfoundland. ▧

There will never be a national park at Bonne Bay

February 7, 1969   *Democracy*

The United States of America is not wealthy enough to do it. But the Smallwood government thinks Newfoundland can afford it.

The US is the richest country in the world, but a long time ago they realized they could not afford to do what the government of Newfoundland seems bent on doing.

America was not rich enough to allow every part of that country to be laid open to mines, lumbering, pulpwood cutting and industrial development. They realized that vast areas of the country were far more valuable if kept as close as possible to what they were when the white men came.

The US has iron-clad laws that preserve these vast tracts of land and defend them against the speculators and "developers." They realize that these areas are worth far more as national parks than as mining areas or pulpwood stands.

Canada has done the same thing. The great national parks of Canada are considered to be among the best in the world and models that other countries seek to copy.

Newfoundland has one of Canada's national parks – Terra Nova. It is tiny compared to some of the others and, apart from long saltwater indrafts, the scenery and features at Terra Nova are rather ordinary and common.

Even so, Terra Nova has already become an area of which all Newfoundlanders are proud. It has provided many jobs and brings much money to the area. Thousands of people are supported, directly and indirectly, by it.

The tourist industry is now Canada's third largest money-maker and before long, it is predicted, it will be the largest. The federal government realizes tourism is especially important in the Atlantic provinces, where other industries are lacking.

For this reason, the government of Canada has expressed an interest in establishing a second national park in Newfoundland. A far larger and more impressive national park than Terra Nova.

The government of Canada selected the only area left in Newfoundland where such a great national park would be possible. It is the area that contains the greatest forests, mountains and scenery on the island of Newfoundland – Bonne Bay.

Those who are experts in these matters say that if properly done the Bonne Bay park could become one of the most spectacular and famous national parks in Canada.

This may surprise many Newfoundlanders who are used to the rocky and often barren east coast and who have never seen Bonne Bay. But it is a fact that the area has been compared to the best of Scotland or Norway, or even parts of the Rocky Mountains.

All the millions of city dwellers in eastern Canada and the US would have to travel nearly across a continent to find such a place as Newfoundland's Bonne Bay. Yet they are only a few hours away from Bonne Bay by air.

The Canadian government realizes this and had already taken the first steps toward establishing this great national park at Bonne Bay. But the Smallwood government has stopped it dead in its tracks.

The Smallwood government seems clearly determined that there will never be a national park at Bonne Bay. Why? When the government of Canada is in favor of it? When parks experts, naturalists, biologists, tourist officials are in favor of it?

When the people of the area themselves see the great value of it and want it? The only excuse for stopping the park the government has given so far is a cock-and-bull story about "silica."

Mines and Resources Minister W.R. Callahan has come out with a vague and half-hearted statement that there's silica in the area; therefore it can't be turned over for a national park.

It has been shown conclusively by now that this talk about silica is nothing less than a half-truth and a bluff. It is merely an excuse to stop the federal government from going ahead with a national park at Bonne Bay.

If this silica business is only a bluff, what other reason can the Smallwood government have for barring a national park? Since we are not told the whole truth, we can only speculate.

Bowater's and Lundrigan's want to strip the Bonne Bay hills of timber? Maybe. Both companies are great friends of the Smallwood government.

But there's an even more likely prospect. An even closer friend of the Smallwood government, John C. Doyle, wants to build a chip mill at Stephenville.

Or at least the latest proposed location for this proposed mill is Stephenville. Once it was Labrador. The wood for this proposed mill is to come from the middle of Labrador, we hear.

But Bonne Bay is a lot closer to Stephenville than Labrador. Could this be the real reason the Smallwood government is trying to wreck the Bonne Bay national park plans?

Can it be that Mr. Doyle, who already owns so much of Labrador and Newfoundland, is the real reason? Is this area, the only chance we have of getting such a park, being sacrificed to Smallwood's buddy, the wheeler-dealer bail-jumper, whose first and foremost aim is to make more millions for himself?

If you believe that a great national park at Bonne Bay would be worth far more to Newfoundland, please write to Honorable W.R. Callahan, Minister of Mines and Resources, Confederation Building, St. John's.

Many people have already written Mr. Callahan. Will it make any difference? If it doesn't, what hope is there for us? RG

You can smell the jungle

Culture and History

I've never been much of a fan of ice hockey – perhaps because I got off to a bad start. Seeing my second real game at the St. John's Stadium on Saturday didn't help, I'm afraid.

The first real game I ever saw (on an indoor rink as opposed to a pond) was about 14 years ago on Bell Island. This is no reflection on your district, Stevie boy. It could have happened anywhere.

I forget who played against Bell Island, but anyway the visitors won. To get back to the dressing rooms the winning visitors had to walk through the spectators.

By the time these unfortunates had run the gauntlet, they had been struck in the face by drunks; little high school girls, their fingers crooked into talons, tried to claw their eyes out; strings of spittle hung from their uniforms and faces.

Hockey or any other spectator sport (Ole!) leaves me with the vague and uneasy feeling there's more than a touch of mob psychosis involved. I get the creeps from the same phenomena in politics and religion.

An unsavory side of the naked ape is brought out. You can smell the jungle. It may be stretching a point, but there seems to be a connection between the group chants at a religious service, at a political rally or at a sports event.

The individual disappears into the mass. The crowd roars with one voice. Maybe a Freudian trauma makes some of us overly sensitive on this point. From the radios above our cradles came the mass roar "Seig Heil!" and from our parents came a sense of fear.

Enough two-cent psychology. St. John's Stadium. They say sport is a substitute for war. "Britain's wars were won on the playing fields of Eton," and all that. How are we fixed for warriors in Newfoundland?

Judging by some of the spectators at the stadium we could get together an extremely potent and aggressive force. The only problem would be to keep these citizen-soldiers from biting chunks out of each other while they waited to grapple with the enemy.

But I must try, as always, to be fair. This awesome ferocity seemed most intense in the seats nearest the boards and appeared to decrease in proportion to the distance from the ice. High up in the stands there was more emotional detachment.

Buchans and St. John's were playing. The place was blocked. By direction rather than choice I found myself jammed into the benches near the boards. A Tokyo subway train. A sharp set of knees in the kidneys.

A bunch of drunks came in bundled up in parkas and wearing the blissful smiles of pigs in clover. Before long there was a falling out among them. One of them was kicked out of the nest and came tumbling down around our ears.

Spectator sports seem to provide instant "they." The other side. In sports, as well as in politics and religion, there's always got to be "we and they." I didn't notice any touch of religion at the stadium, but there was a dash of politics.

"Ya damn baymen! Joey's boys! Joey's boys! Why can't you get a goal, baymen? You're used to handling nets. Ya !*!?** fishmongers." All directed, of course, at the well-known fishing community of Buchans. Or was it?

The more agitated of the spectators screamed and roared an endless string of obscenities at the players who never gave the slightest indication they heard them. Tremendous intensity in the screams of some of the spectators.

Surely they weren't roaring at players in a game of hockey, but at savage, inhuman demons who were raping their daughters and mutilating their sons. Who were burning down their houses in front of their eyes and torturing their grandmothers.

The rhythmic clapping. A few fans start and the multitude takes it up until the stadium echoes. Two long and three short is the message of the tom-toms. Whack. Whack. Wak-wak-wak.

But suddenly the puck was launched off the ice and smashed into the crowded benches only a few feet away from me.

There was a horrified murmur as a half-dazed spectator was helped over the boards and across the ice to the first aid station. His face and chest were a sheet of blood and it looked as if his eye was knocked out.

A second injured spectator half-stumbled through the tightly packed crowd toward the exit, his lip split and his teeth loosened.

The murmur subsided and the game went on. There were spatters of blood on the ice from the injured men. There was a deep and hopeful growl nearby from the throat of one of the fanatics whose daughters were being raped: "Arrrhhhh! A bit of blood on the ice! That should touch it off!"

But although there were a few minor scraps among the players I'm afraid he didn't get his kicks. It wasn't one of your better 18 or '0-stitch games.

It'll be another 14 years before I go to my next hockey game. Even if ... no, especially if, by some great quirk of fate, the Arnold's Cove "Catastrophes" were pitted against the St. John's "Capitals."

In that event, wouldn't I find myself sitting in "our" section roaring obscenities at the pinky boys, the stupid got-a-nickel-mister townies, the "gutter scum?"

Yes. I think if the Catastrophes and the Caps ever meet, I'll play chicken and stay home. It could be too demoralizing to get such a close-up look at the naked ape in the mirror. ▧

Pip pip and all that, y'know

The Throne Speech. Her Majesty's representative read it. This is part of his job. But it was written by Joey, who has written them all for the past 20 years.

The Throne Speech didn't sound much like Joey. You'd hardly say, at first glance, that it was Joey's handiwork. No baby talk. Like this. But it is surprising how baby talk can be dressed up for show.

We all know how Joey talks. Sound and fury. Chop. Chop. Chop. Repeat. Repeat. Repeat. When we read the Throne Speech, we see how Joey writes – when he tries to be grand and imposing.

When he wants us to believe the whole thing was scratched out on parchment with a goose feather. When he wants us to believe that something of the tradition of the British Empah is behind it. Grand and imposing.

The effect is ludicrous. Just like when you use grand and pompous language when you want to make something look comical. Or like the young outport girl (or St. John's girl, for that matter) just back from a month in Boston.

Pompous, twisted up, out-of-date phrases. Sham-traditional. Ye olde dignity. Pseudo-British colonial office. It all fits in with Joey's childish delight in rubbing shoulders with the nobs.

A stab at apeing Churchillian prose. An attempt to pass as a squire to the manor born. There's one curiosity of speech that always turns up even when he's talking baby talk.

"The government ARE considering ..." By Jove. By Gad. Pip pip and all that, y'know.

It turned up all over the Throne Speech. "My Government believe ..." "The Company are considering ..." Jolly good. But the sham falls down on page one where we read, "The Government of this province was represented ..." WAS represented? The "grand" lady is caught drinking from the fingerbowl.

The document is riddled with pompous and curious phrases. Hot air. Sentences that mean absolutely nothing. Stuffing. Hot air is common to Joey's writing and to Joey's speech.

But there's a difference. When he's talking, he can rant and roar and swing his arms about and put on a one-man performance that draws some people's attention away from the fact that it IS hot air.

Some people are so bemused by how he says it that they forget to listen to what he says. University students are no exception. That has always been three-parts of his secret.

He hasn't got the advantage of these tricks when he's writing. He can't resort to all those distracting bellows and whispers or to whipping up his clothes to show his belly button.

So when he writes, he tries to muffle the hot air in a lot of pseudo-dignified phrases and archaic gobbledegook. It's a poor camouflage job. He's better on the jaw than he is on the pen.

If you had to rewrite that Throne Speech as if you were sending it across Canada as a paid telegram, you could boil it down to a single page. It would still be hot air, but refined hot air without the phoney-grand gibberish. Baloney is still baloney no matter how thin you slice it.

It was a remarkably empty Throne Speech – even for Joey. Without the stuffing it could have been read in five minutes. As it was, the members hardly had time to warm up their seats before they had to stand again for the departure of His Honor.

It's hard to single out specific examples of this gobbledegook stuffing because the whole thing is riddled with it. On page one we read about a "conference held in Ottawa a forthnight ago."

Forthnight? We'll put the spelling mistake down to a printer error but what was wrong with saying "two weeks ago?" Fortnight is a word you'd use if you wanted to be quaint and comical. Ye gads. Who wrote this? Dr. Samuel Johnson?

"This is the part of wisdom for Newfoundland, and I believe that all thoughtful people will agree and approve."

"My Ministers hope that these reports and recommendations may be received in time to permit of careful consideration …"

"They engaged in very many meetings and conferences, and it is therefore a matter of keenest possible pleasure to them …" Hmmm. Did they all have mental orgasms?

"In Stephenville, the dwelling-house construction factory is getting well into its stride …" Up the Stephenville dwelling-house construction factory!

Nit picking? OK. But just one more before quoting a more juicy example of flim-flam. "My Ministers are very much disinclined to have Newfoundland become a permanent supplicant at the door of the Government of the nation …" Beautiful. Equal to the best of *The Pilgrim's Progress*.

Now try this on for size: "My Government believe that there does NOT as yet exist in this Province sufficient taxable capacity to enable the public needs of the people to be served by tax revenue gathered within the boundaries of the Province."

What the devil does that little prose gem mean? It means: "If we try to squeeze much more taxes out of Newfoundlanders, we'll be buried so deep in the next election we'll greet the resurrection morning in Japan." That's what it means.

And so it goes. The biggest bit of pompous over-stuffed malarkey it has ever been our pleasure to read. But if he wrote like that and meant it to be funny, it wouldn't seem funny at all. Funny about that. █

This is a crusade?

Grandmother used to tell us that if we screwed up our mouths at someone and the wind changed, then our faces would stay that way.

If the wind had veered suddenly on Friday afternoon, Joey might have been left with a very unlovely expression on his face. He could have been caught with his mouth turned up in a perpetual sneer.

They were talking in the House about this Bonne Bay park business. Willy Callahan declared that "in spite of an attempt to have people write to me complaining about (the delay over) the park I have received only 86 letters."

"This is a vast crusade?" sneered Joey.

We'll take it for granted that Willy Nilly received "only 86 letters." He's a Minister of the Crown, and has the title "Honorable" in front of his name. We won't follow his own example over the weekend and bandy the word "liar" about.

We'll say that Honorable Willy received "only 86 letters." But is this something to sneer at?

The people who wrote those letters thought they were just as good Newfoundlanders as Joey is. And just as good as Will Callahan, one of his more supercilious jumping jacks.

They were sincere in what they did. They believed they have just as much right to say what should be done with their own province as Joey or Callahan have. They took the trouble to write a letter about it.

A few of them sent along copies of their letters to me. There was no abuse or ballyrag in the ones I saw. I think Mr. Callahan got his fair share when he got "only 86 letters."

It takes a pretty big piece of controversy to stir individuals to write even a dozen letters on the same topic to the press. For every one who writes there are a hundred who would have written but "didn't get around to it."

Joey didn't curl his lip at me when he sneered at the "vast crusade." He mocked the sincere Newfoundlanders who did take the trouble to write Will Callahan. But they're in high company. Joey also sneered at Pippy, Lundrigan, Roberts, Martin, Moores, Justice Higgins, O'Dea, Mifflin, and others who expressed their opinion on what should be done with Newfoundland.

If those big shots prefer to ignore Joey's abuse, OK. If he wants to belch his hot air at me, splendid. I'm in the hot air business, too, and will always endeavor to bloody well give him as good as he sends.

The difference between my hot air and Joey's is that if you don't like mine you can always pass on to the other comic pages, but every puff from Joey costs you dearly.

He can abuse the big shots and sneer at me to his heart's content. But when he stoops to abusing and sneering at school kids (at least half a dozen Grade Eights from the west coast wrote letters), he's stooping pretty low.

The part of wisdom for you now, sir, is to keep a civil tongue in your head. It won't cost you a cent extra. The people have gagged on your 20-year diet of bull and baloney. Don't try to stuff abuse and sauce down their throats now.

Where deceit and malarkey have failed, what hope of success is there for lip and bluster? Who's afraid of the big bad wolf now?

Afraid! Newfoundlanders haven't got the sense to be afraid of the likes of him. They're angry. Angry and ashamed of having been duped and made fools of for so long.

Ashamed of a government's philosophy that always puts the quick dollar and the sure vote ahead of everything else.

The time and the tide have run out. Newfoundlanders are ashamed of having been taken for fools for so long. Of having left Newfoundland entirely in the hands of a person the size of whose head is exceeded only by the size of his kisser.

Joey calls me his third greatest asset. Me and my miserable little efforts here in this corner of *The Telegram*. Maybe he takes me for some kind of a safety valve through which some of the hot air and shame and anger of Newfoundland escapes.

Perhaps he figures that people read this trash and feel just as relieved as if they had said it themselves. One shrill and off-key whistle is better than one big explosion.

Or maybe he thinks that I make such an ass of myself in railing against him that others will be discouraged from doing likewise.

What sorry nonsense! There's a hundred times more shame and anger on a single stage head in Newfoundland today than could ever get vent through my little tin whistle. The explosion will come.

And if I make too big a fool of myself … does one squashed mosquito mean there are no more in the woods?

The "vast crusade." Never mind, youngsters. That sneer – considering where it came from – was one of the biggest compliments you will ever get in your lives supposing you live to be 100.

Something did get Joey off his butt and sent him rushing off to Woody Point, Bonne Bay, didn't it? His two little boys, Willy and Gerry, wouldn't face it alone. They had to take Big Daddy with them.

Whatever sent him to Bonne Bay, I wonder? He usually prefers the climate in Jamaica or Panama at this time of year. Could it be that you helped send him to Bonne Bay?

Yes. And please God and for the sake of Newfoundland you'll soon be able to help send him somewhere else. ▩

One of the finest collections
of apes in captivity

March 4, 1969   *Democracy*

Far be it from me to criticize our Tourist Development Office. In general, it does its job very well. So it comes as a great surprise to find that it is completely ignoring what must be the most unique tourist attraction in Newfoundland.

In fact, so little publicity has been given this remarkable attraction that it was only by chance that I learned about it.

This untapped gold mine of tourist revenue is known as the Newfoundland Provincial Zoological Gardens and was established through public subscription.

On a recent visit to the Gardens, which occupy some three acres on a site near Rocky Harbour, Bonne Bay, we spoke with the zoo curator, Uncle Elazer Bishop, a grizzled and wise old gentleman, and learned many interesting facts about it.

"What is unique about the Newfoundland Provincial Zoological Gardens," said Uncle Elazer, "is that we have here what the experts admit to be one of the finest collection of naked apes in captivity.

"Other zoos have their chimpanees, urangutans and baboons," continued Uncle Elazer, "but none of them as yet display the naked ape or Homo Sapiens, as it is known to science."

We discovered something of the interesting history behind the establishment of the unique Zoological Gardens from the doughty curator. The zoo was set up some years back – in August 1970.

At one time it was thought that a great national park would be established in the district. The federal government was prepared to set up and manage such a park if Newfoundland would give it the necessary land.

But for some strange reason – many wild, weird and ridiculous excuses were given – the provincial government wouldn't accept the offer from Ottawa.

At first, the federal parks board requested enough land to make a first-class national park. But the provincial government wouldn't have it. It refused to turn over any land that had trees on it.

All it was prepared to turn over for a park was an area of 480 square miles – about 1/90 of the area of the island and equal to one-third of one per cent of Bowater's cutting rights. It consisted mostly of spectacular but barren mountains facing the sea.

It was a puny area compared to the 17,300 square miles of the Wood Buffalo National Park in Alberta, or even the 4,200 square miles of Jasper National Park, or the 1,500 square miles of Prince Albert National Park in Saskatchewan.

But the National Parks Board said it would take even this much and do the best it could with it. Still the provincial government persisted in flogging its strange and mysterious policy. Another stumbling block to the park appeared.

Silica! The provincial government declared it was going to open an eight-square-mile rock quarry directly across the only possible road into the proposed park area. A quarry that might, at best, employ 15 men.

This proved the last straw for the National Parks Board. It threw up its hands in disgust and abandoned the idea altogether. Newfoundland lost its chance of getting a national park.

The province also lost the most beautiful and attractive scenery to be found in eastern North America. You can see what has become of it today. The sides of the mountains have been stripped and the valleys have been gouged by bulldozed woods roads.

You drive through miles of tree stumps and through a huge unsightly gravel pit that has long since been abandoned. The wind howls continually among the barren hills and a few crows and ravens scrounge around deserted garbage dumps.

Anyway, to make a long story short (said Uncle Elazer), the people of the west coast and indeed of the whole of Newfoundland were outraged and heartbroken when they saw that their heritage and birthright had been squandered and destroyed forever.

"They got together and determined to salvage what they could and make the best out of what was left. It wasn't much. They purchased these three acres you see here from the owner, Mr. J. Doyle, cleared off the tree stumps and set up the Newfoundland Provincial Zoological Gardens."

They couldn't afford to stock the zoo with the usual chimpanzees or crocodiles, but they were able to trap many fine specimens of the naked ape which at that time ran wild in Newfoundland, causing much damage. In fact they once controlled the whole province – preposterous as it may seem.

"Here we have them. This is one of our most interesting exhibits. His scientific name is Dupus Supercilious Callahanus. We call him 'Willy' for short. He sleeps most of the time in the corner.

"Quite different from when he was running wild," chuckled Uncle Elazer. "His job used to be to set up some sort of diversion or smokescreen for the rest of the pack. Ah, he was full of tricks.

"Here's a petty but typical instance of how he always twisted and turned and laid down red herrings. Once, when he was asked how many people had written, pleading for the Bonne Bay Park, he declared that 'only 86 letters' had been received.

"The truth was that one of those letters alone (from Corner Brook) was signed by 25 people. And another letter from Gander contained a similar number of signatures. Ah, yes. Getting the full truth or a straight answer on anything was like squeezing water from a stone."

There were many more intriguing exhibits – including the most interesting of all, the Only Living Fraud, whose antics delighted children of all ages – but space does not permit a description of them all.

It is enough to say that if the Tourist Office does its duty and advertises the Newfoundland Provincial Zoological Gardens, tourists by the thousands will flock to the Bonne Bay area to view the many marvelous specimens contained therein. 🆁🅶

An infant megalomaniac

March 6, 1969   *News and Propaganda*

Hoooo, boy! It's almost a risk to go in to the House (of Assembly) these days. You don't know what minute you might get a custard pie in the face.

Premier Smallwood ran off a superb comic skit yesterday wherein he played the role of an infant megalomaniac. He rattled the bars of his playpen and shook his rattlebox at the bestial, partisan and biased world outside.

It was definitely the finest bit of entertainment provided in the House so far this session. We hope the trend continues. If our loyal and humble servants can't give us sane and sensible debate, the least we can expect is a jolly good show to brighten up the hungry month of March.

Yesterday's performance was better than "Red Skelton," "Dr. Findlay's Case Book," and "The Beverly Hillbillies" combined. A regular "Rowe and Smallwood Laff-in." All it lacked was underarm deodorant commercials during the intermission.

As usual, Premier Smallwood got all the best lines – the real rib-ticklers. He carried the running gag. It's an old joke but still good for a laugh: "The *Newfoundland Bulletin* is unbiased, non-partisan, unslanted and carries all the news you need to know."

The premier really laid 'em in the aisles when he quipped that the *Newfoundland Bulletin* is the only real newspaper in Newfoundland. He followed this up with a gut-busting one-liner: "Other newspapers aren't fit to read because they don't follow the *Bulletin*'s example of giving only the straight and pure facts."

Taking this piece of merry nonsense to the ultimate, we can imagine what the other news media in Newfoundland might be like if they took (or were forced to take) the premier's little joke seriously:

THE DAILY NEWS: A page one headline – "Unemployment can be fun, says father of 12." A large front-page picture: "Miss Sylvia Knucks, a grand old Newfoundland lady who celebrates her 27th birthday tomorrow, says she'll be buried with a photograph of Premier Smallwood clasped to her bosom, shown here (1-r), because I think he's really super-dooper and the greatest!"

Letters to the Editor – "Dear Sir, It's time something was done about this great dirty Tory conspiracy. I am a widow with small children and it's getting so bad that I have to get up three or four times a night and search under the bed with a flashlight.

"They're everywhere, sir. Spreading poison. Assassinating characters. Telling lies and trash. Criticizing our premier. They must be stopped before it's too late!"

Wayfarer – "It never ceases to amaze me how quickly the present generation has forgotten the terrible poverty, animalistic degradation, et al. of but a few years ago as compared with the comfort, stability, high standards of living, education, health and welfare now enjoyed under the present ..."

THE CANADIAN BROADCASTING CORPORATION: "Ladies and gentlemen, tonight 'Here and Now' takes a look at the fishery. Our special guest is Premier J.R. Smallwood.

"We'll have many thought-provoking and illuminating questions and I'm sure a lively and fast-moving discussion will result. Here's our panel ... on my left: Ed Roberts, Dr. F.W. Rowe, Aidan Maloney, and our special guest expert tonight, Mrs. J.R. Smallwood. I'm your moderator, Bill Callahan.

"Here is the CBC news. Premier Smallwood, in a logical and well-reasoned announcement, today expressed grave concern over the obviously growing tide of poison, character assassination, trash and dirty Tory lies being spread in a great foul, dirty conspiracy that has its tentacles in every corner of the province.

"The leader of the dirty Tories replied to the premier's charges in a press release today. But our news time is up. We'll have the leader of the dirty Tories' comment in our 3:30 a.m. news bulletin sometime early next summer.

"And now the weather. Premier Smallwood announced today that the low pressure system stationed just east of St. Anthony for the past several days will move off slowly during the night and ..."

THE NEWFOUNDLAND HERALD: Front-page headline – "Smallwood's friends swamp Crosbie supporters."

CJON RADIO: "And now, our first caller of the day. Hello. Open Line.

"Hello, Mr. V. I think 'tis something shockin'. Yes, I do. I t'ink 'tis something scandalous. That what the premier told us yesterday. Something really should be done about it. The newspapers dumpin' poison into Windsor Lake!"

"And now the news. Premier Smallwood called a special press conference today to announce that he has received a letter of warm congratulations from the editor of *Pravda*, the official government newspaper in Russia."

THE EVENING TELEGRAM (The Premier's Paper): Front-page headlines – "Government with a heart announces Neary to run on Bell Island again." "Figures prove Smallwood government most wonderful in the world." "Still another success for Smallwood government – burning rectal itch relieved in minutes."

Editorial – "Don't go, Joe." "Of Smallwood and Statues." "Who Owes Our Everlasting Gratitude?"

Ray Guy – "Great news, my duckies! Premier Smallwood struck still another blow for truth and common sense today when he defended to the hilt that most estimable example of journalistic excellence – the *Newfoundland Bulletin*. Oh, yes!

"Did us all proper credit, did dear Mr. Smallwood. Yes, he did. The good old *Bulletin*. Fair, unbiased, non-partisan, factual – the only real newspaper in Newfoundland and … and …"

(EDITOR'S NOTE: Sorry folks, but we're afraid Mr. Guy has just lost his cool again. A moment ago he started to turn green around the gills and was then seized with the dry heaves. Something he wrote must have disagreed with him. With the help of the proper physic we hope to have him revived and on deck again tomorrow.) █

Aunt Cissy: The devil has come
for me at last!

March 11, 1969   *Aunt Cissy*

They've calmed down for a few days in there at Mrs. Dilly's Hilltop Nursery School, so we're left to our own resources. If we want a bit of nonsense to tide us over until classes resume, we'll have to look elsewhere for it.

There's not much doing besides, unless you want to hash over red herring, national parks, centralization, and the high cost of peppermint knobs. Dull as dishwater.

I was tired of knocking around the office. For some strange reason, the newsroom personnel seemed to be more interested in work than in the finer things of life. Spring fever must be overtaking them.

So I got into my horseless carriage and drove out the Trans-Canada Highway. I found myself in the vicinity of Witless Bay Line when inspiration seized me.

Why not take a dodge down the Line, I said to myself, and pass a few hours with that grand old lady of the gowiddy, Aunt Cissy Roach, or "Aunt Cissy" as she is commonly known to her host of enemies.

She lives a far piece down the Line. Even then, you have to leave your conveyance and traipse 13 miles in over the barrens to get to the dear old soul's domicile, she being a recluse.

It is always a pleasure to visit Aunt Cissy. It reassures you to know that no matter how foul and filthy the weather, or how grim and gruesome the times, she will always make things look brighter. By comparison.

I spotted her from a distance, standing in front of her humble cottage amid the boulders and bog spruce and shaking a gnarled fist toward the low overcast. I came upon her unawares.

"Be God, the divil is come for me at last!" she croaked at my approach. "Stand back, or I'll cleave your head to match your hocks! You won't take Aunt Cissy without a scuffle."

Since she was swinging a double-bit axe around her aged head at the time and is extremely nimble for one so advanced in years, it took a fancy bit of footwork on my part to avoid being decapitated.

"Aunt Cissy!" I cried. "Don't you recognize your darling boy come to pass the time with you for a few hours? It is I. Be not afraid. Can't you see the resemblance to my poor grandfather?"

It took some persuasion to convince her, but finally the dear old matriarch, one of the last of the fighting Newfoundlanders, calmed down.

"Oh, 'tis you, is it, batter face? I'd sooner see the divil any day. Come in. Come in. Sit down. Sit down. And keep your hands to yourself. I might be small but I'm wiry.

"What in the name of zounds have ye got on your face? I seen better lookin' armpits. Call that a chin whisker! Poor Arnprior – he crossed over in '21 – had one right down to his quarters. Caught it in his fly one day, tried to straighten up quick, broke his neck. He's in a better world now. What did ye bring? Get it out. Get it out."

While there are certain hazards entailed in visiting the dear old lady at any time, it is sheer folly to turn up at her "pied de terre" without an appropriate offering. I had come prepared with four bottles of the best the BLC has to offer – Eau de Steeped Toad Guts.

Aunt Cissy eagerly accepted our libation and tossed down a glutch. She gagged ever so slightly and a look of disgust crossed her remarkable features.

"Curse I the flamin' dyin' sleeveens!" she exclaimed. "Keelhaul 'em and part 'em from their testimonials. Waterin' it down again! Never mind. By the taste of it, the miserable pig's knucks'll be dead within a 12-month of diabetes."

For all her complaining she took another draught and even sprinkled a drop off her finger into the five-pound tea crate wherein reposed her pet carey-chicken, Sunny Jim.

"I suppose ye come here to pick my brains again, ye lazy slump of a no-good layabout. Why don't ye do your own work for a change? I know you. Ye don't come out here for the pleasure of me company. No. Ye come here for information. Well, damn the little you're goin' to get. This is one of me off days."

Despite her rather gruff exterior, the doughty old soul is as cheerful and as harmless as a cornered lynx, except when her blood is stirred. Still, if you catch her on one of her off days, you have to pick your steps, as it were.

"Tell us, Aunt Cissy." I said, "what do you make of all the goings on these days, at all, at all. Did you ever see the like back in your time? Whatever do you think is going to become of us?"

"Times!" she snorted loudly and commenced an assault on her second quart of BLC special. "Don't you prate to me about times. My time! This is my time! Yesterday was my time and, be God, we'll see yet if tomorrow isn't my time, too!"

I realized straight away that I had gotten off on the wrong foot with the dear soul and decided it was useless to pursue the conversation further. I occupied the rest of my visit in admiring the many curiosities and objets d'art scattered about her humble abode.

There were the original scalp-locks, for example, from the unfortunate polls of some of Peter Easton's crew; the hand-tinted likeness of Kaiser Bill over the Waterloo; the identical dagger employed by the late, great Sarah Bernhardt in her depiction of Lady Macbeth.

I left Aunt Cissy's in an extremely buoyant frame of mind. Although it had been one of her off days and I had secured nothing from her by way of information, the memory of her swinging a double-bit axe cheered me inordinately.

I'll sleep a little better at night knowing that she's still out there somewhere on the Witless Bay Line. A strange thing about that. ▨

How much do the old owe the young?

March 13, 1969 *Resettlement and Rural Life*

The government is willing to sacrifice the old for the sake of the young.

Speaking about centralization, Bill Rowe, the 27-year-old minister of community and social development, admits that the mental and emotional pain it causes those of 50 and over is great ... but necessary.

To be fair to young Mr. Rowe, he did not put it so bluntly or as brutally as that. I don't mean to suggest that he is without the usual human allowance of pity and compassion. But he has stated the cold and clinical "facts of life" as he sees them and the statement is frightening.

Mr. Rowe says that because of centralization, the older generations suffer from being torn away from their old homes and friends. But he says they must be prepared to endure this so that the younger generation may benefit from better schools, hospitals and a chance of jobs in the new "growth centers."

How much does one generation owe another? It is sometimes argued that parents willingly submit themselves to a lifetime of cheerless drudgery for the sake of their children. Or that in time of war the young are ready to suffer and die for the sake of the old who stay at home.

Perhaps this has been a general rule. In time of war the young get the dirty end of the stick. In time of peace it is the old who come off second best. Must the see-saw continue?

No one seems to be able to figure out quite what we have now – war or peace. But one thing is sure, the emphasis is overwhelmingly on the young. "The young are people, too," is one of the slogans. We're "building a brighter future for our children." Oh yeah?

Perhaps the great emphasis now is placed on the young because everyone seems to be deathly scared of old age. Not death, but old age. And perhaps old age has been made a frightening prospect by society and through governments.

Efficiency. Economy. Precision. Statistics. Statistics are the great passion of governments these days. People are complex, cranky, slow to change, complicated, diverse. Statistics are uniform, precise, efficient, easy to handle.

Because society has become so big and unwieldy, governments can no longer cope easily with people. People are not easy to handle. So governments tend to take the easy way out and treat people as if they were statistics.

There is a great fear and abhorrence in government of what they term "emotionalism." Too often this derogatory word is applied not to an "ism," but to plain emotion. No doubt people would be more manageable and efficient if they had no emotions. Like computers.

Centralization. One of the first stories I heard about it concerned a grandmother of 80, long black dress and her hair in a "bun," who was caught up in the great exodus from the islands.

During the last week as the family was busy packing boxes and moving furniture down to the wharf, she showed little signs of distress. But when the moment finally came and she was led out the door, she suddenly seized hold of the door frame. It took a strong man to pry her old hands loose. How much do the old owe to the young?

In the new "growth centers," I have seen people, not really old, but men of from 50 to 75, sitting around in a daze, dispirited, afraid and without hope. I have seen it. I know of not a few who have been driven to the brink of mental breakdown and over. They've paid their debt to the young generation – a living death.

We see this to a lesser extent in the case where an old outport couple has no choice but to go and live with a married son or daughter "in town." It is certainly not true in all cases and may not even be the general rule.

But what emotional and mental distress some of these old people must suffer. They greatly miss what they have been used to all their lives. Puttering in a garden, yarning with old friends, cutting up a bit of wood. It is late in life to have to learn new ways.

In the city they often find nothing to do but to walk down the street for the paper or to watch television. Perhaps their married children live in "modern houses."

These are the little pastel boxes built to contain an absolute maximum of two young adults and 1.4 children. Even a limited "modern" family is a tight fit in one of those. They're confined together to tread on each other's toes and grate on each other's nerves. Stuff in one or two grandparents and what do you have?

In the "modern" society, the size of the family must be limited. There's no room for the big house of the outport or the city that had room enough for parents, children, grandparents, a maiden aunt, an adopted merrybegot, a retarded cousin and God knows who else. There were enough chores to be done to make everyone, from the youngest to the oldest, feel useful.

There is hardly enough room in these efficient modern, economical, logical pastel boxes – hells of our own manufacture – for a family of 3.4 people to stay sane. Grandparents? Special buildings must be provided for them.

So the old are segregated to special buildings. Moved to great institutional waiting houses where they "wait for their time to come." Again, I'm not suggesting that old people can't be happy and content in these homes. They're certainly better off there than in the little pastel psycho-boxes.

But it is often an unnatural and depressing end. To see nothing but old faces around you. Not to hear children crying and laughing. To come down to the dining hall in the morning and see another empty chair.

This is the "modern" way of life. This is progress and efficiency. This is also part of the debt the old are called on to pay to the young.

Uncle John was a small and jolly man, always cheerful. He was the best storyteller or teller of "yarns" around. People would sit for hours and listen to his great old stories.

When he became very old, his memory started to go and he became very deaf. But he still used to come over to our store just about every day and tell his yarns to anyone who would listen.

We had heard them all before. We knew them all by heart. You couldn't talk to him because he was deaf. But there was always someone who would volunteer to sit beside him for half an hour or so and listen and nod and look interested. Always someone. He kept it up until the week before he died.

Perhaps we listened out of respect for his old age. Maybe out of gratitude for all the pleasure and merriment he had given.

But I think we listened because it made us feel good, in a way, to be making Uncle John happy. It was a fair and comforting exchange. What else is there between people?

I'm only two years older than young Mr. Rowe, but sometimes I think I can see what it could be like to be 80. I'm old enough to know that emotionalism can be a dangerous thing.

But to attempt to disregard or ignore emotion completely is to admit that you are ashamed of being human. There is only one terrible course open after that. To be anti-human. ▨

Then along comes Harry Hibbs

March 25, 1969   *Culture and History*

When they weary of standing around with their hands in their pockets whining that "there's nothing to do," young Newfoundlanders sometimes bestir themselves to take part in those new inharbor and outharbor juvenile delights – hockey and guitar playing.

No, no, no, my pretty. I'm not talking about YOU. Even if you do play hockey or the guitar you have no cause to think I'm picking on you. I'm speaking in general terms. I'm talking about "them," not you. The average mass. That's not you. You're OK, Jack.

Hockey and guitar playing have lately swept the province's acne generation. Youngsters not even in their teens struggle toward the nearest rink laden down with $100 or more of the requisite gear.

The young have also taken to playing guitars and drums. Youthful rock and roll groups have sprung up with surprising rapidity. The amount of money spent on this type of gear is also amazing.

It is dangerous to read too much into any such trends or to stretch the implications to the limit. But if you want to do that, who am I to stop you?

If you wanted to see a connection between these new, imported fads and the whole Newfoundland situation, go ahead. If you choose to suggest that instead of building on the distinctive foundation we had scrapped it all and tried to import and impose a new one, that's your choice.

Far be it from me to bring "great new industries" – centralization, the mania to create some sort of southern Ontario society on these fog-bound rocks, the delusions of building a Pittsburgh on the bog – into it. As always, I'll stick to the facts.

Keeping it down to the fad field we see that there are many instances where pale imitations have replaced the genuine article. Student unrest. A big thing elsewhere. The news reached our own campus and some decided that it would be up to date to have a bit of unrest.

Every one so far has been a comedy of errors. Ludicrous. Because they were not spontaneous. They were merely copies that had some of the external appearance of the real thing but no content. Nobody stopped to see what there was on our own campus to be restless about.

Just as with the local "hippies." More pale imitations. Copied from the campuses of Los Angeles and the streets of San Francisco where they might have had some spontaneity to begin with. Not here. String on a few beads, rip a pair of old jeans in the proper places – Presto. Instant pseudo-hippy.

To get back to young Newfoundland guitar players. They're serious and intense about it, no doubt. They feel they're being creative and original and getting in on a great universal trend in music.

There are little "bands" all over the place with outlandish names that are copies because they are all splitting a gasket to be the same thing – "different." If there's any difference it's all the same.

They're putting themselves to an unnecessary strain. One way they could be different is to look around them and draw on the differences in their immediate vicinity. The differences in the Newfoundland foundation that so many are so eager to scrap.

Still, hundreds and perhaps thousands of young Newfoundland guitar players are feverishly copying groups they see on television which, in turn, are pale imitations of the Beatles. They tend toward long hair and, in various Newfoundland accents, remember to sprinkle their conversations with "Like, man …"

Then along comes Harry Hibbs. Well done, Harry. Harry is 26 years old and lives in Toronto, to which he moved from Bell Island six years ago. In that golden city of the blessed he has found employment as a factory worker and night watchman.

Harry doesn't know music by note and he plays a red $40 button accordion. You know the stuff. Newfoundland jigs that are different from the Irish and not at all like Don Messer's renditions.

Enthusiastic. Wilder and more rowdy. There's a bit of fire in them that's almost Spanish. It's low-brow, of course, and like, man, square, but the least you can say about it is that it's different.

That's what Harry plays and it seems that Harry has it made. Oh, yes. Because Harry has made a recording with his red button accordion that in one month has outsold 95 per cent of the Canadian albums ever made.

There are even news stories about it. According to one, by the Canadian Press, Harry's record "has sold more than 30,000 copies in Toronto alone – a spectacular figure in a country where a 5,000 sale is a success."

They say it's a mystery how it happened because, at first, none of the radio stations would play it and this had always been necessary to make a record a success.

But the strange (to them) and enthusiastic un-Messer, un-Irish, uncommon sound got around somehow and people started taking to it. Perhaps it isn't all so mysterious.

Perhaps it happened because Harry was not trying to copy anything else. Because he came from one part of Canada that is not the same as the rest and he was not ashamed of it. Because the difference wasn't beaten out of him by the great sea of sameness around him.

It might have happened because Harry was honest and that is a rare thing in people these days. Or because Harry was himself and that is a rare thing even in Newfoundlanders these days. Anyhow, there it is and it can't be no tizzer.

Well done, Harry, my son. I don't allow you'll be another Beatle but … not bad for a local. Perhaps when the local radio stations down here see that your record has got the great Toronto seal of approval, they'll even play it.

We'd certainly like to hear it. I think that between the jigs and the reels there might be a valuable message in it for all Newfoundlanders. Yes, sir, I do so. ▨

Long Harbour – A sea of death

March 26, 1969

Great New Industries

Nearly two months have passed since the first of the mysterious red herring began to appear in Placentia Bay. Nobody is any the wiser yet – or if they are they're not talking.

In the harbors and coves in the northern half of Newfoundland's largest bay, great schools of herring were stricken by some strange calamity that nobody has yet explained.

When the malady struck, herring were seen to rise to the surface and twist and spin crazily about on top of the water, darting beneath and dashing to the surface again, skittering and shuddering about as if in frenzied agony.

Gradually their struggles against the sickness that gripped them became more feeble. They became weaker and weaker until, one by one, they turned belly-up on the surface. Waves brought them nearer to shore. Most of them were dead by the time the sea washed them up on the beaches in their thousands.

Their eyes were red and bulged from their heads like ugly clots of blood. Their silver bellies and white fins were startlingly changed to a bright scarlet. The dead red herring.

The manner of their dying and the difference between a healthy dark blue and silver herring and these deformed and monstrous specimens created a sort of awe and dread in all who saw it.

What disease or what poison could have had such an effect? They were blind, no doubt about it. Fishermen were quick to note that red herring found in the stomachs of cod had been swallowed headfirst. Normally, cod have to chase the fleeing herring and gulp them tail-first, they said.

What blinded them and turned them red, as if every blood vessel in their bodies had been ruptured in a massive hemorrhage?

In their thousands they washed ashore on beaches around the northern half of Placentia Bay. They have been dredged up from great depths in the middle of the bay, where they lie in unknown numbers on the bottom. They were caught in nets as they struggle around in their blindness, their eyes turned to blood clots.

It began nearly two months ago and lasted for about two weeks. Now there are no great reports of any herring, alive or dead, in Placentia Bay. Those that washed to shore have either decomposed or have been carried out again by the tide.

The only red herring to be seen now are those that are held in freezers for further examination, their gaudy death colors dulled by the frost.

It is the duty of the federal department of fisheries to investigate and report on such matters. They began investigating as soon as the first red herring were seen, and are still investigating. But there have been no reports.

Why? Why the delay? Why the silence? It could be just another natural phenomenon, or it could be a matter of greatest urgency. Who knows? But what is taking so long?

Laymen, who have not the slightest knowledge of marine biology, are asking: Would it take nearly two months to find out whether a human had caught some disease or whether he had been poisoned – and isn't a human a more complex piece of machinery than a fish?

If there is as yet no solution to the mystery, why not at least an explanation for the delay? It has been charged that the Long Harbour phosphorus plant is creating a sea of death. Rumors spread daily, and our inshore fishermen have still another worry added to their traditional burden of troubles and uncertainty.

Until there are some answers, most of the fishermen directly concerned are pointing to the Long Harbour plant as a potential monster.

This belief, whether justified or not, is founded mainly on a frightening "accident" that occurred late last year, just after the $40 million phosphorus plant began operation.

The "accident" turned the waters of Long Harbour a milky grey. The stench that rose from the polluted harbor was at times intolerable. It was a sharp, acrid smell like brimstone or the stink caused when a box of matches explodes.

After a time the water cleared to reveal the bottom of the harbor littered by dead fish. Flounder, smelt, eels and other varieties. All dead.

When the red herring started to turn up a few months later, the Long Harbour plant was the first thing that sprang to mind. Why is it taking so long to prove or disprove these rumors?

Of course, there is no doubt that the Long Harbour plant IS polluting the waters of Placentia Bay. But what harm this pollution is doing and whether there is any connection between it and the dead red herring is another matter.

I saw the pollution first-hand late last week. Two waste pipes of two or three feet in diameter empty directly into Long Harbour waters. The continuous discharge through these pipes turns the water a milky grey and makes the sea cloudy within an area of several hundred feet of the outlets.

A smell rises from the polluted water, which, directly over the outlets, is sharp enough to make the eyes smart and breathing unpleasant. It is not unlike the stench caused by an exploding box of matches.

The federal department of fisheries takes water samples daily. It has moored crates of lobsters at Long Harbour. It has sent water samples and dead red herring to the mainland for examination. It has sent a fisheries research vessel and crew to investigate. Fisheries officers send a continuous flow of daily reports.

But two months is a long time. Too long. ▦

John Crosbie: Dispatched with balloons and party favors

April 1, 1969   *Liberals and Pea Seas*

A few bad heads on the go today, I expect. More than one aspirin tablet swallowed this morning, I dare say. A scattered queasy stomach here and there, I imagine.

From one end to the other the country was aflame last night with gaiety and revelry. The like has not been seen since the official opening in 1956 of the Kumquat Quay public convenience.

It's the sort of thing that puts a needed dash of sparkle and color into the final days of Lent. Its gets Holy Week off to just the right start.

But after the balls were over … hang on. There's a fine distinction here. They weren't balls. They were banquets. Balls, I do believe, are where you dance and banquets are where you eat.

Even that needs to be qualified. You don't stoop so low as to "eat" at a banquet. No, sir. You dine. You sit there and dine with the minstrels fingering their harpsichords in the background and you fling a scattered bone to the Tories under the table.

In the capital city the general merriment had to be seen to be believed. There were incredible scenes of jubilation in the public streets. Celebrants danced and sang and reeled along the thoroughfares in gleeful abandon.

Reports are not in yet from such far-flung outposts of empire as Corner Brook and Marystown, but in St. John's, at least, both a banquet and a ball were held. Oh, yes. Both barrels.

They paid $7.50 for the banquet and $2.50 for the ball. They dined on roast duck at the banquet, after which they heard Donald (Duck) Jamieson read poor Pierre's speech. Music to digest by.

It was all flashed across the province live by means of the modern miracle of television. Due to an oversight on somebody's part I did not receive an invitation and being rather miffed at this I refused to take it in via TV. Pure peevishness.

Because of this bit of pique readers will have to make do with a second-hand account. Beautiful enlarged color photographs of Mr. Smallwood were distributed to the lucky banqueteers. Suitable for framing.

Mr. Smallwood was in receipt of a lovely engraved tray which cost somebody $1,100. There was plenty of pinky to go around. John Shaheen and John C. Doyle purred in the background.

The foreign press was represented. A Toronto reporter inquired of a local newsman: "How many fishermen do you figure are here tonight?"

Maybe he was just naive, but you can't trust these Canadian reporters. I suspect he was trying to be smart alecky. Making fun of us, again.

Meanwhile, out in the sticks, the other banquets went ahead with special Liberal personalities being shipped out from St. John's to serve as centerpieces and gladden the hearts of the outharbor diehards.

John Crosbie, as we mentioned, was dispatched with balloons and party favors to Marystown. It is not known whether or not he was allowed to go out unaccompanied. Perhaps he has at last regained that purity of thought and steadfastness in doctrine which does away with the need for a chaperone.

While it is never our intention to sow the seeds of dissension and strife between the urban and rural elements of our populace, we are constrained by the precepts of factual reporting to note that once again the baymen got the dirty end of the stick.

Whereas in St. John's the banqueteers banqueted on roast duckling, rum frappé, beaujolais and port, the co-celebrants in Harbour Grace, for example, had to make do with cold ham, potato salad and Jell-O.

And whereas the St. John's revelers were entertained by at least four separate sets of gilded tonsils and a ball at Holiday Inn, the Harbour Grace contingent had Ed Roberts and a minute's silence for the *Southern Cross* which went down 55 years ago to the day.

As I say, far be it from me to dwell on these things but it seems that the just society still has its haves and have-nots.

Never mind. The festive spirit and the unadulterated joy that swells the bosom of every Newfoundlander on this, the 20th anniversary of Conglomeration, is what really counts.

In the humble cottage of the outport peasant the best tablecloth was brought out and a few rounders, selected and watered for the purpose, were consumed reverently and with thanksgiving as a candle fluttered before a portrait of the Only Living Father.

In the mansions of the wealthy, both old and recent, the same air of sanctity mingled with festivity prevailed. What a celebration it was! Never has Newfoundland been so united in a general and spontaneous display of merrymaking and adulation.

Perhaps it is a good thing that such anniversaries come only once in two decades. It will take at least another 20 years before we all get over this one.

Poor Pierre. He doesn't know what he missed. 🆁🅶

Too late for praise and lollipops

April 21, 1969   *Democracy*

Last week I got this letter from a schoolteacher in Labrador.

"The students of my Grade 8-I civics class recently sent you (a copy of) a petition they forwarded to Mr. William Callahan concerning their views on a Bonne Bay national park.

"Neither of you have seen fit to reply commending their participation in civic affairs. Unless they receive some sort of recognition, even as intangible as a letter, they may very well be deterred from joining other more important crusades.

"These students are very young and their beliefs and goals are, as yet, not cemented. I trust that you will acknowledge their effort and thereby aid them in their attainment of positive rather than negative values."

Well! I can't really answer for poor old Silica. Perhaps his apparent indifference to public opinion doesn't allow him to answer. On the other hand, maybe his secretary has wrist cramp from answering so many other similar petitions about Bonne Bay. But here's mine:

Dear students,

I had not the slightest intention of writing you a letter of praise for sending Mr. Callahan your opinions regarding the Bonne Bay national park. I still haven't. Please don't expect any thanks or praise or commendation from me for being "civic-minded."

In fact, any thanks or praise you get from anybody for being civic-minded won't be worth the paper it's written on. It will mean absolutely nothing. It will be only an empty formality, a meaningless piece of etiquette.

You can't expect to get meaningful praise from anybody for doing these things. Because they are no more than your natural and simple duty. Praise for duty done is always meaningless.

In Newfoundland, I'm afraid, it was often looked on as a rare and exceptional thing for the average person to be actively interested in civics, to learn about and to take part as much as possible in the workings of government at all levels.

There was a tendency to stand back and let something called "the government" make all the decisions, to allow it to rest smug and secure on its last victory at the polls and to be the source of all thought, opinion and action.

We were satisfied for a long time simply to be told what to do. And it follows that if you don't make an effort to get what you want, you will have to put up with what you get.

In the past, this effort seems to have been too much for us. Perhaps we shouldn't be too hard on ourselves until we are able to get a good look back at our history. Living under various forms of dictatorship – fishing admirals, colonial rule, commissions – for a few centuries is not good training for democracy. Whatever that is.

People stand back and let something called "the government" do what it will under two basic situations. One is in time of a dictatorship. The other is when people get too fat and apathetic to care much what a government does.

Our involvement in civics was simply to trot along once every three or four years to the polling booths and go home content in the knowledge that we had done our civic duty.

When we spoke of this thing called "the government" we forgot we were speaking about our servants and not our masters. It was the great Newfoundland sickness.

The helpless, indifferent shrug: "Oh, we can't do anything about it. The government will go ahead and do what it wants anyway." This unhealthy awe, you see, this touching of the forelock whenever the word government was mentioned.

Naturally, when you have this kind of situation you can expect "the government" to take full advantage of it. "The government" easily forgets that it is supposed to be the servant and the people are the masters. Arrogance feeds on itself.

But now something new is taking place. We are beginning to see who should be the servant and who should be the master. Whether it has changed anything or not, Bonne Bay was one example. But there are many others.

If you pay attention to the news, you will see that all over Newfoundland, people, either as individuals or in groups, are at last taking an active and lively interest in civic affairs. They are making their opinions known on issues that concern them and concern Newfoundland.

It's new. It's what's happening. But we see a conflict. We see a clash between the new people and the old government. We are treated to the outrageous spectacle of a government sneering at, heaping scorn on, trying to trample down, ridiculing, disparaging, belittling, ranting against any form of public opinion it doesn't agree with.

Because, you see, it is far, far easier for a government to be the master than it is for a government to be the servant. Being the master is not a position a government will give up without much bitter kicking and screaming.

In our own particular case we have a government that refuses to acknowledge and adapt to this change. It is understandable. A government that was "the master" for so long will be shocked and jarred by the change.

It may refuse to accept reality and cast about wildly for things to explain the change. It may see "nests of dirty Tories" everywhere or even a whole public misguided by "the dirty Tory press" – or other outlandish excuses.

Such a government will be both desperate to hang on to its old role as master and conditioned to think of any differing opinion or criticism as coming from the only opposition it is used to – "the other party."

This is nonsense, of course. The change has nothing to do with party politics. It has only to do with the fact that people can mature politically.

It may still be a bit novel in Newfoundland for school students and other people to show interest in civic affairs. Yours may have been a rare thing to do even a few years ago.

A concern by every citizen about civic affairs is not something which in any situation you get a pat on the back for; it is not something you can expect praise for. It is always a natural duty.

In our case it is our natural duty to Newfoundland. What's Newfoundland? It isn't the Long Range Mountains and it isn't the Churchill River. Newfoundland is the people who live in Newfoundland.

That includes us. So when we do our duty toward Newfoundland by learning as much as we can and becoming actively interested in civic affairs we are only doing our duty toward ourselves. Where does praise or commendation come in?

Would you praise yourself for eating all your cornflakes in the morning? Silly, what? Perhaps a few years back your mothers might have praised you for forcing down the last soggy spoonful. But that's only for little kids, isn't it?

Commend you for your participation in civic affairs? Not bloody likely! I wouldn't insult you. You may be young, but I think you're too big already for lollipops.

In civic affairs in Newfoundland we are all getting too big for this reward and punishment bit. It is too late for scorn, sneers, diatribes, ridicule and ranting from the former "masters." It is also too late for praise and lollipops.

So I, for one, won't praise you. I hope this won't spoil it all, but it was one heck of a struggle not to.

Yours truly,
RAY GUY

Everybody gets the same six feet
of ground when it's over

May 7, 1969   *Resettlement and Rural Life*

Doggish, degrading, miserable, primitive, soul-destroying, inhuman, back-breaking, hand-to-mouth, brutal, crude, outdated, cruel, bitter, hopeless, deplorable.

These are some of the terms that have been applied to the fishery in Newfoundland – particularly the inshore fishery. It doesn't sound very appetizing, the way some people talk about it.

A vast and unbalanced backlog of revulsion has been built up against the fishery in Newfoundland. It has been pictured as something less than a fit occupation for human beings.

A young person hearing all this lopsided and biased propaganda about the fishery would probably choose slavery in the salt mines of Siberia rather than go in the fishing boat.

Some of these horror stories are justified, of course. But much of the stigma now attached to fishing has been manufactured.

For the past 20 years at least government and other sources have treated the inshore fishery as if it were a repulsive and embarrassing relic of a poverty-stricken past.

Those early political slogans set the pattern for the discouraging of the fishery: "Burn your boats! There'll be three jobs ashore for each and every man! We will take the poor women off the fish flakes!"

I don't believe all the boats have gone up in flames yet; I don't think there are three jobs ashore for every man yet; and not all the women have left the fish flakes.

The fishery was disparaged and sneered at. It was thought unworthy of notice and left to wither on the vine. All the attention and effort was directed toward those "great new industries."

And so an industry that had survived every conceivable sort of abuse and natural disaster for centuries was brought to the edge of extinction in just 20 years.

As in so many other cases, the foundation (such as it was) that was there was allowed to crumble, while the great heft of the time and money was poured into whims and fancies and castles in the clouds.

The fishery was practically forgotten and left to rot away in a corner. On top of ignoring it, this steady diet of propaganda – with all the disparaging words – was pumped out.

Fishing is no bed of roses but it is not, or need not have been, the chamber of horrors, the fate-worse-than-death, the living-not-fit-for-humans, that some have painted it.

It may not be an easy living, but what is when all is considered? Everybody gets the same six feet of ground when it's over. Who's had the best deal at the end? A fisherman or an office worker caught up in a dismal rat race, chained to the treadmill of the city where the air has been so polluted it burns his eyes?

The truth is that there are advantages and disadvantages to both ways of life. And if both are given the same chance it will be found that one is not necessarily superior to the other.

The test of it all comes at the end when the six feet of ground is opened up. Who has gotten the most out of it?

The fisherman winds up with his hands gnarled, his face weather-beaten. He's never played golf, he's never owned a $6,000 car and he believes that God never intended man to go to the moon.

The big city office worker, before he has been put underground, acquires a potbelly with an ulcer, paid off his mortgage five years before, has striven rather frantically to get to "the country" on weekends, and after retirement found the shock of getting out of the rut in which he had been chained almost unbearable.

So if there's any difference, isn't it all the same? The strike against Newfoundland fishermen, of course, is that someone decided some years back it was impossible for them to keep the old advantages and have some new ones, too.

Either they joined the rat race or they couldn't have even a $2,000 car. Either they picked up their lunch pail and trotted to the factory or they couldn't have proper medical attention when they needed it.

Either they chained themselves to the treadmill and learned to breathe polluted air and drink polluted water, or they couldn't send their kids to a decent school.

The big city office and factory worker is going squirrelly as the disadvantages of his way of life multiply and he's struggling desperately to get some of the advantages the Newfoundland fisherman had. But it's a hard struggle and is blowing his big city and himself apart.

The Newfoundland fisherman naturally wanted to hang on to the advantages he had and add to them some of those the city dweller had. Somebody decided this was impossible.

Somebody decided that if it wasn't impossible it should be. Smug young men who sneer at "pastoral romantics" in a rather frenzied attempt to convince themselves they are right. Who are part of a regime that doesn't like the smell of fish. Who speak of fishermen who lived on islands, by inference, as if they were some sort of animals.

As if they had lived in sod-roofed hovels in filth, ignorance and degradation, had chopped holes in the floors for toilets, whose children came up ignorant, uneducated. As if they had to be herded into "growth centers" for their own good.

Someone decided that the fishery was not a fit way for human beings to make a living. So the fishery was disparaged and ignored until it came to near collapse.

The government piously and vehemently protests that the fishermen of the islands moved to these new Jerusalems or "growth centers" of their own free will.

Trash! They were forced out just as surely as if some Gestapo had held a gun to their heads. One way or another, they were forced to burn their boats.

The fishery was let down, schools were let down, transportation and communications were let down. It was "too expensive." The die was cast in somebody's hot little head long ago. The fisherman had to be transformed into a factory worker.

The fishery has been nearly destroyed. The fishermen are not allowed to be fishermen. There is no turning back. But where are the factories?

There is one at Long Harbour, Placentia Bay. ▯

Another bloody whale on our hands

June 19, 1969

Culture and History

In nine fathoms of blue water just off from the cobblestone beach of St. Stephen's in St. Mary's Bay a trapped monster dies slowly of starvation and torture.

Two thin strands of rope are apparently all that hold the monstrous beast in its death trap. But it is a rope of fantastic strength. A modern "miracle" – nylon.

Even one of the largest creatures now living – or that has ever lived on earth – has thrashed about helplessly for 10 days and cannot break this web which is a product of modern technology.

The federal department of fisheries, which has its hands full elsewhere with red herring, has so far made only one magnificent contribution.

It has graciously and nobly offered to provide St. Stephen's fishermen with as much .303 ammunition as may be needed to torture the whale to death.

How long will it take to kill the monster with .303 bullets? How long would it take to stab a man to death with a sewing needle? Already more than 30 rounds (some say 100) have been pumped into it.

Ho hum. So we've got another bloody whale on our hands. A pity, so soon after that rather unpleasant business at Burgeo. Ah, well. We'll have to call for Farley again. Or else put the damn thing on welfare.

If you're the type who shies from what you take to be sentimentality in such cases as stranded whales and centralization, perhaps this may pinch you where you can feel:

The "damn thing" in its death throes is incidentally destroying $5,300 of your money.

It is tangled in the leader of a cod trap of the Japanese design which is owned by the government and was loaned to fisherman Ron Flemming of St. Stephen's to see how it would work out.

The modern net is made from the best and most expensive materials available. And the strongest. Had it been an older trap made of linnet and manila the 50-foot whale would have ripped through it as through floating kelp. But nylon is stronger than steel.

Mr. Flemming says that since the whale blundered into the government-owned trap he has called repeatedly to the fisheries department in St. John's for help.

The department has told him, he reports, that it has no boats available. The only help offered was .303 ammunition free of cost.

St. Stephen's is now caught up in the near-frenzy of work that comes at the height of the cod-trap season. All its fishermen are working practically non-stop far into the night while the run lasts.

Mr. Flemming says that perhaps if he could get a half-dozen men to help they could cast off the leader of the trap, freeing the whale and saving the rest of the expensive gear from destruction.

Perhaps. If the fishermen were not caught up in the frenzy of summer work. And if it were his own trap instead of government-issue, they might make time.

They tried bullets. A few days ago several men in a dory rowed in close to the thrashing whale and pumped more than 30 bullets into its head.

With a snap of its mighty tail the tormented animal struck the dory and knocked it completely out of the water. Those aboard were not hurt but the tough spruce planks of the dory bottom were split and now there's a more healthy respect for the starving monster's power. They give it a wide berth now.

So we've got another bloody whale on our hands.

If the fisheries department doesn't see its way clear to try and salvage a net that cost $5,300 of your money, I'm sure you'll object to the waste.

But I believe that the bill we'd have to pay for those government-issued .303 bullets would cost us far more. ▩

Human kindness fairly oozes from that great corporate bosom

June 30, 1969   *Culture and History*

We sometimes think of big business as being cold, calculating and self-serving. Of being concerned only with making a profit by whatever means are open and, in the immortal words of one of their number, "the public be damned."

How gratifying it is, then, to see the gracious blossoming of a warm social conscience on the part of that enterprise at Long Harbour.

It touches us with a rosy glow to see that the captains of industry who run this concern had the interests of the public in mind all along.

Indeed, we rejoice to see that the milk of human kindness fairly oozes from that great corporate bosom. It was there from the start waiting only to be tapped.

The good neighbors at Long Harbour have recently issued a pious assurance that they "don't want to harm anybody's fish." And they're sticking like grim death to their story that they never did.

However, out of the sheer goodness of their hearts they're going to spend $1 million "for social purposes." Not that anti-pollution measures are needed, of course. They won't admit that they HAVE polluted anything.

We could almost believe that flatfish frolic under the pier and conners gambol in the shadow of the loading dock. As soon as the weather gets warmer we could expect the company to do it up brown and stick a few swans on the harbor.

No, they're going to spend $1 million "for social purposes." A noble gesture. A manifestation of social charity. Pollution really hasn't got much to do with it.

Why, they could have achieved the same thing by erecting a $1 million combination arts and culture center and snack bar at Long Harbour.

But it just happens that this great social gesture is to stop pumping raw and deadly poison into the sea around Newfoundland. "Social purposes!" How many sleepless nights did their public relations hack spend cooking up that one?

And how much more of this type of clap-trap are we expected to swallow? It comes at us from all angles in big juicy lumps. If governments slack off for a moment, someone else is there to fill the gap.

How long before we have to start looking at the whole lot of them as a load of sly, greasy liars – and their every utterance a lie until it is proven otherwise?

This "red herring" business is only one example of efforts to stuff distortions, half-truths, and lies down the throats of the public. But it's a good example because nearly all the boys got in on the act.

The company? The one fact we do know is that they would have saved $1 million by pumping their waste directly into Placentia Bay.

Federal fisheries? It was their duty to see to it that the plant would not kill fish. They apparently stamped it simon-pure and allowed it to be opened.

Now, more than six months later, they tell us that less than 25 parts of phosphorus to one billion parts of water can kill herring and trout. And that the acid water pumped out by the plant could be just as dangerous. Twin streams of poison.

So who takes the blame for that little foul-up? Which "experts" can that be pinned on? The one thing governments are expert on is buck-passing. Trying to corner a top civil servant is like chasing a frog through a bog.

The ever-smilin' Jack Davis is the logical target. But what satisfaction is there in trying to slam a swinging door? He's afflicted with the famous Trudeau shrug of indifference.

Our own dear leader prefers to escape the stink of red herring and scuttle off to Red China. The master architect of it all, father of this "great new industry," would rather be elsewhere.

A timid tack for someone who gave Labrador to a US bail-jumper, who gave Shaheen such outrageous concessions that even some of his own cabinet ministers gagged, who paid Holiday Inns to come here, who …

You'd think it would be a simple one to talk around. You'd think he'd be able to talk his way out of this one with one arm tied behind his back – with his tongue.

After all, the enterprise at Long Harbour is a "great new industry" in the flesh. That Newfoundland pays them twice as much in subsidized electricity as they pay out in wages is beside the point.

So is the fact that the Long Harbour plant has done untold harm to the fisheries of Placentia Bay and Newfoundland. That it has robbed hundreds of fishermen of immediate income and has placed their whole futures in jeopardy. Never mind. It's a "great new industry."

For the past week a vessel appropriately named the *Ottawa* has been taking aboard thousands of tons of poisoned fish in Placentia Bay. She steams down the bay and dumps the polluted saltbulk some 50 miles off Cape St. Mary's.

Meanwhile, the bay has been "opened" for business again. The federal experts have reported that fish are back to normal.

The truth is that codfish being caught there now show the same signs of red·death by phosphorus poisoning that they have for past months; that the stomachs of some cod are rotted away and that fishermen cleaning them have a struggle to hang on to their own guts because of the stench.

Federal fisheries say things are back to normal; the company makes a gracious gesture "for social purposes;" and the father of great new industries is in Hong Kong buying knickknacks for his mantel shelf. ▨

Do not rest in peace

July 3, 1969   *Roads, Rails and Water*

I intended to make light of it all, my love, but I am not able.

After all the fuss and letters to the editor and protest rides and loud words in the Parliament at Ottawa you had a quiet wake. It was a Presbyterian wake, not an Irish Catholic wake.

But a wake it was. Somebody wrote a verse to the papers last week calling you "you," like you were a person or something, and here I am foolish enough to be doing the same.

Don't think, you poor comical monster, that we are calling a mess of wheels and machinery "you." You are all the people you ever carried and the country you carried them across.

You were more than a machine and that's the closest we can come to it. You took us away from home and you brought us back for a long time.

You shook up our livers and lights and you shook up our emotions at the same time whether you brought us east from Port aux Basques or west towards it.

And you were such a funny and outrageous collection of clatters and squeaks and rattles and quirks and anecdotes that we had to laugh at you even when you were jolting and jarring us half to death.

But everyone knows why we thought of you as "you" and not "it." Do you think we'd have a wake for a heap of machinery? And a wake it was.

There weren't big crowds at the stations but there were people all along the way. And not two in 10 that did not wave at you for the last time.

And the cameras! There were never so many pictures taken. You'd think you were royalty. Even past midnight as you passed three small houses in the darkness there was the white blink of a flash bulb as someone tried to take your picture.

A man in Port aux Basques, who had white hair and a red face from the weather and creosote, walked along the tracks slowly before you left, looking at the switches and the rails very carefully.

Then he took off his glasses and wiped his face with the back of his hand. And a nun with her trout pole trouting in a brook in the morning waved at you.

And I saw a man with black ribbons tied about his arm for you. Or perhaps not for you. But it didn't take imagination to see that many along the way did not regard you as a piece of machinery.

Canadian National didn't make a fuss about your wake, which is understandable. Their public relations people were there and they had a rather nasty little job to do and they did it as best they could.

But they made some smart cracks about your many faults which I thought were not appropriate considering the occasion. We made all our jokes before, so where is the need now that you are finished.

The CN provided $105 worth of free booze to the press to help the journey along, but I think there was still some left. They told us that "nearly all" the railway men put out of work would get other jobs.

But they did not mention the big layoff that is to come in September. They told us there would be an upgrading of the freight service but they didn't tell us how many semi-trailer trucks they have on order.

Perhaps there wasn't a big fuss over your wake because you've been dead for some time. You were killed off by degrees, not quickly and decently, but slowly poisoned so that your end would not be noticed.

If the bit of fuss that was kicked up over your demise had come 10 years ago instead of two, it might have helped. But by the time it did come, you were so far gone that it was foolish and useless.

In September 1966, I wrote a piece saying you should be buried. It wasn't that I had anything against you, but the people who couldn't afford a sleeper and tried to get two hours sleep out of a miserable 24 frightened me.

And you were dead then. It was disgusting that your corpse had to be dragged about and squabbled over for so long.

They had you spruced up for the wake. Even the windows cleaned. But the potatoes were a spongy dab known as "instant," the carrots came out of a tin and so did the ham.

When we tried, in all innocence, to get another cup of tea later, the steward snapped so that all in the diner turned to look: "You're trying to pull a fast one, eh?"

He was going to be out of a job the next day, I suppose. It was unusual because to the last the service given by the men who kept you operating was about the only good thing people mentioned about you.

But perhaps there have been the scattered insult and abuse here and there these past years by men made irritable by the knowledge they were working on borrowed time, and that helped kill you, too.

Anyway, there's not much sense hashing it over anymore. You're dead. We're too poor a rock to afford a train, according to the CNR. They'll sit us in plastic buses on plastic seats and have us gobble food in plastic restaurants and they'll trundle us through a 500-mile-long gravel pit.

They talk about "transportation" and the passenger-mile ratio and cost factors and efficiency, not about people and trips. We are at the tender mercies of computers and the men they operate.

Do not rest in peace. Curse them with a long and howling curse like your whistle in the night. 🆁🅶

Being a political sex symbol is one thing

August 15, 1969   *Liberals and Pea Seas*

Ladies. Restrain yourselves. Yield not to temptation. You may (as they say at the Playboy Bunny Clubs) look but don't touch.

Now that the leadership candidates have pulled out all the stops to woo and seduce you (politically speaking), you'll need all the self-restraint you can muster.

Both main candidates are out to win over the ladies. And, following words with action, they have blossomed out in splendid array for your delectation and titillation. Keep cool, ladies – if you can.

The most astonishing transformation has been made by Mr. Smallwood. From sartorial ugly duckling to cock of the walk, almost overnight. Never known as a natty dresser, he has bloomed of late.

Gone are the baggy black suits of Hong Kong manufacture. Gone are the frayed collars and dowdy neckties. Gone are the street-sweeper cuffs. The Khrushchev cut is out.

In his new campaigning gear, Mr. Smallwood cuts a dashing figure. The ensemble is done in a delicate beige, although it comes over as near-white on television. Some viewers mistook the last Great Announcement for a fried chicken commercial.

But this is only a small disadvantage. Joseph's shirt is even more stunning than Joseph's coat. Blazing, aggressive, vital vermilion. Rooster red. Altogether devastating.

And topping of the whole concern is the frightfully debonair bow tie bespeaking the continental élan of a Charles Boyer or the smoldering Latin charm of a Ramon Navarro.

Some who have had occasion to come within range also claim to have detected a whiff of aftershave lotion. If only he could sing like Tom Jones. But who knows what other campaign armaments are yet to be unveiled?

The ladies have a choice, of course, but it will be a difficult one. For his part, Mr. Crosbie has always been a nifty dresser. Not quite so flamboyant, perhaps, as the new Mr. Smallwood in full plumage, but with a certain restrained elegance.

Electric blues, discreet grey checks, last year's cut. And the sideburns. Early on in the game Mr. Crosbie began to cultivate his sideburns.

So that, by now, at a time when every little extra bit of dash counts, these facial adornments have reached full maturity and the peak of perfection.

Sideburns are a great advantage to at least three extra platform planks or 300 more power pole posters. Designed at first to catch the youth vote, they have been found to appeal simultaneously to both the teenyboppers and the blue-rinsed matrons.

Ben Cartwright and Herman and the Hermits rolled into one. Mr. Crosbie also carries his age well and this is an advantage for spur-of-the-moment public appearances.

A dash of talcum to the dimples, some last-minute teasing of the sideburns and bring on the television cameras.

It is encouraging to see that Newfoundland's first such campaign will skirt petty and often messy issues to concentrate on the things that really matter. It is clear to see that haberdashery will loom large.

All the same, there's a danger that things could get out of hand. A glad-rag escalation gone out of control would be a sticky wicket indeed.

At present, both principal candidates are running neck and neck as regards outer adornments but suppose, for example, that Mr. Smallwood took the lead.

Suppose that in addition to the beige suit, the rooster-red shirt, the bow tie – the works – he came out tomorrow with an Indian headband and hippie weskit.

Would not Mr. Crosbie be obliged to wear peace beads and a Nehru jacket? This could only be countered by faded blue jeans and a Navajo blanket on the part of Mr. Smallwood.

Mr. Crosbie would then be left with no choice but to take to granny glasses, a chest wig and shoulder-length hair. And so forth. You can see where it all might lead.

Meanwhile, the ladies of all ages must feel flattered, if nothing else, to be the objects of such ardent displays. Which of the two political suitors will win their affections in the end remains to be seen.

It has also to be kept in mind that, as someone knowledgeable in these matters has observed, the ladies are rather like Model T Fords in that they are difficult to get underway. But once in motion it is easier to stop an avalanche or stem Niagara Falls.

Let us hope that the two candidates know what they are doing and have not already bitten off more than they can chew. Let us hope they haven't misjudged their own fatal allure.

Being a political sex symbol is one thing, but being torn limb from limb in the course of a shopping center political rally is another. ▪

Dimple, dimple, Happy John

September 23, 1969   *Liberals and Pea Seas*

The writing of folk songs, once a favorite pastime in this country, has fallen off grievously.

But there appears to be a slight revival now in connection with the leadership campaign. This is a heartening sign. A Crosbie campaign worker has pressed upon me a copy of some freshly penned lyrics which he says were sung lately at Smallwood gatherings.

No doubt, he presented them to me as a public service feeling that they were precious bits of Newfoundlandia to be preserved. Colorful sidelights of the great campaign that should be passed to posterity.

Being strictly impartial (since Mr. Barbour dropped out) I present them here in that vein. If Smallwood campaigners have similar interesting tidbits I shall be glad to pass them along also. History must be served.

These ditties, according to the Crosbie worker, were passed out at Smallwood rallies and were meant to be rendered by the audience in massed chorus when the Leader appeared on stage.

The informant says that the sing-song was a flop and that only a few of those assembled warbled weakly along with the master of ceremonies. But we must allow for his bias and present the lyrics here for the sake of their broader significance. Authentic folk art is what they are.

It is not known if a band of music was on hand to provide accompaniment, and the musical score is not given, so we must guess at the tunes.

Note the spare quality, the barebones structure, so very like the old ballads and war chants of an earlier day. The sentiments expressed are simple yet sublime. They speak of fellowship, joy, optimism and purposeful … well … purpose.

These are happy songs. Songs to fire the blood. Rousing songs guaranteed to drive the little old ladies in sneaker boots into an awesome frenzy.

Here is the first on the list, which is apparently to be sung as the Leader enters the hall through an archway of furled umbrellas:

Hail, hail, the premier's here,
Let's give him a hearty cheer;
Hail, hail, the premier's here,
Let's give him a hearty cheer.
(Hip, Hip, hurrah.)

You may see that while the words are stirring in themselves, the tune in general could fall flat without full-throated and enthusiastic participation. It is a piece that should be rendered by the Mormon Tabernacle Choir or else not at all.

This selection is quickly followed on the program by the second rendition of the evening, which is entitled simply "How d'ye Do?":

How do you do, Premier Smallwood, how do you do?
How do you do, Premier Smallwood, how do you do?
We are Liberals to a man,
We'll do everything we can.
How do you do, Premier Smallwood, how do you do?

How, indeed? Here also is a composition that must be sung fortissimo and with feeling or else left alone. Even more is this true of the third piece which, in lyrics at least, is the most complex work on the ticket:

The Liberals are together, together, together,
The Liberals are together and happy are we.
For our friends are Joey's friends,
And Joey is our friend,
And the Liberals are together and happy are we.

According to the program, the musicale ends with "For He's a Jolly Good Fellow" and "Auld Lang Syne." Although not listed, a few snatches of "Abide With Me" would not seem inappropriate to the occasion.

It is hoped that as the great campaign rolls onward toward its climax there will be many more such efforts in word and music. Out of mighty conflicts such as these came the folk songs of our land in days of yore.

Create, create. Go to it. Here's an example on Mr. Crosbie's behalf to be sung to the tune of "Twinkle, Twinkle, Little Star":

Dimple, Dimple, Happy John,
You can really turn 'em on.
With your wavy hair and dimple,
You can charm both sash and wimple.

Or to the tune of "Mary Had a Little Lamb":

Crosbie, Crosbie, is our man,
Crosbie can; he's our man.
Crosbie, Crosbie, is our man,
His fleece was white as snow.

Had Mr. Barbour stayed on I could have really put my mind to it and come out with something genuinely heroic along the lines of "Rossie, Rossie, Über Alles." Alas, he was but a shooting star.

As for the PCs, perhaps we had better simplify because they tend to stumble over the big words. Something in the nature of a high school cheer, perhaps:

P! P! Give me a P!
C! C! Give me a C!
Rah, rah, rah!
Go, PCs go!
(In unison) Unleash Ottenheimer! ▉

Partridgeberries: A great new industry

September 30, 1969 *Great New Industries*

His eye, it now appears, is on the partridgeberry.

On a recent foray into Harbour Grace, Mr. Smallwood mentioned pickled herring and partridgeberries as the likely salvation of that town.

How strange to hear the humble partridgeberry spoken of by one who is more used to telling us about great new petro-chemical complexes, great new orange juice works, great new establishments for the extraction of milk of magnesia from sea water and so forth.

Do we see here a moderation of the vision? Is there a trend from the greater to the lesser? In the space of a few weeks we have heard two of the humbler items – hockey sticks and partridgeberries – mentioned.

However, it is more likely to be a case of the small being made great. A hockey stick is an ordinary item, but what splendor and magnificence the phrase takes on when it is rolled off the Smallwoodian tonsils.

It elevates hockey sticks into the realm of spaceship components. Jobs, jobs, jobs. We can picture a factory no smaller than the Pittsburgh steelworks. Such is the Smallwood magic.

And it isn't likely to stop there. Will there not be more announcements soon on the extension of this great new hockey stick enterprise? Won't it also go into early production of blue lines? Then branch out into the manufacture of first, second and third periods? There are boundless possibilities. Let Stephenville rejoice!

What will happen to the lowly partridgeberry now that it has been singled out for the Smallwood treatment? Great things. Without doubt, 1970 in Newfoundland will go down in history as the Year of the Partridgeberry.

Details of these momentous decisions which are shaping the lives of all of us will be revealed in the fullness of time. But a certain impatience drives us to speculate on them now.

What was the scene in that eighth-floor office as the Great New Partridgeberry Industry (Can it be less?) popped fully fledged from the warm womb of that great imagination?

"Harbour Grace. Mmmmmm. Eberhardt! Eberhardt! Come in here. Your skipper wants you. There's a meeting at Harbour Grace tonight and we need a great new industry. Think up three, give me the list and I'll select the most likely. Get to it. Get to it.

"Wait. See this snap. This is I and Willy and Billy in a rickshaw in Calcutta. Don't you wish you had been there? Eat your heart out. Do a good job on this and your skipper might take you along next time.

"We can't have a meeting without one of three things: (1) A great new industry. (2) What I and God have wrought. (3) Give the little guy from

Gambo another chance.

"Number One is the ticket for Harbour Grace. Eberhardt! Stop thinking disrespectful thoughts! Yes, you are, I can tell. Do you know I'm next to the Queen? Oh, yes. There's the Queen and then there's me.

"Hop to it, Eberhardt. Purveyors of hope and joy are we. Uplifters of the spirits of the toiling masses. How do I know which great new industry? That's your job. Give me a list and I'll make a selection.

"This is my story, this is my song. Talking about industry, all the day long. Dum dee dee dum, dee dum … Eberhardt! Stop sulking and get busy. I know it gets harder to think up something new, but put your mind to it. What year is this?

"There's Her Majesty and then there's me. The Queen and I and the great Sir Richard Squires. Lord, what a combination! Hand in hand through the ages. Enough to make you humble, isn't it?

"God save us, Miss Wilson! What a state of a woman! Were you out on an expedition to find Inca gold or something? What? What? Your daily tramp in the woods to commune with nature?

"What a mess for a secretary to be in. Brambles all over your mackinaw. Burrs in your cotton stockings. And what, pray tell, is that small red sphere caught in the top of one of your sensible shoes?

"What? What? A partridgeberry? You're putting me on! What's that? A wild fruit? Edible? Jam? Sauce? Pies? Even liquor? Land sakes! And the woods is full of them?

"Eberhardt! In here! Heel, boy, heel. Your skipper has it! My God. Do I have to keep dogs and bark myself? Everything left to me. Where would the toiling masses be without me?

"But, you know, I don't feel an inch taller than the least of these, my brethren. Not an inch. My heart beats in tune with the hearts of the common people. Listen here, Miss Wilson. Flub a dub. Flub a dub. Flub a dub dub dub.

"Partridgeberries. Eberhardt! We have been pleased to take notice of a certain berry that grows in the tuckamores and on the barrens and along by that Trans-Canada Highway which is like a great cathedral – never finished.

"This wild fruit will be the basis of a great new industry. We will order a great work to be commenced immediately. A great partridgeberry complex for Harbour Grace.

"J-O-E-Y, Eberhardt! J-O-B-S! There's the Queen and then there's me. Little Joey from Gambo. But I don't feel an inch taller. Not a millimeter. Where's my tambourine?

"This is my story, this is my song. Talking about industry, all the day long. This is my story … What's yours, Miss Wilson, if the worst comes to the worst?" RG

The old are now "a burden"

There's a rock at a certain place off the Labrador coast that's above water only at low tide.

Years ago the Eskimos would row out to this rock with an old grandfather or grandmother aboard and put them ashore on it. Then they rowed ashore leaving the old person to drown when the tide rose.

The old were considered too great a burden to keep over winter when there was only so much food to go around.

Don't say the Eskimos were more barbarous than we are until you think about it. We might have food enough to keep the old people over the winter, but often we don't have the room or the time or the patience. So we put them off in an old people's "home" to wait until their time comes. I'm not criticizing those who put their old people in a "home" when they are sick and need a doctor's care all the time.

But there's something wrong with a system that herds people into an institution as if they were criminals or mental cases just because they're old.

The human race can never seem to take a sensible middle course in anything. It swings to one extreme, then swings to the opposite extreme. Not so long ago it was the older class that was in charge of everything – government, religion, business, the works – and about the only things the younger bunch was considered good for was to cater to their elders or die in wars.

Now the swing is to the young and they get all the show and all the play. The old are now "a burden." Those machine-men, who look into the future and predict, say they can see the time when everyone will get a needle or gas on his 60th birthday.

There might not be too much difference in gassing 60-year-olds and in sending youngsters off to face machine guns. But it sure isn't progress. To consider the old a burden is another extreme.

Who isn't a burden on someone from the time he's born until the time he dies? We try to get clear of our burdens by paying money. It would be too distressing to ask a derelict to dinner, so we put some clean money in a clean charity envelope and keep our hands clean.

We're paying our taxes to keep up these old people's "homes," aren't we? So why shouldn't we ship the cranky old coot off there where "he'll be better off, anyhow." Money is the cheapest thing we can give.

To say the old are better off in old people's "homes" is to say our own home leaves something to be desired. It may be true but only because we have gradually allowed them to become what they are.

Some mysterious thing called "the system" says we have to live in a city where we can afford no more than a little box of a house big enough for only

3.8 people. And even that takes a lifetime to pay off and starts to fall apart in 10 years.

The two adults and the 1.8 children which the system decrees is the maximum size family may not stop in one place long enough to get to know their neighbors. This pared-down family has to skip about the country to earn a living. "There's an opening in our Winnipeg branch."

So we're not even allowed an immediate family of relatives, let alone the greater family of neighbors. This is a new thing. It was never like this in history before.

Well, the gypsies were continually moving, I suppose, but they had plenty of relatives and neighbors and they always took them along.

We have ourselves backed into a corner where every concession we make gives rise to the need for two more. The system is now running us. Take our own case.

Move to St. John's to "make a better living." Get a mortgage on a ticky-tacky box. Put the old people in a "home." Limit the family to 1.8, which is all you can afford. Watch the moving vans come and go at the houses of neighbors you hardly knew. See the people at work come and go faster than you can learn their names. Get another mortgage for a car so you can get out "in the country" on Sunday and bumper to bumper back. Move to Toronto to "make a better living ..." There's no end to it.

What it amounts to is that in a lifetime you don't really get to know another human being. Except for the 2.8 others in this artificial "family" and them you get to know too well.

They're the only ones you continue to see year after year as you change jobs, neighborhoods, cities and provinces. You're holed up in ticky-tacky boxes with this 2.8 family and neither house nor family is big enough.

Before long, someone is screaming for a divorce (it's one in four in the US now, I believe) and the kids want to cut out on their own almost before they get the diapers off their backsides.

People need to know more human beings in a lifetime than 2.8 and getting to know somebody takes much of a lifetime. The system we're caught up in won't let us stand still long enough for that.

We ask "how" when we should be asking "why." "How can we adjust?" rather than "Why must we adjust?"

Hermits need no family at all. But most people do. And they need a bigger family than 2.8 and even a bigger family than their close relatives might number.

A "family," in this sense, is the size of an old city neighborhood or the size of a Newfoundland outport where all older people are referred to as "aunt" and "uncle."

And where living to the end of your days was neither a crime nor a burden to others, but a fair exchange. RG

My dear, what a 'ead that man got

October 8, 1969   *Joey*

While it is never my custom (God forbid!) to eavesdrop on the conversations of others, there are times when it cannot be helped. Yesterday, for instance, I was taking my mid-day meal in a city restaurant when I chanced to overhear the conversation of two ladies behind me.

I report it here as accurately as I can recall in the interests of presenting one view of a current popular topic:

Yes, my dear. I got me card. Indeed I have. Into a lovely wallet. I knows I'll never live to wear 'en out. And I got me pitcher, too. Just like life, my dear, just like life. I got 'en framed and 'ung up in the kitchen. 'Tis some sweet snap. All done out into colors you know.

My dear, what a 'ead that man got. What a 'ead, what a 'ead. I spoze there was no one like him, you know, ever barn before in the worl'. The Man Above send him down, I says, to rule over us. We should be down on our knees givin' tanks every minute, I says, if we wuzzent so big in ourselves.

I knows he'll get MY vote. He always did. An' if I had a hundert votes he'd get them, too, and welcome. Yes, an' a tousan more on top of that.

He done a lot of good for Newfounlan, he did. Yes, my dear, an' dass jus' what he did. I mean to say, look at all the good what he done for Newfounlan.

'Tis in all them books wass goin' aroun'. I'm no good to read, meself, but I don't want to read to see all the good that man done for Newfounlan.

I gets me check, John gets hees check, the two boys gets dere checks, John's brudder, Sted, gets hees check AN' the pollin' boot on top of it, and me sister, Murt, she'll get her check now every munt, regaler as the clock, just so soon as she gets out. An' say HE haven' done a lot of good for Newfounlan.

It makes me sick, some people. It makes me bile, das da troot. Miz Smit', now. Do you know what Miz Smit' said to me dudder day? I was talkin' to her, I says, "Look at all the good," I says, "he done for Newfounlan," I says. An' do you know what she said to me?

So help me God, so true as I'm sittin' here. She says, bold as brass, she says, "Don't you think," she says, "somebody else," she says, "could'a done jus' so good and better?" she says. Jus' like that!

Well, MY dear! "Miz Smit'," I says. "You're h'ignernt," I says. "You're nothing but h'ignernt," I says. "You was always h'ignernt," I says, "an'you'll never BE nothing but h'ignernt," I says.

"An' I'll tell you right to your face now," I says. "People like you is nothing but h'ignernt," I says.

My dear, I feeled like clawin' the eyes right out of her 'ead. Dass the kind of people we got in the worl' today. I wish I could talk. My dear, I'd like to be able to talk. But I 'aven't got the 'ead for it.

Yes, he done a LOT'a good for Newfounlan. It come over the air dudder day. I heard it meself. Four more of them paper mills he got goin'. FOUR, no less! An' all them tings he got goin' out in Stephenville. That come over the air too. Even to makin' hockey sticks and one tinganudder.

An' dere's Come be Chance. Tousans and tousans of men workin' there. Tousans upon tousans. Prosperity, my dear. The like was never known. Wass the people too stunned to see it? No. It got to be bet into their 'eads. Certainly we know the Newfounlan people was always too stun' to know wass good for them.

This leadership ting they got on the go now. Wass the good of it? My dear, WASS the need of it? The man is dere. He was send down to us, I says. Yes, send down. An' when hees time is served he'll be took up again.

He got the h'experience. He got the 'ead. Look at the smart people he got in the cabinet, as they calls it. What 'eads, what 'eads. That Dr. Rose. That Mr. Barber. That Mr. Leary. So fine'a man, I spoze, as wass in the worl'. Smart men. Idggicated men.

And here they goes and haves this leadership thing. We was in good hans. What business have DEY got? What do dey tink, they're better'n what HE is? Haven't they got no respeck? They don't know their place, I says.

Haven't they got no respeck for the preemare of their country? And, my dear, the poor man is agein'. That man got a awful burden on hees sholders, that man have. And what he don't have to put up with.

What dirt and abuse. They does everything but call him a liar to hees face. Yes, my dear. And he the preemare of this country! Oh, my dear, sometimes I gets so mad I could fair screech, that's the troot.

Oh, if I could get me hands on them. I'd like to beat the mout' right off them. They should be locked up. They should be hung up, yes, and cut down before the last joog goes out of them and brought to and hung up again. Someone should take a … No. I won't soil me lips to say it.

Oh, my dear, it makes me SO mad, I can tell you. There's nights and nights I cries meself to sleep. That POOR man. After all the good he done for Newfounlan.

A lovely drop of tea, my dear. I wonder, my dear, if you could pay the bill? I don't spect they can change me check in here. �rg

Aunt Cissy: Hello, Mawmouth

October 9, 1969   *Aunt Cissy*

It was the stamps that first caught my eye as the letter lay among others on my desk yesterday morning.

At first glance I took them to be the stamps of a foreign principality. Yet there was something curiously familiar about them. Closer inspection revealed that they were none other than the postal script of our own dear country as it then, more or less, was.

What odd sensations these stamps conjured up. The blue four-cent and the green three-cent bearing the likenesses of Their Highnesses, as they then were, the Princess Elizabeth and the Princess Margaret Rose.

One could almost hear, looking at those stamps, Her Highness's delightfully poignant remark at the conclusion of a Christmas Day wireless message during darker times in the reign of His Late Majesty: "Come along, Margaret. Say good night to the children."

Something more than nostalgia came upon me. Then, suddenly, as my attention wandered from the stamps to the hand-writing on the letter, much sharper emotions were stirred.

It was in a bold and startling script as if scratched upon iron with the point of a harpoon dipped in the blood of a wolf fish. There could be no mistaking that awesome hand.

Even as I tore open the letter I knew I held in my trembling grasp nothing less than an epistle from that fearsome and aged recluse of the gowithy barrens, Aunt Cissy Roach!

There are some things in this life that are better faced head-on at once rather than put off out of cowardice, since prolonging them serves only to deepen the craven terror. So I braced up and forged ahead and read:

Hello, Mawmouth. Hello:

How is the world treating you, you lazy lay-about sleeveen. I am come back here and am settled in now for the cursed winter. Please to come out on the 8th inst. with a little something for me joints.

I remain, as ever, your most humble and obdt. servant.

Aunt C. Roach

P.S. Sunny Jim is bearing up well considering what the poor little devil have been put through. You'll never get forgiveness in this world or the next.

It took me a full 10 minutes to recover. "Humble and obdt. servant indeed! Aunt Cissy WILL have her little joke. But there was no getting out of it. Just as well put aside a summons from the angel of death as to try to disregard a letter from that ancient yet wiry widow.

I looked to the brighter side, if it can be called that. Such is the countenance, deportment and attitude of this doughty anchorite that no matter how hard the times or how dreary the weather, all seems merry by comparison.

More importantly, if there is a more-or-less human on the face of this whole island who knows the score, it is Aunt Cissy.

So that, in these trying times when "the fox in the streets of the city is prowling," as it were, it is something of a sacred duty to get what may be got from this unique, infallible source.

Readers will doubtless recall accounts in these columns of previous visits with Aunt Cissy. The times when she was in one of her bad days and said but little have been reported.

Her departure from her domicile on the Witless Bay Barrens to go up into the Annieopsquotch Mountains to gird her loins has been recounted.

And how, for the duration, I had been put in charge of her pet carey-chicken, Sunny Jim, the most foul and disagreeable bird that has ever been suffered to live. And that she always suspicioned me of ill-treating the little brute whilst he was in my care.

All these thoughts passed through my mind as I picked up a little something for her joints – a fifth of Olde Bilious Haddock, the best the BLC has to offer – and traveled in my conveyance out to the Witless Bay Line, then a walk of some 13 miles over the barrens.

I approached her humble cot warily as, armed with a double-bit axe, Aunt Cissy is on constant watch for the Son of Darkness, who she claims has designs on her person. If true, I would say the gentleman is foolhardy to the point of madness.

But the premises were strangely silent. There was no sound without or within. I listened, expecting to hear her in the distance singing one of her favorite airs:

Hurrah, my boys, the enemy is shaken!
Hurrah, my boys, Sebastapol is taken!

But there was nothing. Then I saw, pinned to the door with the identical dagger used by the late, great Sarah Bernhardt in her immortal depiction of Lady Macbeth, a note:

Hello, Skin and Grief:
Always behind like the cow's tail, you are. I am gone out. I could not wait longer. Aunt C. Roach

So there it is and there's not a thing in God's world we can or need do about it. Both groveling panic and hysterical joy are pointless. The time has come at last and Aunt Cissy Roach is now abroad in our own dear country as it now, more or less, is. RG

Guy's Encyclopedia of Juvenile Outharbor Delights: Tying Cans Onto Sheep's Tails

October 14, 1969

Outharbor Delights

Whereas there is nothing much on the go these days except the same old thing, and whereas the same old thing amounts to a pain in the neck (not to lower ourselves to vulgarity), let us turn our thoughts to a subject of more consequence.

We refer of course to that definitive and exhaustive treatise issued in limited edition, *Guy's Encyclopedia of Juvenile Outharbor Delights*.

Within the pages of these scholarly volumes are found complete accounts of the various and sundry pastimes by which the outharbor juvenile progressed from here to there. Excerpts from this singular work have been presented here before.

Let us turn today to that section of the *Encyclopedia* which dwells on the outharbor juvenile's relationship with others of God's creatures, furred or feathered, wild or domesticated.

If we were searching for a word to describe this relationship, "aggressive" would spring to our lips. In other words, rocks slung at everything that crept or crawled.

It is not the position of the *Encyclopedia* to delve into the motivations behind such behavior. Such things are better left to the Keeper of the Burgeo Whale. The *Encyclopedia* simply records the facts.

On page 867, we come across an item regarding the widespread juvenile outharbor delight of "Tying Cans Onto Sheep's Tails," one of many outrages that may come in for scrutiny after the seal fishery is tidied up.

This activity is carried out after nightfall and when the moon is no more than in the second quarter. Cover of darkness is necessary since this delight constitutes a serious offence punishable by threats of the Ranger being sent for.

A hardy-looking sheep with a stout tail is selected from the flock and some tin cans are secured by twine to the tail. The sheep is released and the juvenile's labors are over. They have then only to retreat to a high vantage point to observe the chain of events thus set in motion.

There is a brief pause at first until the animal takes a step forward, causing the cans to clink on the road. This serves as the starting gun, the triggering device, so to speak, in the nuclear reaction.

A vast river of lambchops and wool gathers momentum, bursting forth from the meadow, pouring through the lanes, spilling out onto the roads, sweeping along the beaches, flattening any of the populace that happens to be in the way.

Onward, ever onward, sweeps the woolly stampede, picking up speed at every furlong, spurred on by the noisemaker in its midst, not to stop until the string breaks or the shores of Notre Dame Bay are reached.

A sheep is the contrariest animal on the face of the earth and will not lead or drive. The outharbor juvenile spends some of the most torturous days of his early career rounding up sheep on the open country and driving them home for the winter.

This is not to say that "Tying Rocks Onto Sheep's Tails" has anything to do with vengeance. Heaven forbid! But recollections of this grueling experience do help to dampen any pangs of conscience.

"Slinging Rocks at Bullbirds" is another juvenile outharbor delight widely practiced around our coast.

A bullbird is like a black and white bunched-up robin, as you may know, or a small turr. They have a fashion of ducking under water when the fancy strikes them and can stay down so that nothing else will.

This knack gives the bullbird more than a sporting chance. Enough rocks have been slung at an individual bullbird to ballast the St. Barbe Highway. The ambitious juvenile may spend the best part of a day following the self-same bullbird back and forth around shore.

A bullbird will dive, leaving only a faint trail of bubbles, and will surface minutes later some distance from shore. The means by which you get a bullbird to come in handier is to say "Gurk. Ana Gurk Gurk."

This is supposed to be a bullbird bawl, although no one has ever heard one bawl. However, it is the thing to do. When a bullbird gets tired of having rocks slung at him and diving, he may take to wing.

When this occurs, the juvenile is left there with his arm hung out of socket and hoarse from saying "Gurk. Ana Gurk Gurk." It is possible to conk a bullbird with a rock, but it is seldom done.

Although a tedious bird to clean, a bullbird makes a tidy drop of soup. Slinging rocks is the only civilized way to deal with a bullbird. Shooting one is like heaving a hand grenade at a bumblebee.

The only thing the author of the *Encyclopedia* ever shot with a gun was a bullbird and the experience turned his blood so that he has never had the inclination to take up arms again.

At a tender age, he sneaked the breech loader out of the house and fired from the top of a cliff at a bullbird no more than 20 feet distant. One second the bullbird is bobbing along on the waves so unconcerned and the next second there's only a few feathers and a small spot of pink water.

It is funny what will turn the juvenile's blood, but once turned it generally stays turned. So small a thing as a bullbird can do it. In the author's case, it has confined him to shooting bull rather than birds. ∎

Wilberforce and Abigail are for Crosbie.
Selwyn and Beatrice are for Smallwood

October 16, 1969   *Liberals and Pea Seas*

A curious sight crossed my bow as I drove around the Bay one day this week.

At the rear of a modest dwelling in a community which shall remain nameless, I spied a hammock slung between two trees and in it a man of leisure soaking up the late fall sun.

Nothing strange about that. But what caught my eye was the fact that this individual in the hammock appeared to be surrounded by a flock of servants and was being catered to as if he were the Sultan of Zanzibar.

I knew him to be neither an Irish sweepstakes winner nor a government contractor and it seemed impossible to believe that able-bodied relief had reached this glorious peak. Emboldened by curiosity, I stopped my conveyance and went around.

As I approached, one of the servants rushed forward and cautioned me: "Don't breathe on him. Watch the germs. Shhhh. Quiet. He's taking his afternoon nap. You can look but don't touch."

Still mystified, I waited around and it was not long before the figure in the hammock bestirred himself. At that, the four servants sprang into action.

One rushed forward with a bottle of beer, another chased away a sandfly from the vicinity, a third came out of the house with a tray of sandwiches and the fourth inquired as to whether the master would like the hammock gently set in motion.

I introduced myself, explained that curiosity had gotten the better of good manners and hoped he would not think the less of me for butting in.

"No, no, me son, no no. Have a seat," said the man. "Selwyn," he said sharply to one of the flunkies. "Don't just stand there like a gawk. Get the man a little something.

"Rest period. Must keep fit, you know. Beatrice! Stand over there. The sun is in my eyes. Abigail! Scratch my foot. No, no, you ninny! The other one. Yes, I must watch my health. This is a valuable property you're looking at," he continued.

"Ah, it's a hardship having all this responsibility on your shoulders. But I suppose we must all brace up and face it. Everyone is expected to do his duty. Nothing less than our democratic responsibility.

"Wilberforce! Knock off mucking around with that TV set and move it over here so we can watch 'As the World Turns'. Hop to it. A little harder, Abigail, and more to the right.

"Yes, indeed. These things have to be put up with. There's too much shirking these days. Our sacred duty and right, I say, won with blood, toil, sweat and tears."

I was no longer able to contain myself so I came right out and asked him what the devil he was talking about and how come all the fancy treatment.

"Leadership convention," he said. "Uncommitted candidate. Two Crosbie and two Joey workers have been tending me hand and foot since I was elected.

"It started out in a small way. One side approached me and offered a free card in an alligator wallet. Then the other side a free card, a wallet and a ticket on a silver service.

"From that it went. On voting night in Pigsqeek Tickle one side sent over a babysitter. The other side sent a car to pick me up. One lot held an umbrella over my head as I got out of the car and a worker on the other side threw himself in a puddle on the road so's I wouldn't get my feet wet.

"By a stroke of genius I decided to remain uncommitted. So far I've got promise of tickets to Las Vegas, a Caribbean Cruise, a color television set and a year's supply of cornflakes.

"But there are problems, I can tell you. Those three days at the convention in St. John's are going to be absolute hell. Decisions. Vital decisions that have to be faced up to.

"For instance, one of the most vital decisions I'll have to make is whether to stay aboard a luxury liner or in the bridal suite at the hotel. Oh, it's no game, I can tell you, to have the future of the province resting on your shoulders.

"I have my troubles with this bunch, too. Wilberforce and Abigail are for Crosbie. Selwyn and Beatrice are for Smallwood. They tend to scrap among themselves."

At that moment, Beatrice was intent on wrenching out a handful of Abigail's hair while Abigail was lunging after Beatrice's jugular with bared incisors.

The man in the hammock picked up a bullwhip lying alongside and aimed a cut in the general direction of the combatants. It had little effect and he sighed wearily:

"Three more weeks of this. Sometimes I think I made a mistake. If I had committed to one or the other all I'd have to put up with would be threats, intimidation, blacklists, Cosa Nostra tactics, skullduggery and terrorism."

When I happened to glance up again I was startled to see that Beatrice had stripped down to her knickers and she and Selwyn had launched into the official Smallwood Campaign Song: "The Liberals are Together and Happy are We."

Not to be outdone, Abigail commenced to divest herself of her garments until she was attired only in three New Generation Of Leadership buttons. She and Wilberforce went into a dance to the tune of the Crosbie Song.

Modesty overcame me and I quickly departed. ▨

Mowat: In search of other noble savages

October 20, 1969 *Culture and History*

CORRECTION AND APOLOGY

I received through the public mails today a brief note which fills my frail carcass with a mixture of shame and terror. It reads:

Hello Pig's Knucks,

You know what you got to do now. Do it and be quick about it. I remain, as ever, your humble and obdt. servant,

Aunt C. Roach.

The bounds of the earth are not wide enough to offer escape from the eye or the wrath of Aunt Cissy Roach. I made sincere and abject apologies for using the dear old soul's name in vain in Friday's column.

My only excuse is that I got carried away when I made reference to a certain "promise" which I attributed to Aunt Cissy. I'm afraid I put words in her mouth. I apologize and beg mercy.

For Aunt Cissy Roach to bring her talents to bear on a person, thing or any group thereof would be a hundred times more devastating (and unsporting) than shooting a bullbird with a 12-gauge at the range of 20 feet. The results would be terrible beyond comprehension.

Pray that she never makes a "promise" in your direction. By the way, have you by any chance caught a glimpse of Aunt Cissy lately, she now being abroad in the land with her loins, need it be said, girded?

***

It may seem irrelevant to pop a book into the midst of the present fun and games, but while a new book on Newfoundland by the doughty and irascible Farley Mowat might possibly be irrelevant, it certainly can't be ignored.

Political campaigns come and go, but the Newfoundland "image" is always there. The "Newfoundland mystique" as Trudeau put it, and put it free gratis, a grant from the Just Society.

So it is always important, if not vital, to see how the Newfoundland "image" fares in the hands of Canada's best-known author. The kind of reception you get when you next go abroad has not a little to do with Mowat's latest Newfoundland book.

This obsession we have with what THEY think of us is a touchy business and one that we sometimes carry to ridiculous extremes. Nevertheless, it does exist … but ours not to reason why right now.

The Boat Who Wouldn't Float is the name of the volume just out. In it Mowat tells of his trials and tribulations after buying a 30-foot sailboat on the southern shore.

It is the funniest piece of literature about Newfoundland that I have ever read (discounting the unintentional humor in certain political speeches). At least, the first half of the book is.

I've been waiting for someone to get wind of the book and again carry the "what THEY are going to think of us" obsession to ridiculous extremes. But the fact is that Mowat is making fun with us, not at us, and anyone who tries to make out differently should be blacklisted.

True, the locals of "Muddy Hole" on the southern shore where this remarkable scow, the *Happy Adventure*, originated are caricatured unmercifully, but the same treatment is also given one Jack McClelland of Toronto.

McClelland, one of Canada's largest book publishers and Mowat's also, was Farley's partner on the boat deal. A classic confrontation results.

Into Muddy Hole rolls Jack, the Toronto executive, radiating optimism and efficiency, clad in yachting cap, sharkskin slacks and hopsack sports jacket, and driving a massive automobile.

The twain meet at last. The west comes face to face with the inscrutable east. It's the best sociology report on the subject yet written. Both Newfoundlanders and "adopted" Newfoundlanders will see exactly how they look to each other at first glance – if they can stop laughing long enough.

More devastating than a hundred editorials "viewing with alarm" is the account of Jack's trek to St. John's for supplies, armed with a list and full of wind and business.

Only to run full-butt into the apathy, the frustrating inefficiency, the complete and utter disdain for the customer with which St. John's business houses reek. McClelland staggers back from the encounter battered but ever game.

For half the book the titanic struggle between east and west continues until at last Jack is summoned back to his Toronto office, his head bloody but unbowed. The east, of course, absorbs the encounter without a ripple.

Mowat's exploits in St. Pierre and on the south coast are amusing, but the great struggle is missing after McClelland departs. The voyage to Expo is an anti-climax.

What our fellow Canadians will think of us after this I wouldn't venture to say. But I for one would far rather they got this picture of us than the one offered by the tourist office's pompous nonsense about "a race apart."

This could be Mowat's last Newfoundland book. He's moved on in search of other "noble savages," at last report either to the Magdalen Islands or Siberia.

We're on our own now and it's a pity. Good old Farley was a wonderful help by making fun with us through our trials and tribulations of trying to keep the *Happy Adventure* above water.

The Boat Who Wouldn't Float by Farley Mowat, McClelland and Stewart Ltd., Toronto. $6.95, 243 pages. ▨

Down in Mr. Moores's hens' pen

Liberals and Pea Seas

As Gerald Irvine Hill, minister without portfolio and Liberal MHA for Labrador South, bustled aboard the aircraft bound from Goose Bay to St. John's and flounced into a seat, anyone could see he was greatly distressed.

What in the world, you well may ask, had so distressed the honorable minister.

For Mr. Hill is one of the most cocky of Mr. Smallwood's loyal Liberals. Though rather short in stature, he positively radiates self-confidence. Some would even say he looks like a watered-down version of John C. Doyle.

With his cigar and his expensive-looking suits, and his pugnacious demeanor, you would have to use the word "cocky" if you were ever called upon to describe Mr. Hill.

The little chore – delegate elections – that he was just returning from should certainly not have distressed him so. Had he not boasted weeks earlier that he had his district all sewed up for Mr. Smallwood?

That all he had to do was go into a community with a $20 bill, buy 20 party membership cards, distribute them to 20 known Smallwood Liberals and his labors were over? No sweat. Then why was Mr. Hill perspiring so freely now?

Cartwright should have been a cinch. For a start, there was the classic Smallwood core – clergy, merchants and government agents – who, as in so many other Newfoundland communities, keep the toiling masses well in line.

And Cartwright was isolated. Should it be necessary to be a little, shall we say, "stern," no disagreeable rumors would pass beyond the boundaries. Word doesn't get into and word doesn't get out of Cartwright that easily.

The only worry, of course, was that Crosbie man. But since that organization had seemed rather lackadaisical about it all, Mr. Hill still saw no cause for worry. He lit another cigar.

His plane had landed at Cartwright and he was greeted as usual by the merchant Fecquet (pronounced "Fecky"), and he went to his usual lodgings at the home of William Moores, representative in Cartwright of the Department of Labrador Affairs.

Some weeks before, Mr. Hill had distributed his $20 worth of party membership cards into the proper hands. Well, $19 worth to 19 loyal Smallwood Liberals.

Such people as the local merchant and his wife; Mrs. Moores, wife of Cartwright's leading civil servant; and Mrs. Waye, the wife of the Rev. Munden Waye. The proper hands.

It would be merely a formality. There were about 300 eligible voters in Cartwright. But no one else had distributed cards. Only the 19 people to whom

Mr. Hill had distributed cards would be able to vote.

Later in the day, the Crosbie man arrived. That evening he held a meeting and found that at least 80 people were angry because they didn't have cards. They said they were never given the chance to obtain them.

They were angry because out of 300 eligible voters in Cartwright, only 19 would be allowed to vote or to be delegates to the convention. So they went across to the hall where Mr. Hill and his 19 card carriers were going to have the meeting.

Mr. Hill was there and so was one Cecil Soper, who had come up representing the Liberal Association to supervise the meeting.

Readers may vaguely recall the name. Mr. Soper is the former town manager of Clarenville who was accused by the Clarenville Chamber of Commerce of setting up a company with the mayor to speculate on land development in the town. A commission investigated and exonerated the pair.

(Not to make the story more complicated, but the mayor was Dr. John H. Swan, who is better known these days as the eastern vice-president of the Liberal Association.)

But Mr. Soper was now in Cartwright in a dual capacity. He was there to supervise the meeting for the Liberal Association, but also, as it turned out, to do some work for his other employer, John Shaheen of Third Mill fame.

Cartwright is rather weary – like everyone else – of hearing about Mr. Shaheen's fabled enterprise. Still, there is not much in the way of surplus jobs in the area and they hang to any hopes that Mr. Shaheen may do some pulpwood cutting there.

So Mr. Hill, his cigar and Mr. Soper now faced a hall packed with people who didn't have party membership cards. Mr. Hill, it is said, was agitated, vexed and furious. His cigar twitched and he spun around and around on his heels.

Mr. Soper ordered the hall cleared, but the 80 people refused to go. The crowd then started calling on Mr. Hill to make a speech. It would be at least something to while away the time.

He ascended to the stage and with his complexion fluctuating (the clergy and the merchants and the civil servant's wife were also aghast), he snapped: "There were plenty of application forms for cards. They were there for anybody who wanted them. That's no excuse. And there's no excuse for this shocking business here tonight."

This gave rise to loud boos and calls and some laughter at the bit about the cards being available. Mr. Hill was unable to continue and the shock was great because he was not used to it. He was in a bit of a state and when he left the stage someone threw him a handkerchief.

Meanwhile, the sharp-thinking Mr. Soper had slipped out and summoned the law in the shape of the lone RCMP constable stationed at Cartwright.

The constable soon arrived and went to the front of the hall. He declared that this was a private meeting and ordered all unauthorized persons to leave.

They did not. Some of the women took out knitting. Some of the men chatted with each other and some had a smoke.

It was, you might say, civil disobedience. It was, you might say, defiance of not only an arm of the law and a Minister of the Crown but of a representative of the man who, as he tells us, stands next to the Queen herself!

So the constable turned and went his way and said that he couldn't very well arrest all 80 people in the hall.

Then Mr. Soper, who is described at this point as being "not tame," called the meeting off. He and Mr. Hill went off through the dark toward Mr. Moores's house with part of the crowd following some distance behind.

The disgruntled duo soon came to a fork in the road. They inquired of some youngsters who chanced to be near which was the right branch, and the children, whether through mischief or no, gave them the wrong directions.

Mr. Hill, his cigar, and Mr. Soper ended up down in Mr. Moores's hens' pen. As they stumbled about amid the chicken wire, a hearty round of applause echoed out of the darkness that hung over Cartwright.

There were reports that potatoes (uncooked) were hurled at Mr. Moores's house after Mr. Hill and Mr. Soper finally got inside. These reports have been denied, however, by one resident who explained: "Potatoes up here cost us more than $7 a sack. They're too dear, sir, for that purpose."

The next morning at 10:50 the Crosbie man met Mr. Soper and asked him when the meeting would be held again. At 11 a.m., in 10 minutes time, said Mr. Soper rather snappishly, and in a private house. The house of Merchant Fecquet, in fact.

The Crosbie man, Joseph Harvey, said that three card-carriers who would have voted for Crosbie delegates – schoolteachers – and three others he had imported from Mary's Harbour had only five minutes' notice of the meeting. Another Crosbie prospect was working five miles away.

So Mr. Harvey made no attempt to attend the meeting, and left the community. The meeting was held at the Fecquet house with 13 card-carriers attending. They elected 10 of their number to go to the Liberal leadership convention in St. John's.

But what then of Mr. Hill and Mr. Soper? Frank Kelly, president of the Coastal Labrador Regional Development Association (better known as CLARDA), says Mr. Soper reminded him that he was making a report on Cartwright for Mr. Shaheen.

Mr. Kelly says Mr. Soper revealed that he had, prior to the incident, thought of Cartwright as a place of "good solidarity and community spirit." But now he feared that his report to Mr. Shaheen on Cartwright would not be very good.

(It is a pity that more details are not immediately available with which to flesh out, as it were, the principals of the drama. All we know of Rev. Waye, for instance, is that he once hit the headlines for expelling a schoolteacher from Cartwright on charges that he was a Communist.)

Joseph Hamel, chairman of the Cartwright community council, says

Rev. Waye, the morning after, brought him a message from Mr. Hill saying that following the shocking behavior in the hall, the council had just lost a government allowance of $1,000.

And that Mr. Hill had a list of all who took part in the protest at the hall and that he would see to it that not one of those on this list ever earned one cent from Mr. Shaheen's proposed operation. Not one red cent, presumably.

Asked about this later, Rev. Waye said: "I did not deliver an official message from Mr. Hill to Mr. Hamel."

Asked if he had delivered a message of any kind, Rev. Waye said: "I did not deliver any official message from Mr. Hill to Mr. Hamel."

Mr. Hill's response, when quizzed on the same point, was chastely simple: "No comment."

So no wonder Mr. Hill was greatly distressed as he winged his way back toward St. John's. It was a messy business and the news had leaked out. He would soon have to face that dreadful meeting with his boss and no good explanation ready.

Meanwhile, back at Cartwright, the people were still talking about that strange night when no one moved when the Mountie ordered them. Nothing like that had ever happened there before.

What did they conclude from it? Perhaps only that it feels rather good not to be afraid any more of the little man with the big cigar. The man from Joey. ■

Elements of Hitlerism
that exist in Smallwoodism

November 3, 1969   *Liberals and Pea Seas*

Events – or stomachs – have not settled down enough yet after the Mad Hatter's Tea Party to figure out what, if anything, really happened.

It proved one basic thing but no more than has been common knowledge for a long time – we have a government that has the support of much less than half the people.

Smallwoodism is dead and won't lie down. More than half the voters voted against Smallwoodism in the last federal election. And now we see that a great chunk of the Liberal party is also against Smallwoodism.

So that leaves us in a pretty pickle. Apparently stuck for up to two years with a government that no more than 20 or 30 per cent of Newfoundlanders want. Something has got to give.

But, as we say, any attempt at peering into the immediate future is best put off to another day when our eardrums stop vibrating and our puddicks stop hopping about like cornered weasels. For today, some tidbits:

We're supposed to be the poorest spot in Canada yet we learn that someone was able to scrape up no less than $3 million (perhaps more) to put off the television spectacular we saw during the weekend.

In a province like this, where does money like that come from? Just to put off the shindig at the stadium cost $323,000, which is $70,000 more than all the Liberals in Canada got together for their leadership convention in Ottawa in 1968.

The answer to it all lies right there. If we could find out where this money came from, we'd know who's really running Newfoundland.

When Smallwood won, hundreds stood and held their arms out at a 45-degree angle, palms down, in the Hitler salute.

Asked about the demonstration later, Mr. Smallwood said it was caused by a few young people who had got into the Crosbie organization only for the privilege of jeering him. He said they were fascist-minded.

He's reached the state now where it's almost a sin to laugh at him anymore. The Pushie report was 90 per cent trash because he didn't agree with it. The Liberals lost the last election in Newfoundland because of tons of hate-Trudeau literature. Newfoundland is going on the rocks because of the war in Vietnam.

Is he really at the point now where he believes his own nonsense? And so out of touch with reality that he sees and hears only what he wants? Or is it still all a bluff on "the bigger the lie" theory?

To interpret the demonstration at the stadium as an indication that those giving the Hitler salute were admirers of Hitler is a little too brazen for even glazed-eyed idiots to swallow.

What, in the height of emotion, the demonstrators were doing was protesting the elements of Hitlerism that exist in Smallwoodism. They were saying it was a disgrace to the memory of those who died fighting Hitler to allow any trace of it to exist in Newfoundland – and in the St. John's Memorial Stadium.

After actually seeing the song and dance at the stadium in person and later seeing bits of the same thing replayed on television, you can spot a few of the differences between the television picture and reality.

For instance, on television, which is the version most people saw, the protest when Smallwood won seemed not nearly so loud as it was in the stadium. Smallwood's voice was picked up by the television and you could hear most of it.

Whereas, at the stadium there were times when, despite the loudspeakers, Smallwood was drowned out altogether by the shouts of "Seig Heil" and the cheers for Crosbie.

The comparison made by the protestors between Smallwoodism and Hitlerism was not, of course, a direct comment on what went on at the stadium. It was a comment on the tactics used during 20 years by the person who once declared: "Hitler was a great man."

But still, for anyone with these tactics in the back of their minds, there were hints (innocent or not) in the stadium to remind them. The Joey placards, for instance, were in the Nazi colors – black, white and red – and the colors were in about the same proportion to those on the banners at Nuremberg. The shape of the placards also resembled those banners.

When the victory was announced, the doors of the stadium burst open and a great and hideous thunder of drums overwhelmed the building. A blare of trumpets drowned all protest.

For anyone who had those other things in mind it was a brief moment of sick terror. But then you saw that the drums were being beaten by little girls in pretty costumes.

Smallwoodism is dead but the skeleton fingers still clutch the throat of Newfoundland. The power of their grip is certainly not supplied by a grey, balding 70-year-old grandfather. Smallwood has no more control over Smallwoodism than has a babe in arms. The creation sweeps the creator on before it.

The power comes from the momentum of 20 years and, more importantly, from the massive batteries that were charged when Smallwoodism was alive and at the peak of its power. ▉

Aunt Cissy: A horrified chill
crept up my spine

November 18, 1969   *Aunt Cissy*

There were so many rumors going the rounds of late that she was either ill or had actually crossed over at last that I could restrain myself no longer.

So once more I boarded my horseless carriage to make that familiar jaunt out to the Witless Bay Line and then another 13 miles on foot in over the barrens.

Imagination can be our worst enemy (memory notwithstanding) and I made the journey with even more foreboding than usual. Aunt Cissy Roach may have her weak points, but it's a bad dog that's not missed.

Not forgetting to bring her a little something for her stomach's sake, I had picked up a crock of fortified bilgewater at the Controllers the evening before.

The sun had just risen as I approached the humble cot of this ancient recluse which stands there on the barrens amid rocks as big as houses and is ever circled by fat soggy ravens the size of vultures.

With a fearful heart I knocked upon the door of her domicile, and there was no answer. But hearing some sounds of activity within, I braced up, pushed the door open and entered.

And there was Aunt Cissy bent over her wood stove and muttering wickedly to herself. "Whoo hoo," I said brightly. "It's me again."

I ducked just in time to avoid being decapitated, she having snatched up her double-bit axe and flung it so that it sunk into the door next to my ear. That's one thing about Aunt Cissy. She keeps you on your toes.

"Ah, 'tis the devil's own boo-beggar," exclaimed Aunt Cissy. "I must be in somebody's black books surely to God. One trouble on top of another. And now the biggest disaster of all appears at me door. Come in, come in, mawmouth, now that you're here. If this keeps up there's going to be talk and me a poor widow-woman here alone. Keep your hands to yourself, sport. I might be small but I'm wiry.

"The sons of breeches broke in while I was gone," she continued. "I just now got it cleaned up. They smashed and ransacked me little house from top to bottom and messed in the corners. A lucky thing I caught them in the very act. The world is better off without 'em."

A horrified chill crept up my spine as I glanced at Aunt Cissy's axe still quivering in the door. But I could not bear to glance at the timeless widow's face to see if she was really joking or not. With Aunt Cissy you can never be sure.

At that moment, Sunny Jim, the most vile and disagreeable bird that has ever been suffered to live, let out a squawk from his cage. Aunt Cissy, being strongly attached her pet carey-chicken, went over to him and started chucking him affectionately under the chin.

"Now, now, Sunny Jim knows how mawmouth here mistreated him, don't he? Yes, yes. Sunny Jim knows don't he though. Now, now, Aunt Cissy's precious lamb," she said in disparaging reference to my supposed treatment of the little brute whilst he was in my care.

Just then the miserable little flamer lunged at her finger with his bill and drew blood. She up fist and clunked him under the beak, driving him ears-over-kettle, back into the corner of his cage with the offhand remark that he was high-spirited of late.

She then turned her attention to the wood stove and the placement of kindling in it. "The cursed wood in this cursed flamin' country. Soggy, mildewed, good-for-nothing. What you haven't got to put yourself through to get a spark going."

Were this not a genteel journal I would record her subsequent remarks here, and it is a pity that they must go unrecorded since they far transcended vulgarity and blasphemy to pass into the realm of pure poetry. With this and the shaking of her fist, the kindling burst into flame.

"Tell me, know-it-all," says Aunt Cissy, applying more wood, "what's going on. I've been abroad and know but I'll humor myself and see what you got to say."

"Well, Aunt Cissy," I said, "there is a growing opinion in many quarters that the events we see are not reality at all but merely the by-product or spinoff, if you like, of a more basic trend.

"This has to do with the theory that the active populating of the peripheral areas of the world such as Newfoundland, which began back in the days of Elizabeth I, Francis Bacon and William Shakespeare, has now reached a peak and a reverse action has set in.

"That is to say that whereas people once flooded out of the crowded cities of Europe to settle in and inhabit the far reaches such as Newfoundland and Tierra del Fuego their ancestors are now caught up in a move away from these areas to the new cities such as Boston and Toronto.

"It is said that in our case, the government at Ottawa is engaged in a scheme to encourage this trend of which centralization on the local level is one step. Consequently, whatever the surface details of local politics may be, the basic fact is that we are attending upon the wake of Newfoundland which is bound to become a desert once more. Many have already bought their one-way tickets to the mainland."

Aunt Cissy appeared not to be listening to this piece of long-winded intelligence at all as she was engaged in fitting a large piece of plank into the stove.

It was a solid piece of wood and obviously hardwood of a type which does not grow in the soil of this country but had driven ashore as driftwood from across the Gulf.

Finding it too long for the stove she took an end in each hand, went into a semi-crouch and brought it down smartly across one (ugh!) bony knee.

There was a fearful crunch and rending and splintering noise and I was aghast for it seemed that the limb of that aged and frail-looking recluse had given way.

But instead, I was forced to duck again as splinters and fragments of the wood flew to every corner of her abode, knocking askew a likeness of Her Late Majesty the Empress of India and glancing off a picture from the *War Cry* on the wall – although she is not of that religion or any other that I know of.

I was surprised both at the strength of her aged bones and the forcefulness of her action since there was hardly enough of the plank left to burn.

She showed no signs of distress whatsoever at the blow or else disguised it by clearing her throat with a long and magnificently resounding hawk after which she spat vigorously over her shoulder without looking. Had I not again been on my toes, I would have doubtless been nailed to the wall.

Whatever else, it will be a long time before I have worries about the condition of her health despite the fact that viewed from a distance she might appear to some to be cheating the undertaker. █

Dover says "no." Robert Wells of the provincial attorney general's office discusses resettlement with a group of Dover residents in August 1961. Unlike many communities, the people of Dover successfully resisted government pressure to move. Wells became a cabinet minister in the Moores administration in the 1970s and later a supreme court judge.

"A Train Load of Dominion Rubbers for Parker & Monroe." One of many attempts by Smallwood to introduce manufacturing to Newfoundland during the 1950s included the Superior Rubber factory in Holyrood. Massive cost overruns and the installation of obsolete manufacturing equipment doomed the factory, and it closed in 1956 after less than two years in operation.

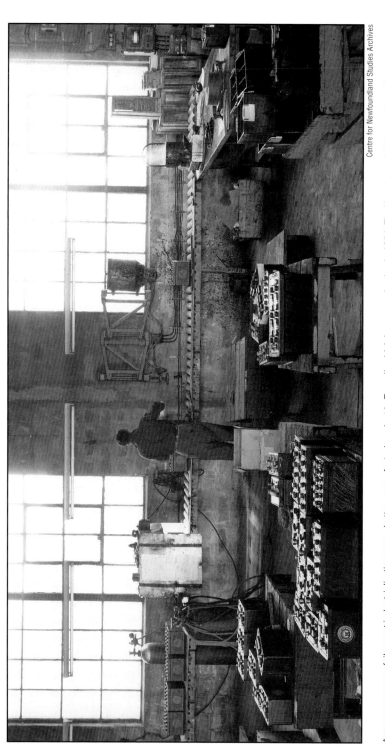

Among numerous failures at industrialization was a battery manufacturing plant in Topsail, which began production in 1954. The Hanning and Kahl operation, like many such ventures during the 1950s, was funded by Germans, who were lured to Newfoundland by a former Nazi collaborator, Alfred Valdmanis.

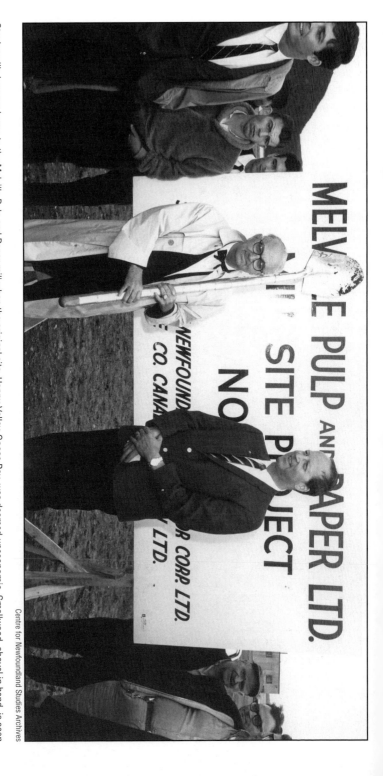

Stephenville became home to the Melville Pulp and Paper mill when the original site, Happy Valley-Goose Bay, was deemed uneconomic. Smallwood, shovel in hand, is seen in 1967 marking the official start of construction of the plant, which became known as the Labrador Linerboard mill. It began production in 1973, but lost millions of dollars before being converted to a pulp mill in 1978. It closed for good in 2005.

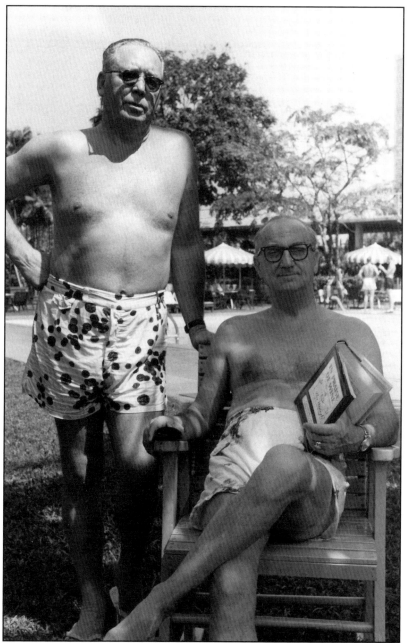

Civil servant and ex-convict, Oliver Vardy, vacationing with Smallwood in Panama in 1960. Vardy later fled to Panama and successfully fought extradition to Canada, where he faced fraud charges in connection with construction of the Stephenville Linerboard mill. In this photograph, Smallwood is reading In Praise of Wine and Certain Noble Spirits by Alec Waugh, supposed inventor of the cocktail party and brother of novelist Evelyn Waugh.

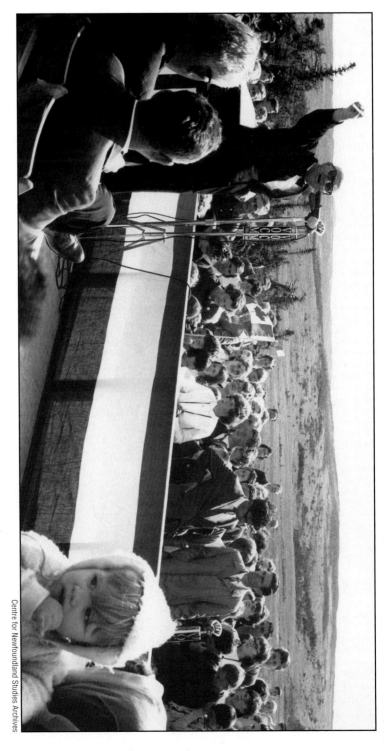

On August 1, 1966, Smallwood presided over sod-turning ceremonies at Long Harbour for the ERCO phosphorous plant. Subsidized electricity from the new Bay d'Espoir hydroelectric project, along with millions of dollars in federal and provincial government grants, lured ERCO to Newfoundland. ERCO closed the plant in 1989.

After years of rancorous negotiations with Quebec, Newfoundland signed an agreement in principle in 1965 to proceed with the Upper Churchill Falls hydroelectric power project. It provided construction jobs for Newfoundland, while Quebec received long-term access to cheap power, much of which was exported to the United States.

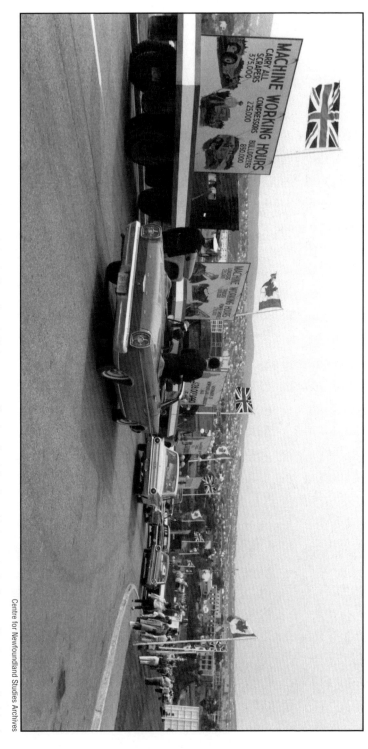

Centre for Newfoundland Studies Archives

"We'll Finish the Drive in '65" was the slogan for completing the Trans Canada Highway across Newfoundland. Smallwood led a cavalcade of cars and trucks across the island in 1966, and was joined by Prime Minister Lester Pearson in Grand Falls. The first stage of the cross-island celebration is shown here at the steps of Confederation Building in St. John's on July 11, 1966.

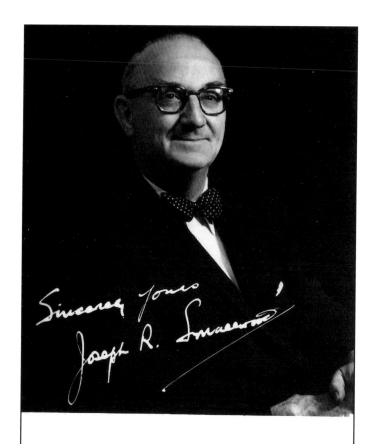

Hon. Joseph R. Smallwood
PREMIER OF NEWFOUNDLAND
Leader of the Liberal Party

humbly presents himself to the voters of St. John's West as candidate of the Liberal Party.

He stands for Newfoundland's RIGHTS . . . .

Smallwood never backed away from a fight. The 1959 provincial election was contested over Term 29 of the Terms of Union with Canada and, to prove a point, J.R. Smallwood challenged PC incumbent Malcolm Hollett in the Tory stronghold of St. John's West. Hollett, who had backed Prime Minister Diefenbaker over the key election issue, was soundly defeated.

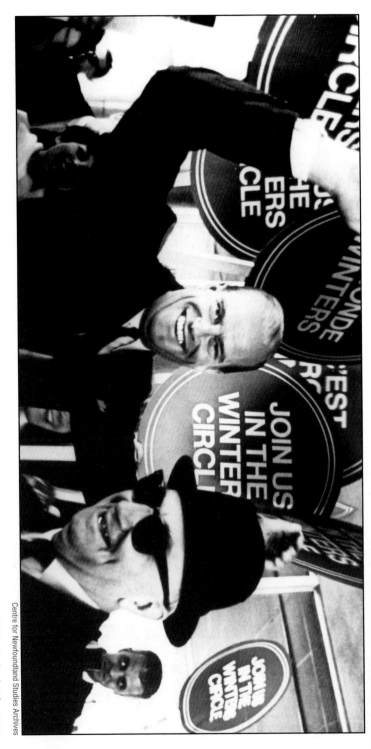

Politician-turned-businessman-turned-politician, Robert Winters brokered an agreement between Newfoundland and Quebec on the Churchill Falls hydroelectric power project. In 1968, he finished a close second to Pierre Trudeau in the Liberal leadership contest to succeed Prime Minister Lester Pearson. Winters is seen here at the convention with Smallwood, who, despite the smile, was supporting Trudeau.

Being "heart to heart" with Smallwood did nothing to help Pierre Trudeau win seats in Newfoundland, in what was a precursor of the electoral disaster awaiting the premier in 1971. The federal Liberals, who had won all seven of the province's seats in 1965, lost six of them in the 1968 election.

A bitter campaign for leadership of the Liberal Party in 1969 pitched former cabinet minister John C. Crosbie against Smallwood, who was running to succeed himself. Crosbie lost and later joined the Progressive Conservative Party. Crosbie is seen here at the leadership convention entering Memorial Stadium with his wife, Jane. Their daughter, Elaine (who married businessman Craig Dobbin), is second from right.

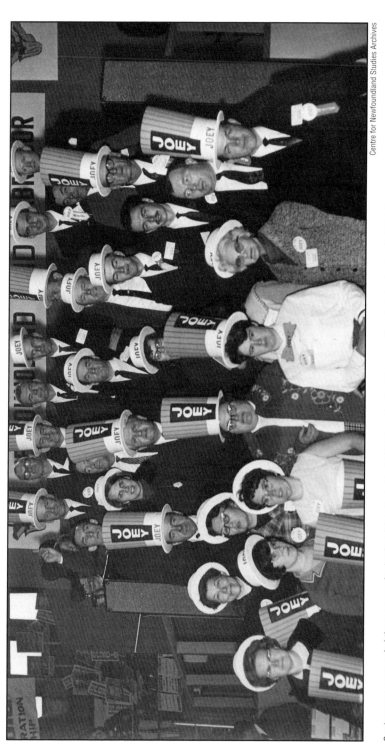

Controversy surrounded the process of selecting delegates to the 1969 Liberal leadership convention. In Labrador South, MHA Gerald Hill provided party membership cards solely to those who favored Smallwood, and they alone were allowed to elect delegates. Labrador South's delegation is seen here at the leadership convention in St. John's.

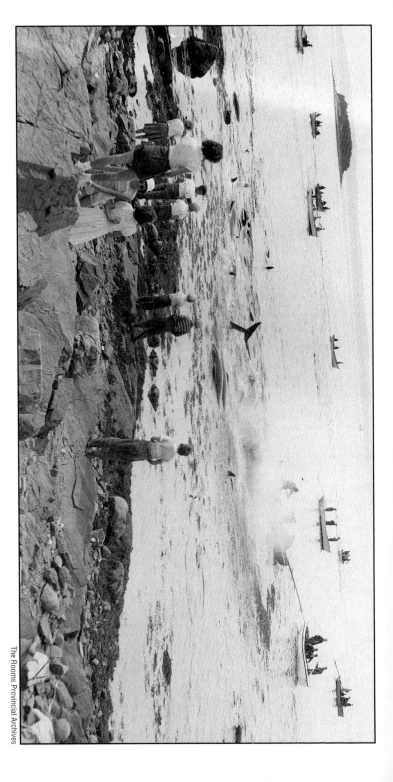

The Rooms Provincial Archives

Whale drives, such as this pothead round-up in the 1950s (possibly at Bellevue Beach), were conducted with little controversy until the mid-1960s when author Farley Mowat moved to Newfoundland.

The Evening Telegram, February 1, 1967

When a fin whale became trapped in a saltwater pond at Burgeo in 1967, a call for assistance from Farley Mowat – who was living in the community – resulted in a pledge of $1,000 by the provincial government for the care and feeding of the animal. The assistance came too late for the whale, as residents had mortally wounded it by firing hundreds of shotgun rounds into its body. Mowat's book, A Whale for the Killing, which described the killing of the whale, made him a pariah for many Newfoundlanders.

Well now: "Cootchy, cootchy coo..."

The Evening Telegram newsroom, in 1963, was located on Duckworth Street in St. John's. Left to right: Ray Guy, reporter; Bob Badcock (standing) sports editor; Gary Callahan (background), reporter; Bob Ennis (seated, rear view), news editor; Tommy Power, copy editor; Maurice Finn, desk editor; Mary Deanne Shears, women's page editor.

The Telegram

My mother didn't rear me
to be election fodder

November 28, 1969   *Liberals and Pea Seas*

Purely by accident I happened to overhear a curious conversation the other day in the offices of a certain political party.

Whilst it is never my practice to go around listening at keyholes (save us and keep us!), I chanced upon this unique scene by accident.

There I was, walking down the street, minding my own business and looking for a sale on day-old bread when I heard muffled cries and the sounds of a skirmish in this building.

Since there are so many stories in the news today about people being beaten up while the public either stands around watching or passes by, I forced myself to stop and see what was up.

I went around through the alley to the back of the building and by standing on a garbage can could see in the window. There were four men inside and three of them had the fourth backed up against the wall.

My impulse was to call the Constabulary, but I hesitated to make sure the situation was really as serious as it first appeared. You have to be certain of your ground before you go so far as to take several constables away from the parking meters.

The three "attackers," as I took them to be, did not seem to be overly violent but the man against the wall was greatly distressed.

Placing my ear against the window, I picked up the following conversation:

"No, boys! No, no, no! I can't do it. I won't do it. It's not civilized to ask me to do it. Anything else. Anything else in the world!

"I'd sharpen pencils in Ottawa the rest of my life. I'd volunteer for scrutineer at the seal fishery. I'll push the Newfie Bullet to Port aux Basques and back," said the man against the wall.

"Look at it this way, Nelson," said one of the other three. "It's a dirty job, we know, and nobody wants to do it. But it's got to be done. When we agreed to draw straws you could have backed out then. Brace up, man, and take it on the chin."

The man against the wall was sobbing gently: "I never thought I'd come to this. Never, never, never. How low can a man go before he's called to his reward? No, I can't, I can't. Anything, anything …"

At this he broke away and made a dash for the window and it seemed to me that he would have dived through it headfirst had not the other three managed to collar him.

They got him over to a chair and lowered him into it. After a few minutes he seemed to be more composed, but was still in a hard state.

"I know it's my patriotic duty," he said, his voice still quavering with emotion. "I'm a loyal Newfoundlander. I'd do anything for Newfoundland. But this would mean I'd have to live here. The weather is bad enough in Ottawa on times, we know, but, my God …

"Couldn't we work out a compromise?" he pleaded. "Couldn't I just sort of wander off and disappear and never be heard of again? I wouldn't bother you. I'd get a job in a herring factory in BC."

"Nelson!" said one of his three captors sternly. "Stop trying to weasel out of it. It's unbecoming. You lost … er, I mean, won fair and square and now you must take your medicine."

"Have a heart, lads," wailed the poor unfortunate. "Can't you see my situation? My mother didn't rear me to be election fodder. I'm too young to join the list of party immortals who have dropped by the wayside.

"I had a good career ahead of me. Even got an invitation to Dalton Camp's New Year's cocktail party. It was a good life up there on Parliament Hill away from the foggy, foggy dew. My asthma had almost cleared up.

"Now, what have I got to look forward to? I might as well order my casket right now. Those long, drawn-out springs, those constituents you actually have to meet every day, those nasty things Mr. Smallwood is always saying about you."

"Enough of this nonsense, boys," snapped one of the three. "Get a good armlock on him and stand over here behind the desk so's it looks like we have a hand on his shoulder. One false move, Nelson, and I'm afraid we'll have to be rough.

"Pull yourself together, man. Look on the bright side, such as it is. You could win the leadership and there is a chance, you know, that you might not lose a provincial election."

At this, a heartrending wail escaped from Nelson: "Ooooooow! Please God I will lose. Whose afraid of losing? It's winning I'm afraid to face. Imagine … me as premier and this party forming the government!"

"With the state she's in we'd never see daylight again. Why do you think it's so hard to get anyone to run for leadership? Because they might have the bad luck to win an election."

One of the other three took a firmer grip on his hammerlock on Nelson and said to his comrade: "Phone the press, Sinbad, and tell them to come down for a press conference. Tell them we've got another candidate for the PC leadership." █

There has been much exaggeration about outport life

January 20, 1970

Resettlement and Rural Life

Outports have been practically ignored in the news and in the House for a long time. The concentration is either on St. John's or on the sites of those "great new industries."

The news media is often inclined to say: "Nothing ever happens out there apart from a whale coming ashore or someone lost in the woods." This is what comes from having a narrow view of what is "news." The outports are "where it's at," as they say, if they were looked at properly.

Count how many members of the House actually live in their districts and you may be surprised. Another reason the outports have been ignored is that they have been officially condemned to death.

It is stated government policy that all outports are to be wiped out and the people herded into 10 or 12 "growth centers." Much damage has already been done. This is one of the greatest crimes ever committed against the Newfoundland people.

But now it seems that the outports are coming into the spotlight. In some areas we hear more of regional development committees and later this month the university is holding a long series of discussions involving many people on "Conflict and crisis in the Newfoundland community." Perhaps at this late date we'll see where the real "news" is.

How could the total destruction of Newfoundland outports become the policy of the government? First and foremost, it was the result of the whims and brainstorms of one person so established in power he could ignore anything that didn't fit in with his wild whims.

Then there are the "planners," the boys who stick pins in a map and refer to the pins as people. There must have been much opposition to the slaughter among the "planners and experts," but opposition you can hear is a rare commodity in Newfoundland.

Those who objected were silenced. Those who agreed ... well, they must state their reasons more clearly than they have in the past. They've worked all their lives to achieve a certain level and type of "success." Perhaps they wish to convince themselves that it hasn't been a waste of time by seeing everyone else aspire to a watered-down version of their way of life.

But success is merely the ability to wrestle as much contentment and happiness out of life as can be got. When you see a very old person who neither longs for nor fears death, you see success. However it's accomplished.

There has been much exaggeration about outport life. There were all sorts of outports and in some the people were dispirited, mean and slovenly; in others, bright, content and lively.

In one you would see an unmarried mother shut away with all the scorn and reproach of relatives and community turned against her until she could bear the weight no more, and died. Just as surely so if she had been in the middle of Africa and cursed by a witch doctor.

In another you would see the people say it was a shocking thing but it happens, and they would call the little one no worse than a "merrybegot" (there are worse things to be called) and it would be taken in with normal joy to get a fair share of whatever a family and community gives.

They say there was privation. But it is hard to starve when you can produce everything yourself except tea, sugar and tobacco. In the "hard times" when some people in St. John's could not earn enough to buy a pound of beans, some people in the outports had roast partridge to eat, and wild ducks and hares, lobsters, smoked salmon, herring roe, saddle of deer, lambs fattened on the salt marshes, dishes of steamed mussels, "cow's butter," joints of beef and fresh eggs.

They say there was sickness in the hard times, but much more than even now in the slums of the great cities? They say there was hard work, but how is it that the fishermen looked as well in his box without the undertaker's cosmetics as the factory worker who went back and forth with his lunch pail for 50 years?

It was no small thing we had hold of and it is no small thing to be slaughtered out of hand at the whim of a single person. Some say it is too late and that it is all dead and young ones can never have a shore to walk around with the addition now of dentists and schools.

But most say they can and, despite it all, their hope grows stronger. Despite the grim scenes of houses dragged away from meadows and coves and set up ridiculously in the bulldozed mud of a growth center "subdivision" side by side on 50-by-70-foot lots.

With pollution and no water, inadequate sewerage, fishing impossible, living costs never heard of before, unemployment and beer for the young, dole and despair for the middle-aged, and sorrow for the old. And only a chosen few to profit from the millions spent.

It'll take a lot to repair the damage and not enough forgiveness under the sun to cover the crime of those who thought they could plunge in like mad bulls and tear asunder a delicate thing.

"Change," we hear. "This is a time of change." Like so much else this is a phrase that has been imported from the mainland and its meaning twisted around to the opposite by idiots here.

The "change" they talk about in the troubled cities of the US is more toward what we have than what they have got. There is a concern and awareness there for the land – so much that President Nixon says it will be the vital project of the US in this decade.

We have here a luxury and an advantage and a head start that we don't often appreciate. The real "change" is that people are going back. The inexorable exodus from the real "death center" has already started.

The drive in people to search for some measure of contentment and happiness and to make a living as they find best cannot be directed by decrees of governments and compromised planners.

That is why people are already drifting back to settle again on the islands of Placentia Bay (Yes!) and why ERCO will go from Long Harbour and the chain saws and bulldozers must never tear into the shores of Bonne Bay. We'll have dentists and schools, too, and cheaper beer.

That is why the bosses are amazed and puzzled that Newfoundlanders do not stay for the "good money" at Churchill Falls … "worse than Indians or Eskimos," they grumble. Yeah, worse, but not that much worse.

Newfoundlanders have gone in droves to Toronto, which is, in a way, admirable. Who would expect to tell a 20-year-old what the other side of the hill looks like and see him content not to take a look for himself?

The first year they save and buy a second-hand car and come back for their two weeks' holidays and go away muttering about "dullsville, man, like how can you stick it back here?"

And they work in the factories of Toronto, and scrape up a bit more and sit around and help good old Harry Hibbs sell 100,000 records and talk about trouting up the brook and out in the boat and the next summer they drive 2,000 miles nonstop in these rattletraps again. And they mutter "Like dullsville, man" again.

But there is not one in 10 of them who dares chop off the mooring line to dullsville. How many leave, but how many are coming back to stay? People who have been in Boston and Toronto for 40 years come back to spend the last of it where they started.

And St. John's had better watch it. It's getting to be a more disagreeable place to live, sprawling out heedlessly without thought, getting from one place to another a misery. St. John's had better stop and think and, for one small thing, make that grass on Water Street permanent.

"The older generation must be sacrificed for the sake of the young," says at least one young idiot. And where do city people with the largest houses and most money send their young in the summer? They send them out to the outports where there is supposed to be "privation and poverty and misery."

There are many in St. John's whose only hope is to survive the slush and misery of winter. Yet, there are places "out there" where the snow is not dirty and the winter is just as splendid as the summer.

Is the only thing worth giving the young a square of asphalt inside a chain-link fence and a "seement pond" with enough chlorine to sting and redden their eyes?

When there are conners to be caught, plenty for all, and long grass on the cliff-tops to sit in and warm bogs to jump barefoot into and caplin on the beaches and boats to go out into, fooling around? Be careful of committing crimes against the young.

There are a thousand things to hurl against the slander and distortion and a thousand things with which to batter the madness. Now that the outports are coming into the spotlight there's a chance to examine some of them.

For we WILL have our soul back, Uncle, although you are now dead and gone, but perhaps are helping us still. In some outports they seem strangely partial to the song "We Shall Overcome."

Yes, indeed. And maybe for the sake of variety we shall Undercome. In either case, we will go back and by this means we will have gone ahead. ▮

Panic has broken out on the floor

January 30, 1970   *In the House*

Good afternoon, ladies and gentlemen. We are speaking to you from the eighth floor of Conglomeration Building to bring you live coverage of the third session of the 34th General Assembly of Newfoundland which has just resumed.

The visitors' galleries are packed for this, the first sitting of the House, since last spring. There's an air of tension and great expectation among the spectators as the big question is – Who will sit where?

As you know, the premier has declared that not one seat, not one red seat – that is to say, not one of the actual articles of furniture with which the anatomies of honorable members come in contact, as opposed to the use of the term "seat" in the abstract as it refers to a particular electoral district (if you follow), will be moved.

In other words, if some honorable members wish to cross the floor, they may not take their seats with them. New seats will have to be provided for them on the other side.

They will either have to obtain new seats or crouch on the carpet for the duration of the session. It is interesting to note in passing that in the Newfoundland House, the government sits to the left of the Speaker rather than to the right as in other Commonwealth parliaments.

Listeners may probably know that that comes from the days when the House sat in the old Colonial Building and the governments of that day broke tradition and sat on the Speaker's left because the fireplace was on that side.

Now we see that members have already taken their seats as they await the arrival of the Lieutenant Governor. From this point we can see no change whatsoever, ladies and gentlemen. The three PC members on one side and the rest on the other.

Wait. Just a moment. A member on the government side and to the rear has started to fidget slightly. He seems about to make some move. Yes ... Yes, he's ... he's standing up ... the spectators lean forward. Now he's making his way ... he's crossing the floor. He's taken a position on the Opposition side.

Now, there's a general stir. There's another standing up. Can't quite make out who it is from here. Could be Mr. Wells or Mr. Crosbie. And there are two more, ladies and gentlemen. Two more government members are just crossing the House.

There's another one up ... and another. It's gaining momentum. Three more. Four ... no, five more. There goes the member for ... now, there's a surprise, ladies and gentlemen. And now they've broken into a bit of a scramble as ... they're racing for the other side in droves.

One man is down. Someone has stepped on his fingers and he instinctively puts them in his mouth. A mistake. Someone else just stepped on his head.

This is a regular stampede. I think it's settled down a bit now. It looks like … yes, I would say, by a quick count that the majority of members are now on the Opposition side.

Some of the confusion has subsided. The mavericks seem to be still rather awed by their actions. I may be wrong on this but I would think they now form the government. The government has changed sides.

Several of the rebels, apparently emboldened by this realization, are now making faces at the few remaining across the way. A few have their thumbs in their ears and are wagging their fingers.

Now, the premier … yes, the premier is standing up. He's waving some sort of file folders – black-covered file folders, I believe, at the deserters.

This seems to have some sort of effect across the way. Most of the jeering has died down and the colors of some of the mavericks are coming and going. The colors of three or four seem to have gone and stayed.

But now, they're regaining confidence. Looks like they won't be swayed. Some are making faces again. In the general excitement Mr. Burgess has stuck his thumbs into Mr. Wells's ears.

What's this? It appears that the premier … yes, the premier has left the chamber. He's gone out. No. He's back. The premier is back and he's … ladies and gentlemen he's carrying a bulky object.

It appears to be … yes. The premier has returned carrying a fireplace. He has set it down in front of his desk. He's motioning to Justice Minister Curtis.

Now he and Mr. Curtis are making motions of warming their hands in front of an imaginary fire. The premier has taken a rearward … he's taking a rearward stance in front of the fireplace, raised his coat tails and is, in pantomime, reveling in the warmth.

Good … gracious! What's happening now? The premier has picked up the fireplace again. He's picked up the fireplace again and has carried it across … The premier has crossed the House and has taken a seat on the opposite side with the majority.

Panic has broken out on the floor. There's a mass stampede back to the other side of the House. The premier has again picked up … He's following the majority back across. They're making another dash now back to the other side … followed again by …

Absolute confusion down there, ladies and gentlemen. My temples are pounding. I don't feel at all well. We return you now to our studios for an interlude of might loosick, loose mightick, moose loosick … Ah … (beep)! 🆁🅶

A quarter of the Newfoundland population should be "persuaded" to leave

February 6, 1970   *Resettlement and Rural Life*

At a time when most people criticize and complain rather than offer alternate plans for the betterment of us all, it is refreshing to hear someone say something constructive.

Such a welcome gust was the announcement yesterday by James (Jay) Parker, new president of the Newfoundland Board of Trade.

Mr. Parker spoke to the St. John's Rotary Club, an organization consisting largely of city businessmen, and was warmly applauded when he said that a quarter of the Newfoundland population should be "persuaded" to leave the province.

Already, as might be expected, there has been some carping at Mr. Parker's modest proposal. But there was little mention by those who criticized the finer points of the plan.

Humanitarianism shines forth at one point in particular in Mr. Parker's address. Families should not be broken up, he says, but should be moved away in a group – parents, children, other dependents, grandfathers and grandmothers and, presumably, any household pets.

A small point but an important one.

Not only would moving them in bulk lots be more efficient and give a better return for the transportation dollar (as containerization has shown) but it would do away with some of the messier aspects which marred an otherwise excellent system in the southern US before slavery was abolished.

There, family groups were often broken up and individual members sold to buyers in distant areas of the country. This helped put slavery in a bad light. We needn't make that mistake again.

The Board of Trade head notes that more than 5,000 Newfoundlanders are leaving the province each year. Much as this warms the cockles of his heart, he would rather see 50,000 leave every year until we are rid of 120,000.

They will have to be "persuaded" to make their exit in much greater numbers, he says. What form this persuasion will take remains to be seen. These and other little details will have to be ironed out but we trust it will stop short of machine guns.

Mr. Parker contends that the province can support no more than 380,000 people. Since we now have more than 500,000, it is obvious that something has to give.

Forced sterilization of all males over the age of 12 would seem to be another step in the right direction coupled, perhaps, with legalized mercy-killing of all those above the age of 60.

That we are grossly overcrowded is evident from the many complaints about inadequate housing, unemployment, inadequate schools and the like.

And where do most of the complaints come from? Right. From St. John's. It is no small coincidence that the number of people we must dispose of almost exactly equals the population of the St. John's metropolitan area.

Therefore it seems fairly logical that St. John's should be moved away as a body. Think of the problems THAT would solve. Mr. Parker has a university degree in agricultural science. He could plant cabbages on the site when all the folks have gone.

He does show a decided preference for moving fishermen and their families. But common sense tells us that civil servants and office workers would have a better chance of a job in Toronto than fishermen ... who could do no more than stand around Lake Ontario with bamboo poles.

We, like Mr. Parker, are thinking only of the greatest good for the greatest number. No doubt a large number of the Rotarians who warmly applauded him are ready to make the sacrifice for the benefit of those who will stay behind.

They probably have their shaving cream, toothbrushes, stock certificates and bond coupons packed already and are prepared to take the next flight out.

The Board of Trade president did make mention, however, that the concentration should be on those who can't make a "decent" living in Newfoundland. There's something to be said for that, too.

You know the kind. The crofters and the peasantry who have nothing better to do than poach deer from country estates and muck about the landscape absolutely ruining fox-hunts and frightening the horses.

Dr. Sametz and young Billy Rowe must be put in charge of the project immediately. They have much experience of moving people and in this have displayed the necessary traits and inclinations that would be essential to the success of the exodus.

Of course, there might be a problem in finding "growth areas" willing to take (FOB*) 120,000 Newfoundland fisherfolk and-or Board of Trade members. Toronto springs naturally to mind, but perhaps Mr. Parker had other areas in view. Perhaps New York or Calcutta?

He didn't specify them. Never mind. Once across the Gulf this troublesome 120,000, this irksome excess human baggage, would be someone else's problem.

Ticklish and minor details in an otherwise admirable plan. By no means insurmountable. For instance, all these transportees would have to be deloused and showered prior to being dispatched.

An opportunity, need we say, presents itself right there.

* Free On Board is a transportation term indicating that the price of goods includes delivery at the seller's expense. 🆁🅶

Back to the jungle

February 10, 1970   *Policing*

A shudder ran down my back on first receipt of the news yesterday that the constabulary had gone on strike. Obviously there would be an immediate breakdown in law and order and all that that entails.

No police. No restraints. Anarchy. Back to the jungle. As chance should have it I was sitting in *The Telegram* newsroom when the news arrived. All the more reason to shudder.

I noted an immediate change in my own attitudes. I was out of cigarettes and at that moment one of the slighter communications clerks (they used to be called copy boys in the days when you could send them out for coffee) passed by.

A lawless thought flashed into my mind. How easy it would be, I thought, to stick out a foot, trip the little beggar, snatch his ciggies and be on a plane for Rio before he came to.

I attempted to borrow a nylon stocking from one of the desk editors to haul over my head as a disguise. But she was wearing the more modern garment and the pause which ensued gave me time to wrestle with my conscience.

It also allowed me time to give thought to my own situation. Now that the police were on strike, I, like everyone else, was open to naked aggression.

If such acts of lawlessness could occur to me, what mischief might be going through the minds of people around me – chaps who perhaps flunked out of Sunday School even worse than I did.

I glanced about. Reporters and editors alike were making furtive movements. Their eyes were narrowed. They knew. There I was with a sum of money and valuable papers on my person. A total of $3.78, in fact, and a receipt for two orders of fish and chips.

Slowly, very slowly, I looked around for some means of defence. I found just the thing in the office of the chief librarian in the shape of a heavy hardwood table leg.

It is used, in peacetime, for propping up a window to afford the ladies a cooling draft in summer. It came originally from the punch-up at a teenage dance at Kelligrews a few years ago – which readers may recall – an exhibit brought back by the photographer who covered it.

So I sat with my back to a corner and the weapon across my knees, determined not to give up my valuables without a scuffle. The situation gave me a new slant on nuclear weapons stockpiling. It was a crude defence but it would have to do until the next day when I could obtain and strap on a pair of six-shooters.

Other effects of the police walk-out dawned on me. With some despair I realized I would not get my customary parking ticket that evening.

It is a cold world with little enough communication between people. I had come to look forward to that little scrap of cardboard on the windshield every evening.

Even though I had never met him, I knew it was placed there by a warm human being who cared. I'd miss it now and, at the thought, a wave of nostalgia overcame me. I suppressed a sob as the world grew a little colder.

Violence in the streets should be breaking out around now as the news of the police strike spread. I looked out the window onto Duckpuddle Street and, sure enough, a little old lady with a shopping bag emerged from the bank across the way.

"The Grandma Bandit" had lost no time. A passing car splashed slush over her oxfords and she made a swipe at the offending vehicle with her walking stick. I turned away from the window unable to witness any more raw aggression.

It grew later, darkness closed in and I realized with another shudder (not unlike the first) that I would soon have to leave the relative security of the building. I would have to venture out into the unpatrolled streets where chaos reigned unchecked.

A sobering thought it was. I couldn't very well take my table leg with me. I would be mistaken for a vandal and set upon and thoroughly pummeled by the hastily formed people's militia.

So I would have to venture out under shot and shell with no protection. I tried to recall that neat judo trick from the "Avengers" in which the hero kicks his assailant in the knee and runs like heck. But, under stress, I couldn't remember if it was the right knee or the left.

At last the time came. Members of the staff were moving out in groups for mutual protection. I decided to go out alone for, when law and order are suspended, who can you really trust?

I edged out the door. The edging bit was necessary because I had pushed a yardstick out into the shoulders of my jacket. I figured that would make them think twice.

The violence and looting were not immediately evident. As I moved up the street toward my conveyance I practiced the "Avengers" judo kick on two parking meters along the way.

This had an immediate effect. Two passers-by looked at me askance and gave me a wide berth and were obviously not ready to tangle. Two hoodlums, they were, cleverly disguised as women shoppers.

I kept to the middle of the sidewalk under the street lights and avoided dark alleyways and put on a brisker step as I neared my horseless carriage.

Suddenly I saw three figures approaching. My heart gave a jolt. Ominous indeed. The one in the middle was wearing a maxi-coat, the two others were clad in mini-skirts.

The color drained from me. I could see it staring me in the face. There I was with nothing with which to defend my virtue. Was I now to meet a fate worse than death in the lawless streets of St. John's?

For what (if you objectively consider the package) has protected me all those years from the assaults of sex-crazed females if it is not the full weight and majesty of British law? The threat of the police, court and a jail sentence makes them think twice, that's what.

Now, fear froze me in my tracks. There was not a policeman in sight. As they came abreast I prepared for the pounce. I could do no more than offer up a silent prayer.

Nearer they came until I could see that the right nostril of the one in the maxi-coat was flaring slightly. They passed on by! My knees were weak, my palms perspiring and I couldn't believe it.

Dumbfounded, I turned around and walked back past them. Still no reaction. Needless to say, I was severely shaken when I finally made it to my auto and locked the door behind me.

It is satisfying, in some ways, to see how well the general citizenry is holding the line in the face of a police strike.

In other ways, rather disappointing. ◼

The last refuge of scoundrels

February 19, 1970 *Democracy*

On the first page of Newfoundland's latest contribution to great English literature and philosophic discourse, the Throne Speech, the word "patriotism" crops up twice.

If "patriotism is the last refuge of scoundrels," then we can take it as a sign of the times.

For we have a plethora of scoundrels hunting around for a refuge these days. Scoundrels who are graduates with top marks from our most excellent school for scoundrels. An abundance of scoundrels per square mile.

Patriotism can't possibly shelter them all. The United Nations or the Red Cross will have to set up refugee centers for them. Or some charitable group might open a retirement home for professional and long-time scoundrels.

But they usually balk at retirement. They try to hang on at all costs. When the going gets rough they try to take refuge in patriotism.

They wrap themselves in flags. They muffle themselves in bunting in an effort to escape their just deserts. We'll probably hear more direct and indirect references to "patriotism" in the near future.

As it comes to the pinch, they'll really bear down. "Patriotism" has been used to some advantage as a camouflage in the past. Some have tried to excuse all their skullduggery and whitewash all their misdeeds by saying they meant well and were only trying to do their best for Newfoundland.

True blues. Love it or leave it. And the "it" they refer to is not a piece of geography but the scoundrel system they've set up and which they defend with the desperation of cornered weasels.

"Mistakes of the heart!" cried Don Jamieson at that Liberal shindig in Grand Falls a few years ago. How can you beat that kind of logic?

To take it a step further, they stitch their patriotic blanket to make it appear that any criticism of them is a criticism of Newfoundland. Freddie Rowe has proven himself a dab hand at this ploy in the past.

Bristling with indignation (and, boy, can Freddie bristle!), he was prone to denouncing questions about the government's dealings with its two favorite carpetbaggers, Doyle and Shaheen, as foul blows at the fair and maiden form of Newfoundland.

They try to set up themselves and their schemes as the naked and pulsing heart of Newfoundland. Stick a pin in their machinations and they scream that you're going to give the whole province a cardiac hemorrhage.

There's mileage in "patriotism" yet. We'll hear about times of crisis and peril and of the danger of changing horses in mid-stream and that we must abandon "destructive criticism" and all pull together and not bug the captain while the storm is raging.

Rally round the flag, boys. But it would look better up a pole than as a security blanket for a sorry bunch of harum-scarums.

Never fear! Salvation is nigh: The Throne Speech also informs us that DREE is on the way. It seems that DREE isn't really a polite name for a runny nose but is the chubby-cheeked issue of those fun-loving swingers, FRED and ADA.

DREE is coming with jobs, jobs and more jobs. Just when we thought that the bottom of the Ottawa barrel had been reached, along comes another handout with which we're supposed to patch the craft and try to keep her afloat.

In the past, Ottawa's handouts weren't often put toward repairs to the old tub. They were expended more on naval grog, which was lavishly dispensed among crew and passengers. This gave all hands a cosy glow so that they didn't feel the cold water creeping up around their haunches.

Now, when the honey in the jar is down to the last licks, there must be loud and mighty lip-smacking in cabinet over the juicy prospect of DREE.

Why, DREE might even be the shot in the arm needed to carry that election which must be faced within the next 18 months – and which the latest product of the St. John's rumor factory says will be in the early fall of this year. (As time gets shorter, the rumors are bound to get more accurate.)

Adding to the unbearable excitement, the Throne Speech tells us that a great conference will be held in the near future. Another gathering of the clans with the Pied Piper performing upon the bagpipes.

From hither and yon they'll be summoned to the capital to discuss inflation and economic prospects and why the sea is boiling hot and whether pigs have wings.

We hear that preparations are already underway for this great conference. A new technical device is being installed and should make the proceedings run smoother than ever.

It will cut down on much wasted time and eliminate much useless verbiage. All conference delegates will be wired for sound and connected to a master control switch.

While a speaker from the floor is delivering his 10 per cent pure gold, his words will come out over the public address system loud and clear.

But whenever he gets to the 90 per cent utter trash, the master controller will flick the switch, causing the speaker's tonsils to automatically quadruple in size. In consequence, he'll peep like a beached bullbird and have to sit down. ▉

Aunt Cissy: A House is a House and a pimp is a pimp

February 23, 1970   *Aunt Cissy*

I went out to see Aunt Cissy Roach again this weekend and I'm hardly the better of it yet. It takes a lot out of a person.

For a start, I received a bad turn even before I reached the humble abode of this aged recluse, which is some 13 miles on foot in over the Witless Bay Barrens from a point midway along the Witless Bay Line.

I was no more than 500 feet away from Aunt Cissy's secluded dwelling when it happened. There was the scattered dwye of snow and dark up ahead as I passed through this small droke of woods.

A sudden rending and cracking in the tuckamores made me look up just as a heavy beast of some sort, much too large for a dog, coal black, lunged across the path and into the trees on the other side.

It was gone in a flash, crashing off through the woods in what seemed to be blind terror. What it looked like, I couldn't say. I had like to perish on the spot and was still shaking by the time I got to Aunt Cissy's door.

I pushed it open but there was no one inside. So I looked around out back and there was the ancient anchorite, her double-bit axe in hand and a slight but curious smile on her weathered face.

"Well, well, well!" she said. "Look at his honor. Washy around the gills. Not a well man, you're not. Come in. Come in. Sit down. Sit down. I was just conductin' a bit of business out there. I'm still in trim … although SOME, to their sorrow, might think otherwise.

"A drop of tea mightn't do you any harm. I'll put on the kettle. Oh. I see you brought me a little something."

I always bring Aunt Cissy a little something in an effort to keep on the good side of her, if possible. But she usually grumbles about the liver pulverizer marketed by the BLC. She accuses them of adulterating it with all sorts of foreign substances such as fermented sculpin guts, saltpeter and water.

This time I brought her a crock of a little something homemade according to a recipe held by one of the oldest families in the country. She down-hatched a tumblerful, looked at me and, for a change, passed no remark on it.

"What a state, what a state, what a state," said Aunt Cissy. "I've a-seen parboiled squids with a better color. Abusin' your health again, I dare say."

"I'm alright now, thanks," I replied. "I thought I saw something on the way in."

"Yes. Well, we know what thought done. Too much thinking is not good for your complexion, seems like. What are you up to those days, mawmouth? Anything or nothing? Or is there any need of asking?"

"Well," I said, "the House is open again. I'm in there, off and on and ..."

"That'll be enough," said she. "Knock off washing your dirty linen in front of me, a poor widow-woman living alone, trying to get me inflamed. I'm warnin' you now. I might be small but I'm wiry.

"You got your handicaps, we know; but surely God you're not driven to visitin' a House yet. Laziness! Run a rake through your hair now and then. Put on a bit of talcum powder and blacken your boots.

"There's lots of young maids on the loose, blind as bats but too much vanity to wear eyeglasses. I'd say that's your only hope ... if you got one at all. When they gets close enough to see what they're up against, it'll be too late – if you're on your toes. 'Pride goeth before a fall'."

"My dear woman," I said, put out. "When a person gets to this age they have more elevating things on their minds than ..."

"Oh, my god!" cried Aunt Cissy, clapping one hand to her brow and grabbing for the bottle with the other. "Hopeless, hopeless, hopeless. But why should I worry? This is a free country. Everyone can go to hell in their own jauntin' car."

"The House I was referring to," I said, "was not that kind of House. It is the other kind where they sit about and abuse each other. Where the government goes on."

"Small difference," sighed Aunt Cissy, picking her teeth with the identical dagger used by the late great Sarah Bernhardt in her immortal depiction onstage of Lady Macbeth. "A House is a House and a pimp is a pimp and you can tell that to young Squires or whoever is running it now.

"A House of ill repute or a House of dead repute. Haven't you got anything better than that to do with your time? But I suppose there's no such thing as shame left in the world."

It was duskish by the time I left Aunt Cissy's for the 13-mile hike back to my conveyance. I had hoped to find out more from her about what is going on for if there is anyone who knows it is Aunt Cissy.

But the most I got from her on that point is that she was looking after her own little corner and that she was still in trim although SOME, to their sorrow, might think otherwise.

Despite the bad turn I received on the way in and the fact that I am, if anything, on the timid side, I went back over the Witless Bay Barrens with no more fear than if I was sitting down in my own home.

For I was left with the feeling that Aunt Cissy's little corner extends no less than to the Four Capes. And after all those years, she is still in trim. 🔲

⟨⟩ **Richard Nixon, John Shaheen, Adolf Hitler** ⟨⟩

March 4, 1970   *In the House*

I was half an hour late getting in to Conglomeration Building yesterday for the House proceedings and a curious sight met me as I got off the elevator on the 10th floor.

Several spectators were staggering out of the visitors' galleries, pale in the face and their eyeballs revolving rapidly in opposite directions.

A little further along, some other spectators were in a collapsed state in the corridors, being given cold water in small sips, and pleading that they'd tell all they knew, if only the noise would stop.

The noise, loud enough to ripple the surface of Burton's Pond, sounded like a rat-tailed file interfering with a cheese grater. And by no means a consenting cheese grater.

Stepping carefully over the casualties and around the walking wounded, I made immediately for the press office inside, where I inquired as to what the horrendous din out there was about.

A colleague informed me that it was, in truth, coming from a speaker on the floor of the House. Although it sounded vaguely familiar, none of the newsmen seemed ready to venture out and see who was making it, due to the risk of eardrum injury.

But a second newsman offered the guess that it might be Liberal party whip, Walter Hodder, in another one of his tantrums.

He also suggested that if I hoped to avoid shell shock and inner ear damage I do as some of the more seasoned reporters had done. So I stuffed my earholes with a quantity of wet toilet paper and cringed against a far wall with the rest of them.

Every time the office door was opened the blast of acid rock from the floor of the Chamber forced us to drop into the fetal position with hands over the ears until the door was closed again.

Through the open door we caught glimpses of spectators attempting frantically to escape, struggling from their knees in the corridor only to be dropped again by a renewed blast from below.

Between the jigs and the reels and the heart-rending groans of those who would never again hear the gurgle of a mountain stream – or even the delicate tweet of a foghorn at six paces – I managed to pick up a few scraps of what was being said. SAID?!?

"What would they do, Mr. Speaker, WHAT WOULD THEY DO if I suddenly ceased to exist? They'd be lost! They'd be absolutely lost. They'd curl up and perish. PERISH, Mr. Speaker, from the face of THIS EARTH!!!

"I, Mr. Speaker, I myself, I, me, little me, am their only reason for being! They should worry about my health because if anything happens to me they've had it. IT, Mr. Speaker, IT is what they will have had. And they do, ah, yes, they do. They worry, all right. Make no mistake about that.

"Do you know, does this Honorable House Know, KNOW, yes know, that just the other day the great Richard Nixon said [to] the brilliant John Shaheen – the ABSOLUTELY brilliant John Shaheen and … Do you know what the great Richard Nixon said, Mr. Speaker?

"Do you know WHAT HE SAID? Do you know, Mr. Speaker? DO YOU KNOW??? Do you? DO you??? Well, don't just sit there like a ninny. Either you do or you don't. I'll tell you what the great Richard Nixon said to the brilliant John Shaheen. He said: 'How's my little friend Joey?' He said that! Richard Nixon said that!!! Ah, yes, Mr. Speaker, they worry. They worry.

"And do you know who else worries, Mr. Speaker? Do you know who ELSE worries??? Do you know … does this Honorable HOUSE know? Does this Honorable House know what His ABSOLUTELY High Highness – One of the highest highnesses I suppose this world has ever KNOWN – the Duke of Edinburgh said to me in the truly great men's room at Gander Airport???

"I'll tell you and Honorable Gentlemen across the way what he said. I'll tell you what he said. He said: 'They're out of bloody towels again'. That's what he said. And then, after asking for the loan of my pocket comb, he added: 'I say, old man, hadn't you better do something for that loose hair?'

"And so it goes, Mr. Speaker. They worry. They worry. At the White House. At the Palace. And I could go on and on but I don't want to bore the Honorable House.

"The great Adolf Hitler, Mr. Speaker, on the morning after the bombing of Coventry, turned to the almost-as-great Reichsmarshal Goering – as he then was – and said … Do you know what he said? Do you KNOW what the great Adolf Hitler said??? I'll tell you what he said.

"He said: 'Never mind about the list of Luftwaffe casualties, you ninny. Tell me, how is the great Joseph Smallwood this morning?' Ah, yes. They worry. They all worry. And well they might, Mr. Speaker. AND WELL THEY MIGHT!

"They wouldn't exist without me. I'm the keystone. If anything should happen to ME … The sun … The sun in the sky, Mr. Speaker. Are there any ignoramuses opposite who still believe that the SUN doesn't worry …"

At this point there was a particularly piercing cry of agony from the corridor as still another set of eardrums caved in and I made a bolt for the elevator.

Who would have thought Walter Hodder had it in him? ▓

The dictatorship and the toadying

March 5, 1970   *Democracy*

Former finance minister Val Earle doesn't sleep WELL.

He's got a heavy burden on his mind, he told us in the House yesterday. His conscience troubled him while he was in the government and now that he's out it still won't let him rest.

Earle implies that the skullduggery he saw while in government and which was hurtful to 500,000 Newfoundlanders is what troubled him then. The fact that he can't tell anyone what did go on makes him toss and turn at night now.

All cabinet ministers take an oath never to tell what goes on in there. Mr. Earle gave us an example of the pickle he now finds himself in.

He says he knows that the premier gave the wrong answer to a recent question but he's still bound by the oath and can't give the rights of it. A dreadful burden would be taken off his mind if he could tell all, he says, but he can't.

Both Smallwood and Rowe have borne down heavily on the cabinet oath of secrecy. These two unlikely preachers on the subject of political morality went on and on about it until you could almost see the radiant beams shooting out of their noble brows, particularly when they got to the part about "a solemn oath taken on the Holy Bible, Mr. Speaker! The Holy Bible!!!"

Do we detect a slight note of panic in the pious and self-righteous warnings to former intimates by these two some-time Testament thumpers?

Perhaps Earle is not the only one to miss a few winks. If there's anything that might disturb the sweet dreams of the Smallwood clique it may be the thought that any one of the five former cabinet ministers now across the House might kick their insomnia by blowing the roost.

No shattering revelations, perhaps, but a bit here and a bit there might add up and have the effect of transferring those sleepless nights from one side of the Honorable House to the other.

The simple fact that five Smallwood cabinet ministers did cross and are now lacing their former master with more vigor and enthusiasm than ever the natural-born Opposition did in 20 years should be enough to make some on government benches count sheep.

"FIVE, Mr. Speaker! No less than five ministers of the Crown! SENIOR ministers of the Crown!!! No less than the minister of finance, Mr. Speaker. Five. Not one, not two, not three, not four, not four and a half ... but FIVE!!! Was ever the like known in any parliament in the Commonwealth, Mr. Speaker? Even the most stupid ignoramus, Your Honor, must see what that means."

The five, along with backbencher Gerry Myrden, have all made general statements about the view from the inside ... the machine, the dictatorship and the toadying. And they've made them with the enthusiasm of recent religious converts.

But the thing is, the toiling masses aren't quite used to thinking in abstracts. One single juicy illustration complete with facts and figures and nouns, proper and improper, and length of the principals' sideburns would carry more weight than 10 generalities about shoot, croup and corruption.

"… a solemn oath taken on the Holy Bible, Mr. Speaker! The Holy Bible!!! They dare not, Mr. Speaker, they DARE not!!! Unless they're lower than the low; unless they're lower than a dog! They dare NOT, Mr. Speaker. They WILL not!???"

So you can see why all hands concerned are a little more on edge than usual and how come some of them are pacing the floor in the wee hours.

Some of those ex-cabinet ministers torn between baring their souls and their solemn oath of secrecy (taken, as the Rev. Mr. Black informs us, on the Holy Bible) must be used to the Hamlet bit by now. They crossed the House but brought their insomnia with them.

They may also be nagged by the thought that they didn't cross soon enough, that they swallowed too much. A commentator in the US recently wrote on that aspect of it.

He was concerned with top-rank civil servants rather than elected officials … the ones who disagree sharply with government policy and must decide what to do.

Some quit. Others stay on. Those who stay on say to themselves: "Well, if I do quit they'll put someone else in the job they can push around. I might just as well swallow some more convictions and stay on and get in my licks where I can." They don't sleep well, either.

The solemn oath taken on … etc., etc., on the one hand. And on the other, the fact that you know that something has been done – and is being done – that is, in some way, hurting 500,000 Newfoundlanders.

How do you get off that sort of hook? Do you read Immanuel Kant and Aristotle and Machiavelli … and the Holy Bible? Or do you walk down a street or road and glance at the faces of people to whom an extra morsel of hurt is being added?

A few days after Mr. Smallwood kicked him out of the cabinet Mr. Earle was photographed on the golf links (it was a mild fall) looking very relaxed. He was quoted as saying he never felt so free and relieved in his life.

It isn't that easy. Eric Jones is now in the position held by Mr. Earle this time last year. All we can do is wonder if the sandman comes early to Mr. Jones. ▨

Rotting fish guts and sewage

March 10, 1970   *Culture and History*

Mention the stink and inconvenience of city buses … and someone screams you're making the situation worse by discouraging people from riding them.

Mention the lunacy of some of the government's soggy-brained schemes … and someone screams that you're damaging the credit of Newfoundland.

Mention ERCO's dead red fish … and someone screams you're damaging the province's market for fish.

The screamers cling to the theory that such things should be gone at behind the scenes, through "the proper channels," or kept hush-hush, or mentioned only to "the people at the top."

It DOESN'T WORK THAT WAY. Those "behind the scenes" or "at the top" have had every chance in the world to correct what needs correcting. But they are not going to do a damn tap more than they have to.

Improving and correcting spells inconvenience. Coasting along in the same old rut spells comfort. Unless enough incentives or pressures – or both – are applied people will not choose the inconvenience of change over the comfort of slogging along in a familiar rut.

This applies to civil servants and cabinet ministers and fishermen and factory heads alike. Especially when they get to the point where the comfortable rut is well-worn and so deep they can't see over the top of it … let alone get out of it without strenuous effort.

"It's always been done this way" or "these things have to be done in stages" are some of the excuses you'll hear from people who are comfortable and apathetic and slogging along in a familiar rut. From people who don't want to be inconvenienced.

Anyway, the quality of fish was mentioned in the House yesterday by Alec Moores (L-Harbour Grace). The handling of fish in Newfoundland is one of our more obvious ruts.

It's so obvious that it goes unnoticed. Perhaps the only way some people can see over the top of this deep rut is to stop for once and consider the obvious – that fish is an article of food – and to imagine a side of beef being put through the same process.

If they knew, or even suspected, that the tin of meat they buy was put under the same conditions as fish, salt or fresh, they'd turn green around the gills and choke with indignation.

For the methods used in handling fish would make a starving hyena retch.

The fish is taken off the lines or from the nets and thrown into the middle of the boat where the wood is impregnated with slub and blood. A few buckets of cold water and a filthy mop or broom are the only means used to clean the boat.

On the way in, the fish slosh around in gurry and perhaps in gas and grease that has run back from the engine. It is pitched up over the wharf and then into the stage.

The floors and walls are impregnated and encrusted with the slub, gurry, blood and slime of years' use. The familiar stench of a fishing stage may bring on nostalgia to those who have always been used to it, but it will bring up the guts of those who have never visited one before.

The fish is split and gutted and washed in water drawn up over the wharf. Drawn up from among the rotting fish guts and sewage below. The trunkhole, a few feet away from where the fish is being handled, is used as a toilet.

Swarms of flies, green and blue and fat, infest the stages, being drawn by the rotting guts and sewage below in the beach, the filth of the stage itself or the barrels of decomposing cod livers outside the door.

Some fishermen are disgusted by the flies and try to discourage them. They liberally spray windows, splitting table, floors and the piles of salted and of dried fish with DDT.

Sometimes dogs, cats and sheep walk about on the fish as it dries on the flakes. Or a pile of dried fish will be used as a convenient seat in the storage shed throughout the winter.

Fish that is sold fresh doesn't fare much better. It is brought in in the same boat and greeted by the same swarms of flies. It may lie on the wharf and decompose in the hot sun for hours.

The boxes of some of the trucks that take the fresh fish to the plants are not what you'd like to eat off of. The fish is pitched aboard and a tarpaulin thrown over it.

If the driver goes to lunch before leaving for the plant, the mess of fish is left to fester a bit more in the heat. It is already getting soft and the gurry may be dripping out the bottom of the truck.

Then off we go toward the plant 40 or 60 miles away. The softening mass gets softer as the truck sways on the pavement. And when it hits the dirt road, the fish are further pounded around and beaten to a near mummy.

Clouds of dust come in over it. The flies that have come along for the ride get fatter. The driver stops for a beer and the sun beats down on the tarpaulin.

At the fish plant, this cargo of food may sit around in the sun and the flies and rot for a few more hours before unloading starts.

It is little wonder that some frozen fish or fish sticks bought in the supermarkets have a sour taste. We are likely to blame it on the freezing and say that frozen fish never tastes as good as fresh.

Some fishermen may be hurt and angry at these remarks and declare that THEY always keep their stages clean and scrubbed down. But the fact is that due to the methods used even the cleanest stage is not much better than the one described.

They may say it has always been done this way, that they eat some of the same salt fish themselves and nobody has ever been poisoned by it.

But if they took a tour of a meat-packing plant and saw meat put up under the same filthy conditions, they might not relish their next slice of bologna or tin of bully beef. It depends on what you're used to.

Familiarity breeds contempt and we are so used to fish being handled in this way we don't even stop to think about it. Yet there's no difference in bloated flies crawling over, spitting on and laying their eggs in a piece of meat than doing the same thing on a fish.

Screams anyone? 🔳

Bow down, if supporting a government is bowing down

March 17, 1970   *In the House*

In today's installment, we continue the thrilling episode from Hansard taken from Premier Smallwood's famous 10-hour speech in the House recently.

When we left Honorable Gentlemen on Monday, Mr. Speaker had just made an attempt to restore order and the star of the show had reminded spectators that, as his mother had told him when he was a little boy, they should be seen and not heard.

We continue the hair-raising drama of "As the Mind Collapses" and we hear Mr. Smallwood say:

"And visitors who have not been elected to this House are only to be seen and not heard and they look and they listen and they are warned not to be seen or heard – not to be heard, just seen."

(We skip most of the next page which is along the lines of "When Bond built the great Courthouse Building on Water Street he was denounced; when the Colonial Building was built it was denounced ..." etc.)

"I want to pose a serious problem to the Honorable Members opposite. A pretty serious problem for them, all 10 of them. As I say, the one thing they have in common is their dislike for me, the distaste they feel for me.

"It is extraordinary no one else does, but they do. Nonsense. It is this one thing held in common by them that keeps them together and, if necessary, this same dislike they have in common for me may bring them together in one party.

"I would like to be able to attend the convention that is going to elect the leader of that party. I will try to get a job as a reporter to go in and cover it, just to see it. And if not, of course, I will follow it on television when they come to choose a leader.

"If necessary, the only way they can achieve putting me down is to get together in one party, they will do that. They will do it."

An Honorable Member: "For what good will that do?"

Mr. Smallwood: "For the good of themselves. Lincoln was assassinated by a man who did it for the good of America, do you remember? He assassinated Lincoln for the good of America.

"Every assassin always does it for some great and patriotic and worthy motive. Robert Kennedy was shot for patriotic motive. A good, fine motive – he was doing a good thing to shoot Robert Kennedy.

"And I have no doubt that the man who murdered John F. Kennedy set himself to be a real patriot. He did that for America's sake. So the Honorable Gentlemen opposite, if it is necessary, if this is the only way they can see that might give them a chance to get rid of me, they will come together in one party.

"Now, there will be some bloody scenes when they will try to see who will be the leader. But, nevertheless, they will come together and they will form a party. But, sir, here is – Look, if I were the Honorable Gentleman's leader, by now I think I would have assassinated the Honorable Gentleman.

"And do not think, Mr. Speaker – The smile on his face shows that I hit the nail right on the head. Right on the head, because he will not stand the Honorable Gentleman much longer. He will not, believe me. Oh! I am a Leader and I know why. I know why.

"Now, here is the serious problem, Mr. Speaker, I pose for them. The only thing that brought them together – the only thing that keeps them together, the only thing that will keep them together – is their common dislike for me.

"Now, here is the serious problem. Suppose I die. Suppose I drop dead. Suppose I resign. Suppose anything – that I cease to be the cement to hold them together. What then? Where does that leave them?

"Utter chaos. The only thing they have in common is their dislike for me. So their very lives depend on me. Their fortunes, their future, their strength, their unity depend entirely on me."

An Honorable Member: "On who?"

Mr. Smallwood: "On me. Yes, on me. If I die they will be at each other's throats so fast, Mr. Speaker, a donnybrook would look like a Sunday School Party, a Sunday School period. It is true. It is true.

"You see, they may indeed dislike me but they dislike each other more. They may mistrust each other but not as they mistrust me. They may be jealous of each other but not as jealous as they are of me. And I am, therefore, the linchpin. The linchpin of the Opposition. The one cementing element that can keep them together."

Mr. Wells: "I am not a Tory. I am a Liberal."

Mr. Smallwood: "Yeh! A Liberal who fights the Liberal Government. God save us from that kind of Liberal. The Liberals that fight the Liberal government."

Mr. Wells: "I do not have to bow down to him."

Mr. Smallwood: "Bow down, if supporting a government is bowing down."

Mr. Wells: "That is right."

Mr. Smallwood: "If supporting a government is bowing down he can never support a government. He can always be Independent. Independent and in Opposition. He can always be Independent and in opposition because supporting a government is bowing down and this he will never do. The great Independent."

Mr. Wells: "Not in other Independent democracies. Not quite so here."

Mr. Smallwood: "I have never, since I have become premier, and for about three years before I became premier – that is now – 21 and three are 24 years – the best part of a quarter of a century – not once have I been without some crackies snapping at my heels.

"Never have I been without a lot of crackies snapping at my heels. I must say, honestly, I would miss them if they went away."

An Honorable Member: Inaudible.

"I am not quite 21 yet – add, say, five years, that will be 26, and three before I became premier will be 28 years – say after 28 years I go and the crackies go, then when the barking and the snapping and the snarling of the crackies die away into silence, and they die away, and they disappear, and I am gone, and the crackies are gone, then a lot of people perhaps will begin to say, you know he was not all bad, he was not all wrong …"

Mr. Wells: "This is hard to believe …"

(Don't miss tomorrow's gripping episode in which we continue the incredible adventures of Honorable Gentlemen in the People's House. And in which the Honorable the Premier surmounts the incredulity of the Honorable Liberal Independent Gentleman representing Humber East and goes on to use a word which even the broad-minded People's Paper may balk at printing! Stay tuned!) 🅁🅖

He hauled up his kilt and he said, "Bite, you little buggers, bite"

March 18, 1970   *Joey*

Still another episode in the continuing story of "Joey in Wonderland" taken word for word from Hansard, the official record of what is said in the House.

Yesterday, we saw how Mr. Smallwood had likened himself to a rather heroic and majestic figure with a swarm of crackies snapping and barking around his heels.

When we left the thrilling drama yesterday, Mr. Wells was saying ...

"This is hard to believe."

Mr. Smallwood: "No, it is hard. The Honorable Gentleman does not believe that about anybody. And I warn his Honorable Leader, beware of him, beware of him."

Mr. Wells: Inaudible.

Mr. Smallwood: "Well, I believe that. The Honorable Gentleman is his own leader. No, the Honorable Gentleman is his own leader. That Honorable Gentleman is a scalp hanger on his belt.

"That is what the Honorable Gentleman is. He likes collecting scalps to hang them in his belt. That is what he likes. And I know the next scalp he is going to get – not far from where he is sitting now. That will be the next scalp he will be after.

"That will be the next scalp he will be after. Crossing the House – the Honorable Gentleman who made that remark should never make that remark about crossing the House because it reminds people – brings it fresh to their memory that he has crossed the House three times. Three times. Three times …"

Mr. Speaker: "Order, please! I would like to remind all Honorable Members of the House that words uttered in this very dignified debate are recorded in Hansard, and I hope that their behavior will be governed by what they will be reading in a year's time, or five years' time, or what other people will be reading.

"I think that if they would remember that for a few minutes it possibly would add to the dignity and to the decorum of the House."

Mr. Smallwood: "Yes, the Honorable Gentleman from Humber East, Mr. Speaker, who is so insistent upon maintaining the dignity of the House, fully agrees with Your Honor and Your Honor must be relieved to know that. It must be very reassuring to Your Honor.

"Mr. Speaker, the Honorable Gentleman who is the member for St. John's West made an unfortunate remark there a moment ago about crossing the floor. Not crossing the bar but the floor. And every time he speaks of crossing the floor I am reminded …"

(And here we omit another page of Hansard in which Mr. Smallwood goes on at length about Mr. Crosbie's crossing the House, about how he is a dead duck and about how four opposition members will not run in another election.)

"The people of Newfoundland – whatever they are or are not – the people of Newfoundland are very fair-minded. They are very fair-minded. These crackies that keep barking at my heels, you see. I said as long – until I go, these crackies will be barking at my heels.

"Bite? That reminds me – about bite. Sir Robert Bond, the great Liberal premier was speaking in the House of Assembly once, when someone on the other side of the House kept snapping at his heels that way. And finally, Sir Robert got annoyed.

"He ignored it as long as he could with contempt, with silent contempt. But finally he got annoyed and he said, Mr. Speaker, the Honorable Gentleman reminds me of the story of Sandy the Scot.

"Sandy was an ardent fisherman and he was up in the Highlands beside his favorite stream fishing for trout, wearing his kilt. And he was fishing and paying all his attention to the trout and to the business of fishing.

"But the mosquitoes were numerous and he (wearing a kilt) he was really not too well protected against the onslaughts and the bites of the mosquitoes.

"So he would change hands and he would slap – then he would try it again and then he would slap – and he kept this up trying to keep his attention on his trout but these mosquitoes would keep biting him and biting him.

"And finally he said, Mr. Speaker – and as Sir Robert Bond said this, he suited the action to the words – he said, finally, Mr. Speaker, Sandy lost his patience and turned back on and as he said this, Sir Robert turned back on to his tormentor across and he hauled up his kilt and he said, 'Bite, you little buggers, bite'.

"That was – the snapping at the heels is still going on. This is the mosquito biting again. Mr. Speaker, we are 21 years old, we will be shortly. We have put in 20 years and are now starting on our third decade as a Canadian province and as Canadians.

"What lies before us? Not just 10 years more of this sort of thing. There has to be something better than that. We have laid a foundation. It is not the best foundation but it is a foundation.

"It is not the best one in Canada but it is the best one that we ever had in Newfoundland. We never had a foundation as good as the one we have now. We spent billions to do it. Billions. Literally thousands of millions of dollars …"

And here we leave this particular episode as the rest of it is pretty much a re-run. Readers who saw that inspiring document *To You With Affection From Joey* can guess what came next.

For the rest of our program period we continue with another brief excerpt from Hansard with the promise that tomorrow we'll return to the more frivolous matters which can only be found outside the Honorable House.

Mr. Hickey: "Mr. Speaker, is this a question?"

Mr. Smallwood: "Just sit down."

Mr. Hickey: "Mr. Speaker, out of order. Out of order."

Mr. Smallwood: "Sit down. Sit down."

Mr. Hickey: "Mr. Speaker, out of order. I am not sitting down. I go by what the Speaker says. You sit down for a change. I have a point of order, Mr. Speaker."

Mr. Smallwood: "I am on a point of order. There can be only one at a time."

Mr. Hickey: "Mr. Speaker, the premier did not rise on a point of order. I am not deaf and I did not hear it. This is just another game. Sit down."

Mr. Speaker: "The Honorable the Premier interrupted the Leader of the Opposition. He could only do that on a point of order. Now, will the Honorable the Premier now state his point of order."

Mr. Smallwood: "Mr. Speaker, will the Honorable Gentleman not just say there is a rumor. Will he make a charge?"

Mr. Murphy: "No, no, definitely."

Mr. Smallwood: "No, he will not. He will not make a charge so where does that leave us, Mr. Speaker? Is this parliamentary? Is it in accordance with parliamentary practice, and precedent and procedure for a Leader of an Opposition to say there is a rumor? He does not say who says it. He says there is a rumor. It is anonymous as far as this House is concerned."

Mr. Hickey: "Mr. Speaker, this is a long point of order."

Mr. Smallwood: "So far as his speech is concerned it is anonymous. We do not know. He says merely there is a rumor. I suggest to Your Honor that this is highly improper. In the extreme it is highly improper. He ought either make a charge so that we can have it investigated or not mention it. Not talk about anonymous rumors."

Mr. Hickey: "Is this a point of order or is he making a speech?"

Mr. Smallwood: "Sit down. Sit down. Sit down, ignoramus. Sit down."

Mr. Hickey: "I have heard that before. I am not sitting down when the premier says so."

Mr. Smallwood: "Mr. Speaker, protect me."

Mr. Speaker: "Order please."

Vestal virgins standing by at the airport

March 19, 1970   *Great New Industries*

Please God, we'll be relieved of this terrible burden of suspense before the week is out.

Much longer and I'd say we'd be on the hand of going to bits. You can only stand up under such a strain for so long a time. And there's not many on this island who have been sleeping well these past few days.

The whole province is in a state of tension and agitation as we await the return from overseas of the Shaheen-Smallwood entourage. No one seems to know what's keeping them and public concern has reached fever pitch.

A local journalist who accompanied the party has returned to these shores ahead of the general congregation. He seems to have nothing large to report and the citizenry is left all the more agog.

Many stories are making the rounds. With a clutch of cabinet ministers and the Economic Genius himself out of the province, some people are asking: "Who's in charge now?"

On top of that we have late word that Deputy Premier Dr. Rowe has taken off to the West Indies for the good of his health. Some say that Mr. Barbour has been left in charge of the keys but we can't get confirmation of that one way or another.

All in all, if there's a rumor that these chaps have all taken out citizenship papers in Liechtenstein, it won't do the public morale one little bit of good.

However, we must hope for the best and trust that if we leave them alone they will come home sooner or later, wagging their duty-free imports behind them.

Details about the whole business are scanty. Just how many altogether are dashing around Europe at public expense is not known. The purpose of the mass migration, we have been told, is the signing of "final papers" for Mr. Shaheen's proposed riboflavin, niacinamide and camphorated oil complex at Come By Chance.

On that account alone we hope for a good outcome. All Newfoundlanders want to see disparity and inequality abolished and fair play and justice done. So we hope that Mr. Shaheen will prosper.

Mr. Doyle has got a nice private plane out of it. Lundrigan's has two, including a private jet. But until now Mr. Shaheen has been the odd man out, without even one measly little DC-3 to call his own.

In any case it will be a thrilling scene when they all bundle off the plane at St. John's Airport – that is, if past triumphal returns are any indication.

For the past two days (uncertain of the exact time of arrival) the Liberal Party has had 24 vestal virgins standing by at the airport. They are barefoot and clad in five yards each of curtain scrim in pastel shades.

Their job will be to strew rose petals and election campaign pamphlets in front of the returning heroes as they walk in from the plane. It's none too warm out there and last evening I was moved to take one of them into the snack bar for a cup of hot cocoa.

There were goosebumps all over her poor little person but she said she didn't mind the wait as it was all for a good cause. Her father operates a public house in the west end.

According to present plans, Mr. Shaheen and Mr. Smallwood will be carried off the plane on a canopied litter borne by four cabinet ministers with Ed Roberts, in blackface and jeweled turban, waving a fan in front of them.

At one stage it was planned to have Mr. Smallwood ride into the city on an ass. However, reception organizers decided this would be redundant and likely to confuse the public.

Mr. Smallwood will no doubt have his arm in a sling from signing all those "final papers." His head, too, perhaps. After all the talk and great expectations it would be more than his political neck is worth to come back empty-handed.

The chaps on the other side of the bargain are possibly not so dense that they don't realize this. Might they be tempted to up the price a bit? And guess who can't afford not to pay it?

Anyhow, just about the whole population is standing by on tenterhooks, waiting for the troops to come back. To gauge the intensity of public interest I took a "mini-poll" down on Water Street this morning.

One citizen declared: "It's no odds to me one way or another so long as they don't cancel the Bingo."

Another said: "Where's Dr. Valdmanis now that we need him?"

And the third, an elderly citizen with a flask of Trouter's Special sticking out of her shopping bag, maintained: "We wouldn't be in the mess we are today if Joey Smallwood was still alive." RG

My "Joey" hat was out to the cleaners

March 28, 1970   *Liberals and Pea Seas*

Alas, I didn't get out to the airport Friday to help welcome home the conquering heroes. My "Joey" hat was out to the cleaners and I couldn't think of a good slogan for a placard off hand.

So I spent that eventful afternoon in the serenity and tranquility of my domestic establishment washing a few socks, sipping a small tomato juice and reading the latest issue of the *Anti-Vivisectionists Journal.*

All the while, the airport was aswirl with colorful pageantry, tumultuous receptions, cheering multitudes and weary but jubilant cabinet ministers thankful to be back from the rigors of life in the ritzy hotels of London and Paris.

Consequently, I have had to get my information on this momentous occasion second-hand. Had I known it was going to be such a lively affair I would still have been of two minds about going to view it.

For it is surprising the amount of wear and tear we impartial, objective, passive observers come up against at such functions. At celebrations following the late, great Liberal leadership conference, for example, I was spit at by a Liberal supporter.

Of course, this may have been because he had two teeth missing in front and the force of his utterance of a string of unusual words directed at me produced a fine spray through the gap.

Another Liberal supporter, with a drink in each hand, advised me that if I didn't make myself scarce he would spoil my face for me – no small feat considering its present condition. And this was in the Hickman "hospitality suite."

On this basis I decided to forgo the Smallwood "hospitality suite" altogether. The worst I got, apart from the above-mentioned, were some hard looks from a couple of outharbor "Joey" supporters who were, despite the abundance of free booze, quaffing Aqua Velva shaving lotion in a washroom of the hotel.

So you can see that when spirits are up it is often the unbiased, neutral press observer, such as myself, that gets some of the spinoff. A shocking state of affairs. Rather like shooting at a Red Cross medical supplies truck.

Anyway, from what I hear the airport reception for our boys back from overseas was a sunshine-shadow affair. For a start, although the backroom boys put on some desperate pressure to mount a show worthy of Caesar's return from Gaul, they fell short of their quotas.

Before the grand vizier's flying carpet touched down, Uriah Strickland, parliamentary assistant to Mr. Smallwood, nipped out for a look at the cars coming along.

Hughie knows what nervous tension is all about, having won his seat in the last election by less than 100 votes. But he was clearly on edge, they say, and kept an anxious eye out as the cavalcade was forming up.

"We're going to get 100 cars at least," he remarked, after one of his peeks around the door jamb. But only 49 turned up, which wasn't bad, I suppose, but not good either when you consider that Great Announcements are not as plentiful as they used to be.

It seems that some of the trappings from the Liberal leadership convention have been saved up and were taken out of storage and dusted off for the occasion. Some of the Smallwood delegates, too, by the look of it.

Lower and lower swoops the great silver bird bearing the greatest collection of financial brains Newfoundland has ever seen, back from their encounter with the economic heads of Europe.

A door swings open in the side of the craft and down the ramp, awash with vichysoisse, and pâté de foie gras and aglow with the warm feeling that they have done something really great for Newfoundland, come the victors.

Among the joyful band in the terminal, varicose veins are forgotten, arthritis is discounted, biliousness disappears as they flutter their plastic boaters and bubble over with anticipation.

Then the university crowd take over where they left off at the stadium last fall with the chants and the placards and it is all one tumultuous scene with students, having greater lung power, clearly getting the upper hand.

It got out of hand when one of the protesters expectorated at Mr. Smallwood (a definite misuse of phlegm) and another obstructed the police.

Finally, they got it straightened out and the show hit the road, with horns honking, toward the Laurier Club to celebrate the great something-or-other in proper fashion.

All in all it was a newsy affair. And all that was needed to put the cherry on the top of the whole piece of business was a statement from the Bell Island jackass.

Mr. Neary popped up on the radio and television stations to use his well-known talents in an attempt to smear the whole university and liken Smallwood to Jesus Christ being betrayed and set up for the crucifixion, it being Good Friday and all.

It all helps pass a weekend, I suppose, but there are some things I'd just as soon hear about second-hand. ▪

Utterances of the Bell Island blatherskite

March 30, 1970   *Liberals and Pea Seas*

By a stroke of good fortune, I have had placed in my hands a copy of a recent statement made by S.A. Neary, minister of welfare for the welfare province.

I had feared that Mr. Neary's words would be scattered on the radio and TV airwaves, heard once, then lost to mankind forever. It is nothing less than a privilege to commit the utterances of the Bell Island blatherskite to the printed page for the study and consideration they deserve.

There is no lack of such statements from Mr. Neary. At the drop of a hat he will present himself at the television and radio studios with his latest observations on whatever tickles his fancy. Or he will stuff them into the mailboxes of the newspapers.

His prolific observations, both in and out of the House, are generally steeped in mawkish sanctimony and stewed in political piety – which gives them a ludicrous odor when you consider the source.

Mr. Neary's many announcements, pronouncements and denouncements produce two effects on his listeners. On the one hand, there is the inclination to regard them as natural, if gross and grotesque, sources of amusement.

On the other hand, there is the stark realization that all this purple grotesquerie is coming from the lips of a cabinet minister – a person who is responsible for making the laws that govern us all and deciding how the resources and energies of Newfoundland are to be directed.

It is not that Mr. Neary is much more deficient than his cohorts in cabinet. It is just that he seems to lack that small but tremendously vital extra most of the rest have – the ability to conceal their deficiencies or at least not flaunt them in public.

Who but the present minister of welfare would pounce so eagerly upon, and heavy-handedly attempt to wring nuances, profundities, philosophic observations and overwrought political propaganda from a gob of spittle?

His colleagues may have been content to count their blessings, as it were, and let the situation speak for itself. That is, that the whole protest at the airport had been discredited by one ill-mannered lout.

But Mr. Neary was not content to bask with the rest in this "fortuitous" incident. He had to belt it for the nearest TV station and wallow in it. His colleagues must have cringed as they heard him make a shambles of the delicate balance of political advantage the incident afforded.

However, that is the impetuous Mr. Neary. Many of his pronouncements seem to indicate a burning desire to rise head and shoulders above the rest of the dwindling band of zealots in the Smallwood cabinet.

His admiration for his Master knows no bounds – or at least the compulsion to profess such admiration seems to be unbounded. While the rest of his cabinet brethren are often content to nod and clap and beam and chuckle in the proper places, Mr. Neary seeks to rise by stooping to boot polish more often than anyone else.

By being so blatantly obvious about it he may be defeating his purpose. In any case, let us see exactly what Mr. Neary had to offer an anxiously waiting populace who must hang in a state of breathless anticipation in the short intervals between his momentous pronouncements.

"From my standpoint," declares Mr. Neary, still panting slightly after his urgent dash to the TV studio, "I admire the good sense and self-control exhibited by the premier of our province under great provocation.

"Apart from the damage to his feelings, which must have hurt him to the core since he was the one who fought so hard to make possible a real provincial university, the outlandish conduct of such a small minority damages the image of all students at a university of which the people of this province are so anxious to be proud.

"People with common sense know that the sacrifices we have made to have a university are justified through 99 per cent of its graduates, but that one per cent, who have neither good manners nor good taste, damage the hopes and prospects of all their fellow students.

"That spittle on the premier, a man who both because of his age and achievements, is entitled to more than ordinary respect, could very well go down in Newfoundland history as in a class with the Judas Kiss of which so many of us are thinking these days."

Thus spake Mr. Neary, who then presumably retired to work on his next profound observations and/or tend to the affairs of the welfare department.

Even though some of the basic elements are there, there's no possible way that Mr. Neary's gross and heavy-handed statements could fit the category of effective political propaganda – which is a fine art.

His sole piece of raw material was that one person – who happened to be a university student – spit at Mr. Smallwood. Even in the hands of an expert, stretching this much beyond the obvious would be a tricky business. But it didn't daunt the would-be lily-gilder from Bell Island.

First he makes the delicate point that Mr. Smallwood "was the one who fought so hard to make it possible a real provincial university." He's beating a dead horse there, which is the well-worn myth that if it wasn't for Smallwood the sun wouldn't rise.

By now, even the most politically gullible have a fairly realistic view of the role of a politician … which is to get himself ensconced in public office and, by various means, keep himself there.

Apart from this prime consideration, his job, once elected, is to figure out how much money he can collect from the people and how to spend it. And decide what use to make of the resources that belong to the people in general.

This nonsense about politicians "fighting" for this and "fighting" for that and putting their kids and aged parents out to work to raise some money toward building roads, hospitals and universities doesn't hold water any more – not even for Mr. Neary's purposes.

He also takes a clumsy stab at those useful words "per cent." One per cent of the students, he said, have damaged the hopes and prospects of all the students at the university.

Since the total number of students is 6,000, he must want us to believe either that 60 students (one per cent) spat at Mr. Smallwood in unison, or he is attempting to make the one person who did the representative of everyone at the airport not wearing a "Joey" hat.

Butterfingers Neary also attempts to do along the way what others have tried with much more subtlety. That is, to attempt to stamp out by smear, innuendo, veiled threats, manipulation of public opinion and convoluted theories, anything about the university that is not either passive to or non-critical of the present political regime.

The last paragraph of Mr. Neary's contribution to the thought of western man speaks for itself. It would be interesting to see if he would have said the same thing had it been a custard pie. Probably.

All in all, most people are at least as worried about the percentage of those in the cabinet who heap even more noxious substances on the heads of Newfoundlanders as they are about the percentage of spitters at the university.

And Mr. Neary, all by himself, constitutes no less than five per cent or one-twentieth of the total body of cabinet ministers.

A sobering thought. 🅡🅖

Fortify the Funks! Call out the Piper's Hole Militia!

April 7, 1970

Liberals and Pea Seas

A scant 24 hours ago it seemed certain that the transactions in the Honorable House which resumed yesterday would demand our attention above all else.

Not so. Profound and vital and fraught with great consequence though yesterday's business in the House may have been ("Sit down, sit down. Shut up, shut up."), a matter of far greater urgency has been brought to our attention.

It is none other than the startling observation by F. Howard-Rose, one of the 267 PC leadership contenders, that the fair and maiden form of Newfoundland lies naked and defenceless against the evil intent of any nation, great or small.

At first glance we were inclined to pass over Howard-Rose's warning lightly. More sober reflection on it, however, brings the import and gravity of the situation to us with a shock.

"Newfoundland and Labrador today stands quite defenceless before any power in the world who may wish, for one reason or another, to invade our shores," Mr. Howard-Rose declared in Corner Brook during the weekend.

"We are completely and absolutely without any effective means of repelling any kind of attack. We would be at the mercy of even the most rudimentary attacking force," he continued, sparing us none of the gruesome facts.

"Our federal government would find it totally impossible to hold on to a defenceless Newfoundland. We would have to submit to being occupied and ruled by enemy occupation troops … while waiting to be liberated."

There it is! What is to be done … and done quickly?!! Our first thought may be to issue a call to the Colors. But the hitch is, if you run up a flag in Newfoundland the most you'll get is a crowd setting up Crown and Anchor and Bingo booths around it.

Howard-Rose suggests that a tunnel be built immediately under the Strait connecting with Labrador so that we may have a chance of escape when "the Assyrian comes down like a wolf on the fold," as it were.

But this is retreat! Never, sir! What assurance do we have that we wouldn't be harpooned by Labradorians and/or bludgeoned with empty pinky bottles by the Frenchmen when we popped out on the Labrador side?

Craven retreat through a hole in the ground is not the way for true Newfoundlanders! Let us resolve ourselves that if we have to go we'll each take one of the enemy with us. Then we'd at least have some help in driving to Toronto.

Since the US forces are leaving it is true that the "Fortress Isle" is caught with its posterns down. Should a warship with aggressive intent appear on the horizon tomorrow the most we could do is stuff Neary with cannon balls and aim him in the general direction.

We're in a shaky position, especially when the word of our defenceless position gets around. I shudder to think what will happen if the French island of St. Peter's loses this year's soccer playoffs. A sticky wicket, indeed!

Nations great and small are ready to pounce on this precious diamond set in the northern seas. In one fell swoop the invaders would corner the pickled herring market and have access to our vital stockpiles of defunct cabinet ministers.

The only thing for it, since we lack the armaments, is to wage guerilla warfare. Let us follow the example of our stout-hearted country-woman, Mrs. Antigone Parsmits, widow, of Plasterville on the southern shore.

Upon receipt of the news of the imminent invasion Mrs. Parsmits rigged up a bucketful of a nasty substance over her front door to dump on the heads of the invaders. She took it down on second thought.

"It is bad enough to fall prey to the sinful lusts and debauchery and depravity of the invading troops," she told a reporter, "but worse with them stinked up like that."

She now plans passive resistance and intends to sing "The Ode to Newfoundland" as an act of defiance for the duration of the occupation.

We must make the most of what we have. Every longliner should be equipped to deal with enemy submarines: a woolen sock to haul over their periscopes and a brace and bit for drilling holes in their bulkheadings while they are thus disabled.

Fortify the Funks! Call out the Piper's Hole Militia! The Bonavista Unfencibles! The Fogo Fusiliers! We shall fight them on the beaches! We shall fight them in the hills! We shall fight them on the landing fields and in the streets! We shall put rocks in our snowballs!

An excellent master plan of defence may be along the lines of the Russian ploy against the French invasion of 1812. We would retreat, retreat, retreat, letting the enemy advance into the interior as far as Grand Falls.

When they realized there was nothing for 300 miles both east and west of them but typical Newfoundland restaurants, the poor wretches would gulp their suicide pills without hesitation.

Meanwhile, as we make determined plans to defend the sacred soil of the Motherland, let us examine all possibilities. There may not be such a big lineup of potential invaders, you know.

And far as I'm concerned, anyone who can subjugate Port aux Basques deserves it. RG

Anniversary of the birth
of Adolf Hitler: Part I

April 20, 1970   *Democracy*

I don't know if you plan any sort of a little celebration today or not. Today is, of course, the 81st anniversary of the birth of Adolf Hitler.

(No, junior. He isn't the new quarterback with the Baltimore Colts or the lead guitarist with the Purple Poop. He was long before your time and he was a troublesome fellow.)

We read (pronounced "reed") that on April 22, 1945, two days after his 56th birthday Der Fuehrer fell into a state of nervous collapse and refused to leave his bunker under the chancellery. On the evening of April 29 he married Eva Braun, the woman he had been knocking around with, and at about 2:30 p.m. the next day the happy couple killed themselves.

Mrs. Hitler took a swig of poison and the Big Cheese himself stuck the barrel of a revolver into his mouth (under that smudge of a moustache) and pulled the trigger.

When the news was announced on May 1 (according to the *Encyclopedia Britannica*) … "The government of Portugal proclaimed two days' mourning. Officials in Madrid and Tokyo were saddened. Eamon de Valera extended condolences to the German Embassy in Dublin. The rest of the world rejoiced."

But before Herr Hitler blew his mind, 15 million military men, six million Jews and several million other civilians had been killed. The ugly flamer was also responsible for the loss of my big rubber ball with the man-in-the-moon face on it.

They came and collected it during a "rubber drive" when I was four years old and bawled unpatriotically and couldn't care less that they were short of tires for Bristol bombers.

For the first six years of my life, the Hitler war went on. We in that age bracket were steeped in the war and soaked it up although we didn't have much clue about what was going on.

I do remember the day the Americans came to the Cove marching out the road from the Station with their guns on their back, and hairy great boots on their feet and passing on through the place, kicking up dust out over the bog to the Otter Rub.

They put up telephone poles and the fishermen marveled that the poles were all hardwood. The only bit of hardwood you'd see before that was a small piece that drove in around shore.

My younger sister used to be taken up in their arms with her thumb in her mouth to have her snap taken. But I was timid and would always run upstairs and crawl under the bed.

They put up big guns and camps out at the Otter Rub and the tracer bullets would make streaks of fire and a while later you'd see the gulls go up from the rocks a mile away across the harbor.

The older boys said the Americans would give them 10 cents or a chocolate bar for a dozen conners to eat. One of them said he was out to the Otter Rub and they let him try on a gas mask. And one soldier pinched the tube for a joke until he nearly smothered and it just about turned his blood.

They were bigger, had white teeth and were browner in the face as if there was more sun where they came from. Their clothes were strange, not being sheep's wool sweaters or anything, and I remember thinking that all the same color of clothes was ugly.

Like a crowd from another planet they were rich and bringing new stuff with them like comic books, bully beef, chocolate bars and movies which a big warship brought up twice a week from Argentia.

Once, one of them did something to one of the older girls and the men in the harbor said that the captain said he would be sent over to France right away and put in the front lines. I got the feeling that the men in the harbor felt that this was punishing the chap too much.

You could only feel a few simple things in the air like fear at times and joy at others because you were too young to understand what was going on. Simple but strong. There were submarines around and they might come ashore. "If you see a stranger run and tell me right away."

"What will we do if they come here, Momma?" "Daddy will take us all up to Grand Falls into the woods. He knows where to go and they won't find us. And they'll get lost and they'll starve because they won't know where they are and then they'll go away." "Will they come soon?" "No. Hush, hush. They won't come. They won't come."

Being of tender years, my first notion was that it might not be such a bad thing if the Germans did come as they'd probably bring some more bully beef and chocolate bars. But I was soon put in the light of the fact that the Germans were a different kettle of fish than the Americans. They were bad because they listened to Hitler.

It was all very complicated. I couldn't understand it any more than I could understand what the news man said on the Silvertone battery radio. He was talking a different language that didn't sound at all like that I heard around the house. I was six or seven before I became bilingual.

Anyway, "Old Churchill" was over there giving it to them hot and heavy. Here was the bloody mad monster, Macbeth, and Churchill to growl at him: "Turn, hell-hound, turn!"

(To be concluded tomorrow.)

Anniversary of the birth
of Adolf Hitler: Part II

April 21, 1970   *Democracy*

(Continued from yesterday: In which we mark the 81st anniversary of the birth of Adolf Hitler April 20, and the 25th anniversary of his blowing his brains out in the Fuehrerbunker, April 30.)

By the time they had the "big new bum" and dropped it on the Japs ("Little black specks fall out of the sky, my dear, and burn you to the bone and if you look out the window your eyes melt in your head. It came over the radio last night!"), I was old enough to feel that in the Cove they were glad that was the end of it but also a bit sorry for the Japs who were further away than the Germans.

While it lasted there was no need to read books of dragons and knights and gods and devils and ogres and beanstalks and David and Goliath. You could feel in the air that something huge and frightening and exciting was going on around you.

There was perfect black and perfect white. Absolute good and absolute evil. There was a God and there was a Devil and these two gentlemen took sides depending on what country you lived in.

Now, not many years later they said that Churchill was just a windy old boozer and Hitler simply a neurotic with a poor upbringing who was swept along by circumstances.

The "big new bum" put an end to this black-white business. Seeing things that way is a luxury of the past. The bomb put both God and the Devil out of business on earth.

If you're going to set up a group that is absolutely in the right with God on its side, you've got to have another group to fit into which has the Devil on its side.

You've got to go after the Devil's boys with no holds barred or else you're only half-hearted about it and you can't be half-hearted about absolute right and absolute wrong.

In other words, what you need for a satisfying single-minded all-out war is to think you are a good God and find an evil Devil to fight with who thinks it's the other way around. Plus even a slight chance of survival and victory.

The Bomb has spoiled all that. The Hitler war was the last chance we'll ever have to see all of the people of the world put the very last ounce of their interest, enthusiasm, energy, mind, resources into one big project. To see the spirit and will of all the world brought into a single focus.

Far more than half the resources of the world are being directed toward war still. More than half YOUR tax dollar will go toward "defence" this year. But the spirit isn't in it on account of the Bomb.

The Americans speak of the Godless Communists and the Communists speak of the American Devils. But both are scared to act on their convictions. The world stews in frustration because it is too chicken to grapple with the Devil.

The US gets rid of some of this frustration by picking on Vietnam instead of going after China. A disastrous mistake mainly because the Vietnamese are pretty people, only five feet tall. They have the same built-in weapon as the whitecoats (even Dr. Goebbels couldn't have made a whitecoat out of Hitler).

It's a half-hearted effort. The Vietnamese don't make good substitute Devils. But there seems to be a human craving for black-white God-Devil. Some Americans are driven to trying to find the Devil among themselves and a segment set up Lyndon Johnson, "whitey," the older generation, or the negroes, in that useful capacity.

Or they try to set up substitute "wars" against poverty, pollution, hunger, crime, lawlessness and disorder, or at least "races" to assemble arms, get to the moon or outsell your Volkswagon, mine Fuehrer.

Alas, all of this is half-hearted substitution and none of it satisfies. The Russians and Chinese have the same trouble. There's a craving by all the world to get on with the one big thing all hands can pitch into with full spirit and resources and energy.

The only thing that did it in the past was a full-scale last-ditch war and now, because of the Bomb, a big satisfying war is impossible. "Wars" on poverty or pollution just don't fill the bill somehow. We've always been used to the real thing and aren't satisfied with less.

In any case, by the time we could break the habit of history and make a Napoleon or a Hitler out of poverty and pollution, it would be too late. We'd be starved and poisoned.

A threatened invasion from Mars is the only thing that could put the energies and spirit of the world into one focus. If Martians had at least half-human faces. That's the only kind of war we understand.

What the world craves now is WAR. But the kind of war it needs doesn't satisfy it. And the kind of war that satisfies it is impossible. St. George was satisfied with a dragon but, after all, he was a saint.

We sit about stewing in frustration and manufacturing enough bombs to blow up the world ten times over. There's probably a hydrogen bomb cocked and primed and ready to go closer to where you're sitting at this moment than Grand Falls is to St. John's.

Never mind the continuously circling H-bombers that operate out of Goose Bay or the armed Russian submarines that cruise off Cape Bonavista. Or the waiting ICBM missiles.

Both the Godless Communists and the American Devils have satellites orbiting a few hundred miles up that contain hydrogen bombs which can be set off from the ground. One of them probably passes over your head every hour or so. Ho hum.

No wonder the people in the Cove, in the midst of being glad that it was all over, also gave off vibrations of fear and pity when they dropped "the big new bum" on the Japs. There was the same hint of instinctive fear when the dead red herring washed ashore and I wondered where I had felt it before, until I remembered.

After the Bomb, the world was reduced to only two persons and each one of these persons has a loaded gun held against the other's head. And each one knows that if he pulls the trigger the other will do likewise at the same instant.

No, the world is reduced to less than this. It is reduced to only one person who is both God and Devil who sits there in a state of nervous collapse with the barrel of a revolver in his mouth. ▩

Petro-chemical complexes bursting forth from the bakeapple bogs

April 23, 1970   *Great New Industries*

Shaheen and his group have apparently decamped.

Mr. Shaheen, who is, among other things, North American agent for the Sheik or Sultan or Shah or whatever of the Middle East oil country of Kuwait, appeared before us out of the mists for a few days, then struck his tent and left again.

It had like to break the tender heart of Premier Smallpox to see the rude way these gentlemen from America, Britain and the burning sands of Araby were quizzed by the Opposition.

"Outrage!" he howled passionately, that these "invited guests" should be so discourteously treated. And with one eye turned heavenward and the other turned toward the TV camera he was at last driven to invoke the sacred principles of "Newfoundland Hospitality."

Anyhow, what did we get from the special TV production of "Camelmart Capers?" For one thing there's not going to be many permanent ... er ... ah ... ahem ... well ... JOBS on the Come By Chance hydrogen cracker.

We'll admit that, Mr. Speaker, sir. We'll end up with 425 jobs for which we have gone in debt to the tune of $155 million so far. Assuming that all 425 will be filled by Newfoundlanders, the great Come By Chance oil refinery could provide permanent jobs for about half the people laid off at Argentia.

These 425 jobs are little enough when we consider there are 16,000 people unemployed in the province and 7,000 or 8,000 are leaving for the mainland each year.

But the cost of creating jobs has risen greatly. Gone are the good old days when we could put a measly $1 million or so into something like the Harbour Grace boot and shoe works and confidently predict that 800 jobs would be created. Now we have to put in 154 times that amount to predict half that number of jobs.

Never mind, never fear, never blanch, Mr. Speaker. We must not dwell too long on these petty details. We must let our minds and imaginations soar above such mundane facts. The great Come By Chance refinery is really insignificant by itself. We freely admit it.

You see (and here you must force your tiny little minds to expand, to blossom, to inflate) what we should now be turning our attention to is the great, the really great, the truly vast petro-chemical complex that will grow up around this wee seed of an oil refinery.

Tremendous, stupendous, horrendous petro-chemical complexes bursting forth from the bakeapple bogs of the Isthmus of Avalon like toadstools from a manure pile on a sultry night, Mr. Speaker! That's what we should be thinking of now.

What kind of great new petro-chemical complexes? What will they produce? How many jobs will they provide? How much more will they cost us?

Imbeciles, Mr. Speaker! Impoverished minds, Mr. Speaker! Irrelevant and petty details is all they dwell on. Great new petro-chemical complexes must follow as surely as the night the day. It's as simple as that.

Then that old trouper, Freddie Rowe, never one to overlook the election campaign potential of a Movable Prospective Industry, tries to get the visitors to suggest that the petro-chemical works might be located in any of a number of districts. After all, the Isthmus of Avalon has only so many votes.

The visiting experts, however, refuse to bite. What will they produce, those great petro-chemical industries of which we hear? "Can't say," and they blush and look down at their toes. How many might they employ? "That depends on many variable factors."

How much might this great petro-chemical works be worth? "Couldn't even hazard a guess."

Enter Joe Smallwood:

"Hundreds of millions!" he shouts. "Hundreds of millions of dollars, surely!" in a parody of himself from the time of the Lightfingered Latvian to the present: from the era of rubber plants and gazelle-skin gloves to the era of linerboard mills and petro-chemical complexes.

Where lies the blame? Think about it. ⬛

Our Joseph has entered into mortal combat

May 7, 1970   *News and Propaganda*

These are troubled times in which we live.

Wars and rumors of wars on every hand. Shot and shell and discontent and open hostilities and naked aggression and raw carnage and downright unpleasantness wherever we happen to look.

On top of it all, we received the doleful news yesterday that the Benefactor of the Toiling Oppressed Masses has declared "open war" upon the Canadian Broadcasting Corporation.

The frail flame of peace on this turbulent globe grows weaker still. The battle-weary human race staggers under yet another burden of hostilities.

Our Joseph has entered into mortal combat with a section of the cool media. The lights are going out all over St. John's East. We shall not see them re-lit in our time.

Far be it for me to arouse still darker fears in the public breast, but we would be burying our heads in the sand if we did not consider the grim prospects of escalation.

Events leading up to yesterday's declaration of war are well known to all. The Four Horsemen of the Apocalypse were let loose when the CBC made the unilateral decision to allow John Crosbie to appear on that station.

Crosbie should not be allowed to, as Joseph put it, "squirt his poison into the air." We must have nothing but the benign lavender-scented elixir of Dr. Smallwood wafted to us upon the breezes.

Massive retaliation against the CBC began immediately. The Corporation reeled and staggered under the severest blow that can be dealt to any institution, group or person in Newfoundland. Mr. Smallwood refused to speak to them.

He went instead to CJON and made his Great Announcement there while the CBC struggled under the havoc wrought by the blitzkrieg. Ed Roberts did manage to parachute into Channel 8 last night on some sort of a weird peace mission but no doubt he'll have his head shaved in public for fraternizing with the enemy.

I am afraid we are going to see the Domino Effect. The CBC was the first to fall but even now Mr. Smallwood may be preparing for another lightning thrust at the soft underbelly of the local news media, VOCM.

"Conversations" has been scandalously treated. It is not introduced by a snatch of the Triumphal March from *Aida* and ended with a recording of 200,000 fans cheering at the Chelsea Manchester United soccer finals. A mortal blow will be struck and VOCM deprived of "Conversations."

Next to topple into the fearsome abyss of war will be the *Daily News*. It takes only a spark in this powder keg. The relentless savaging of government policies (particularly the Saltfish Marketing Board) by their political columnist "Wayfarer" may be the match at the touch-hole.

CJON will be caught completely by surprise. This erstwhile ally and bedfellow may show too much hesitation in using the terms "ranted" or "sniveled" on mention of Opposition members in its news broadcasts.

And within a fortnight, Joseph will have declared war on the People's Paper. Ambassadors are likely to be recalled without notice after the latest villain in Dick Tracy appears in a bow tie.

Civil war appears imminent – two nations warring within the bosom of a helluva state – when the *Newfoundland Bull–etin* is bombed without warning. Mr. Smallwood wanted a full portrait of himself attired as Zeus seated on clouds of glory on the front page.

The blowup occurred when it was suggested to the premier that people might then mistake the *Bull–etin* for the Round Church and Christian Transcendentalism Review. The first shot to be fired in that skirmish was Jim Thoms.

We predict that as escalation continues, other journals both large and small will be drawn into the fray. The *Monitor* cannot expect to stay neutral for long considering its lopsided ratio of photographs of the pontiff compared to those of the premier.

It is then only a matter of time until the ultimate weapon is turned upon the House. Our Joseph will shake that institution to its very foundations when he refuses to make any Great Announcements there.

Total war will then be upon us. Mr. Smallwood will declare that he will never again make a Great Announcement in the House or through the news media. From henceforth, government aircraft will be employed to write Great Announcements in smoke in the sky.

If we presume to see into the immediate future, skywriting will turn the tide for a time until a foggy spell during the Dog Days when all aircraft are grounded.

Dark Days indeed. Our Joseph will have need at that very moment to deliver himself of a Great Announcement on a great new tiddlywinks works to be located at the great industrial complex at Bumblebee Bight to be undertaken by a great Swaziland consortium.

What to do? He will rise to the occasion and this will be his finest hour. He will deliver his Great Announcement in person:

"Fellow Newfoundlanders. My government have decided that this province is to launch into the greatest single enterprise ever conceived on these shores and furthermore I say to you tonight that …

"Clara! Clara! Leave that bloody geranium alone and pay attention here!"

RG

The "final solution" for Bell Island

May 8, 1970   *Liberals and Pea Seas*

Neary has come up with the "final solution" for Bell Island.

God knows where he found the time after his stupendous contributions in the House but the Wabana Warbler appeared before the Senate committee on poverty yesterday and told the honorable gents a thing or two.

Why not, says Neary, put the Bell Island unemployed to work digging a tunnel under the Tickle from Bell Island to Portugal Cove? To make the most jobs possible he suggests that no machinery be used.

Just the lads a'hackin' and a'hewin' down below with picks and shovels for their government cheques. He figures the tunnel would take 10 years to finish by this means.

One up on mushrooms, which were doomed to failure from the start due to the lack of horse manure. But Neary's tunnel solution to unemployment is absolutely smashing. It should give the Canadian Senate committee something to chew on.

However, it doesn't go far enough. In 10 years when the tunnel is finished, what then? We'd be right back where we started, with all the tunnellers unemployed.

Had Mr. Neary given it a little more thought he would surely have seen that the answer is not a tunnel under the Tickle but a causeway over it.

If Bell Island's unemployed were to start now with picks and shovels and perhaps a little dynamite to help things along they could hack away Bell Island bit by bit and push it into the Tickle to form a causeway.

In 10 years' time when the causeway was completed to Portugal Cove there'd be no return to unemployment on Bell Island for the simple reason that there'd be no Bell Island.

And if Mr. Neary had a brilliant mind rather than a brilliant heart (as his Master puts it), he would have taken his great heart-felt unemployment solution still a step further and applied it to Newfoundland in general.

If the 16,000 or so unemployed in Newfoundland were put to work hacking away at Port aux Basques and dumping it into the Gulf of St. Lawrence and taking it on from there we could have a causeway across to Cape Breton in 10 years' time.

And, of course, by that time all the island's economic and employment problems would be solved because all the island would have been dug up to form a road across the Gulf.

With a little help Neary might well go down in history as the savior of his country. All he needs is a bit of encouragement. His solution to the problem of poverty on Bell Island was at least as sensible as anything else to come out of the House this week.

We have heard of killing time but this is nothing less than outright premeditated murder. This week, like the week before, our humble and devoted servants have fiddled about talking about everything from caribou sex organs to their schoolyard girlfriends.

When they haven't been spitting at each other across the floor, that is. Most of the action centers around Joey and a few of his henchmen and Crosbie and one or two of the gang on that side.

The PC opposition has been in a rather comatose state, a sort of languid hibernation, since they got a bit of help against the Gambo Conch. They seem to be lolling in this new-found luxury now that the heat is off them.

On the government side, a few of the Queen's Ministers like Rowe and Callahan lend orchestral support to their patron now and then but most of the rest of them don't seem to know if they're punched or bored.

They lounge about for the most part, snickering and guffawing among themselves reading the "Dear Abby" columns in the newspapers and generally looking like they wish they had access to the government's Gander River fishing lodge … if not an invitation to Nassau for a few weeks.

A strange experience to gawk over the rail at all this pageantry below. It is like a mini-world to itself, having nothing whatsoever to do with the reality outside.

We can have no serious objections to this, of course. There's probably no other way the House can now operate – if that is the word. Smallwood has been in complete control of it for 20 years and he's not about to give way to cooperation.

While there are enough members opposite to, if not to blast this stumbling block to some semblance of cooperation, then to stick in their heels and turn the House into a mixture of stagnation and chaos.

There seem to be only two possibilities under the present set-up. Either give Mr. Smallwood the free rein that he has had for two decades or decide that chaos is the lesser of the two evils.

Fine and dandy if that is the only alternative until an election or a causeway across the Gulf. But we do wish that the quality of insults and name-calling would improve. As she stands they're squabbling on a level that is far less imaginative than a shindig between two mesdames squalling over a backyard clothesline.

It's boring and, considering the salaries we pay them, not a good return for the money. As long as the House is bogged down in an unholy deadlock, why don't the chaps resign themselves to this fact and do their duty accordingly?

Let them abuse each other with the vim, vigor, vitality, vulgarity, originality and nobility of your average inflamed Newfoundland fishwife. Such half-hearted, whey-faced, restrained, hackneyed billingsgate as we have seen so far is a disgrace to our national image.

Unleash Rossie Barbour!

To be frank, Moores lacks color

May 14, 1970   *Liberals and Pea Seas*

As delegates from across the province arrive in St. John's for the great Pea Sea leadership convention in a church basement, we are left with the uneasy feeling that there's something lacking.

A moment's thought will disclose that what is missing from this conservative convocation is color. Most definitely. Perhaps the hour is not so late that the deficiency may not be remedied.

Color has served the Liberals well and the Pea Seas could do worse than follow the example. Premier Smallwood has always been noted for his colorful ways but we recall that before the great Liberal leadership convention he redoubled the effect by wearing a beige suit and a red shirt.

The bow tie "trademark," the use of the diminutive "Joey" and other such devices do much to create the warm, loveable and (as the mainland magazine writers never fail to put it) puckish image that we have come to know and cherish.

Although the time is short, much could still be done to brighten the rather dull and colorless image of the Pea Sea party and the grey neutral picture we have of the leadership candidates.

An obvious start, given the success of "Joey," is to adjust the candidates' names so that we have Hubie Kitchen, Hughie Shea, Wally Carter, Jacky Carter, Frankie Moores, F. Howie-Rose and, the newcomer, Joey (mercy, no!) "Guiseppi" Noel.

Trademarks would make candidates stand out more clearly in the eyes of the public and, in the case of the two Carters, avoid confusion. The agricultural gentleman, for example, might always appear in public carrying a pitchfork and chewing on a stalk of alfalfa, while the Ottawa crusader could make the sealskin coat his campaign uniform.

Space is limited as well as time so that we can do no more than offer our forthright suggestions at random. The problem is a troublesome one. To be frank, Moores lacks color and it would also be a pity to see Kitchen sink for lack of hue. Shea, on the other hand, could do better with a running mate to counterbalance his radical tendencies.

If there is anything to the rumor that newsman and erstwhile political activist Brian Goff plans to team up with Mr. Shea, his chances in a dual Shea-Goff candidacy would be greatly improved.

Punchy campaign slogans are sadly lacking to date. It is surprising that John Carter has not yet promised to "knock the stuffing out of unsavory politicians" and even more so that Walter Carter, who was once Premier Smallwood's chauffeur, has not hit upon the slogan: "Put Carter back in the driver's seat."

Candidates' policy statements to date have been vague and ill-defined. Both John and Walter Carter have placed great emphasis on the need for smaller industries such as lumber enterprises employing, say, a dozen men on the shores of our wooded brooks and streams.

But so far, the public has not been given enough details and particulars to make up its mind on the feasibility of Carter's little river mills.

Cheerleaders, fetching young girls in attractive costumes, play an important part in any political convention. We trust that candidates have each made arrangements for cheerleaders and that the supporters of each will be led in their applause by such groups as the F. Howard-Rose Buds, the Moores-Maids, the Shea-vettes and the Kitchen Wenches.

Theme songs for the various candidates do much to liven up a convention. Catchy ditties for F. Howard-Rose might run along the lines of: "Howard-Rose, Howard-Rose, he's the proper man, To keep the Commies and the French out of Newfoundland," or perhaps "Onward, Pea Sea Soldiers, marching as to war, With Colonel Josh O'Driscoll's Boy Scouts on before."

Frank Moores, who maintains a number of residences in various parts for the sake of variety, might be hailed by the following:

I'm at Carbonear and Ottawa, Toronto and Gatineau Hills,
And once I even took my seat for passage of some bills.
I like to move around, you see, and get a bird's-eye view.
But once I get the premiership my wandering days are through.

For Hugh Shea, that patriotic air, "The Star Spangled Banner," might be employed with a few adjustments. "I'm Shea and you'll see if you cast your vote right, that the scoundrels who graft'll get their lounge licence cancelled …"

Poor stuff, we admit, but this business of trying to inject color into the Pea Sea leadership convention has been driven out to the eleventh hour and we can only do the best we can under the circumstances.

On numerous occasions in the past, I have offered through these columns a plethora of sound, sensible and valuable advice to the Liberals including loyal, real, reformed, Smallwood, renegade, dissident, stalwart and defunct varieties.

All free gratis, need I add, and all prompted by nothing less than Christian charity, Hebrew honesty and Moslem magnanimity. Putting aside a certain natural modesty I may say that a number of these helpful hints and priceless pointers were used to the betterment of last year's great Liberal leadership convention.

So in the interests of giving both sides an even break, I can do no more than offer the same assistance to the Pea Seas as regards color. Otherwise, I fear, we'll get nothing more original than "It won't be long again, now." RG

Are we doomed to swing from one extreme to the other until hell cracks?

May 18, 1970   *Democracy*

After more than 20 years of that sort of thing, those short hairs on the backs of our necks tend to crawl whenever we hear of anyone winning any sort of an election by a "landslide victory."

Burned children dreading the fire is what we are, and we flinch instinctively whenever any crowd gives its "overwhelming support" to any one of its number.

Moores's grossly lopsided victory on Friday carried a faint reminder of singed flesh with it. Those who will cry out about unfair comparisons must remember that we have our scars.

Perhaps we react this way because we have been conditioned for the past two decades by one "landslide victory" after another. More hopefully, it is because we have learned at least something from past mistakes.

If the latter is not the case, then we might as well inquire right now after the price of one-way tickets to Australia. Because Toronto wouldn't be half far enough.

There is an unhealthy air, hard to define, in the fact that one person out of seven received more than 400 votes out of 600 on a first ballot – even allowing for the one or two "novelty" candidates that always crop up in such campaigns.

For three candidates to get five votes among them, for two others to get less than 50 each and for the closest runner-up to get less than 100 of the total is a trifle weird, no?

In a normal state of politics – if there is such a thing – no one is that good. And no one is that bad. No one will become that bad unless enough think, at the start, he's that good.

True, Newfoundland politics have been abnormal for a long time. But does it follow that one deformity must breed another? Are we doomed to swing from one extreme to the other until hell cracks?

Not to belittle the merits or efforts of either Moores or the Pea Seas but their excellent chances of winning the next provincial election by one of those "landslide victories" is due more to circumstances than anything else.

"There is a tide in the affairs of men which, taken at its flood, leads on to fortune," or something like that. (Wayfarer would have it letter-perfect and probably in Latin.)

Out came the prepared buttons. "Premier Moores." The old slogan "It won't be long now" was altered to "The time has come!," which is something of an admission that the Pea Seas had long done little more than sit in the ashes and wait for their ship to come in.

From the start and for years afterwards Joey got in on "landslide victories" with a vast majority time after time. And for 10 years or more most of us gleefully burbled and chortled and were content with it.

Then the bloom started to fade and the reaction began. But it was found that on the strength of the first 10 years or so of "landslide victories" Joey was able to wedge and jam and root himself in there.

Grumbling and opposition grew but was blocked from expanding, so the reaction was confined and stored up and gathered energy like a compressed spring.

Pressure built up and up. Joey managed to cling on long past his time until he was at last popped out like a bung from a keg. Swept to a "landslide victory" by this outburst of over-ripe reaction will be some convenient party like the Pea Seas or some convenient person like Frank Moores.

Nothing succeeds like success so that Moores may find himself in the same position Smallwood was 20 years ago. And away we go again.

The Pea Seas already have won a Newfoundland election with a "landslide victory" of six to one when the pent-up and over-ripe reaction against Smallwood found some vent a few years ago.

Smallwood knew well enough what a liability to the party he was even then, but his basic instincts got the better of him and he was tempted to show himself in one of the seven districts.

It is significant that Moores, who happened to be in that district, chose to hold up the fact as his trump in this leadership campaign. A face-to-face brush with Smallwood is as good as a stuffed ballot box these days.

The party that happens to be standing in front of the bung when it pops in the next election will get its landslide. The leader of such a party will be a rare bird in politics if he doesn't garner what credit he can for such a victory.

Since the party gave him his own landslide last week, he'll be in nearly as strong a position as Joey ever was to run both the party and the province as a one-man show. And the apparatus will still be there.

What an uncharitable thing to say! What tortured reasoning and what a convoluted projection from such little basis! What extreme pessimism and what a gloomy-guts attitude!

Sure. We'll admit it may be an extreme view and that there are plenty of other more cheerful possibilities. But we certainly don't apologize for at least considering such an extreme.

Because talk about being burned in the past! Among the mass of ugly scar tissue on the body politic of Newfoundland, it is natural that there be plenty of worry warts.

Aunt Cissy Roach: Reaming out her ears with the handle of a common table fork

May 21, 1970   *Aunt Cissy*

We have been taking vitamin pills for some months and have made it a practice in recent weeks to sleep with the window slightly ajar to allow of healthful circulation.

It is all part of a regimen to get in a supremely fit condition in preparation for another visit to that doughty dowager of the gowithy barrens, Aunt Cissy Roach.

We intrepid correspondents may approach such petty and routine assignments as the House, political conventions, state visits, World War Three and the Second Coming without such preparations, but, when planning a visit with Aunt Cissy Roach, you have to be in top-notch condition.

Sound of wind and limb and reasonably blithe of heart we set off out over the Trans-Canada in our conveyance, taking with us from the Controllers two crocks of Old Reserve Sculpin Sweat, dark, as a medicinal gift to the redoubtable and ancient widow.

We proceeded as usual to the Witless Bay Line and to a point midway along it and from thence some 13 miles on foot in over the tuckamores to the spot where lies the humble abode of Miss Conception, 1891.

The weather being clement we did not make haste but rather dawdled along the way, pausing now and then to savor the aroma of the steaming bogs and to admire the lesser-breasted lurchers flitting through the alders, the leaves of which are already the size of the old Newfoundland five-cent pieces.

Now and then a dumbledore, or "busy bee" as they are called by some, propelled itself across our path, they being extremely large and heavy this year. We saw several the size of a small child's mitten and could clearly hear them changing gears on the turns.

Midway along, we stopped and turned slightly off the way to view the self-same spot where in 1919 the famed Italian aviator Commandatore Vespucci Gioconda came down on the barrens in his tri-winged Vercompte-Plutz while en route from Long Island, NY, to any place suitable.

Scarce touched by the ravages of time, the dismal scene took on an almost cheerful aspect in the bright sunshine. The Commandatore is still sitting there among the remains, his right arm raised as when he lifted a glass of vermouth in that final gallant toast.

We pressed onward until we came at last to that secluded cot wherein is domiciled the object of our journey. It lies amid huge boulders and a few juniper trees grow here and there, their tops all bent in the same direction as did that of their ancestor when Judas Iscariot hanged himself from it.

Rapping smartly upon the main door of the estate we were greeted by a not unpleasant "Come in, come in, come in," and there sat Aunt Cissy Roach reaming out her ears with the handle of a common table fork.

"Well, well, well," she said. "We know the fine weather can't last when look what's out beatin' the paths. Sit down, sit down, sit down, you cod of misery, and take the load off your feet. Did they let you out or did you make a run for it?"

We accepted her gracious invitation, sat down, and could not help but remark to ourself on how well madam was looking, comparatively speaking, of course.

Although it is difficult to spot signs of anything particular in her remarkable physiognomy, she appeared to radiate an air of well-being rather like the glow from a deceased haddock at midnight with a storm brewing. It was nothing less than heartening and a joy to behold.

"What stirs you out, lantern jaws, and don't know but I will have a drop of tonic. Never seen hide nor hair of no one all spring, thank God, without it was Aunt Attie. She come out there the latter part of March and stayed overnight."

I took this to be a reference to Aunt Attie, as she is known to her host of friends, or Mrs. Atrocious B. Plimsoll of Bung Hole Tickle, D.W. Bay. A remarkable woman is Aunt Attie who, despite her great age, is still not able to read fine print with or without the aid of glasses, she being completely illiterate.

"Well, Aunt Cissy," we said. "We see you're still here."

"Talk sense, mawmouth," responded Aunt Cissy. "Yes, I'm still here although some, to their sorrow, might forget it."

"Tell us, Aunt Cissy," we continued, for if there is anyone who knows it is she, "what do you make of the present state of affairs in this country?"

"Never you mind the state of affairs in this country. The affairs of this country is what they always was. Worry about your own state. Something shot at and missed, is what you are. Your great grandfather would turn over in his grave if he was in any position to.

"Keep a decent stitch on your back. What a slovenly and lazy hangashore. Brace up and look alive, man. Are you takin' your meals regular or not? Well, you might as well stay to supper as I got two nice stuffed twillicks in the oven."

So we partook of the evening meal with Aunt Cissy, passed words with her and even took a turn around the premises in company with her, it being a fine day. However, we failed to get much in the way of comment on the state of affairs of this country.

We were feeling rather mellow as we took our leave of the ancient recluse: "Farewell, Aunt Cissy. Do you know there are times when we look upon you as "Señora da Boa Viage," as our Portuguese friends say, or "Our Lady of the Good Trip."

For this we received a sharp box in the ear and the reprimand: "Watch your language, pickle-face, or you'll be able to count your teeth without a looking glass. I'm small but I'm wiry. What a way to talk and me a poor old widow-woman out here alone. Don't forget me drop of medicine the next time."

And so we passed on in over the barrens feeling exceedingly light and hopeful in the knowledge that Aunt Cissy is still there and to see, as we progressed toward our vehicle, that the sun is so late in setting in the western sky. ▨

Guy's Encyclopedia of Juvenile Outharbor Delights: Footwear

May 27, 1970   *Outharbor Delights*

Having an hour or so to spend during a wet afternoon yesterday we found ourself leafing absently through a volume of that renowned thesis, *Guy's Encyclopedia of Juvenile Outharbor Delights*.

Turning at random to page 264 of volume three of that remarkable work, we were struck by the section, "Footwear as Regards the Outharbor Juvenile and Vice Versa."

It is nothing less than surprising to read within these pages the extent to which footwear loomed large in the life of a juvenile of our outharbors in those times.

We quote verbatim: "Good ankle support was greatly stressed in the early years. From the time an infant was able to toddle he was laced into what was called 'a good sturdy boot' for the sake of ankle support.

"By the age of five or six, he was wearing such sturdy boots affording unexcelled ankle support that if knocked out by, say, a beach rock thrown by a companion, he would not topple over but merely flop forward from the waist.

"Indeed, many outharbor juveniles reared strictly according to the principles of good ankle support and a sturdy boot often fell flat on their faces the first time they put on shoes. They had two extra joints down there they had never used before.

"Shoes were not much favored even in later years for the simple fact that they were useless, except for show. It was impossible to walk 100 feet in any direction without sinking past the insteps into one viscous substance or another.

"Lumps were almost as bad. These items were apparently hacked out of solid blocks of gutta percha rubber with little eye to the differences in foot size or the shape of the right foot as compared to the left.

"The main virtue of lumps is that they 'stood up'. Which is to say that even the most ambitious and active outharbor juvenile could not hope to wear out his lumps inside of five years.

"On the other hand of the scale from lumps were long rubbers. Business executives may have their private jet planes but the outharbor juvenile knew the supreme thrill of being presented with his first pair of long rubbers.

"There is a certain buccaneer swash to long rubbers whether they are folded down once, allowing the white linings to show in a rakish fashion, or folded up again with the straps flicking nicely and the buckles jingling at every step.

"There is always the job of testing them during the first several weeks of wear. The testing of a long rubber involves seeing how far you can walk out into the water without going over the tops.

"Since there is absolutely no way to tell what the extreme limits are without going beyond them and backing up, a proper test of a long rubber entails getting it full of water. For how do we know what is enough until we have had too much?

"Another piece of footwear much favored by the outharbor juvenile was the logan, which consists, essentially, of two refined rubber lumps attached to knee-length leather uppers.

"They are secured by means of great yellow laces, six feet or more in length, which are crisscrossed through numerous eye-holes and then hitched back and forth through rows of hooks near the top. With a set of new laces your logan boot cut nearly as much dash as your long rubber.

"A favorite of the author was always the knee rubber. Here, to his mind, is an item of footwear ideally suited, except for the depths of summer, to year-round use in the outharbor.

"While not so jaunty as the long rubber, it is far better suited, with two pairs of stockings inside, to the slushy footing of winter than is the logan. It affords more protection from seepage whilst traversing both beach and bog and is less heavy than the long rubber.

"The knee rubber – of 'Hood', 'Blue Bar', or 'Miner' manufacture – was a constant piece of equipage in the writer's wardrobe from earliest days onward.

"As for the depths of summer, which in hardier times extended from the middle of May to the middle of October, the sneaker boot was the only item of footwear into which the outharbor juvenile would suffer himself to be forced without a struggle.

"The new feminist, discarding her foundation garment by way of protest, scarce knows the great feeling of liberation experienced by the outharbor juvenile transferring from the long or knee rubber to the sneaker boot for the summer. Having dropped some 20 pounds of weight he could easily up his top speed by 15 miles per hour.

"Curiously enough, the favorite summer footwear among many juveniles was no footwear at all. With two weeks' practice, your average outharbor juvenile was able to maintain a steady trot barefoot along a gravel road.

"And this to the startled profanity of older folk such as 'Good Glory!' or 'Blessed Fortune!' Blood poisoning was greatly feared should the juvenile tread on a nail or piece of glass. However, on every possible occasion off came ..."

The end of our space being reached we must lay aside our volume of the celebrated work *Guy's Encyclopedia of Juvenile Outharbor Delights* until another day. ▨

Dear O.L.F.

May 28, 1970   *Joey*

From time to time I receive letters of a personal nature from troubled and anxious souls seeking advice on rather intimate matters.

Most of them, for some reason or other, come from political personages. Far be it for me to set myself up as an expert in such matters, but still, when these plaintive calls for advice come in, a person would have to be pretty callous and stony-hearted not to answer them as best he can.

Here are but a few examples of the many such touching pleas for advice which cross my desk:

Dear Uncle Crabby:

Please help me as I am at the end of my tether. For some time now I have made it a point to be seen in public in company with a friend whom I shall refer to as "Bonavista Boss."

My reason for this is that he is, though a genial fellow, somewhat on the "slow" side, if you know what I mean. I try to associate with him as much as possible because I feel he makes me look rather bright by comparison.

Now, Crabby, my problem is this. Lately, I get the uneasy feeling that when we appear together in public some people confuse me with good old "B.B." There is altogether too much snickering in the wrong places. What am I to do?

Wabana Warbler

Dear Warbler:

Yours is not at all a peculiar problem. Only the other day I received a letter very similar to yours:

Dear Uncle Crabby:

I have a friend who we'll call "Wabana Warbler." He is a handy chap to have around because, to put it bluntly, he does not have a "brilliant mind," if you get the picture. Next to him I show up as a near genius.

This has worked out well to my benefit until recently. Crabby, I get the disturbing feeling that some people are mistaking me for him. Yesterday, I caught him winking behind my back. Please advise as I am nearing the end of my rope.

Bonavista Boss

Dear B.B. and W.W.:

What you two crackers need is a third party as a foil against whom you would both show up as persons of at least minimal intelligence. But, alas, the age of miracles is past. Even among your associates there seems little chance of finding someone still at large to fill the bill.

Make the best of a troublesome situation and remember that each of you would look even dimmer, if possible, without the other.

Dear Uncle Crabby:

I am seeking your advice as my mind is in constant turmoil of late. It concerns the matter of a statue. I have no doubt whatsoever in this world that when the time comes the people will erect a statue of me.

A splendid statue, be it of Vermont granite, solid bronze or Carrara marble. When one is the brightest comet ever to flash across the political firmament of the western world as I am, one takes these little gestures of public esteem for granted.

But, Crabby, the question that haunts my mind night and day is how big? How big a statue? Fifty feet? Sixty feet? Sixty-five feet? Seventy feet? How big will it be?

I could resolve the whole question, I suppose, by following the example of the great Sir William Coaker and building my own. Do you think this would be a trifle gauche?

O.L.F.

Dear O.L.F.:

Your glaring inferiority complex to one side, you do have a problem as regards statues. To be on the safe side, your best bet is to put one up yourself and as soon as possible. With your experience, you should have no trouble getting the item through the estimates.

Admittedly it might be considered a bit gauche but better to be safe than sorry. Thousands of tourists go away disappointed each year at not being able to find that solid gold statue of Dr. Valdmanis.

Dear Uncle Crabby:

Lord bless us, sir, this is not a thing I like to be talking about, God knows. But I feel I got somewhat of the dirty end of the stick, so to speak, in this particular deal.

Here I've been toiling away all these years through thick and thin and just recently they nearly doubled the salary for the job to something like $20,000. Just as I start getting my just deserts it looks like they're going to get someone else to take over the job. What do you make of that, bless the mark?

Anxious Ank

Dear Anxious:

Look at it this way. There are many needy people in this world. You will be standing aside to let someone probably far more in need of this pittance than yourself have it. Take comfort in the humanitarian aspects of the situation.

By the way, please wish your fellow-countryman, "Me" of "Me 'n Ned," a speedy recovery. Between the three of you, you hold out evidence that the pernicious and peculiar race known as Townies are not entirely without redeeming qualities.

And so it goes. Hardly a day passes when I am not in receipt of similar cries for help from puzzled politicians. Clearly, politics is no bed of roses, and takes its toll in diverse ways. █

Dear Uncle Crabby

May 29, 1970   *Joey*

Yesterday, we offered advice to political persons who are constantly writing to us with their problems.

We continue today with a few more examples from our vast backlog of appeals from politicians in distress:

Dear Uncle Crabby:

One of my favorite diversions while doing the housework is listening to open line programs on the radio. Sometimes I phone in and it is really great because you don't have to give your name and nobody knows who you are.

The other day I phoned in and told them a thing of two about that wretched Mr. Crosbie, I can tell you. Well, Crabby, the problem is they recognized my voice and mentioned my name over the air.

My husband, who is in politics, was furious and has put his foot down. He says I am not to go near the telephone for a whole month. Do you think this is fair?

Wilica

Dear Wilica:

This is severe treatment indeed although a politician's wife can be a troublesome thing if completely unbridled. During the time that you are deprived of the telephone I'd suggest you get your licks in by writing anonymous notes and stuffing them into the appropriate mailboxes. It's nearly as much fun as open line programs.

Dear Uncle Crabby:

I am beside myself and need advice desperately. For many years I have been following faithfully in the footsteps of one whose boots I am not worthy to unlace. I did so with the understanding that one day I would step into those shoes.

But, Crabby, as time passes it grows more unlikely every day and my chances are fading. The worry is so great that I am losing my hair. What should I do?

Frustrated Freddie

Dear Frustrated:

It may well be that all these years you have been chasing a tinsel star. The office of premier (if that is indeed the position to which you refer) carries with it more headaches than rewards.

You would be poverty-stricken, according to the present holder of the office, and be left with not enough money to pad a crutch. The cost alone of keeping tires on your car would be something fierce and you would not get your snap in the *Newfoundland Bull–etin* that much more often.

Perhaps you should make other plans for your future. Have you considered the ministry? In any event, sign up with a good pension plan.

Dear Crabby:

Here is my problem. I have come across a good chance to bring a great new industry to the west coast of the province but I don't quite know how to put it over.

As you know, there has been a rumpus in Alaska recently because the US navy plans to store 13,000 tons of nerve gas there. Some say this is dangerous and an accident could wipe out the whole population. Others say it could mean 400 to 600 new jobs for the area.

Anyway, Crabby, I think a nerve gas depot would be just the needed addition to our great national park and silica quarries at Bonne Bay. It beats even a golf course and timber concessions.

The problem is, how can I convince people the future of the historic coast is secured if the US accepts our offer to store their nerve gas at Gros Morne?

Silica Bill

Dear Silica:

For the life of me I can't see where your problem lies. With your winning ways and completely straightforward manner you should have no trouble convincing people that an H-bomb test range and a national park go hand in glove. Look at your success so far.

Tell them nerve gas is the main ingredient used in the manufacture of nerve food pills. That should do it.

Dear Uncle Crabby:

In my present position I am supposed to get along with the baymen. But, Crabby, I just don't seem to be able to fit in. Daddy has been a cabinet minister for most of my life and I live in a rather nice house in town.

When I go out to the outharbors and tell them things like the old must be sacrificed for the sake of the young, it just doesn't come across, if you know what I mean. How can I be accepted as "one of the boys" out in Kumquat Tickle?

A Hard Row to Hoe

Dear Row:

Try to break the habit of shooting your cuffs. Stick herring scales to your patent leather pumps, acquire a salt and pepper cap and play Kitty Wells records on the jukebox at every opportunity.

And above all make certain the elderly gent to whom you are talking about being sacrificed doesn't have a fish fork in his hand or you are bound to make a complete hash of it.

And so it goes. Politicians have their problems the same as we common folk. Uneasy lies the head that wears the crown, although they usually manage to do so with a straight face. RG

Mr. Neary's book for berry picking

Resettlement and Rural Life

Another episode in the continuing drama of "Newfoundland on the March!"

In which we interview Mrs. Porkentine T. Bitts, housewife, mother, and one of Newfoundland's growing band of jolly paupers who, with the invaluable aid of S.A. Neary's booklet, *S-t-r-e-t-c-h Your Dollar Hints*, is learning to make ends meet.

"Well, my dear, I'll tell you, Mr. Neary's book was a great help to us. We have been on the dole, or social assistance as some calls it, these past 15 years.

"Bless Mr. Neary. We knowed all along that he was conscious of the problems met by his clients in living within the limits that must necessarily be set to our present scales of Social Assistance. But what a treat to read it in black and white in his new book.

"Anyway, when it comes along in the mail with our dole cheque I said to Pork, me husband, Pork I said, we are going to folly it word for word and better ourselves and make ends meet. That was my very words.

"So we sot out on all them self-help activities in the book. First was home vegetable growing. We got a hold of them 'few simple tools' recommended – spade, digging fork, hoe, rake, trowel, planting line, hand weeder, hand duster, wheelbarrow, combined garden drill and wheel hoe and garden tractor.

"It seemed logical that because of its greater bulk and general availability that cow manure is most generally used. And we planted the corn, staked tomatoes and pole beans on the north side where they would not cast shade on smaller plants.

"We put in asparagus and rhubarb and side-dressed the Wilhelmburger turnips with ammonium nitrate and applied boron to prevent brown heart and watery core. We sprayed the Danish ballhead with diazinon to knock out the cabbage looper, imported cabbage worm, purple-backed cabbage worm and diamond-backed moth.

"Well, my dear, before you knew it the time had come to folly the instructions in Mr. Neary's book for berry picking. We got a taxi out to beyond the overpass and charged it to the welfare.

"We brought home half a gallon of blueberries since the hills was crowded and the berries was scarce and spent the best part to a week decidin' whether to use the solid pack method, the dry sugar method, the cold pack method, or the sugarless method.

"Then I went along with the section on 'Knitting and Sewing, Etc.' and took lessons at the vocation school on weaving, leathercraft, crocheting, smocking, embroidery, knitting, millinery and sewing.

"The best part of the whole book was the part on 'Fishing and Hunting' where Mr. Neary tells you that with the price of meat so high people on the dole should go out and shoot it.

"Let me read you the piece on fishing. It says: 'There are three types of fishing carried on in this province (1) inshore (2) nearshore and (3) offshore. The most appropriate type for persons who are unable to engage in nearshore or offshore is the inshore fishery'.

"My God, I mean to say, don't that make sense? Pork nearly jumped off the settle when he read that 'Lobsters are caught in traps which can be handled by one man and one man can catch salmon or trout in a river'.

"He spends half the day up the brook with the pole after he comes in from the fishing grounds in the dory. In the fall he's in on the hills after partridge, moose, caribou and bear and it's a rare day that we haven't got a ruffed grouse for the pot.

"As time passed we took note that a good cow, well fed and cared for, pays for herself. Then we read that goats may be even more convenient and economical than cows so we got some of them, too.

"Along with the sheep we had plenty of manure for the Wilhelmburger turnips. They says in the book that 'Raising pigs can be a problem – local laws may forbid such an enterprise and your family and neighbors may object to the smell'.

"But we haven't had no trouble on that account. You can hardly notice the pigs on account of the goats. We got some chickens, geese and ducks, too, as Mr. Neary suggested, and knocked up a green house, 15 feet four inches wide by seven-and-a-half feet high covered by .004-gauge polyethylene plastic vapor barrier.

"We follys all the instructions in Mr. Neary's book. We even puts a drop of food coloring and a half-spoon of sugar in the youngsters' milk to make it more exciting and brushes our teeth with salt or baking soda to save on toothpaste.

"All in all, we are making ends meet and it is more interesting since we started reading that little blue book. There is the scattered hitch, of course, but that is to be expected.

"The other day the cow got into the turnip patch and one of the goats made a standing jump clear through the greenhouse, capered up onto the fish flake and leaped from there on to Duckworth Street.

"The city council bunch came around in a hell of a tear but I says to them, I says, don't you tell us what we can or can't do – you can go in and have a chat to Mr. Neary.

"Then meself and Pork dolled up and went along to the curling rink to take part in the big Dole Recipients Bonspiel. If our rink don't get four rocks by the second end I allow we'll be knocked out of competition." ▣

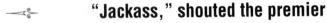 # "Jackass," shouted the premier

June 4, 1970   *In the House*

When it is brought home to you that you are falling down on the job, the first reaction is remorse and depression. This is soon followed by a determined resolve to do better in the future.

Tuesday in the House of Ass–embly, Mr. Smallwood declared that the press was misleading the people as to what goes on in the House.

He said it plays up the "catchy phrases" and this gives readers and listeners the impression that nothing else goes on in the House. The main points of debate are "not snazzy and catchy enough to get reported," says Smallwood.

This is where I let the side down badly, I fear. The reporters feel compelled to report all the "catchy phrases" because there are times when they are overlooked in this corner.

If I had been on the ball and taken note of all the "catchy phrases," the news reporters would have been free to concentrate on the news stories in the profound, sublime and dignified debate that makes up at least six per cent of each sitting.

Looking back through the files, I blush to discover how many of these "catchy phrases" I missed, leaving it to the reporters to put them in news stories and give the public the wrong impression.

In February, for instance, Smallwood was calling Hickey an ignoramus and a jackass and accusing Ank Murphy of the "quintessence of McCarthyism" – catchy phrases all.

"Shame," cried the Opposition.

"Stupid," shouted the premier.

"Shame," cried the Opposition again.

"Jackass," shouted the premier.

It is catchy phrases and snazzy rejoinders such as these that give the public the impression that the House proceedings are something they are not.

Billy Rowe, by mid-February, was accusing Murphy of implicating every Honorable Member by innuendo, of destroying the dignity and respect of the House, and declared that he would live to regret it.

Smallwood was saying that Crosbie had made a jackass of himself and Crosbie was accusing Curtis of unbridled tyranny. Silica Callahan declared there was "in progress a plan, a plot, a policy, to deliberately obstruct, delay and impede the business of the House."

Joey was crying that Val Earle's disclosures were "dishonorable … It is utterly a dishonorable thing in the extreme." Crosbie called Neary "crown prince 12" and Wells said the Opposition was "treated with contempt and disdain that would make any South American dictator blush" and said it was all "based on the bitterness of one man."

Not to be outdone, Smallwood said Wells was overcome with "blind, partisan hatred" and, while he was at it, said Crosbie was a dead duck, politically. To which Crosbie responded with the catchy phrase: "Quack, quack."

The premier said that when Ed Roberts was through with him, Wells would walk out of the House with his tail between his legs. He also declared: "We are paying our way and balancing our budget."

To this, Wells responded, "Ho, ho." Which prompted Smallwood to counter with "Ho, ho, ho, ho, ho… five ho's." All catchy stuff, although there's some question as to just where it would all catch you.

"Shabby trash," "utter guff," "rotten nonsense," "walking slime," "big sook," "big bully," "trash, trash, trash," "cheap political tricks," "dirty scoundrel" and "filthy liar" are other endearments I may have overlooked.

It isn't that all these catchy phrases are attention-getting and bound to strike the headlines. It's just that after the sixth or seventh time they tend to lose some of their original freshness.

Some time in February, for instance, Tom Hickey made a motion to have Joey kicked out of the House for calling Wells a liar. This seemed reasonable since the year before Hickey had been suspended for three days for calling Smallwood a liar.

But the Speaker ruled Hickey out of order. Since then, hardly a day passes when some Honorable Member does not call some other Honorable Member a liar.

And not your regular garden-variety liar either. Filthy liars, rotten liars, dirty liars. Before she clews up someone is going to go for the record and call someone else a "sawed off, hammered down, unmitigated, baldfaced, miserable, dirty, stinking, contemptible liar."

If I'm on my toes I'll make note of it here first to save the reporters the trouble of putting it in the news stories. It's the least I can do.

After all, we wouldn't want readers to get the impression that these sorts of catchy phrases are really bounced back and forth in the Honorable House.

Better to lump them all together here where there's a chance that they'll be taken for pure fantasy. ▧

The 234th annual Caplin Supper
and Fecundity Dance

June 9, 1970   *Culture and History*

One of the social events of the season took place on Wednesday past in the shape of the 234th annual Caplin Supper and Fecundity Dance at Bung Hole Tickle.

I have been looking for reports and snaps of it in the St. John's press but, due to the slowness of the post, these accounts must not have arrived yet.

However, I had the privilege of attending the gala event in person and have taken the liberty of knocking out a piece on it here. Photographic views of the "crème de la crème" of Bung Hole Tickle society at the annual formal event will doubtless appear in city journals before the week is out:

"The ballroom of the F.U. Hall in downtown Bung Hole Tickle was the scene of the 234th annual Caplin Supper and Fecundity Dance on Wednesday past sponsored by the True Blue Latter Day Fructification Society, Ladies Auxiliary, Crocheting and Whort-Jamming Branch."

"Among the notables attending the glittering event were the international Sacrosanct Madam of the T.B.L.D.F.S., Lady Godiva Twiddlepease-Smythe from the Old Country; His Worship Henry Alfred Sunks, mayor at Bung Hole Tickle and Skipper Gotterdamerung Jinks, J.P., patriarch and town elder.

"Guests of honor also included representatives of the 17 religious denominations in the community. The Extremely Reverend Praisegod Barebones of the Round Church What the Devil Can't Corner, was to have sung grace to open the banquet but forgot his lines after 'Be present at our table, Lord ...'

"An embarrassing situation was neatly avoided and the shoe-shuffling silence broken when one of the guests at the lower end of the table slung a pork bun at an acquaintance at the upper end. At this, animated conversation broke out and the guests were quickly seated.

"The ballroom of the F.U. Hall was charmingly decorated for the occasion with spruce tops festooned with illustrations clipped from Eaton's Midsummer Sale catalogue.

"An innovation at this year's ball was the introduction of a kerosene bracket lamp in the porch, which was aimed at cutting down on the incidence of smooching (or worse) in the heretofore-darkened foyer, a feature of other years.

"Following the banquet, which included soupe des pois, sautéed caplin livers and Duffe a la Figgi, there was a gay scamper for the dance floor as guests were encouraged by an exuberant Uncle Bill Joe Perisher, D.C.P.M.G., Esq., shouting: 'Last one on the floor gets my boot ...'

"Sacrosanct Madam, Lady Godiva, was the center of attention as she led off the Grand March escorted by His Worship, Henry Alfred Sunks. Her Ladyship won the hearts of all for her charm and grace but more particularly for the coarse expletive that escaped her lips when a hot flashbulb from the camera of one of the guests popped down her cleavage.

"During intervals in the dance a 'Grab Bag' at 25 cents a grab was run off and such items as a face cloth from a box of detergent and a block of Good Luck butter were put up on tickets. Mrs. Fungicide Tittle, chairwoman of the fundraising committee, said the proceeds would be sent off to help the Christian Blacks in other parts.

"The Belle of the Ball was Miss Didoes McGee, 14, daughter of Mr. and Mrs. Teutonic McGee, who looked absolutely ravished (as well she might) in a fetching off-the-shoulder orange taffeta with the ever-so-in hemline of the season described locally as 'up-around-her-quarters'.

"Another charmer of this year's Caplin Supper and Fecundity Ball was pretty Miss Geraldine Scupper, 16, daughter of Mr. and Mrs. Beatitudes Scupper and/or His Worship Henry Alfred Sunks. The Scuppers reside at "Crabshaven" Bung Hole Tickle Extern.

"Geraldine chose a delightful 'basic black' in tie-dyed curtain scrim, loosely fitted, which allowed her to coyly lean against the foyer door and snap the elastic waistband of her stepins as she charmingly popped her upper dentures in and out.

"The annual fight stared at 10:30, some 10 minutes behind schedule. This part of the ceremonies was led off by Mr. Buck Turgid, 18, son of Mr. and Mrs. Aloysius Turgid of nearby Qualmish Gut, a place long noted for having a 'hard crowd'.

"Young Mr. Turgid, snappy in hip-hugging corduroys and black leather jacket studded with bottletops, wrapped the coal scuttle around the ears of Mr. Jacobean Knucks, 19, of Bung Hole Tickle proper. Mr. Knucks responded with a knee to the parts and bit off the top joint of Mr. Turgid's left index digit.

"Not the last to join in this part of the entertainment was Uncle Percival John Scurvy, 94, 'Grand Old Man' of the community, who playfully struck Skipper Thomas Joseph Piebald, 87, in the nose with his fist, remarking wittily as he did so: 'Here, smell that!'

"The spirited altercation was enjoyed by all present. Lady Godiva remarked afterward that she was much taken by Skipper Gotterdamerung Jinks, 79, who kept wringing up his fist and shouting 'Be the Lord Liftin' *****! I seen the time when I could put it through a inch board!'

"There was a break for refreshments at 3:45 after which the wounded were attended to and dancing resumed. The 234th annual Caplin Supper and Fecundity Dance concluded on Saturday morning with the singing of the National Anthem. A good time, need it be said, was had by all." ■

Drinking beer and carrying out indecent acts

June 12, 1970   *Policing*

Indecent acts have broken out in the parks of St. John's. Some of the parks at any rate. The increased incidence of indecent acts was noted in a story in yesterday's *Telegram*.

So that Weekend-only subscribers are not deprived of this piece of vital intelligence, we repeat the news story here in part:

"The police moved into the area (a mid-city park) after receiving complaints from residents that young people were visiting the area during the day, drinking beer and carrying out indecent acts.

"The young people usually go to the park during lunch hour and again after school hours apparently after stopping somewhere to buy beer, according to the reports. Apparently after eating and drinking they usually took part in indecent acts.

"Wednesday afternoon the police moved in, a patrol car at either entrance, and by means of a loudspeaker, asked the young people to stop what they were doing and leave the park.

"One woman, whose property borders on the park, said that when the police arrived the young people arose from the grass and shrubs like a swarm of locusts."

So there you have the bald facts. There is something to be said, I suppose, for confining indecent acts to the city parks. At least it is better than having indecent acts on the public streets where they could cause rear-end collisions and bent parking meters.

However, it appears that residents and the police want no part of it in the parks either. For the sake of decorum in the public prints, the news story does not give further particulars.

We have only the barest outline. When it comes to indecent acts we are into an area that may be better imagined than described. Surely our youth have not gone so far as to besmirch their minds by leering over passages of Hansard or passing clippings from newspaper reports of the House from hand to hand in dark alleyways.

We can only hope that the acts referred to are not quite so indecent as that. In any case, we are told that "after eating and drinking they usually took part in indecent acts."

From this we may gather that indecent acts are not to be taken part in on an empty stomach. We also note that two police cars rolled up at either end of the forum and "by means of a loudspeaker, asked the young people to stop what they were doing and leave the park."

According to reports, this had a singular effect indeed. The indecent actors, as the loudspeaker boomed out, "arose from the grass and shrubs like a swarm of locusts."

Surely, there's a possibility of a tourist attraction in this situation. It remains only for some enterprising person to sign up tourists for safaris through city parks.

A line of beaters, as we see in the movies of African hunts, could progress through the tall grass and bushes, beating on tin pans and yelling loudly, to flush the "game." The tourists, cameras at the ready, would be ready to capture trophies they would treasure a lifetime.

To find out more about this phenomena of indecent acts in city parts we consulted Professor Vassily Deferens, head of the debauchery and insectology branch of the university.

Professor Deferens says that it is all connected with the increased use of pesticides and insecticides in today's world. The whole ecology has been upset, he says.

"Before the introduction of insect sprays your indecent acts were performed – during the months of June to October – either indoors or underwater," the professor explained.

"This was particularly true in Newfoundland. To put it in layman's terms, your average indecent act entails the removal of protective garments. As everyone knows, before the introduction of insect sprays and repellents, that was impossible in your grassy fields, your woodsy copses and your verdant dells.

"The incipient indecent actor would be set upon by swarms of mosquitoes, sandflies and cowbees to the detriment and, usually, to the immediate termination of the indecent act. I might refer you to the works of Benson, Crocker, Collins, Martin, et al., with regard to further research.

"In brief," continued Professor Deferens, "we see that the introduction of DDT drastically reduced the number of creepy crawlies and wingy stingies in our parks and the incidence of indecent acts increased in proportion.

"Truly, we are all part of the warp and woof of creation," he said. "From the smallest insect to the merest blade of grass we are all part of the great chain of life. Alter one link and the whole universe is shaken."

So much for the warp and woof. Meanwhile, until insecticides are banned entirely and the balance of nature is restored, we would be advised, according to the professor, to either whistle loudly or jingle the loose change in our pockets while walking through city parks.

Barring these cautions against embarrassment, the professor says there is nothing for it but to include a large tin of DDT in the picnic basket. ▊

Guy's Encyclopedia of Juvenile Outharbor Delights: The Fine Art of Doing Nothing

August 7, 1970   *Outharbor Delights*

There is no need at all in this world for me to make mention of it.

Everybody privileged to be reared on these shores knows all about it just so well as they know the backs of their hands. I don't know why I'm wasting my time bringing it up. There is no need for it whatsoever.

These two weeks in the first part of the month of August, of course. The top notch, the peak, the height, the zenith, the Everest, is now.

Wherever you go, sir, and whatever you do these two weeks in the first part of the month of August are stamped and impressed and sunk into your frame just as sure as if you were run over by a double-headed east-bound freight with 34 cars.

Here and now and from cape to cape and up the shore and down the shore and across the bay and around and about and from top to bottom, topside, downside, outside, inside and backside.

This is the peak of the year, the high church days, the Holy Season for Juvenile Outharbor Delights. These two weeks above all out of the 52.

Absolutely sinful it is and too much of a good thing to be wholesome. Delights now streaming down upon the heads of outharbor juveniles, awash and brimming over, blinding as the sun before dinner and as dizzying as a game of "Turning Around and Around Until We Gets Stomach Sick."

Chinched to the hatches, at this time of year more especially, and so plentiful that it is downright sinful. Grab one, take two bites, sling it down and grab another. Out and gone from daylight to dark.

There's hardly an outharbor juvenile in sight to be caught and sent to the store. Light in the heads, they are caught up and made drunk as lords by the festivities of the Holy Season.

The most you can do is ask the useless question: "What have you been doing all day?" And the most you'll get is a brazen confession of the ultimate sin: "Nothin'." Artisans, masters, doctors, maestros, holders of signed, sealed and delivered certificates in the sinful art of doing nothing.

Juvenile Outharbor Delights hit their stride in the two weeks while the year is turning around. A week before the peak the grass in the meadows and along the shore is green as paint and a week after it is brown and red and yellow.

Doin' nothin' is having a pet frog into a pickle bottle and saying: "If he feeled like jumpin' all you'd have to do is poke him in the ears with your finger and he'd ... he'd ... he'd jump over yeer house! Ha!"

(You have to wait 30 years before you say: "I keep him at the books and he manages to get a 75 per cent average. Not bad, I suppose, but he could do better if he put his mind to it.")

The fine art of doing nothing is dominated by the juvenile, outharbor and otherwise, but most people never stop trying to regain the lost knack. They try to do it by means of ever more expensive and elaborate toys.

Going downhill on the loose gravel on a second-hand Raleigh with your feet on the handlebars gives way to making it from Gander to St. John's in three hours in a 12-mile-per-gallon Chrysler.

The bough house out back of the hill is replaced by the "shack" in the country with an asphalt driveway and a bath-and-a-half. Nothing but an 800-pound tuna fish will take the place of the sardine caught in the brook on an alder and a worm.

And does it? Ah, ha. There's the rub. How big would a tuna fish have to be? As big as the church with two heads and two tails and King Neptune sitting on his back wearing a fitout all done out with lumps of gold as big as hens' eggs and eyes as big as bowls of lime jelly playing Patience with a large deck of marked cards. That's how big a tuna fish would have to be.

People fly in to Labrador to catch trout weighing 10 pounds each. But all they catch is trout. Except perhaps for the scattered glimpse and remembrance of what they're really after.

The sooner the knack of doing nothing dies away the more frantic the attempts to get it back. When sticking your head in an empty pork barrel and yelling, or clouting an empty oil drum with two rocks no longer does the trick, there is a desperate tendency toward "high fidelity" gramophones, amplified guitars and echo-chamber howls.

It is all useless, of course. No amount of expensive toys and pastimes can recreate what was once second nature. Once the knack of doing nothing goes, it is gone.

Easy it was and second nature without having to try. Every minute of every day there was nothing to be done and done well and enjoyed. And these were not times when a day went fast, mind you.

These were times when a day was as long as a week and a summer was without end. The only problem was going to sleep fast enough so you could get up early enough and start in again.

It wouldn't hurt to have a look at outharbor juveniles going about the business of doing nothing. (Townie juveniles, too, for all I know, but that is out of my jurisdiction.) But you are permitted only a glance now and then out of the corner of the eye.

Be warned that staring is a sacrilege and attempting to join in is a desecration. Have you no reverence for the sacred rites and rituals of the Holy Days? ▩

Probing resettlement for
effects on intelligence

August 13, 1970

Culture and History

You miss a lot if you don't read the People's Paper from cover to cover.

Yesterday, for instance. On page 30 I came across a piece of great interest to myself and, I am sure, to readers everywhere. It was headlined: "MUN group probes resettlement for effects on intelligence."

I recognized it in a flash. What a coincidence. Truth is always stranger than fiction and make no mistake about it. For no more than a month ago I came across what I take to be this same MUN group out in Bung Hole Tickle, G.D. Bay!

After reading the piece I was sure of it. It said that the "Institute for Research into Human Abilities" at the university was making another study of people in "resettled" outharbors.

The gist of the story was, as one of the chaps put it, that "there is usually the Darwinian notion behind theories of intelligence that intelligence is adaptable and even that adaptation is the essence of intelligence."

Right. And the words had a familiar ring indeed. A month ago I was in Bung Hole Tickle and had gone down to get a small fish for dinner. Young Sylvester Codpiece (mentioned here before) is home on furlough from Toronto and is fishing for the summer with his grand-da, Uncle Anchorite Codpiece, or Uncle Rite as he is known, a slight man of advanced years but extremely wiry.

Uncle Rite was splitting and young Sylvester was gutting. It was a hot day and they were out on the stage head when a knock came to the stage door.

Young Sylvester answered it and called out: "Uncle Rite! Chap here from Sin John's, tam on his head, pimple on the top of it, chinwhisker on his jaws, wants to see you."

The older fisherman said nothing but spat forcibly over the splitting table and wiped some intestines from his face with the back of his hand. The visitor came in carrying a tape recorder, a briefcase and a note pad.

"Well, my good man," he said. "I'm Professor William Scrod from the university and we will shortly be launching another important study into resettlement. I am the pathfinder of the group, as it were. I understand that you, sir, relocated here in Bung Hole Tickle some 12 years ago.

"I should like to ask you a few very simple questions. Now ... tell me in your own words whether or not the Darwinian notion behind theories of intelligence that intelligence is adaptable and even that adaptation is the essence of intelligence applies in your case."

"Lot of that on the go," said Uncle Rite. "Got a touch of it meself this week. Loose one day, seized up the next. Be jeeze, them Atom bums is what I puts it to."

"Deaf as a haddock," explained young Sylvester. "Deaf in one ear and can't hear in t'other. Har. Har, har."

This attempt at robust humor was lost on Professor Scrod, who took another tack: "Young man, kindly pass my questions on to your uncle. Ask him whether or not his ability patterns have altered since coming to Bung Hole Tickle in accordance with theories which predict that intelligence will change with environment."

"Uncle Rite!" bawled young Sylvester. "Chap here wants to know whether or not your ability patterns has altered since you come here to Bung Hole Tickle in accordance with …

"I don't allow you'll get much out of him," said young Sylvester, ducking smartly as Uncle Rite spat in his general direction. "Cross as the cats. Got a touch of this complaint and he suspicions Uncle Bill Jinks for cuttin' off a spandered new set of our lines this mornin'."

Professor Scrod was clearly out of patience, too. "Look here, young fellow," he said. "You're wasting my valuable time. This survey is of immense value to Bung Hole Tickle and places like it. All I want is your simple cooperation. I have better things to do than sit here in this abominable stench and banter with you two cretins all day."

Young Sylvester was getting impatient also. Like lads of his age he was anxious to complete his work and be off for an ale or two with his fellows and there was a chance, if he finished soon, of cornering Miss Florabunda Tittle, the village vamp, down behind the old wellhouse.

"Now," said Professor Scrod testily, "try him again. All I want to know, purely and simply, is whether he feels that he has adjusted to the new environmental alternatives here or if he thinks his abilities will have to be developed, if possible, to correct the situation."

Young Sylvester hove a long sigh and shook his head wearily. Then he brightened up slightly and I do believe that the means of his salvation occurred to him at that moment. He laid down his knife and backed up a pace.

Taking several deep breaths such as skindivers do to hyperventilate the system before going under water, he worked himself up to the necessary effort.

"Uncle Rite!" he roared at the top of his lungs. "What he wants to know is whether you're so damned stunned since you moved in here as you always was!"

It happened in a flash. All I remember is that Professor Scrod and his tape recorder turned three complete somersaults before they hit the water. ∎

The Ninth Cinch: Part I

Spy Thriller

(In which we continue a new Spy Thriller of Intrigue and Suspense set amid the Political Squalor and Savagery of the Happy Province – with a vivid description of a Stark Naked female poll captain chucked in on page 57 to keep the ball rolling.)

Chapter Seven: Mr. Wonderful

At the very instant, N.D.S.T., that the Boss of Bonavista South was lying prostrate on the pool of pink and green Congoleum and reaching under the Simmons Beautyrest Kingsize for the corrugated carton wherein lay the Ultimate Weapon basking in its own malevolent purple glow, another far less sinister-looking figure was contemplating his appearance in a Louis Quinze ormolu.

Incredible as it seemed, he too was a key cog in the feared Apparatus. To look at him few would think so. Could it be that this innocent-looking cherub was numbered among the top echelon of the organization? Some said he stood next to the Skipper himself.

The soft light of mid-morning shone through the half-opened French doors and caught the dark brunette curls at an angle. A stray beam of sunlight reflected off the red lettering on a torn tinfoil packet of stomach powders on the dresser and lent a downy blush to the cheek.

From as far away as St. Anthony and the Strait Shore, little old ladies sent him parcels through the mail containing double-knit mitts or small chocolate cakes sprinkled with hundreds and thousands.

Once, a female admirer had even sent him a pair of Sea Island cotton underdrawers whimsically patterned in a colony of ants. He seldom wore them. What would the chaps in the locker room think?

"Croppy" they called him by way of endearment. Some gave the "O" an umlaut, others pronounced it as a broad "a." Which ever way you cut it, "Croppy" was nothing less than a bundle of charm.

As he sized himself up now in the Louis Quinze ormolu, he reflected that his main attributes were his air of earnestness and innocence. The answer to the old test question "Would you buy a used syringe from this man?" could be nothing other than the affirmative.

"Hmmm. A bit too much sun in the wrong place," he remarked to himself. Indeed, his heavy crop of hair and his dark glasses plus that 523-page report had shielded most of his features yesterday on the terrace. Except for the top of his nose. It had turned a toasty brown.

Despite his tender years, Croppy was jaded. He had crammed much into a short space. His rise in the Organization had been astronomical. Now he was bored. His only diversion these days was seeking out the Boss of Bonavista South once a week and trapping him into a logical fallacy.

Never mind, he thought, shaking the tin of Ice Blue Secret as the instructions directed, maybe this new job coming up would be just the thing to get him out of the doldrums. It had proven a tonic in the past and he knew this one would be the grand daddy of them all.

A faint yet persistent sound hung on the air, rather like a miniature buzz saw slicing a leprechaun in two lengthwise. Croppy looked down and there, amid the aids to personal daintiness on the dresser, was an exceptionally large bluebottle spinning around on its back.

"Drat!" he said aloud. Full well he knew that if anyone had entered the room at that moment and had seen the expiring fly, they would immediately have accused him of using DDT. While he in fact used only piperonyl butoxide, a non-residual, he knew that in his position he couldn't afford to take even the slightest chance.

The plump insect struggled momentarily as the pressure between thumb and forefinger increased. No less than three micro-drops of the pyrethrins bearing the piperonyl butoxide had entered its respiratory system a full 30 minutes before and the eight hairy legs had been greatly weakened.

"Hmmmmm," said Croppy as he briefly examined the resulting purée. "Fancy that.

Chapter Eight: Don't Be Talking

Fever pitch was but a mild phrase to describe the indignation of the Boss as he discovered the likeness of himself, a one-column by three-inch mug on page 28 of the city's leading daily journal.

He was incensed to the last degree and flung the sheets of newsprint to the floor. Time and time again he had told them that his left profile was his best side. They never listened.

Never mind. The day would come – and come soon – when they would listen. They all would listen. The Ultimate Weapon would see to that.

Not that there wasn't a 50 per cent chance of failure … and the penalty for failure was enough to make even the doughty Balmy Alcock quake in her cossack boots. But the Boss didn't dwell on the possibility of failure. He had made up his mind.

He was going to put all his eggs in one basket and go for the Grand Slam. Better that, he had decided, than continue to dribble out his substance over the long years in hopes – hopes that were always deferred.

"Always the carrot on the stick," he thought to himself, "and always the donkeys had gone for it … Silica, Croppy, the Wabana Warbler, all of us."

"But they won't get me again on that," he mused aloud. "Au contraire. Now it's my turn. Little do any of them know that I and I alone …"

(Continued tomorrow when we at last come to page 571. Are you ready for .. Angelique? …)

The Ninth Cinch: Part II

August 18, 1970   *Spy Thriller*

(In which we continue the new Spy Thriller of etc., etc., etc.)

Chapter (if memory serves) Nine: Pluck it Out ...

Angelique knew it was a hard, cutthroat business. That was why she liked it. What she didn't know was that at that very moment two red-rimmed and unblinking eyes were lustfully following her every move.

She had wrapped the last lock of her auburn tresses around the last of a dozen empty Campbell soup tins, tops and bottoms removed, and was preparing for bed. As the purple and black corduroy dressing gown slid from her shoulders and dropped to the floor, the sinister figure lurking outside the window gasped perceptibly.

With good reason Angelique was proud of herself. She was the most efficient poll captain, male or female, the Organization had ever produced. Her mere presence at the polling station was enough to strike terror into the enemy agents.

And with good reason, for Angelique weighed 18 stone in her combat boots if she weighed an ounce. She often wished she could whittle off a few pounds and regain the svelte 190-pound figure she had at 16. But she knew that her heft was her biggest asset.

There'd been the bit of a dust-up down at the station at the last election. One of the enemy agents had been making a fuss about irregularities. In the commotion, Angelique had seen her chance and suddenly backed into him. They had to sandblast what was left of the poor devil off the wall.

Her stature wasn't the only weapon in her arsenal, however. One of her fondest memories was of the way she had handled what could have been a touchy business back in 1958. The top agent on the other side had started to raise a cry about ballot box stuffing.

She smiled as she recalled how, in the press of the crowd, she had deftly removed one of her garters and snapped it on over his head. The poor brute was in the final throes of strangulation before they finally managed to claw it off.

As she finished her toilet for the night, she noticed a piece of paper on the side table. It was an application form from a ladies' organization in the US – W.I.T.C.H., the Women's International Terrorist Conspiracy from Hell.

"Damn sissies!" snorted Angelique, crumpling the paper into a ball and pitching it away from her. These pantywaists with their namby-pamby methods disgusted her. She split the night table with a karate chop and felt the better for it. Then she tossed off her usual nightcap of a triple J and B on the rocks.

Outside the window, the miserable wretch of a Peeping Tom cowered lower in the hydrangea bush as she let go the latches of the elastic sky-blue garment that girdled her titanic torso. It was not unlike the sudden breakup of a particularly complicated log jam on the Upper Humber. All that covered her voluptuous frame now was a pair of blue cavalry twill knickers.

As these slid to the floor with a dull thud, the wretched creature crouching on the other side of the half-open venetian blinds sagged slightly, then retched into the Lonicera hybrid, or Dropmore Scarlet Trumpet honeysuckle, as it is more commonly known.

With some effort, he scrambled to his feet and scuttled off through the bushes into the darkness. It was enough to make a chap take up footwear or bicycle seats.

"God, you do get acne in the damndest places!" remarked Angelique to herself as she noticed an angry rash on her left elbow. Never mind. Otherwise, she was supremely fit and would be ready to swing into action the moment the Organization called on her. She knew the call would come soon.

Chapter Ten: What Goes Up

It was now 23 minutes before noon and, as the overhead sun beat mercilessly down, the intrigue and depravity which hung over the old seaport of Sin John's shimmered in the mid-August heat.

The Boss was still seething inwardly over the likeness of himself which had appeared in the last issue of the city's leading daily journal. He had told them repeatedly that his left profile was his best side but they had gotten it wrong again.

In any case and at this stage of the game publicity of any sort was the last thing he wanted. He switched on the television but there was no news of any sort. However, he was just in time to catch the end of his favorite show, "Disneyland."

It was a re-run of "Ole Red, the Barn Owl who Thought he was a Defrocked Episcopalian Clergyman." Next week, according to the previews, they'd be showing "Ole Green, the Story of the Little Cockroach Who Thought he was a Diabetic Republican Senator."

However, there were no news bulletins, just a commercial for a dog food containing "tender, husky, hearty pieces of fresh red beef," followed by another commercial showing Lotta Hitchmanova dishing out barley soup in the slums of Calcutta.

His mind was made up as he switched off the television. No later than tomorrow the Boss of Bonavista South was going to pay a call on the Skipper himself.

Beads of perspiration stood out on his purposeful forehead, for in all these years he had never done so before without an invitation. ▩

HAIR: Part I

It is nothing short of surprising the rate at which fashions change in this modern age. I had it brought home to me sharply this present week.

Not so long ago a chap with long hair was looked at askance on the public streets. Now, of course, bank managers and magistrates sport curls down to their collars.

Schoolteachers and chartered accountants cultivate mutton chops that would put the late Prince Consort in the shade. Even your political leaders and your managing editors are all a'bristle in the most debonair way imaginable.

Hair, it seems, now is the thing. A few years ago it was only the scattered violin player or the callow Bohemian youth who ran around in ringlets. But the fashion caught on in no time.

Almost any stretch of sidewalk looks like the international Old English Sheepdog trials. You see a large bush coming toward you and you expect someone to jump out from behind it and say "Boo!" They can't. They're attached to it.

As you may have gathered I have never given much thought to my personal appearance. When I first saw what I had to work with I gave it up for a bad job. Nothing would have helped anyway short of a complete transplant of everything above the ankles.

So far forth as hair is concerned I found it economical in years past to get it all mowed down, smack smooth, in what was called in these far-off times a "brush cut." Then I would let it all grow out again.

By this means I was able to get by on two haircuts a year. Apart from the savings gained, it was an interesting process. It was an education in itself to watch those two yearly crops grow and come to maturity.

Those first delicate sprouts in spring, watered by the gentle rain, nourished by regular applications of Vitalis, carefully mulched with brilliantine, invigorated by the summer sun. Then, in the fullness of time, came the harvest.

Another brush cut and the cycle of nature began again. What need for boredom, what room for ennui with a full crop always under cultivation immediately above? Many's the time I have sat for hours and watched it grow.

These past few years, however, it has been more than your face is worth to get a "brush cut." You would be mocked and jeered in the marketplace. But just how far the pendulum had swung I didn't know until Saturday.

It was about time for another harvest at home. The weeds had been kept down nicely but I feared that in the case of an attack of cutleaf beetles the whole crop might be wiped out. So I went along to the barber.

"I'd like it rather on the short side, my man," I said, "cut close on the back and sides and watch out for the rocks in the mower. Heh, heh, heh."

I always make it a point, upon settling into the chair, to pass a few such pleasantries with the barber. It puts me at ease. When you only go along a few times a year you don't get to know these lads on a first-name basis.

And the idea of a stranger standing behind you with a straight razor held six inches from your throat does tend to bring out a touch of the old paranoia. Jack the Ripper might have escaped and tied up the real barber in the back room, for all you know.

But after passing a few words with them and failing to note any sinister movements, I am able to settle back and relax and let them go to it. But we digress.

This particular barber must have been overjoyed at my instructions. I dare say they took him back to the good old days. In present times, with long hair the rage, barbers have to practice on Yorkshire terriers just to keep in shape.

Anyhow, he took to the job like a starving man taking to a sirloin steak. There weren't many hairs out of place by the time he had finished, I can tell you. Rather fetching considering the material, I thought.

Oh, it wasn't a brush cut by any means. Not at all. Just an ordinary plain and simple haircut suited to the summer months and which would allow Halloween to come and go before I had to undertake a similar expense again. Or so I thought.

I had no sooner stepped outside the door into the street when I started getting sharp glances. Some people were even turning around to get a second look. A few giggles broke out here and there.

When I got a chance I glanced down and was relieved to find that the trouble did not lie in that region. Everything secured. My memory for these small but important details is not what it was.

They were obviously taking umbrage at the length of my hair. Four youths stood directly in my path, their locks down to their shoulders. I decided to put on a bold front and indicate by some means that despite the state of my head I was one of the beautiful people, like even unto them.

So I broke into a snatch of something I considered appropriate … a tune which I believe is still high on "the charts." "Adolf Hitler's beeyouteeful in his own way; Terminal acne's beeyouteeful in its own way" … and so on and so forth.

However, …

(To be continued tomorrow.) ▩

HAIR: Part II

However, as I say, it made little difference to them. The stoutest among them, a chap standing six-foot-two with a coiffure like that of Rita Hayworth in the early 1940s, jostled me rudely as I passed.

"Yaaa, yaaa, sissy!" cried the one with the Prince Valiant. "You some kind of a creep running around with your hair like that."

I had occasion to visit the bank but found conditions little better there. It was surly and suspicious looks all round and the manager, sporting Ben Cartwright mutton chops down to his collars, stood ready to lunge at the alarm bell the minute I made my move.

One of the tellers served me but with obvious distaste. The whole establishment was on edge. I distinctly heard one of the girls mutter something about … "escaped from Salmonier."

It was a relief to be outside again. But the disparaging remarks continued. "Disgusting." "Should be horsewhipped walking about in public like that!" "The world is gone mad!" Etc., etc.

As I came abreast of a little old lady in front of the Court House steps she gave me a nasty cut across the quarters with her umbrella which, fortunately, was furled.

"Go home for shame's sake, you short-haired weirdo!" she cried, winding up for another drive down the fairway. "You're nothing but a disgrace to the parents what reared you!"

As, indeed, I soon found out I was. That evening I dropped in on the folks and although their colors rose the minute I darkened the door, they said nothing right away. It all came to a head, as usual, at the supper table.

"By God, if I didn't think it would come to this sooner or later," declared one of them. "That crowd you been hanging around with. A bloody disgrace. Them two ears sticking out naked as the day you were born. Not enough hair on your head to hide your shirt collars, let alone cover your shoulders."

The other parent said nothing but sobbed softly. I received orders not to set foot in the house again until it grew back to a decent length. I walked off into the sunset. They might have known when they had me that they'd have a hard row to hoe.

It was even worse down at the office. The minute I stepped into the newsroom the sanitary maintenance engineer passed some clever remarks to the teletype girls and there were snickers all round. The city editor glowered at me from under his tousled locks.

When the message came that the managing editor wanted a few words with me I knew I was in for it. I waited for him in his office, admiring the "Lukey's Boat" pin-ups on the wall. When he arrived I took the appropriate stance …

eyes on low beam, hands behind back, toe digging into the carpet.

"This is a newsroom, we know, but it is also, in a way, a business office," he said. "We have all sorts of people coming and going here and even making allowances for your … ahem … artistic temperament we must keep in mind the overall impression our visitors receive.

"The business office is no place for short hair. It looks untidy and unprofessional and besides that it's dangerous. You could get your ears caught in the typewriter keys. I suggest you either buy a wig or stay home until it grows to a decent length."

So here I am confined to my place of residence knocking out bits on my portable typewriter. It isn't so bad once you get used to being shunned and avoided. But I fear the electricity bill is going to be heavy.

I have to keep the lights on all day since the blinds are tightly closed. The neighbors complained that my short hair was setting a bad example for their youngsters.

At the rate fashions change these days I may not have to stay here long. Short hair may be catching on again. Yesterday, while peeking from behind the blinds, I noticed two avant garde college students going past with their tresses shorn.

Of course by the time short hair becomes the rage mine will be too long to qualify and still too short to squander $2 on at the barber shop. So you see my situation.

The old saying is true: "Better to be born stylish than rich." I'll settle for either one. ▨

Aunt Cissy waved her double-bit axe in greeting

September 8, 1970 *Aunt Cissy*

After Labour Day the summer is supposed to be over.

As a general rule, we then get the fall. It occurred to me that it would be a good idea to find out what this fall has in store for us. So naturally I made my way out over the Witless Bay Line and from thence some 13 miles in over the Barrens.

Getting the lowdown on things of this nature is not the easiest thing in the world, especially since the only certain source is that wiry old trollop of the tuckamores, Aunt Cissy Roach.

As I neared the secluded domicile of this ancient recluse, I could not help but note once more the grim aspect of the countryside in which she resides. The rocks are the size of bungalows and the trees are as crooked as sin's self. Even the dogberries growl at you.

Nearing her humble cot, I saw that Aunt Cissy was out in the yard and obviously in an elated frame of mind. She saw me coming at a distance and waved her double-bit axe in greeting.

"Ha, just in time, lantern jaws," she croaked. "Just in time. Come along here and see something. Hoo hoo. I got the ringleader his self. The rest is all turned tail and took off like bats out of hell. Heee heee. They'll have to eeleck another chairman."

Hanging by its heels from the limb of an extremely twisted rampike was a dead raven of prodigious size. Its neck seemed to be awry. Come to think of it, I hadn't noticed the customary flock of ebony birds wheeling above the rustic abode of the aged widow.

The sky is usually thick with them and there are times when you get the uneasy feeling that they are waiting for the old soul to kick the bucket or perhaps to catch her with her back turned.

"Hard laws, Coalpound, my son, but we all got to come to it sooner or later," cackled Aunt Cissy, dancing a bit of a jig around the unfortunate bird. "Brief life, Blackarse, old trout, is here our portion."

"A fine catch no doubt, Aunt Cissy," I said, "but of course all wild creatures are only following their instincts when they stalk likely sources of sustenance. It is a law of nature.

"I am put in mind of a story in the lesson books," I continued, "first when the Canadian books came in. It concerned a small youngster on the hand of being eaten by two mountain lions. The child was saved, if memory serves, by the late Sir John A. Macdonald who fell upon the ravenous beasts and beat their skulls to a pulp with an empty rye bottle.

"Meanwhile, back at the cave, several lion cubs starved to death waiting for their parents to come back with a small youngster or two for lunch. The piece was entitled 'They Seek Their Meat From God' and contains a lesson for us all.

"And did you know," I went on, "that a famous figure in the Indian religion is said to have calmly delivered his person up to the jaws of a hungry tiger, philosophizing as he did so that all life is one, so what odds?"

"By God, was you nippin' at the little drop of something you got for me on the way in," inquired Aunt Cissy, "or is you just havin' another one of your bad turns?

"Come in the house. You better sit down until it passes off," she chortled, pausing to look up and shake her fist as a thunderclap rent the black and purple sky. "You're lookin' greener than usual about the gills."

I had, of course, stopped in at one of the BLC's brown paper baggerys and purchased a small present for Aunt Cissy in the shape of a crock of Ye Embalmers Special, Very Old. She takes a drop for the sake of her joints.

Having poured a good portion of this substance into a tumbler, she tossed it off, made a disparaging sound, belched, and as far as it is possible to determine, a grimace crossed her remarkable features.

"Phaaaaaaaa! Gurk!" she said. "The country is on the skids when they starts waterin' the spirits. An outrage against Nelson's blood. And they're not satisfied to put plain water in it. They must wring out the sheets at Murphy's flop house, strain it through six pairs of trawlermen's socks and mix the whole concern with the spinal tap from a dead cat."

I commenced to get queasy. "My dear woman," I said, "I was never one to check up on a person in her own home but I must say your language is coarse in spots."

"Haaaaa," she cackled in glee, "have another drop to settle your stomach. And if you heaves, be sure to heave to leeward. I'm up to you before now. Either you're makin' out you're a townie or your mother was frightened by a Wesleyan."

I decided I had better mention the main purpose of my visit before she lowered her crock at half-mast, after which she is apt to become mischievous. "Aunt Cissy," I said, "tell me, if you will, what is in store for us on all sides during the months which lie ahead."

"No such thing," she said. "I am just in shape for celebratin' and be damned if I puts meself to work now. Come out in a fortnight and I'll have it all for you."

On the way back over the Witless Bay Barrens, I caught a glimpse of some black shapes bobbing among the rocks on the top of a hill. The election of a new chairman was apparently in progress. ▓

The bottomless gullibility
of the Newfoundland people

September 24, 1970   *Democracy*

One of these days when the roll is called up yonder, all things made plain, the low places made high and the high places made low, the seven mysteries revealed and all that jazz, do you suppose we'll get the drift at last on this Come By Chance scheme?

It might seem like the height of folly to pay any attention at all to the whole farce. Perhaps we'd better leave it all to the grand farceurs out of whose hot little heads it is spun. But you can't help but worry sometimes if for no other reason than that this is our country, too.

A columnist in another paper seems to have resigned himself to the will of Smallwood and/or Allah where Come By Chance is concerned. He says the deal is of such magnitude and complexity as to be far beyond the ken of ordinary mortals.

So he's willing to leave the whole mess in the hands of such mental giants as Smallwood, Les Curtis and John Nolan. Presumably, he goes to bed contented. Ours not to reason why; ours but to read prayers in the churches for "those who are set in authority over us."

The *Journal of Commerce* takes a similar line, at least on Come By Chance. In a recent editorial they allowed that the average person understands little of this great project. Even the commodores of commerce on Water Street can't wrestle with the fleece that passeth all understanding.

It must be admitted that the local press hasn't done much more than dutifully set their tape recorders going whenever Smallwood steps off the plane and send the results out over the air waves or commit it to black and white as it rolls off the assembly line.

To look through the files on the volume of prattle about Come By Chance since 1953 is to partake of hallucinogenic substances. It includes a vast wonder in the reader at the bottomless gullibility of the Newfoundland people.

People who flung their arms to the skies, made little groans of ecstasy, dropped their drawers and otherwise went cracked in celebration at the first announcement of "a great new industry for Come By Chance" in the early 1950s will probably go through the whole drill at the latest pronouncement this week.

They've been through a dozen or more of these announcements and half as many elections. But they're always on tap to go into raptures whenever the Master tickles their fancy again. The most outrageous and bizarre contradictions and embellishments don't faze them a bit.

It would be useless anyway to trouble such a tribe with a few facts. They're fueled on blind faith and as long as their palms are kept greased by one means or another and expectations of much greater spoils held out before them they'll perform on cue.

Even the outward and visible signs are hard to keep track of, let alone the esoteric details. Quick, for the grand prize of a second-hand pair of panty hose, how many times has the wrangling gang and that "battery of lawyers" winged across the Atlantic for signing of final papers since March?

Sometimes the queen bee alights in London with a clutch of cabinet ministers and some of his lesser satraps and sometimes he's off to Norway or France or back to Montreal or New York "on public business."

But let the public ask what this business is and they're told it is none of theirs. Four or five names keep cropping up in these mad giddy whirls through international airports. Les Curtis, E. Moxon Roberts, Rowe Minor and John "Dancing Dollars" Nolan.

What an exhilarating life it must be for these jolly jet-setters popping back and forth the Atlantic like a bunch of yo-yos, sipping their free beverages in first class over the Azores, breakfast in bed at the Savoy, nipping across to Paris for a bit of business and pleasure, whirling off to New York to dazzle the financiers there.

Then plunk down at Torbay between trips to announce that they've saved Newfoundland $20 million on the deal so far, that within 10 years Come By Chance will employ at least 30,000 persons – which is exactly 20,000 more than the number in Smallwood's 10-year forecast 10 years ago.

A glance at the files to refresh our memory: In late March the House closed and the five wheeler-dealers were London-bound for final papers. There was great concern since they were gone so long but eventually they returned and the Liberal ladies flocked out on the tarmac with their stockings rolled below the knee.

Shaheen and the lads appeared in the House the latter part of April and people who never bothered with politics before saw it all going on before their eyes … and their guts rolled. That show did more than anything else to make people uneasy.

In June, some of the Shaheen lieutenants who had been wheeled in to take part in the TV special either resigned from his company in disgust or seem to have disappeared from Newfoundland.

Capt. Wallace, the marine superintendent, who tried to put it in "baby talk" for Neary; Ingster, the construction superintendent; Reid, the office manager; and Pretty, the accountant, haven't been heard of since their TV debut.

In mid-June, it was off to New York, then back to open the House again and get some "imperative changes" made in the contract, then off to Paris and Norway somewhere in between; a bunch of them in London on July 30; Smallwood, Roberts, Nolan and Curtis back in London for more final papers in mid-August but back empty-handed; back to London again at the end of the month.

They return and final papers are signed in St. John's on September 1, at which the grand vizier declares: "I thank God for the great deed done today for the people of Newfoundland."

Then six cabinet ministers back in London this week for more final papers and equally great deeds and who knows right now if they're coming or going.

One thing sure, they're having more fun than those two night watchmen sitting in the middle of a twillick bog at Come By Chance all this while. All they have to do is watch the fog roll in over the Foxhead and Whiffen's Droke. RG

We're what they calls baymen

October 5, 1970 *Democracy*

The state of the post in this country is nothing less than a scandal. In this day and age, the number of letters that go astray in the mail is a disgrace.

Take my invitation to last week's Liberal seminar, for instance. It was probably posted a full fortnight ago, but I still didn't receive it in time. If my guess is correct, it will reach me later this week.

I could have obtained a personal invitation to the seminar from Mr. Barbour, of course, but I don't like to be all the time asking the man for favors.

So I decided I would try and slip in to the Canon Stirling Auditorium unnoticed and mingle unobtrusively with the 125 delegates. The proceedings were well underway when I got there. Mr. Smallwood was reiterating his "develop or perish" policy.

No one noticed as I ducked in the back door and made my way directly to the nearest washroom, not so much to have a wash as to compose myself before I took my seat. If you don't want to stick out like a sore thumb at Liberal dos these days, you've got to put on a slightly anxious look – as if you didn't know where your next contract was coming from.

To my surprise, the washroom was in darkness. Just as I entered the door, one of the three shadowy figures in there struck a match and a flash of blue flame rent the gloom.

Gales of robust laughter followed the explosion and the first thought that came to me was that some dastardly fellows were having a dry run for another Gunpowder Plot.

With much trepidation, I switched on the light and there, rolling around the floor in a fit of hilarity, clutching a box of Sea Dogs in one hand and his sides with the other, was none other than young Sylvester Codpiece of Bung Hole Tickle, G.D. Bay.

I don't know who was more surprised but it took young Sylvester a full five minutes before he stopped laughing and got enough breath to extend a greeting.

"Hello, then. Hello, then. Hello then," he said cheerily, the tears rolling down his cheeks. "By God, we're all here now then. I never hear tell of it before. No, I tell a lie. I heard tell of it but I never seen it done before."

"Good Lord, man," I said, quickly appraising the situation. "Do you realize what would have happened if you had struck a match and someone had opened the door with Moxie Roberts and the Wabana Warbler out there on the same panel? The cream of the Liberal party would have been reduced to a dish of fried onion rings.

"The safety counsel advised that the proper way to do it is to sit in the bathtub with a box of matches and ignite the bubbles as they come to the surface. Not only is that method safer but it is much more esthetic."

"By God, byes, now there's what it is to have a education," declared young Sylvester, addressing his comrades, Patrick Calamitous Sunks, also of Bung Hole Tickle, and a third party who was introduced to me as one Nooky McAllister from the west coast.

Patrick was in the corner still in the throes of laughter and McAllister was casting anxious glances back over his shoulder. When they had finally composed themselves, they must have guessed my question.

"We're what they calls token baymen," said young Sylvester. "The delicate from our place said they wired him to bring in two up-and-comin' young outharbormen to dress up the proceedin's so me and Paddy came along.

"They told us to part our hair in the middle and sot us right up for'd where the TV cameras is and told us to look as intelligent and concerned as possible. But it got tiresome. Nothing goin' on except Joey talking and you can hear he every day of the week on the radio.

"We met up with McAllister here this mornin' and he passed some remark about them speeches and one thing led to another so here we is. Care for a swally?"

Young Sylvester produced a flask and as one of the keynote speakers outside could still be heard through the washroom door I gratefully accepted. It must have been a drop of stuff from St. Peter's and me with an empty stomach because I thought I could hear Freddy Rowe say:

"Translated into simple language this has meant that Liberalism has always been afraid of unbridled competition, whether that competition has been among individuals or among corporations and in particular between profit-oriented business on the one hand and society in general on the other!"

"Yes, we druv in with the delicate from our place," continued young Sylvester. "That's Calvin Waddle you know and he was in one hell of a state. Nervous about that contract comin' up for the piece on the breakwater. Had like to put her off the road by the passover, as they calls it.

"Dumped us off down here and he took off for Confederation Building like a bluearse fly. Says they're gettin' a bit strict on it lately but he 'lows he'll have 'em straightened out be dinner time.

"I could'a been in for the PC convention, you know," continued young Sylvester. "They was lookin' for token baymen for that, too, but happen so it was caplin scull. Uncle Rite didn't think too well about me comin' this time but we wanted a stuffin' box for our three Atlantic."

After another swally all round it seemed that Dr. Rowe was saying: "It becomes necessary, in my view, for us to restate and reaffirm some of those basic concepts before we can enunciate or formulate ideas and programs in the light of present circumstances and in anticipation of what the next 10 years will require."

"Not a patch on Reverend Rex Humber," declared Paddy. "He got the wind but he haven't got the punch. Listen, byes, listen, byes, we goin' hang around here all day or what?

"What say we take a dart downtown? I got to get a new suit of spring-and-fall and Sylvester here got to get his stuffin' box and McAllister here got to look up his aunt who runs a boardin' house. Then we'll go around and see the sights."

By this time it sounded like Dr. Rowe was talking about the need for revolutionary measures, at which young Sylvester passed a coarse remark about taking one complete revolution and the complete disappearance such an acrobatic feat would entail.

Anyway, we left unobserved by the back door and I gave the lads a lift in my conveyance down to the suave, swinging sophisticated heart of the capital city.

By this time, all hands were feeling quite jolly and after hot turkey sandwiches and a tour of the public houses, young Sylvester was all for getting back to the seminar. He was bound on striking a match in the front row during the keynote speech by Dr. Jamieson.

I had all I could do to persuade him against it and we spent the rest of the afternoon at the Belmont. Lucky for all concerned, I'd say. Had young Sylvester gone ahead with his merry prank, there'd be nothing left today except a big crater in the ground where St. John's once stood. ■

Mickey Mouse, eat your heart out

Great New Industries

"J.R.S. wins acting award."

Ever since word came through that he had won an award for best actor in the film "A Little Fellow From Gambo," he could think of nothing else but a new career in motion pictures.

As he took the air down a woodsy October lane at the north end of the estate, he thought of the possibilities. He especially admired Disney movies and had been much taken with Ole Puce, the Yellow-Bellied Sapsucker Who Thought He Was a Grand Banks Doryman.

Ole Turquoise, the Lesser-Breasted Nuthatch Who Thought He Was a Syracuse, NY, Chiropractor, had also been a dramatic and exciting Disney film. Yes, no doubt about it, he would prefer Disney movies as they were good, wholesome family entertainment.

There he would be traipsing over hills into the sunset, his faithful spaniel, Freddie, trotting behind, in search of his long-lost pet buffalo. There wouldn't be a dry eye in the house.

As these and other fancies ran through his mind he rounded a bend in the path and came suddenly upon a stooping figure clad in tweed knickers and smoking a crooked-stemmed pipe.

"Good day, sir. I'm Professor Galbraith of Sacramento, California, here on vacation. I was just admiring your schist."

"Eh?"

"Your schist, your schist. You have some lovely schist around here. A kind of rock. Look it up in your Funk and Wagnells. Medieval literature is my profession and geology is my hobby.

"Do you know that I have never seen such really great schist specimens as I have seen here in Newfoundland? The whole island is just full of it. What a pity that no one here seems to appreciate it."

"Hmmm. Tell me professor, is this schist valuable? I mean to say, can it be used in great new industries and the like?"

"Oh, my goodness gracious yes. Schist can be extremely useful if got at the right way. Full of all sorts of minerals and what not. There is hardly any limit to what you can do with schist."

After the professor took his leave the new and rising star in the film firmament made his way back to the house. But thoughts of a film career were put out of his mind for the time being. That night his head was filled with nothing but schist.

Next morning he could hardly wait to get back to the office and immediately called for the minister of mines, the deputy minister, the assistant deputy minister and the acting assistant deputy minister as well as a large number of subordinates in the department.

He demanded that they tell him everything they knew about schist. They produced a large volume of facts and figures but nothing really important. He already had all the information he wanted which was that schist could be the basis of a great new industry.

Far into the afternoon he pondered the possibilities. When the minister of finance looked around the door about to inquire about a mislaid final paper, he received a brusque brush-off.

"Get out, get out, get out," snapped the little fellow from Gambo. "Can't you see I'm up to my ears in schist? No, on second thought, come back here. And get the rest of them up here at once."

When the cabinet was assembled he put it to them: "Gentlemen, you have always looked to your little old leader to pull your chestnuts out of the fire and I don't expect thanks for it. But always remember who put you where you are today.

"Now, while the rest of you have been sitting on your duffs or engaging in sciamachy as usual, I have been doing my homework. Gentlemen, we are going to the country on schist!

"From now on we will think, talk, sleep, drink and eat schist. Our platform will be based on it. I have just now been on the line to the great Lord Sciatica in London, England, who is known in European mining circles as the King of Schist.

"I fly to London this evening to hold talks with the great Lord Sciatica.

"A great new industry based on schist will be the watchword. Schist will be writ large in the future of Newfoundland. We must make it a household word throughout the province ... surpassing hockey sticks, magnesia, linerboard, petro-chemicals and even orange juice.

"I want figures immediately on the number of jobs (not forgetting the multiplied effect) that such an enterprise will create. Including the vast number of persons who will go back to school to learn the elements of schist production. I think we can talk in terms of 30,000 jobs.

"The House will be called into session next week right after I go on television with the great announcement. Develop or perish. Our salvation through schist. That's good. I like that. Ed, make a note of it.

"Our ever popular colleague has earned the affectionate nickname 'Silica' due to his connection with that other wondrous mineral. I shall go down in history in like manner. We shall win the next five elections on it.

"And you are looking at next year's academy award winner. Why should I go to Hollywood? Let Hollywood come to me. Gentlemen, what celluloid drama can compare with the great real-life epics we unfold here year after year?"

Mickey Mouse, eat your heart out. ▨

Guy's Encyclopedia of Juvenile Outharbor Delights: The Road to Health and Strength

October 8, 1970   *Outharbor Delights*

While it can hardly be placed under the heading of Juvenile Outharbor Delights, there is, nonetheless, a section in Guy's celebrated *Encyclopedia* dealing with the means used to keep the juvenile on the road to health and strength.

The principles of hygiene were widely practiced and much emphasis placed on preventive medicine. Twofold were the paths to sturdy development, namely, purging the blood and keeping the juvenile away from "too much sweet stuff."

Purging the blood was maintained on a year-round basis although the process reached a head in late March at an annual grand clearance when the most potent physic available was brought to bear against the manifold impurities that had accumulated in the juvenile's person during the winter.

As the time for spring cleaning approached, the juvenile was closely studied each morning for signs of "bad blood." Listlessness, swallow complexion, cold sores and general irritability were certain indications.

Stark terror of the purging caused the patient to put up as bold a front as possible. As the dreaded dosing approached, he feigned boundless energy and high spirits in a futile attempt to forestall it.

The fumes of hell wafted through the kitchen on that black morning when the time had arrived at last to do battle against the noxious substances coursing through his veins.

Sulphur, a vile yellow powder stinking of the lower depths, was mixed in a china cup with blackstrap molasses. As the physician approached, sleeves rolled to her elbows, and the physic at the ready, every ounce of strength left the patient's legs and he could do no more than sink into the nearest chair.

However, the last reserves of strength in his trembling carcass were called to the fore and concentrated in his resolute jaws. They were clamped shut with a force that caused the back molars to crumble in a death grip that no amount of fearsome threats could loosen.

A smart judo chop to the back of the neck about the seventh vertebrae down usually did the trick. At the instant the jaws flew open, a soup spoon rolled up in a blob of the universal blood cleanser was thrust inside.

Our highways would stand up three times as long if they were paved with the self-same substance. Once the despicable mass was inside the teeth there was nothing for the patient to do then but swallow or suffocate.

By this time, the cringing guts of the patient had shrunk to the size of a walnut and were hiding somewhere behind his left kidney. However, the great black sulphuric glob slid slowly downward and sought them out and hammered them against the backbone like a boxing glove filled with large lead chunks.

Stunned and dazed by the whole ordeal and by the titanic struggle between the forces of good and evil now raging within him, the dosed juvenile was then left to stagger outside into the air and reel about the roads and lanes while his medicine did him good.

Since the crucial day for blood purging usually arrived in all households at the same time, the byways were somewhat crowded with dosed juveniles, all stumbling about with punchy expressions on their faces and sick as dogs as their vital juices underwent their annual and monumental scrubbing.

Glazed eyes, vacant stares, a greenish tinge at the sides of the face and jaws were all signs that the gracious work inside was progressing well. Nor was this the end of it.

Such a massive frontal assault on a year's collection of impurities must take its toll of other physical functions necessary to good health. It generally knocked the plumbing awry.

Still more physic was called for to cure the patient of the effects of the first dose. By this time he was too much weakened to put up even token resistance as senna tea was brewed and introduced into the ravaged system.

Better to be sure than sorry so that the latter concoction was chased closely by two soup spoons of castor oil mixed, if there was a scrap of mercy still left in the world, with raspberry jam.

Then he was left to crawl away to some darkened corner, preferably behind a stack of junks out in the woodhouse, while the whole unholy cocktail seethed and roiled and fermented and heaved among his outraged innards.

Like an activated atomic pile he huddled there while the fissionable materials gathered force and a thin blue smoke issued from his quivering ears. Charity inclines us to draw a curtain over the climax.

Suffice to say that for a week thereafter he went about the affairs of this world in a state of stunned remoteness rather like that of the religious fanatic who has fasted on a mountaintop in sackcloth and ashes for three months.

Dirty blood had been conquered. Whatsoever the whole realm of bacteria and contagion and pestilence and infection brought to bear against him in the twelve months ahead were as dust in the eye of a hurricane.

Of course, other less drastic hygienic regimens were employed as booster shots from time to time but it was clearly evident that if he had survived that herculean purge in late March nothing short of a hammer on the head would stagger him for the duration. ▓

He has to work in a ghost town

October 9, 1970   *Resettlement and Rural Life*

"What we should have done is we should have all hove ourself on the government and broke the bloody Country and have it done."

"Well, there's not the hell of a lot left to break now, is there, George?"

The hardness dissolved, as usual, in a laugh. George said he had six different guns aboard and he pitied the Mountie who would come to drive him away. It was his place and his father's and grandfather's before him and there were papers with the King's Crown on them to prove the rights of it.

For all that, he probably would not have taken up arms if Rose Marie's lovers had come on the patrol cutter to evict him. No need to. He could have nailed the unfortunate constables to the side of the old Co-op store with a stream of Stag tobacco juice.

Nothing personal, you understand, but a person can be backed up only so far before he feels the wall behind him.

"I have to laugh when I thinks about it now. I said 'Here, give me that lamp' and I put my hand to the top of the chimney and I blowed out the light for the last time in Isle Valen.

"You have to laugh at it. The clergyman wasn't going to leave anything behind. There was two gallons of kerosene up in the church and he said 'Boys, go up and get that and bring it down and put it aboard'.

"But the boys said to theirselves, 'No, Sir', and just as everyone was having supper they went around and cut the tires off every boat in the harbor. They didn't leave one. Fourteen tires they got into a pile. And they went and slung the kerosene over the works and sot a match to it."

So the flames roared up in a column over the boats loaded in the harbor to take the last people away from Isle Valen. Perhaps only a prank, perhaps a protest or perhaps a reminder to a clergyman too interested as such a time in Caesar's goods.

He has since been transferred from the parish by his church and sent off to enlighten the blacks in the West Indies.

"As much as $40,000 in savings for the one fishing family was taken out of Isle Valen when they moved them away," says Harry Wareham, whose family were the merchants at nearby Harbour Buffett.

"Others had $10,000 and more saved up. From that to $40,000.

"It was one of the richest places in the Bay, Isle Valen. They had one of the best small boat harbors you'll ever see and they were right on top of the best grounds in the Bay. The place and the houses might not have looked like much but they worked and were in a position to work."

It depends on how you look at it. Isle Valen is uphill and downdale and the graveyard occupies about the only level piece of ground in sight. But in the millpond of a harbor you could almost tie up the *William Carson* to the shore.

Some 40 families once lived at Isle Valen. The last of them was "resettled" by the government four years ago. They moved to "growth centers" like Arnold's Cove and the government squirms and lies blatantly and tries to cover up its criminal insanity like a cat covering up her dirt.

In the September issue of the magazine *Atlantic Advocate* there's a long story with photographs about the beautiful job the government has done on resettlement at Arnold's Cove.

It would seem that in this new heaven on earth created by the Smallwood government there is but one slight flaw ... the small boys have to stay home and mow the lawns and clip the hedges when they'd rather be off swimming.

This rosy pack of half-truths was written by one Robert Johnson. We phoned the *Atlantic Advocate* offices in Fredericton, NB, to ask where we could contact this Robert Johnson. We were told there was no such person.

The magazine informed us it was a nom de plume used by someone who could not sign his real name because he was an "information officer" in the pay of the Newfoundland government. They try to smuggle their propaganda into real papers and magazines ... of which more later. (No, it wasn't Jim Thoms.)

George Lockyer was the last to leave Isle Valen and now has a house at Arnold's Cove. But he has to steam back across Placentia Bay in his longliner to his old home to make a living.

His house there is gone. He and his brother and nephew have to live aboard their longliner for weeks on end. They must bring all their supplies with them. Government bait depots have been closed down and wharves are falling into disrepair. He has to work in a ghost town, the corpse of the village where he was born and lived. You have to be able to laugh.

According to Wareham about one-third of all the saltfish processed in Newfoundland last season came from Placentia Bay. And 95 per cent of that was caught by people like George Lockyer who have had to go back to their old homes.

Next summer, Wareham has twice as many fishermen lined up for supplies ... 100 crews, about 400 men. They'll go back to the government-created ghost towns to work, whether final papers have been signed or not.

Mr. Lockyer was joking. There's still the hell of a lot left to break in this bloody Country.

(To be continued on Monday.) 🆁🅶

We've got our homes here and are comfortable enough

Resettlement and Rural Life

The spirit was willing but the flesh was weak.

General Booth said yes but corporal stomach said no.

The bearded long-haired type sat on deck in his faded blue jeans huddled against the cabin, a glazed far-away look in his eyes, nodding slightly and seemingly beyond speech. You could say he looked dopey.

The young Salvation Army lieutenant – with the small moustache – leaned nearby against the gunwale of the dory on the deck of the longliner pitching and rolling and heaving in the middle of Placentia Bay. Despite chewing gum and the open air, he was deathly seasick.

From time to time he glanced at the forlorn bearded figure huddled against the cabin. Duty clearly called. The trip would take two or three hours and in less time than that many had been saved from a life of depravity and set upon the straight and narrow.

Finally, the lieutenant put the question which had been bothering him to me: "Isn't that Robert Sinclair who wrote the stories on drugs in *The Evening Telegram?*"

"Yes," I admitted, "that is indeed the self-same personage." The devil whispered to me at that moment. I had but to infer that this talented *Telegram* staffer had been reduced to his present sorry state through indulgence in the very drugs he wrote about.

His suspicions confirmed, would the young lieutenant then double his struggle against the physical miseries which encompassed him round about, and rise to his duty and try to save this poor bearded backslider on the spot?

Christian charity overcame my baser mischievous instincts. Never say that being laced to Sunday School in earliest years does not now stand me in good stead.

I told the truth. Mr. Sinclair's present condition, I assured the lieutenant, stemmed not from indulgence in evil substances but solely from the rigors of ocean travel. He was just as seasick as the lieutenant himself.

You had to pity the two poor perishers. There they were, the one from the shores of that muddy pond known as Lake Ontario and the other from a substantial but far lesser Bay on our northern coast.

Not much used to conditions here on this superlative body of water, this paragon among Bays, this most noble work of Nature, in short … Placentia Bay!

Needless to say I was enjoying every moment of the voyage. Equally needless to say, I had taken the precaution of tacking down my guts with a stiff shot of spirits and a handful of Gravol tablets before departure.

In sickness and in health, we were all bound from Arnold's Cove across to Monkstown on the western side, the only community there still intact and still standing against what the government considers to be mercy-killing and calls "resettlement."

The lieutenant was on the way back after attending a conference in St. John's during the weekend. In addition to his church duties at Monkstown, he also taught in the two-room school there.

We wanted to see what an "isolated" community looked like and perhaps to find out why it was still standing when those around it had collapsed like a deck of cards under the government's onslaught.

I knew for a start that the Salvation Army had long been prominent there and that Monkstown had contributed no less than 15 officers to the Army during the years ... more than any other settlement in Newfoundland.

In addition, many teachers and social workers had come from there originally. I must apologize for not having more information on this aspect of the community. Perhaps someone at Army HQ will write a letter to the editor giving more details on this interesting side of it.

Anyway, Monkstown is a unique place in more ways than one. People say: "How is it with these places that many residents say after resettlement that they didn't really want to move but that the government forced them into it?"

Here was a chance to find out. Our visit was brief to say the least but the half-dozen or more people we talked to at random in Monkstown all seemed determined on one thing ... they had not the slightest intention of moving.

If a sampling of a half-dozen opinions seems inadequate, the fact that the place still exists when others have been abandoned long ago must be considered.

One man said: "They sent a government feller over here some years ago to see if we were interested in moving but he went back and told them that you couldn't prize us out of Monkstown with a crowbar. There's been no one around since. They must have give up on us."

A woman told us in the shop: "There's no one here wants to move out as far as I know. There'd be no sense to it. We've got our homes here and are comfortable enough."

There are about 30 families in Monkstown, which is located on the mainland at the bottom of Paradise Sound. Four families had moved away during the past five years or so and another house is to be floated out this fall.

Those who gave us this information emphasized that the ones who had moved out did so because their health required they be near a large hospital or because they had retired and gone to live with relatives.

Yet Llewellyn Guy of Arnold's Cove, on whose longliner we traveled, was certain that "when that government barge comes here to move that one house this fall, you'll see them all join in and Monkstown will be cleared out in no time."

This prediction didn't seem to tally with what the residents were saying but

Mr. Guy has had a first-hand look at the way it happened in other places.

There may also be some wishful thinking on his part. An influx of some 30 families from Monkstown into Arnold's Cove would greatly increase the Salvation Army congregation there of which he is a leader.

Anyway, those who speak of deprivation and poverty in "isolated" places and expect to see ragged hillbillies and tumbledown shacks on the rocks, would be set back on their haunches by Monkstown.

The houses are substantial, modern and comfortable; the children are healthy and bright; the gardens are neat and kept up … in short, it is exactly the same as any of a half-dozen communities you would see on the Southern Shore, out around Trinity Bay North or anywhere else by a road in Newfoundland for that matter.

The one big difference in "isolated" communities is the lack of cars and all that goes with them. This is not altogether an unmixed blessing … not that the people in Monkstown don't want cars, as we shall see when we continue the story of "We Have an Anchor" tomorrow.

(By the way, some of those long-promised snaps of places we saw around the Bay should appear in *The Telegram* soon. They came out rather well, if I may say so, especially those taken by Mr. Sinclair who, brick that he is, rose above mere deathly seasickness and stuck to his duty.) RG

Bears are reasonable people

October 13, 1970   *Resettlement and Rural Life*

More of Monkstown.

One of these days someone is going to get smart and make a large fortune simply by acquiring a piece of land and building houses on it.

The only difference would be that all streets and roads would end at least a half-mile away from this community. Those too old or too lazy to hoof a half-mile would have to be lugged in on stretchers or pony carriages.

Besides the people living there, weekend tourists would line up and pay an entrance fee to walk in and see this remarkable place free of those 20th-century lice, the motor car.

For all its advantages, the automobile, more than anything else, makes a community an irritating place to live in and changes it from a habitation for human beings to a set-up geared to machines.

Few people today ever get to see such a place. The car is just about everywhere. If they do find an unblighted corner it takes a few hours for the shock of a car-less environment to sink in.

And it is a shocking experience, make no mistake about it. The quiet, for one thing. And the cleanness for another. No dirt, dust, mud, potholes or getting splashed, no stopping to look to see if two tons of machinery is bearing down on you. Just a wide, grassy path through the community, neatly graveled in worn spots with handrails to help pedestrians along the steep parts in winter.

Monkstown has, as far as we could see, only one vehicle and that was a small pickup truck which looked extremely well rested. Not that the people in Monkstown don't want cars. In fact, getting cars was the main theme of everyone we spoke to.

Or at least a road. A 15-mile road to link them up with the Burin Highway on the other side of Paradise Sound. Except for the lack of a road they were perfectly comfortable and content to stay where they were.

But they had made do without one ever since time began and were willing to wait longer. There didn't seem to be much hope of getting one in the immediate future.

It seems that the Liberal MHA, Pat Canning, who is the member for Placentia West, takes a reverse tack from that of his colleagues who never tire of promising their constituents roads. He promises Monkstown they'll never get one.

"Pat Canning says we'll never see the day," said one man as he leaned over his gate. "He says it would cost $1 million and he talks like the money would have to come out of his own back pocket."

The government was not always so hesitant in doling out roads. Seven years ago they gave Monkstown one. It still exists, in good condition for the size of it.

This road is seven miles long and it runs to nowhere. It used to connect Monkstown with Davis Cove, but now Davis Cove has been "resettled," except for some fishermen who come back to fish in summer.

So we have a seven-mile road (costing upwards of $500,000 if Mr. Canning's calculations are correct) which leads to nowhere and which runs in the opposite direction from one which would connect Monkstown to the Burin Highway and the fleshpots of Marystown and St. John's.

Unlike some nearby places, it seems that Monkstown never did depend entirely on the fishery. The cutting of pit props and other timber along the Paradise River used to be the big thing.

Monkstown was also famous for its dories, the best in Placentia Bay, which is to say, the best in Newfoundland. One winter they turned out more than 20, which sold at the time for $25 each. Now the price is closer to $150, although we saw only one being built while we were there and that by a man for his son in St. John's.

The news they had for us when we landed was that bears had come out of the woods. A bear had got into a man's garden and killed a man's sheep. He had jumped over the fence with the sheep and eaten her on the road and then came back the next night for the scraps.

We might have thought that Monkstown would have been in an uproar at the news, with a party of men got up to go and shoot this bear and traps and snares set all around.

No such thing. The man whose sheep had been stolen had done what has been set down in these cases for a very long time now. He had made a flag and stuck it on a stick in his garden.

It was a sign to the bear that if it was all the same to him the man would just as soon that he did not come around taking his sheep. Bears are reasonable people.

Monkstown parents do not rear their youngsters to be et by bloody bears any more than do St. John's parents. But let a bear visit St. John's, let us say, and what is his reception?

He is shot to death upon the spot and dragged off to the university to be chopped up into little pieces. Oh, my dear man, no. There is a civilized way of doing things as well as an uncivilized way. Let us not confuse civilization with neon lights.

Mr. Sinclair, having been restored to some semblance of health after our rough passage across the Bay, accompanied me on a turn around the community. We had viewed the bear flag on the way in.

It was foggy and the drizzle turned to light rain at intervals. As we were returning from our walking tour we heard an uproar ahead and down the lane came six small children of kindergarten age.

One carried a flag on a broomstick and another had a tin kettledrum which he laced with great vigor. They were singing (with more spirit than reverence, if I may say so) that familiar Salvation Army chorus: "There is sunshine in my heart today, more glorious and bright ..."

They fell in behind us and we proceeded back through the community to the accompaniment of this juvenile band of music. I glanced at the bearded Mr. Sinclair from time to time, half expecting him to be overcome by Messianic notions, understandable considering the circumstances.

The remark was passed that instead of Beatlemania these kids had been afflicted by Religionmania. This recalled to me the words of the Founder: "Why should the devil have all the good tunes?" Or the Rolling Stones, for that matter.

Such spirited tunes have an appeal for the young. The Writer, although brought up securely within the bosom of the Established Church, numbers "Playing Army" among his juvenile outharbor delights.

To this day he passes many a pleasant and uplifting hour performing such songs and choruses upon the parlor harmonium. These and other observations occurred to us as we progressed through Monkstown with the young soldiers bearing down on: "There is sunshine, blessed sunshine, and I'm singing as the happy moments roll ..."

On our way we chanced to fall into conversation with young Onslow Masters, 11, a bright and sturdy lad who told us that there were six television sets in the community and they got Channel 6 pretty good; that they didn't play hockey (Good Lord, no Little League!) and that he had never been outside of Monkstown in his life.

It is nobody's wish that young Onslow be deprived. There is altogether too much deprivation in the world today. All those deprived kids in Monkstown who have never seen St. John's; all those deprived kids in St. John's who have never seen Toronto; all those deprived kids in Toronto who have never seen Los Angeles; all those deprived kids in Los Angeles who have never seen ... Monkstown?

We would only wish for young Onslow that he be able to go out and see all that there is to see. But we wish also that Monkstown will be there when and if he wants to come back.

I don't know if that huge and elaborate government barge has been to Monkstown yet to take away the house of the one family that wants to move. They will be at pains to show everyone how simple and how easy it is.

Far be it from me to tell anyone their job. But perhaps when they come the young lieutenant will comb his hair and trim his moustache and take the youngsters over to where all the excitement is going on.

Perhaps, with little buddy lashing it home to his kettledrum, they could stand on the shore and give them a few choruses of "We Have an Anchor."

Or something equally suitable.

Yes, indeed. Why should Confederation Building have all the good tunes? ◼

There are no romantic Englishmen

Culture and History

"Well, Sinclair," I said, "this is it!"

Mr. Sinclair was brushing his teeth with regular Crest just aft of the pilot house. He looked up, foaming slightly, to see what it was.

It would be difficult, I knew, to bring home to him the greater significance of it all and so increase his appreciation of this highlight of our voyage.

"Yes," I said, "this is it. Here we are. Who'd have thought we'd have lived to see the day!

"Do you not perceive, sir," I continued, in an effort to get him into the spirit of things, "that we are now approaching one of the great spiritual shrines, the Plymouth Rock, the Camelot, the Mount Olympus, if you will, of this great island of ours?"

This didn't seem to impress Mr. Sinclair all that much. He is originally from other parts although now one among us. But our two native boatmen brightened appreciably as we approached the spot.

"In song and in story, Sinclair," I persisted, "in legend and in myth and in the pages of our long history few other places are as celebrated as this site to which we now draw near."

He continued to scrub his back molars as the stark cliffs grew closer. How noble and immovable they looked as now I recall that brilliant fall day of but a few short weeks ago.

"Even our writers for the stage have drawn upon it for inspiration. Do we not recall that recent dramatic production by Grace Butt which stirred the bosoms of all who viewed it at the Arts and Culture Centre?"

We were getting quite near now and Mr. Sinclair was wondering where he had put the cap of his toothpaste tube. The inspiring vista stretched before us, the green sparkling water, the blue cloudless sky, the gold and brown hillside grass and sedges.

"Let me recite, at this time, a passage from the Master so that we may better grasp the true significance of it. If memory serves '... no dusty road with cars or trucks will ever bring 20th-century Canada into Toslow. It will be Newfoundland for all time to come'."

Warming up to it, I continued with the passage from H. Horwood's book, *Newfoundland*: "'It is safe in the years that were', Sinclair. 'It will remain forever inviolate, the village that gave us birth, that shaped us, that made us what we are, this happy breed of men that came, somewhere, out of the fire and ice of the past, and stood upon this iron-black land, and looked fearlessly upon the sea and the surrounding hills, and called a little cove a cup of silver'."

Needless to say, I had difficulty keeping my emotions under control at this point. I averted my head and made a pretence of blowing my nose. Mr. Sinclair muttered something about Guy being the only one who can top Horwood in the purple prose department.

Never mind. Our two native boatmen, sturdy lads, burst into the familiar refrain ... "And if we strike bottom inside the two sunkers, thennnnnnn straight through the channel to Toslow we'll go."

I feared that if they didn't pay a little more attention to the wheel we'd be striking bottom for sure. But who could blame them? Here we were gazing upon the self-same sunkers and the identical channel!

The popular theory as to the naming of Toslow is held by Horwood, Harrington, Perlin, Fox, et al. These authorities surmise that the romantic French, taken with the sparkle of sunlight in the harbor basin, named it La Tasse de L'Argent or Silver Cup.

As we sailed through the storied channel an inspiration came to me in a flash. Never mind your sparkling sunlight! There, on the cliff face, was an oddly shaped white marking and it resembled nothing so much as a pewter goblet used aboard ship in those days. A new Toslow theory was born on the spot!

I excitedly passed my theory on to Mr. Sinclair. He was inclined to agree, although, ever the keen and analytical scholar, he pointed out that the shape of bird droppings on the cliff was not likely to have remained the same over three centuries.

By this time we were inside the narrow passage and o'ershadowed by the eternal hills of Toslow. Words failed in the heat of emotion and I turned once more in memory to the words of Horwood: "The great majority of singers have never seen Toslow ... but that did not matter for Toslow existed in the land of the imagination; like the Islands of the Blessed, it was everyone's ancestral village, where his fathers had labored and hoped and loved and passed in the end under its sod or its waves."

The engines stopped and all was quiet in this hallowed place. I turned to Mr. Sinclair to see his reaction. "Hmmmmmm," he said, "small place isn't it? There couldn't have been much else to do here except write folk songs about it."

Mr. Sinclair might have passed in the end, then and there under its sod or its waves but I didn't have the strength to even pass him over the side.

I feared I sulked as we journeyed onward. As we neared Paradise further down the coast, Mr. Sinclair noticed two square rocks off the harbor entrance. He tried to make amends.

"I'll bet you," he said, "that some romantic Englishman saw them and named the place 'Pair-o-dice'."

"There are no romantic Englishmen," I snapped morosely. "Like the ruddy Scots, they're just a bunch of bleeding rock-headed, small-souled perishers." ▩

Please God, it's the army and not the FLQ

October 26, 1970   *Democracy*

How did you get along over the weekend with your civil rights suspended? I didn't find it too much of a burden myself, although I must admit I can never remember what my rights are.

With the War Measures Act in force all across Canada, I did get a bit curious to know just what had been taken away from me. But there didn't happen to be a bun of baker's bread on the premises at the time with the "Canadian Bill of Rights" on the wrapper.

When I got down to the office, I looked up a few particulars on it. Seems that the War Measures Act gives the Canadian army the right to put the boots to your door any hour of the day or night.

Not much likelihood of any of the unpleasantness down in this quiet corner of the country … but you know how some people worry. So the War Measures Act should be a comfort to at least those with nervous conditions.

You know the sort. They're not much up on events but with all the uproar in other parts, they've let their imaginations run away with them. At every crack in the night they lift a foot off the mattress figuring the FLQ has come to kidnap them.

If they fancy they hear the back door being splintered at 3 a.m., they can be 50 per cent less apprehensive now that the Army is on the job. There's a 50-50 chance it's the Army come to take them away and not the FLQ.

While most of us don't have nerves or imaginations pitched quite that high, the War Measures Act will be welcomed by the small minority in any neck of the woods who have.

Crash! Wo … wha … what?!!! They're here! They'll be bursting into the bedroom in the next few seconds with those sub-machine guns under their arms. Martha'll be vexed about them getting mud on the mat.

Please God, it's the Army and not the FLQ. I'll know by the helmets … or do the others wear helmets too? Wonder if I'll have time to fish my upper plate out of the glass before they bundle me off?

So the cat knocked down the broom out in the kitchen. But I dare say that in Quebec these days the things that go bump in the night frighten a larger percentage of the population.

When the cry of "Mad dog!" goes up, the pursuers tend to take on some of the attributes of their quarry. After the despicable events in Quebec, they went a bit ape in Ottawa.

More than half the infantrymen in the Canadian Armed Forces have been moved into Quebec. The famous "Canadian Bill of Rights" that we hear so much prate about in other times is now only … to use another familiar phrase … a scrap of paper.

Normal laws have been set aside all across Canada. The government can send the army or police to padlock or take over any newspaper or radio station, order what will or will not be published or broadcast.

They can arrest, jail, or deport anyone they see fit, they can control all ports and shipping movements, they can control the movements of any or all citizens, they can seize any goods or property they see fit.

Someone said it's like using a piledriver to drive a tack. But that's what happens when the "Mad dog!" cry goes up. A touch of hysteria overtook Trudeau and the boys.

It's catching. The mayor of Vancouver wants to use the War Measures Act to seize and jail other groups of "troublemakers," by which we suspect he means any young people who don't act as he thinks they should.

A Toronto rabbi says the War Measures Act should be used to outlaw certain Arab groups and sympathizers in Canada. Had there been or if there are more kidnappings or bombings in Quebec, how much more hysteria will spring up across the country?

From a distance, it seemed that during those few days last week in Ottawa, it would have taken only another murder or two in Quebec and we might have seen the Army ordered to arrest some Members of Parliament.

"It was entirely necessary," many people said of the introduction of the War Measures Act. "It was the only thing that could be done on short notice."

These are the same sort of people who talk airily yet fervently at other times about democracy and the rule of law and the Bill of Rights and of the sacrifices made in other years on the field of battle to, etc., etc., etc. But when it comes to the crunch, they quickly forget their wine-dipped fancy phrases.

If it's fancy phrases we're looking for, William Pitt, a British prime minister of nearly 200 years ago said, "Necessity is the plea for every infringement of human freedom. It is the argument of tyrants; it is the creed of slaves."

The actions of Ottawa in the past few weeks should make us every bit as nervous as the tactics of those few mad dogs in Quebec. When the heat was on, they proved to be dangerously hysterical and hair-trigger.

Under the War Measures Act, some 300 people have been rounded up. These, we presume, include just about all the people in Quebec that both governments believe to be FLQ members or sympathizers.

Three criminal lunatics could just as easily band together and commit murder and kidnappings and bombings. It doesn't take 300. But whether three or 300, it took the whole German nation on the warpath to prompt such measures, the only other two times in history they were enforced.

If Ottawa admits that it takes the suspension of civil rights all across Canada and half the Canadian army to control three or 300 criminals, they admit there is something greatly wrong with Canada's regular laws and police.

Or if they acted in the belief that conditions are such in Canada that a tiny minority could arouse a large part of the population of the country behind them in civil war, then they admit they have been sadly out of touch with reality.

There had never been a word from the government that such was the case.

While admittedly the man lacked sleep and was under much tension, Mr. Trudeau showed an unexpected side of his nature over the past weeks.

During the election campaign and thereafter, he gave the impression of some sort of Hindu holy man in Mod Squad regalia, bobbing about the country sniffing daisies. Now it seems that flower power has given way to a hint of the jackboot.

"Weak-kneed bleeding hearts" was the advance criticism he flung at those who would question the use of the War Measures Act. "Just watch me!" he muttered when a reporter asked what other steps the government might take.

Not "us" mind you, but "me." It would be a pity if Pierre got carried away. There's no need for him to prove how tough, tough, tough he is deep down. Anyone who skindives, practices judo and invites the formidable Barbra Streisand up to the house for cookies can't be all soft.

Meanwhile, back in our own quiet corner, we'll be watching to see how it all turns out. Seems there might be more to Canada than just Hamilton steelworkers whose taxes keep us in welfare. ∎

Wise Virgins. The Big Bang Theory

October 29, 1970 *Democracy*

One of the most interesting documents it has ever been my pleasure to read came into my possession yesterday. No need for us to mention where it came from.

Suffice to say there is something to be said for infiltrators and "friends in high places." There is little that escapes us here at Information Central.

Of course we reveal only a tenth of what we really know. As Marchand said when asked for evidence of "anticipated insurrection" in Canada – you have to read between the lines.

Anyway, this singular document measures eight by 10, contains 98 pages and is bound in yellow plastic. It is entitled Directive BS-6/82264 – Road Construction re Elections; or Caterpillar Attacks on Newfoundland Greenery. Confidential. Limited Circulation.

A few selections from this interesting booklet will serve to indicate the general nature of its contents.

We quote at random?

Wise Virgins: It is a sagacious government that withholds the heft of its highway spending until the fall. Needless to say, autumn is a favorite time for elections. A farseeing highways department will keep its lamp trimmed and ready, as it were, so that when the call goes out its conserved and concentrated energies may be pitched into the fray.

Acts of God: Election or no, it is better to delay most highway projects until the fall. A great show and bluster may then be made with limited funds, for the winter will soon set in making further construction impossible. The masses are then informed that the Great work will continue "as soon as spring breaks."

Plywood Ploys: Early in the Second World War, when supplies were short, the British camouflaged some of their merchant shipping with wooden gun turrets to resemble battleships, thus fooling the Boche.

So it is that inoperative bulldozers and graders may be parked in view by the highways and byways to create the proper pre-election impression. Plywood cutouts painted in the proper design may also be used if the need is great. However, these should be placed some distance back.

The Big Bang Theory: At 6 a.m. of a calm morning on the road above some tranquil hamlet about 50 sticks of dynamite are set off at once. As the bleary-eyed peasants rush to their cottage windows, they see trucks and equipment silhouetted against the rising sun.

So forceful is this initial salute that the equipment may then be moved on to the next village. With their ears ringing for up to two weeks, the startled citizenry will remain under the impression that "road work is being done." By that time the election is over.

Jobs, Jobs, Jobs: Several weeks before elections, road work is commenced in selected locations. Whether they are needed or not, all workmen in the area are hired. Glowing articles may then be written in the *Newfoundland Bull–etin* about the high employment rate in these places.

Figure Eights: A pile of gravel is produced in a selected pit and a string of dump trucks cart it to another pit some 10 miles distant. When the first pit has been emptied the process is simply reversed and the string of trucks bring it back again. If handled gently, gravel used for this purpose will not wear out and may be used for years and years.

Signs and Portents: Poles, planks, a broken-down tractor or two and other supplies are dumped by the roadside in conspicuous places to indicate that work will start shortly. After the election this gear is gathered up again and sorted for future use.

Flatbed Follies: Heavy equipment is lashed to flatbed trucks, which are sent coasting back and forth over the highways and byways to give the impression that somewhere great works are proceeding apace.

Little Things: Some obscure secondary road or lane is singled out for the deluxe treatment. The proper piece of path must be minor but very much in the public view. A great flurry of activity is focused on it.

This ploy is adopted from that of the famous valet, Jeeves, who not having time to brush and press his master's suit for the next day would take the change from the trousers pockets, polish it, and lay it out in plain sight. "I say, Jeeves, even the change!," says the master, not noticing the rumpled garments.

Grand Slam: All available bulldozers and graders are rounded up and dispatched in groups to the most heavily used roads in the province. Whether or not repairs are needed the pavement is torn up for miles and the detours are made as rough and difficult as possible.

This is known as "Rubbing their bumpers in it." It creates the impression of much employment, activity and progress. On election day, some bulldozers are taken off and sent to run rings around key polling stations.

Frenzied Finale: This tack is used only in hours of darkest need. All the heavy equipment in the province is set into action, the drivers lashed to their seats and hornets nests fixed in place behind them.

The blitzkrieg thus set in motion astounds the whole population as tractors, bulldozers, graders, steam shovels and front-end loaders tear frantically across bogs, swamps, drokes and dells.

Voters, behold! Newfoundland is clearly on the march! ▨

Aunt Cissy: I'm constantly on me toes

November 9, 1970   *Aunt Cissy*

"Gotcha!" whooped the dear old soul as she sunk her double-bit axe a half-foot into the plank door of her humble abode a few inches from my neck.

As the handle lay directly across my throat, hampering my wind, I couldn't make myself known until she came round and saw who I was.

"I'm constantly on me toes," said Aunt Cissy Roach offhandedly as she wrenched the tool of her trade out of the wood and unpinned me.

"You got to be mighty watchful these days. There's not much that gets a'past me.

"I'm eatin' carrots for me eyesight and practicin' me swing. A nice wristy action, don't you think? I could'a shove the top of your head and not drawed blood. Stop study there and I'll try it. Cock your conk a little to starboard, lanternjaws, and knock off biverin'. If you don't stop study I might miss."

"Aunt Cissy," I said, "my nerves are not what they were. Put down that Viking artifact or I may drop this brown paper bag in which, need it be said, is contained my usual present of a little something for your joints."

"Ha! Gettin' timid in your old age, is you, blubber bung? Oh, well, no need to risk losin' that drop of pasteurized goat's drizzle that passes for honest spirits these days. Wipe your boots and come in."

The world's largest precambrian fossil (contrary to other reports) received me in her rustic cottage located halfway along the Witless Bay Line and thence some 13 miles on foot in over the Witless Bay Barrens.

"Well, A.C.," I said, settling myself away on the settle, "the events of these past several weeks have been consequential indeed and in the light of this you will no doubt be able to tell us something of what the final outcome of it all will be."

"Where's your manners, gallbuster?" said Aunt Cissy. "Han't you got the decency to enquire after Sunny Jim? The poor little mortal is still not got over the hard usage he got when you was put in charge of him for a few months two winters ago."

I quickly apologized for Aunt Cissy is extremely touchy regarding her pet carey-chicken, Sunny Jim, the most foul and wretched bird it has ever been my misfortune to come in contact with. I asked where the little blighter was.

"That poor little soul was neglected under your care and one of these days I'm goin' to find out the rights of it," said Aunt Cissy, darkly. "I got him sent off to the coast for the airs in the charge of Aunt Menschivick Poole, a friend of the fambly.

"We'll let that pass for now. What news have you got? Is young Squires still flyin' high or have he been brought to his just deserts, yet? Last time I seen him he looked like he cast his bread upon the waters and the gulls made off with it."

Due to her extreme age, Aunt Cissy sometimes confuses dates. Several months ago, for instance, she asked me if it was true that the Boer War had taken a turn for the worse.

However, when she mentions "Squires" I assume she is talking about politics and respond accordingly. "The premier returned to the place of his reputed birth over the weekend," I said, "and was fêted by the local citizens.

"The mayor of the community has called upon the population of Newfoundland to send in contributions toward the construction of a swimming pool to be known as the Smallwood Memorial Pool. I had thought I would be stuck for topics this week but it seems not."

"I was never one," said Aunt Cissy, passing another half-tumbler of medicinal spirits over her gums, "to gloat over other people's misfortunes. What else is on the go?"

It occurs to me now and then that I am altogether too easy on Aunt Cissy considering what is at stake. If there is anyone who knows what is to befall us during the ensuing twelvemonth it is she. Yet it is a tricky business extracting this intelligence from her.

Perhaps if I were to be more forceful and insist ... However, let those who accuse me of not being forward enough consider the wrath of Aunt Cissy Roach. Would they like to know what really happened to the westbound express of the Newfoundland Railway which left St. John's at 2:30 p.m., October 7, 1932, and was never seen again?

"Oh, not much," I said. "A bit of this and a bit of that. The more things change the more they are the same, as the frogs say. Some think we're going to hell in a handbasket and more think the heft of our troubles are behind us."

"And that indeed," said Aunt Cissy Roach, and I would have almost sworn that a bemused smile flickered across her remarkable countenance although you can't really tell.

"Well, seein' you're here you might so well stop and have some hash before hitchin' your carcass back the way you come. I got a small varying hare and we can have him fried up with cold spuds. Keep your hands to yourself in the meantime. I might be small but I'm wiry."

Needless to say. 🅁🅶

Let the supplicants prostrate themselves

November 10, 1970 *Joey*

Good afternoon, ladies and gentlemen. This live broadcast is coming to you from in front of Conglomeration Building where an estimated crowd of some 25,000 has gathered to watch today's ceremonies.

The temperature here is in the high thirties, most people are wearing heavy clothes and a brisk wind is blowing. Despite that, there's an air of excitement and festivity among the crowd.

A mammoth grandstand has been erected here in front of the main entrance and there are flags fluttering all down the length of the P.P. Parkway. We await the climax of the ceremonies here in about 10 minutes time.

Listeners will recall that two weeks ago on November 5, John Crosbie spoke at the university and indicated he was ready to plead with Premier Smallwood to resign. Many thought at first that Mr. Crosbie had slipped and struck his head on the way in but this was not the case.

Apparently, after a couple of years running his head into a brick wall, Mr. Crosbie was ready to take another tack. Unlike the tomcat eating the grindstone, he has given up the slow and steady approach.

He told the students that although Mr. Smallwood would probably win the next election he should be pleaded with to resign.

"If he retires now, no one will say he's turning his head and running," was the assurance Mr. Crosbie offered.

In any case, he has declared that his behavior in the House this winter will be "statesmanlike." In fact, he went so far as to say that "if necessary, we will let ourselves be trampled on."

Since then, Mr. Smallwood has apparently judged Mr. Crosbie to be ripe. He has said he will consider his plea but only if it is presented formally.

This is the first time the colorful Supplication Ceremony has been presented in public. All is in readiness and Leslie R. Curtis, resplendent in his new university robes, has mounted to the dias to direct the proceedings.

In the background, a massed choir is singing: "Just as I am without one plea, but public tenders waived for me ..." The soft and tender strains rise on the brisk air.

All the cabinet members are assembled. Now we see that Mr. Smallwood is coming to the platform. He wears the ceremonial gold-plated hobnail boots. Now the two supplicants are being ushered forward, barefoot and clad only in potato sacking.

Mr. Crosbie is accompanied by his squire, Mr. Wells. They are now slowly advancing up the steps on their hands and knees as the choir in the background sings: "There is a fountain filled with graft, drawn from the public chest, and sinners kicked out in the draft, can feather not their nest."

Mr. Curtis speaks: "Let the supplicants prostrate themselves." Both are kneeling now and Mr. Crosbie has taken Mr. Smallwood's left foot and placed it on his head. The spectators are presented with a rear view proclaiming "PEI Grade A Sebagos."

"Here and now, at this official public pleading ceremony, do you promise to keep civil tongues in your heads from here on in?"

"We do. We do."

"Do you now plead openly and humbly with the premier to resign?"

"We do. We do."

"And do you solemnly swear that if he does you will not go about saying 'Yaaa, yaaa, old muzzy-guts gave in' and other evil blasphemies of this sort?"

"We do. We do."

Ladies and gentlemen there are true tears of repentance running down the faces of both supplicants at this stage. Mr. Smallwood is demanding that the TV cameras zoom in for good close-ups.

"And if he does consider your plea that he resign will you allow yourselves to be trampled on in the House for the miserable worms you are in atonement for your manifold sins and wickedness in the past?"

"We will. We will."

Ladies and gentlemen, Mr. Crosbie seem to be getting some sort of ecstatic kick out of this. What's this? There appears to be a bit of a scuffle over there. Freddie Rowe seems to be overcome. He has been taken by what is known as a "Gory Fit."

He's doing a little dance and now he's making a rush toward the two kowtowing supplicants … and he's grabbed just in time and restrained by Roberts and Barbour.

The formalities have been given a dash of color by this bit of spontaneity. Dr. Rowe appeared to be enraptured and rushed out shouting "Saucy crackies," apparently intent on fetching a sharp kick to Mr. Crosbie's proffered posterior.

However, this stage of ceremonies, known as the Cabinet Trample, will be done alphabetically. They're lining up now, one by one, their construction boots at the ready. A roll of kettledrums marks time in the background.

The spectacle ends with a pronouncement from the premier: "We will take into consideration your humble plea that we resign. If we decide to do so you two fighting Newfoundlanders will be the first to know. Meanwhile, don't call me – I'll call you."

We return you now to our studios for some light music. RG

The "swinger" has shown himself at last for what he is

November 11, 1970   *Democracy*

Lest we forget.

Forget what? Deviltry of one sort or another, I suppose, all lumped together and tagged with vague words like tyranny, war, dictatorship, destruction, oppression.

Or other equally abstract words like duty, sacrifice, honor, courage, and democracy. At this time of year, to mark the eleventh hour of the eleventh day of the eleventh month we're entreated to "buy a poppy in remembrance."

The First World War now seems quaint and far away. Those tin soup bowl hats, Kaiser Bill, blue puttees, the trenches and musical hall songs.

There used to be one of those old-fashioned pictures around the house in memory of some relative or other which showed a dead soldier in the mud. A buxom angel with really spectacular wings was pensively placing a laurel wreath on his alabaster brow and the caption read: "He loved Honor more than he feared Death."

No one has applied such child-like sentiments to the Second World War. Some 25 years later, plays are being written condemning Churchill as a windy butcher and every history sophomore knows it wasn't black and white but a complicated business involving old mistakes, economics, politics, sociology and Vera Lynn.

About the only thing we're still positive about is that although he was said to be fond of children and had some small talent as an architect, Adolf Hitler was not one of your nicer types. So far there have been no plays with the Nazis cast as heroes.

Persons today about the age of 30 have a peculiar outlook on the Second World War. Impressions gained in earliest years are said to have the strongest impact. Those born in 1940 – even in this isolated corner – took their first breath of air that was laden with a monstrous fear.

Although not understood, this heavy stamp must have made its mark permanently on the back of the mind. It leads them in later years to try and find out what that great black dread was all about.

There is no shortage of information. There are histories and movies and figures to say that 40 million died and film clips of bodies stacked like cordwood outside the gas chambers.

The "why" is not so easy to find. We learn that the years before the war were not so very different, that it came about slowly, that it grew gradually right under people's noses, that few saw it coming, that little and insignificant events taken one by one added up to a hideous climax.

We look for the signs and similarities and mark them and perhaps are over-sensitive. When Mike Cook says he shuddered when majorettes marched out on a US football field with the bands crashing behind them and a single roar went up from 100,000 throats, we know exactly what he's talking about.

The stamp on the back of the mind says beware when the shout from all throats sound as one or when a leader is set up as something larger than life or when a system or an idea is hailed with a single voice.

Be aware of the signs. When people say "desperate times call for desperate measures." When people say "we must put all our trust in our leaders now."

Trust? Trust has nothing to do with it. The whole long bloody rigmarole would not have been necessary had "trust" been enough. An absolute monarchy would have filled the bill nicely and there would have been no need to force King John to sign the Magna Carta.

"In God We Trust" is the inscription on those American monetary medals. "Put not your trust in princes," ... or in politicians with princely pretentions. Never, never, never.

When people say the times are desperate and we must put all our trust in our leaders and shout and cheer and allow the thin chain forged in blood through the centuries (to get corny about it) to be snapped, we tilt and totter on the edge of a steep and slippery path.

Never mind how benign and sensible and homely the leaders happen to be at the time. The chain is all we have and all we have been able to discover so far. Without it, the creep toward the brink begins.

We are often smug and sneer at the excesses and grossness of the US with their Chicagos and their Spiro Agnews. Yet our neighbors are amazed and shudder at how close Canada has come to the edge.

The murder of that poor man in Quebec was a terrible thing, but the baying that went up from every mad dog in Canada at the scent of the War Measures Act was a thousand times more horrifying.

The "swinger" who was swept to power on Trudeau-mania has shown himself at last for what he is, an hysterical and unstable person unworthy of trust even in tranquil times. The PCs scuttle around in what they consider the winds of public opinion. Social Credit want the firing squad without trial. The NDP put up a token gesture and then collapsed under a storm of abuse.

And who is the "swinger" now? An unlikely personage, an old man in Ottawa with kinky hair and comical jowls and old-fashioned rhetoric – the darling of the Canadian Legion and one-time hero of the little old ladies with their Union Jacks.

He seems to know that among the things we must remember at all times are the words of a bishop who lived in Germany under the Nazis:

"I was silent when they came for the Communists; I was silent when they came for the Jews and gypsies and the trade unionists. And finally, when they came for me, I cried out but there was nobody left to hear." ▪

The Ninth Cinch: Part III

November 18, 1970   *Spy Thriller*

(In which we continue a new Spy Thriller of Intrigue and Suspense set amid the Political Squalor and Savagery of the Happy Province – with a vivid description of a Stark Naked cabinet minister's mistress chucked in on page 76 to keep the ball rolling.)

Chapter Eleven: Uneasy Rider

To the keen eye of the Totanus melanoleucus or greater yellowlegs flying at an attitude of 2,500 feet on its annual migration to Patagonia, the car below on the deserted night highway seemed to crawl imperceptibly.

However, the red needle wavered in the pale green glow of the dash lights at 78 m.p.h. The undersea green bathed the driver's face at an upward angle emphasizing the resolute jaw and picking out a rhythmic twitch under the left cheekbone.

His purposeful eyes were riveted on the dashed line although a well-developed peripheral vision allowed him to scan the roadsides for sinister movements among the boulders and brush.

He drove the black rented sedan westward through the night mist with precision and urgency. A small wicker container of crushed lavender suspended from the rear-view mirror masked the slight mold of the carpets, the stale cigarette smoke and the smell of warm oil from the hard-driven engine.

A black raincoat was tossed carelessly across the back seat. The pale wash of green light glinted feebly off a string of neat tungsten links which joined a thin leather briefcase in the front to a bracelet of steel encircling the driver's wrist.

The fine morocco leather concealed the reinforced framework of the case, impregnable to all but the most advanced cutting tools. A thin smile curled the driver's merciless lips as he thought of his mission ... a momentous one indeed and one not altogether unfraught with risk.

Much rested on the secret meeting to which he hastened. It was a tricky caper. Many had played the dangerous game before and lost. He knew well the reward for failure ... a dreary job in the middle ranks of the civil service.

But as the tires of the speeding sedan moaned softly over the thin film of moisture on the black asphalt, the man known only throughout the organization as Herr Doktor smiled balefully once more.

More than once the same chilling expression had struck terror in the hearts of those who had dared question the fabled strength of Herr Doktor. His hands tightened on the wheel. The Roache's Line overpass loomed directly ahead.

Chapter Twelve: Full Fathom Five

Depravity hung like a thick fog over Sin John's and intrigue hovered over every refuse-strewn back alleyway. Down one of these skulked three sinister figures identically and inconspicuously clad in mattress-striped bell-bottomed trousers, heavy corduroy double-breasted jackets, orange shirts and purple neckties. Immersed in any Water Street crowd they would have been all but invisible.

Between them they carried an ominous burden. By the faint lettering on the package it would have been possible to tell that the wrapping was originally jute sacking in which imported hops had arrived at a local brewery.

The waterfront was all but dead. Far off in the distance the crumbling bricks of an abandoned warehouse stood out in relief under the feeble glow of a 40-watt bulb. In the ruddy smear of light beneath it, a wino sat clutching a half-empty bottle of Jordan's sherry.

Faint and muffled sounds of late-night traffic seeped down through the ancient waterside buildings and somewhere, from an open garret window, came the thin haunting strains of Glen Campbell and his poignant tale of a country boy ensnared by a New York harlot: "It was only commercial affection, but she walked away with my heart."

On a signal, the three sinister figures shuffled forward into the light carrying their burlap-wrapped package. Here, in the baleful glare of mercury vapor street lamps, it was plain that the burden they carried was human.

Scuttling over the 50 yards to quayside they paused on the brink and set their burden down. One of them pulled a cord at the top of the sack and flaxen curls spilled out under the cold light of the street standards.

The captive was gagged with an old school tie and, by the fluttering of her long blond lashes, it was evident that she had appraised her perilous situation in a flash. She glanced down with horror at the orange peels, teabags and other detritus picturesquely floating on the surface of the harbor.

In menacing tones, one of her captors spoke: "Whereas you constituted an incipient threat to the whole organization we have taken it upon ourselves, for the good of the aforesaid party, to offer you two alternatives, viz. to wit, over the side or a one-way ticket back to the mainland."

Intelligent fear crossed the lovely features of the trussed captive as she quickly nodded assent to the latter. The wino did not look up as, in the distance, the heavy thunk of a boot lid and the dull roar of mufflers briefly disturbed the fetid downtown night. ∎

Great industries dance before us
like daffodils in the breeze

November 20, 1970   *Great New Industries*

Summing up this week just drawing to a close you'd have to say it reeked of greatness. Yes, if you were searching for a word to describe it, "great" would spring to your lips.

It was a great week and no doubt about it. Just like the good old days. Some people were going about dabbing their eyes with pocket handkerchiefs. Overcome with nostalgia they were.

"Takes me back to that wonderful spring of '55," sobbed one old-timer in a downtown refreshment center. "Revives fond memories right and left. God be with the good old days."

Those were the times when the minister of economic development and a few of the crew would take off for months on end, flitting about Europe in search of great new industries. Back they'd come with rubber plants and machine plants and leather plants and Dr. Valdmanis and Joey.

Halcyon days. The golden era. The classic age. Who'd have thought we'd ever see their like again. Faded, they seemed to be, in the purple mists of time.

Oh, we've had little flashes of former greatness here and there since then … talk of an orange juice works, a hockey stick enterprise, a goat-raising industry and a manufactory for making wristwatches out of pumpkin pips … but nothing like the good old days.

Nothing, you might say, to recapture that first fine careless rapture. Churchill Falls? Javelin? Come By Chance? Not really. They were too big for the average mind to grasp. Too bulky for the proletarian imagination to enfold.

They transcended mere greatness, so to speak, and achieved the heights of cosmic mysticism. No, "great" would be a puny word with which to describe the titanic vision of Come By Chance. Even the *Journal of Commerce* and A.B. Perlin were unequal to it.

Mere greatness is what transports us back to the good old days. This week, like a trip back in time, we had a reminder of those balmy times when the world was still young and cost-plus still a pregnant bud on the bough.

Great industries, or at least visions of the same, dance before us like daffodils in the breeze and we are overtaken by a wave of nostalgia. A dozen or so great new industries in the works for Come By Chance … perhaps including Neary's factory to turn out toothbrush handles.

The minister of economic development and the former minister and a few of the crew all cocked and primed to fly away with Mr. Doyle to talk about great new industries with the Sons of Nippon.

What great new industries may we expect to be forthcoming from the Land of the Rising Sun? The mystique of the Orient tinges our speculation, and fanciful images buffet us right, left and center. Black spruce chopsticks? Ah, so.

As if this weren't enough we have had an airlift of great industrialists into the province to talk turkey right here on the spot before our very eyes. Myriads of entrepreneurs transported here at public expense to be dazzled by the fancy footwork of the new minister of economic development.

Those that aren't lucky enough to hit the jackpot won't go away empty-handed, not with Dancing Dollars as master of ceremonies. A nice pot holder and a seven-pound bag of flour is better than nothing at all.

At least, we have the word of the former minister of economic development that they're a plane-load of great industrialists. Seems like we have to take his word for it. They've been brought in under wraps.

Top secret. No names, no companies, no nothing. Hush, hush. Believe in the word, brethren, and thou shalt be off and running. This surprise package contains a bunch of great industrialists and you just take old Joseph's word for it.

They're here to discuss setting up great industries ... which is never a bad idea when there's a great new election in the works. They could be great civil servants from Ottawa or great furniture salesmen from Spokane, Washington, or a bunch of really great Afghanistan tourists here for the waters.

But of course they're not. They're great industrialists here to discuss great new industries. Would your little old premier kid you? Of course not. Put all your faith in the Pill, as the song goes.

Anyhow, between the jigs and the reels, we've got the stuff that dreams are made of. Just like the good old days. The priming cup of the public imagination has been topped off and visions of kumquat processing works dance in the public head.

Come By Chance industries, Oriental industries, industrialists from upalong en masse. Dark satanic mills sprouting, like the Wabana Warbler's mushrooms, on every hill between this and Bung Hole Tickle.

Ah, Alfred, would that thou couldst see the sight today. The old-timer had another snuffle and knocked off the rest of his Blue Star. Fairly wallowing in a sea of nostalgia, he was.

Anyway, there was a planeful of persons offloaded at St. John's Airport yesterday. And last night, there was a big gang out at the Colonial Inn happily munching little roast partridges in the shadow of Topsail Head.

As any fool can see, the government wouldn't go to all that expense if there wasn't at least a great new monument and marble works to come out of it. ▧

All you've wanted to know about Newfoundland: Part I

November 23, 1970

Democracy

Many persons are always stuck for an answer when their visitors – friends, relatives and whatnot from the mainland – ask them the usual questions about Newfoundland.

This is a common problem. Clearly, some answers are necessary since a mere shrug of the shoulders or hysterical laughter will be interpreted as bad manners.

The thing to do is bluff your way along. If it's answers to silly questions they want, respond in kind. Better still, commit to memory this brief catechism and you'll be ready for all queries.

Of course, there are dozens of different answers you can give to each question and, if you want to make the effort and improve on your own, by all means do so. But why strain yourself? These will fill the bill nicely:

Q: What quaint scenery you have. And there seems to be such an interest in politics in Newfoundland. What is the reason for this?

A: There has always been an interest in politics in Newfoundland. The people have never been involved in politics; therefore, they are interested in it. Nothing kills interest quicker than participation.

Just as self-abusers show a terrific interest in sex and buy such literature as *Playboy*, so do Newfoundlanders show a keen interest in politics. But it is a spectator sport. Politics has always been left to the politicians. The people get their thrills vicariously.

Q: But you have been here for a few centuries. Surely, that has been time enough to get the simple facts of politics and government straightened out.

A: No. We are slow and steady in these matters like the tomcat eating the grindstone. In addition, Newfoundlanders are as foolish as odd socks. We aren't fit to govern ourselves and never will be.

In consequence, we have had every weird form of government in the catalogue, from the Fishing Admirals to the present day. Star Chamber Rule, Colonial government, "responsible" government that collapsed in graft, corruption and bankruptcy, Commission government and Smallwood.

Q: But surely, the people must have learned something from all this. Haven't they benefited from past mistakes?

A: You must try to understand the fact that while Newfoundlanders are interested in politics, politics does not concern them. They watch the parade of political weirdies come and go as if they were watching eclipses of the moon. Interesting to look at but not much they can do about it. They are utterly detached.

Q: This is hard to believe. What, then, is the difference between Newfoundland before Conglomeration and after ... or do you allow there is any?

A: There have been no basic changes in Newfoundland since Sir Humphrey Gilbert landed. It must be the superficial changes you are looking for.

Q: Gad, sir. Do you mean to say you are in the same position as a Canadian province as you were as a British colony?

A: Exactly. The British held on to us for what they could get out of us. They were never against a bit of bluff and hearty plunder. The Brits had a refreshingly candid attitude in this matter ... quite unlike the hypocrisy of the Canucks.

Q: I must warn you, sir, that I am getting warm. Do you mean to say that we Canadians took you over just for what we could get out of this miserable little scrap of geography?

A: Yes. The idea of having a pink smear right across the top of the map of North America was an appealing one. Besides, you needed a little excitement just at that time. The Second World War was over and there was no chance of an Expo '49. After that, when the flag-waving died down, you found to your distress that you were stuck with us.

Q: Sir, I am getting quite vexed. Has Ottawa not poured millions of dollars into Newfoundland? Have we not raised your standard of living immensely and given you the baby bonus and supermarkets?

A: Quite so. Thanks to Mr. Pearson. He was a do-gooder and an appropriate representative of Canada's "charitable works among the poor" binge. How convenient that the urge in the upper-Canadian bosom to uplift the disadvantaged could find an outlet down here. After acting as Canada's Expo '49 and then briefly as a white elephant, we filled the bill as recipients of gracious Canadian charity. Britain kept us for what money she could take out of us; Canada kept us for what money she could put into us.

Q: What a disgraceful statement. Do you mean to say we pumped millions into this godforsaken hole just because it made us feel warm all over?

A: Exactly. Don't know what you would have done without us. Probably would have been reduced to sending CARE packages to Costa Rica, However, that is all behind us now. Times have gotten a bit tough and when times get tough the first things to be closed down are the zoos and the museums.

The cry has gone up in Toronto that "charity begins at home" ... just as it has in the States where people are saying the US can't afford to do good in Vietnam any longer and should concentrate on its internal problems.

Home was never like this. Home is where the heart is and in the heartland of Canada, that is to say, Toronto, it is doubtful if there will now be enough charity to sprinkle around Quebec to try and keep it greased, let alone such an insignificant colony as this.

Q: God, sir, what an attitude. I find it most revolting. Upon what facts do you base such lunatic ravings?

A: Facts are for chartered accountants. However, the fact is that people have no business living in Newfoundland. The British knew this from the start and made it unlawful for anyone to build a house with chimney and windows within six miles of the sea.

Ottawa soon came to realize this also and set about to depopulate it. That is to say, they established the process known as "centralization" whereby people are rounded up and put into holding pens until the old die off and the young move to Toronto.

In fact, everybody – from the 16th century to the present day – has been in complete agreement that to live in Newfoundland is one of the dark and cardinal sins of mankind.

A famous British writer passed through here last year and observed that such a piece of geography was never meant for habitation. The editor of the magazine *Car and Driver* flew over Newfoundland and remarked that the only people who lived here must be those who knew no better.

A former mayor of Toronto says the only thing we and Prince Edward Island have contributed to Conglomeration are rocks and water and 400,000 seagulls. His estimate of seagulls is far too low.

In short, Newfoundland has never had any reason to exist. Just as we became an embarrassment to Britain we have become a pain in the quarters to Canada. Not bleeding piles like the Maritimes or burning rectal itch like Quebec or a posterior boil like the Indians and Eskimos – but still a petty annoyance.

Now, I see, sir, that still another question trembles upon your nether lip, but for that we shall have to wait 'til tomorrow. 🅡🅖

All you've wanted to know about Newfoundland: Part II

November 24, 1970 *Democracy*

All You've Always Wanted to Know About Newfoundland ... but were afraid to ask.

(In which we offer a brief catechism for the benefit of those who are often asked by visitors certain silly questions but which, for the sake of good manners, they feel obliged to answer.)

Part II

Q: From your maniacal ravings so far, I am surprised that you are still at large. Are there no lunatic asylums in Newfoundland?

A: For the sake of appearances we have one. But it is only a clever device to keep outsiders from asking embarrassing questions. The truth is that everyone in Newfoundland is stark raving ... otherwise they wouldn't be here. Mr. Shaheen speaks of "the Newfoundland madness."

Q: I see. Now, you have said that Newfoundland is seen by Ottawa in certain lights. Would you run through them again, please?

A: Of course. First, we filled the role of Expo '49, then as a white elephant (or perhaps a pigmy white hippopotamus would be more in keeping with the size), then as a convenient outlet for the upwelling of charity and noble good works in Mr. Pearson's bosom, then as a small colorful piece of Mr. Diefenbaker's Canadian mosaic, then as a zoo and museum ("this diverse Canada of ours ... from the quaint fishing hamlets of Newfoundland to the ..."), then as a minor conversation piece ("did you hear the Newfie joke about ..."), and now as a minor pain in the quarters.

Q: I take it that you sometimes get the feeling you're not wanted?

A: Would you want someone who picks his nose to attend your next cocktail party? Beggars with scabs beg in person along Water Street but they're not allowed in the new shopping malls. Instead, we have clean, charitable middle-class persons sitting behind neat little stands who beg for them.

A former mayor of Toronto says what the present mayor of Toronto means but doesn't dare mention. All we have contributed to Conglomeration is rocks, sea and 400,000 seagulls. There's nothing in it for us, cries Smallwood, as he refuses to take part in talks on Maritime union.

Truth is, he knows better than to attend. It saves him the embarrassment of being rejected. We're a minor pain in the backside to Toronto but we're a millstone around the necks of Nova Scotia and New Brunswick.

Q: If you are so peevish about your treatment since Conglomeration then why did you vote for it?

A: A change is as good as a rest. We have made these superficial changes on the average of once every 20 years or so. The novelty of Conglomeration now is wearing off and there's a strong move afoot in Newfoundland toward federation with either Borneo or Muscat and Oman.

Anyhow, just so that people like yourself couldn't heave it up to us, we arranged it so that barely a majority voted for Conglomeration. When the time comes to set out on our travels again, we can always claim that the extra two per cent were names from headstones. We always keep an ace up our sleeves.

Q: Are you saying there is a strong separatist movement in Newfoundland? Good God, sir! Will we see riots and demonstrations and blood in the streets?

A: Possibly a bit of gore in the gutters, yes, although not so much as you'll see at a Saturday night dance these days. No, my dear man, we don't go in for anything as strenuous as riots and demonstrations.

We let others do the work. We had Britain scuttling around for years searching for ways to get rid of us. We pretended we made the decision ourselves because you have to hang on to a few shreds of pride, you know. Smallwood has been our false face ever since.

No, what we'll get is a commission of government from Ottawa in about five years time while Ottawa is looking around for the proper wart remover. Then, if Andorra won't have us, probably the UN will pass a resolution declaring us non-existent. No sweat.

Q: Well, I suppose technology will have advanced far enough in the next 10 years that they'll be able to pull the plug and let you sink into ... Arrggg! I think this place has started to drive me bonkers, too. Come now, let's be sensible. Haven't you had a stable provincial government for the past 20 years?

A: Without doubt. But a stable government is foreign to our nature. We always vote against stable government but, despite elections, we continued (until this past year) to have an extremely stable government.

Q: How do you explain this?

A: How do you explain Magnetic Hill in New Brunswick where motor cars seem to run up a slope in neutral gear? There are about 40 seats in the House of Assembly. But the Smallwoodites have always held all but three or four of them. This, despite the fact that 40 per cent or more of the voters have voted anti-Smallwood.

Q: There seems to be something peculiar there, is there not?

A: By Gad, sir, you are indeed a keen and perceptive person. Of course, the same thing happens in other places. I believe the separatists got 24 per cent of the votes in Quebec but only a few seats. However, ours seems to be the greater wonder of nature.

Q: Mr. Smallwood has done a lot for Newfoundland, has he not?

A: Bless the mark, sir, indeed he has. He has been nothing less than the savior of his people. Without him we'd have been snowed under by now in the avalanche of charity payments from Ottawa.

But Mr. Smallwood, economic wizard that he is, found ways to spend all this money. I don't think anyone else in the world could have done it. Of course, anyone could have spent it but … could anyone else have gotten such good value per dollar? Just ask the contractors.

In addition, Mr. Smallwood has put us $1 billion in debt, which is not to be sneezed at. As if this were not enough, he has relieved us of the burden of Labrador. As soon as Shaheen, Doyle and even bigger buzzards like Rothschild smelled the raw meat, they spiraled in.

Q: What of the younger generation? Surely, with increased schooling and the university, they will make some changes in the state of affairs which has heretofore existed since the days of Queen Elizabeth I?

A: You are treading mighty close to sacrilege there, sir. Our national anthem contains the lines "Where once our father stood we stand …" Would you have us turn our backs on these sacred precepts? I can assure you, sir, that we have not. To prevent such a thing we have always relied on a simple safety measure, to wit, we ship our youth away.

Whether to the Boston States, or to world wars or, as now, at the rate of 8,000 or 9,000 a year to Toronto, we have always provided a steam valve to ensure against any blow-ups.

Any few young malcontents who may be left we put them on welfare or absorb them at the university. So you can see that the nation is secure. I see that you now are about to ask, "After Smallwood, what?" Save us and keep us, sir, you don't get the point at all.

There was no "before Smallwood," there is no Smallwood, so there will be no "after Smallwood." Unless you want to nitpick about it. ▧

Guy's Encyclopedia of Juvenile Outharbor Delights: Getting the Outharbor Juvenile Rigged for Winter Months

November 25, 1970   *Outharbor Delights*

As the winter solstice draws closer, we turn to page 244 of volume three of the celebrated work, *Guy's Encyclopedia of Juvenile Outharbor Delights*, and find an appropriate entry, viz. to wit, "Getting the Outharbor Juvenile Rigged for Winter Months."

The secret of draught-free juvenile winter wear is a good set of drawers. Encased from chin to ankle in such a garment he was ready for any climatic extreme. This home-made body stocking was constructed of wool straight from the back of the sheep with some of the twigs left in it.

In a proper suit of home-knit drawers he could have walked to the North Pole and back clad in nothing else. However, this was only the foundation. A well-made suit of drawers is faced down the front with strips of flour sacking and the trap door around the back neatly faced in like manner.

If it looked to be an especially sharp winter, a chest protector was added, which is to say, several doubles of heavy flannel were affixed inside the drawers against the bosom so that the juvenile respiratory system was doubly protected. There is no snugger garment.

Home-knit drawers had only one defect of manufacture. After several years of washings they were affected by a complaint known as fork droop. The garment tended to stretch and sag over the years so that the crotch fell to about the knees. Apart from causing a slight impediment in the juvenile's gait, this was nothing serious.

Then came hose. The inner pair of stockings, also home-knit, were thigh-length and kept in place well above the fork droop line by a set of garters.

The second pair of stockings were knee-length and drawn on over the first. Lucky the lad with a bright red top to these outer stockings which flashed jauntily above the tops of his boots.

Vamps came next. Hand-knit from the self-same material, these socks came to just above the knobs on the ankles and were worn over the first two sets of hose.

Over the flannel chest protector and the woolen drawers went the outside shirt. Today's shirts are mere toys compared to the heft and thickness of these robust garments.

Then what is perhaps pièce de résistance of the whole juvenile winter ensemble was drawn on. The set of briggs. Or "breeks" as they are called by some. These garments were forged from material of an inch thickness which had been woven from quarter-inch manila rope and guaranteed to "stand up."

It is hard to picture the effect caused by this piece of dry goods. They were reinforced at the knees with patches of the stoutest leather with slits in the legs which were snugly fitted against the juvenile calf by means of an arrangement of lacings.

They were supported upon the person from the shoulders by means of another piece of rubber ware ... the braces, as they are called in the US, or suspenders, as they are known in Great Britain. Such an arrangement produced a curious phenomenon.

Since the garment was always purchased two sizes too large, to allow for expansion of the occupant over the course of time, the breeks hung loosely. Whenever the juvenile broke into a brisk trot, the heavy breeks sagged up and down on the elastic suspenders.

These suspenders or braces were adjustable by means of metal clasps. Tension could be increased or decreased depending on how heavy the breeks became which, in turn, depended on how much water they soaked up.

Fitted out in breeks, the juvenile cut a considerable dash. He looked not unlike a veteran drummer boy from the Great War or a dwarf Mountie doing undercover work among criminal midgets. Thus, briggs.

More wool was then applied in the shape of a sweater which went over the flannel chest protector, the woolen drawers, the shirt and the braces. Whilst other wool garments tended to stretch in time, sweaters, for some reason, always shrunk.

Our attention is now directed to the juvenile foot. You may recall that it is encased in the long stocking, the knee stocking and the vamp. A pair of logans – a unique piece of footwear with a rubber foot and leather uppers with rows of eyes, hooks and yards of leather laces – completed the picture.

Alas, it was never the author's privilege to own a pair of logans, the most dashing sort of footwear next to the long rubber. He had to make do with the knee rubber or gum boot as it is called by some ... the same worn by the present Sovereign and family when mucking about Balmoral on weekends.

Into each boot went a felt, which is a hunk of material, purple in color, constructed from the fur of the Australian rabbit and shaped like the sole of a foot. Felts insulated further and absorbed moisture. They were dried behind the stove at night.

In the days before parkas were popularized, the upper part of the torso was topped off by either an old suit jacket, handed down by some older relative, or a windbreaker.

Hand protection came in the form of mitts. If double-knit, one pair sufficed; if single, two pairs were worn. There are few things more unhandy than a new pair of mitts. The palms come to a point about six inches beyond the finger tips – making a good purchase on a snowball impossible.

However, in about a month of wear a strange substantiation takes place in which the new mitt perfectly assumes the shape of the hand. Old mitts smell nice. They get turpentine on them and when drying under the kitchen stove release the scent of balsam fir so that there is no need of synthetic pine in a spray can.

So much for mitts. We are ready for the headgear. There is only one piece of goods equal to topping the fully dressed juvenile in proper fashion and that is the Aviator Cap, q.v., Vol. VI, p. 842.

This dashing leather helmet is designed after the self-same cap worn by Lindbergh on his heroic solo crossing of the Atlantic Ocean. In fact, all outharbor juvenile winter wear was on an heroic model – from the Royal Northwest breeks, to the Scandinavian forester logans to the Lindbergh headpiece, he cut no mean figure.

With the addition of a flannel scarf to cinch any cracks in these cold-weather armaments through which drifts might enter, the outharbor juvenile's winter regalia was complete.

He was set to face the raging blizzards and crackling frost and thy cloak of shimmering white spread at winter's stern command and all that stuff. Blizzards! Lord save us, with the simple addition of an oxygen bottle he was ready for leisurely strolls upon the surface of the moon.

Out from daylight to dark and the worse it came the better, with only two nostrils and one eye sticking out and the drifts building up as high as the houses and the wind 90 knots an hour and it getting darker and colder and the snow still coming down and in the white whirl you can't see a double-knit mitt in front of your face. What? We worry?

Central heating in the houses and schools and heated school buses have come along. But the juvenile, outharbor and in, must still wait out at least a few minutes at the bus stops and that in mini-skirts or grey flannel trousers.

Either the winters are getting milder or the breed is getting still hardier. RG

You Rain Knee Yum

Great New Industries

You Rain Knee Yum. Uranium. That's a you and an are and an aye and an enn and an eye and a you and an emm. Uranium. A mineral. An important mineral. A very important mineral. Uranium.

Well, somebody has got to put it in baby talk for you. Joey is over in Japan and Neary is more concerned with the recent fire at the home for wayward girls. So who else is left to put uranium into simple words?

Uranium has been discovered. You Rain Knee Yum has been discovered in Newfoundland. Uranium has been discovered under the front porch of the old Alex Hickman homestead down on the Burin Peninsula. Isn't that a coincidence?

All sorts of minerals have been discovered. And as luck should have it they have been discovered in the districts of those two former cabinet ministers turned dirty Tories, Hickman and Earle.

It is a sign from Higher Up. Is there any doubt now as to whose side the Heavens are on? When there's a sinner to be taught a lesson at the polls and defeated for the public good, even nature takes sides.

The gentle rains fall from above, floods occur and sweep over the land in the appropriate places, and lo and behold all sorts of minerals are revealed sticking out of the ground. Great announcements are made and the mayors of all the towns rejoice and are exceeding glad.

We see the hand of a greater power in all this. Uranium discovered in appropriate districts. A clear sign that the two sinners should be cast out and the true party elected again.

And we await the announcement that gold has been discovered in Port au Port. It'll take a bit more than silica to get Callahan in again by the skin of his teeth.

Also in the lucky district of Burin, we had news this week of a great upsurge in shipbuilding. The Swiss navy put in an order for a whole new fleet or something. So the mayor of Marystown rejoiced and was exceeding glad for the second time in a fortnight.

At first we heard mention of 10 vessels to be built, then six, then four and then two. It is very confusing. Is this a reversal of the familiar chant? What are we going to hear now … not $10 million, not $6 million, not $4 million, but $2 million?

Anyway, if we were confused by announcements of a great boom in boatbuilding at Marystown, it is nothing compared to the tizzy Mr. Neary has got himself into over wayward girls.

During a fire at the home, some iron-barred cells were found down in the basement and Mr. Neary has been just about going frantic ever since trying to convince everyone they are imagining things.

Poor old Stevie baby. You'd think he'd be able to cover up a stink better than that. I fear he's going to get a good lash across the quarters when Joey gets back from Japan.

All this political nonsense is interesting but the big story of the week appeared on the sports pages of the People's Paper yesterday and perhaps some people missed it.

It seems that a Mr. Raymond recently shot a giant rabbit down on the southern shore in the vicinity of Cluney's Pond. We are told that it weighed nearly 13 pounds and had four broken snares around its neck.

"Biologists were unable to obtain the carcass for closer examination," and said the news item, "because Mr. Raymond wanted to eat it."

There is some talk that the giant rabbit might have been a tame one escaped from somewhere and some of the professors at the university thought from a description of it that it had the makings of a Belgian Hare.

Belgian Hare or no Belgian Hare, it's an alarming piece of news. The thoughts of giant rabbits crashing around through the underbrush, snapping wire snares like thread and thump, thump, thumping under the light of a full moon toward some deserted farmhouse where the unsuspecting occupants lie sleeping is a disturbing one.

We have giant squids and now giant rabbits. If they grow to be as big in comparison, then kangaroos will look small alongside of them. Imagine a giant rabbit big enough to leap Cluney's Pond in a single bound!

I should imagine that by now rabbits are tired of being shot, throttled, wracked up by beagles, hit on the head and skinned to wrap the baby bunting in. After getting their lumps for so long they're going to be out looking for blood now that they've got the heft.

So be wary when you're out in the woods in a few weeks' time cutting one of Mr. Shaheen's trees for Christmas. There's been no word from Shaheen on it so far but we may suppose that he'll allow us to go out into his woods and cut one of his smaller trees. After all, it is the blessed season.

Because, as we have been told, every single tree on the island is precious on account of Mr. Shaheen's great new paper mill at Come By Chance. He has been given charge of all available trees. If you have a lilac bush in the front yard it may not be expropriated but otherwise ...

So when the tree is lit up and decorated and all the presents under it, let us look admiringly and reverently toward it and say to ourselves: "Thank you, dear Mr. Shaheen, for allowing us one of your little trees for Christmas."

Take it easy over the weekend ... and watch out for those giant rabbits. ▬

Chucking them in the clink
or the funny farm

December 3, 1970   *Culture and History*

He slouches at a corner table of the restaurant with his face about a foot above the soup bowl. The spoon shakes as he slops half of it down his collar and over the table top.

Loud wheezes, grunts and sputters come from him. He gives up the effort to eat and slowly pitches forward, his face hitting the table with a crack. He lies there bubbling slightly at the nostrils.

After a few minutes he revives with a snort and takes another stab at the soup with the spoon wobbling one way and his head another. Then he vomits feebly into the soup bowl and gets busy with the wobbling spoon again.

Some other customers in the restaurant turn a faint green around the gills and try to look away. But they keep glancing toward him with a sort of fascinated repulsion. The drunken slob in the corner doesn't do their appetites much good.

Drunks, bums, and offensive cretins and crackpots seem to be an increasing decoration in St. John's restaurants, taverns, public places and on the streets.

Not only in the dives but in the ordinary, middle-class places and in the pretentious posh nosheries and tanking stations too. Some measure of tolerance is admirable but there are limits.

You get some woozy types in restaurants at a late hour having a snack and trying to sober up. They're not causing a disturbance, their behavior is not that repulsive and it could be your case now and then, too, chum, unless you're some sort of teetotaling fanatic.

And you get the harmless mental defectives who just sit there eating and drinking and babbling away to themselves, hurting nobody. Pay no attention and eat your turkey sandwich.

Because the key word is "behavior" and not "appearance." What difference does it make whether a person shaves the top of his head or lets his tresses grow to his navel? Or whether he sashays about in the patented uniform of a young mod executive or the standardized suede-fringed trappings of a hippie?

It's no skin off your nose, is it? You're no raving beauty yourself and I dare say a visiting Martian would go into just as many kinks laughing at the way you look as he would at the people you consider weird-looking.

And if there's any scooping up to be done, the first to be scooped up and carted off should be those who squawk about clearing the streets of all the harmless mutations, oddities, novelties, eccentrics and half-naturals among us. Such squawkers are the most dangerous animals in the zoo.

There's a difference between appearance and behavior. Defining "acceptable behavior" is a tricky business and a topic guaranteed to keep both amateur and professional philosophers going strong at every coffee klatch and classroom from hell to hackney.

Everyone to his own opinion. The poor alcoholic slob who turned the guts of everyone else in the restaurant should be taken away. If that rat hole under the courthouse is the only place we have to put such people, then he should be put there to lie in his own vomit ... and to lie heavy on your conscience and mine.

If the "bum's rush" is the only answer civilization has come up with so far to such cases then the bum's rush it must be. Those in charge of public eating and/or drinking houses sometimes show too little concern for the majority of their customers.

They are too tolerant of the increasing number of offensive creeps who infest their establishments and too inconsiderate of the other 95 per cent of their patrons.

It is not a matter of one privileged lot of people having to be shielded from the nasty behavior of a few "poor unfortunates and cripples." Nonsense. That's the same as saying only the "better classes" eat in restaurants and snack bars and that meals out are a luxury.

Under the present set-up they are a necessity to persons of all classes. Yet, too often, you are tormented and abused by a variety of slobs and creeps. They're allowed to stagger around among the tables and the next thing you know you get a gust of rum breath and spray of spittle in the face.

Whether under the influence of booze or some more exotic top-popper or else sick in the head without such aids, they stumble about bullying women and children and old people.

More often than not they're given a warning by those in charge but are allowed to cavort about long after they've worn out their welcome. Establishments which allow these creeps to annoy their customers for even five minutes are no better than they ought to be.

If they don't feel equal to showing them the door, they should yank a nearby cop off parking-ticket duty. The clink or the funny farm is the only, if not the proper, place for them.

Now, do we hear certain little choked and incredulous gasps in the background? I'm surprised if we don't. Because the sacred precepts of tolerance, and social-consciousness and humanitarianism are as fashionable today as striped flares and midi-dresses.

At least, prattle about them is. But there's a vast difference between chew and do. OK, so your tender sensibilities are outraged when somebody actually objects to being sprayed with booze-flavored saliva or abused by somebody sick in the head.

Good for you. But be careful you don't take it to absurd extremes. Consider a bit before you challenge those who object to roll up their sleeves and get out there with the Salvation Army social workers lifting up the fallen. Or government social workers for that matter.

In this complicated (substitute "screwed up" if it suits you) society, it isn't possible. At least not for the great majority of people. They work eight hours or more a day and then they go home and patch a hole in the roof or shuttle the youngsters home from school or scrape out the basement.

Then, in the few hours before they shut their eyes for the day, they try to prop up their own mental and physical balance by perhaps reading a book or slouching in front of the TV.

For one reason or another an eight-hour day plus homework and problems now uses up as much energy as a person can muster. But, under the set-up, he has indirectly done his bit for society in general ... in case you're forgetting that little item called taxes.

In theory at least, one-third of the ordinary person's work and energy has been for society. One-third of his income has been taken to lift up the fallen, help the unfortunate and to pay the salaries of social workers and civil servants and cabinet ministers.

And if you think that all he pays is income tax, think again. List up all the taxes and tariffs, direct and hidden and the licences and fees and contributions and you'll get one-third or more.

This is going to be a rough winter. There will be 165,000 jobless this February in Ontario. And down here we'll see more and more creeps on booze or off their rockers and made that way by boredom and frustration. Some will annoy you in public places and others will stamp peoples' faces into the pavement outside Saturday night dance halls.

Chucking them in the clink or the funny farm is more of a desperate reaction than a solution. What's the real answer to the real problem? Christ? Pot? Price wars? Barbie dolls? The War Measures Act?

You tell me. ▇

Newsmen have been off on short vacations to Panama

December 16, 1970 *News and Propaganda*

Abroad thoughts from home. Oh, to be in St. George's, Grenada, B.W.I., now that December's here. Stuff this for a lark.

Even the lesser-breasted tom tits have sense enough to hightail it for a decent climate for the winter months. Only such loons as people are foolish enough to hang around and slog through it.

Lord, it's bleak! And such a state as I'm in today. Absolutely browned off. And it struck me, after careful consideration, that one of the reasons is that I am subconsciously jealous of some other members of the local press corps who have been down in Panama the last few days enjoying 80-degree weather.

Oh, yes. There's not been much mention of it in the press. I don't know why. Surely, this little item would be of some small interest to readers, listeners and viewers. It at least deserves a few seconds or a few paragraphs alongside such other articles as "Man's body found, police investigate," or "Presentation made to skipper of *Christmas Seal.*"

But for some curious reason this newsy and colorful, albeit minor, item has not had much play in the local press. Well, I bet you didn't know before now that certain selected local newsmen have been off on short vacations to Panama. Did you?

That's the place where the canal is. It's warm there now, even warmer than our summers and there are palm trees and swimming pools and the hot sun and magnificent hotel bars. Eat your heart out!

Two flights, in fact, have lifted lucky local news people from chilly Newfoundland to cosy Panama. About two weeks ago one flight winged its way toward the sunny south bearing some of our comrades-in-arms.

People went from VOCM, CJON and the *Daily News*. I don't know if the CBC was represented. And another flight left last week carrying still more of the local news people, including a representative from the People's Paper.

Winging their way to the glorious tropics for a few days at a luxury resort. Oh, boy! Lucky dogs. If you wanted to take your wife and follow in their footsteps, airfare to Panama would cost you $350 each. Or $700 for transportation alone.

And rooms in these posh tropical hotels at this time of year can easily run to $30 or $40 a day. A DAY! And that doesn't include those fancy meals and those coolin' drinks sipped at leisure under everlasting blue skies.

It is better to be born lucky than rich, I say. Because none of this is costing the local news lads a red copper. No sir. Some big-hearted person is treating them to the trip and it is all as free as the air. It is nothing less than a dream come true.

And what fairy godmother has taken pity on these poor toilers of the newsdesks of St. John's, Newfoundland? What generous benefactor has snatched those winter-weary, flu-stricken, fishbelly-white news editors and managers away from the slush and frost and damp to a tropical paradise?

Need you ask? Mr. John Christopher Doyle, friend to Newfoundland and benefactor of the Happy Province, that's who. There now, my son. Doesn't that restore your faith in human nature?

And the best part of it is that there are absolutely no strings attached. No sir! Not one. Oh, there may be some crabby, cynical persons who'll say Mr. Doyle will be looking for favors in return for this splendid treat.

But such sour-gobs are no better than they ought to be. Shame on their dirty minds. That's the beauty of the whole deal. Mr. Doyle's sort of trip is a common one. When Air Canada opens a new service to Copenhagen or Moscow, it invites the press along on the first run.

When the president of Ford or General Motors of Canada happens to visit St. John's they throw cocktail parties for the press just to be sociable. When the government cuts another ribbon, it lays on a reception for guests, including the press.

What Mr. Doyle is doing is opening a new wing on his hotel in Panama. They say it costs about $25 million but I don't know if the Newfoundland government has guaranteed the loan or not. Anyway, Mr. Doyle did the perfectly normal thing for the opening.

He rounded up travel agents, travel writers and members of the general press from Newfoundland (and some other parts of Canada, too) and trucked them off to Panama to enjoy a few days absolutely free at his expense.

As I say, there are absolutely no strings attached. If you don't believe it you have only to keep your eyes and ears open. The proof of the pudding is in the eating.

Local newsmen who were included in the first contingent to sunny Panama returned more than a week ago. Now, I ask you: Have you seen any references about what a swell place Panama is for a winter holiday sneaked in among the news stories? No, sir, you have not.

You haven't heard, have you, the chap who gives out the weather forecast say there'll be high winds and blowing snow and slob ice off White Bay tomorrow but that in delightful Panama you could be enjoying another day in the 80s.

So there you are. Here's the first lot of local newsmen back from their splendid free trip courtesy of Mr. Doyle and they're not swayed one bit by it. They're still objective, unbiased and all these things which we hold precious … or, as the French say, "precieux."

While they may have reclined around Mr. Doyle's big turquoise swimming pool with the chrome ladders and diving boards and may have found him to be a warm and wonderful human being, he's not going to get any free publicity for his Panama hotel off them. No siree.

Still, it is a wonder to me that there hasn't been some little mention of these colorful events in the local press. Perhaps the lads are bashful when it comes to making news, however slight, themselves.

They may be bashful but I'm downright jealous. Furthermore, the furnace has been giving trouble. I spent two hours helping get a vehicle out of a ditch and I heard still another 19-year-old Newfoundlander plans to take off across the Gulf like a dose of salts the first chance he gets.

I don't know how to explain it. Sammy's trick knee must be giving him trouble again. Either that or the goalie is off his oats. There's something amiss when substantial but far lesser Bays can best that paragon among … etc., etc., etc.

Then I said to myself, never you mind, self, because in the end that far greater Bay will win if there is still an honest referee left in the world. And one of these days Mr. Doyle or Mr. Smallwood will take you along to some place warm, some place nice.

By golly, don't know but I'd stay down there if I got such a trip. I like it here but I'm sure I could learn to love Montego Bay. They're mostly black persons down in these places but I'm sure I could fit in after a time.

These days, black is white and white is black. No sweat. It is simply a matter of learning to adjust, don't you think? RG

Social Consciousness Season closes

Let me put you in the picture. Last fall the *Atlantic Advocate*, a magazine put out in New Brunswick, carried an article on centralization in Newfoundland.

It was nothing more than an embroidered and puffed out version of an article which appeared in the *Newfoundland Bull–etin* two years ago. This is not surprising since it was written by a former Liberal "information officer" who used a false name.

When Farley Mowat saw it, he whipped off a letter to the *Advocate*, saying they should have someone else write an article giving the other side of it. He mentioned my name along with several others.

Now, when you reach the stage that the mere sight of a typewriter gives you the dry heaves (I'm trying to get them to shift me over to the photography department), you don't want to waste a word if you can help it.

So, to cripple two birds with one stone, I'm writing my letter to the *Atlantic Advocate* here because it will save further clouting at those cursed keys:

Dear Sirs:

It was nice of Farley Mowat to try and sic me against that foul calumny "Outporters go Import," which appeared in your September issue. However, I'm surprised that Farley, who was domiciled upon our poor but proud shores for six years, overlooked an important fact.

That is that in Newfoundland, the Social Consciousness Season closes down for the winter October 31, and doesn't reopen for business until about the middle of June the following year.

By the way, the annual reopening of the Social Consciousness Season in Newfoundland is a quaint and colorful affair. The lieutenant governor fires off the opening gun, and during the afternoon festivities, there's a baby burning. An infant which has shown signs of incipient anti-Smallwoodism or some other congenital defect is roasted alive over a slow fire of damp seaweed.

But anyone who has lived through a Newfoundland winter will see the sense of a closed season. When winter descends we have all we can do to ward off pleurisy and grippe, heat our sod-roofed shanties and reproduce. This takes just about all our energy.

Up in your area, Social Consciousness is fashionable the year round, I believe. This is probably because you have cosier underwear and your spirits are not the sorry watered-down stuff that passes for honest liquor at the bond stores here.

In fact, we note such a bubbling over of Social Consciousness in the Maritimes of late that new and Relevant Journals have had to be set up to take in the slack. Such papers as the Mysterious East and the Fourth Estate, which fairly reek of Social Consciousness, are put out by Socially Conscious writers whose uniform is the bell-bottomed jeans and the granny glasses.

Despite the great effort it takes to be Socially Conscious in Newfoundland during the off-season, I will attempt to give you a short sketch of "centralization."

Some 10 years ago, the government turned its attention to the thousands of happy peasants living in isolated hamlets around our shores. Before that, the government's only notice of them was in keeping incest and moonshining within reasonable limits.

Then the provincial government sold Ottawa on the idea of "centralization" and the federal money received for it was slung around to kick up enough excitement and create enough of an illusion of progress to help carry Smallwood through several elections. The happy peasants were rounded up and shipped by barges to holding pens called "growth centers."

The situation was tailor-made for the Socially Conscious writer – what with these simple but happy souls ripped away from their cozy seaside cots and the quaint ways of their fathers and herded into "growth centers" alias welfare ghettos.

Mowat, in his never-ceasing quest for downtrodden minorities to champion, sprang to it like a shot. On the local scene some others, including myself, took it up on the airwaves and in the press.

We took to this Socially Conscious issue like ducks to water. Here we have on the one hand the Accursed Downtreaders of the Toiling Masses and on the other the Socially Conscious and Relevant Journalists and Writers.

The cut and thrust of it all has been downright exhilarating. Mowat discharged an illustrated book. The government took $150,000 of public funds to publish a monthly journal telling what a successful and high-souled thing centralization is. I have been cranking out suitably indignant articles in the St. John's *Telegram*.

The government's latest volley came in September when you poor innocents were cornered into printing "Robert Johnson's" piece on that New Jerusalem, otherwise known as the Arnold's Cove growth center.

I was just in time for a parting shot before the Social Consciousness Season closed for the year. This took the form of another feature article on centralization in the St. John's *Telegram*.

If I do say so myself, it was nothing less than a magnificent effort which soared toward the Gothic grotesque and invoked the spirits of dead folk-heroes to wreak post-mortem vengeance on Centralizers, those Accursed Downtreaders of the Toiling Masses.

But, as I say, the season is now closed and your request for a further riposte came too late. The Newfoundland winter has set in. You may get in touch with me again in the late spring. Or, alternatively, you might be able to recruit a Socially Conscious journalist from the Fourth Estate and send him down in the off-season. But for the sake of Christian charity, rig the poor devil out in insulated flare pants and let him know what he's up against.

You may ask, in your rather attractive mainland naiveté, what the situation of the happy peasantry is while the shot and shell of the two forces burst over their heads and the battle rages about them.

Well, like Gordon Sinclair during the present supermarket discount war, they're sticking around and enjoying all this. They haven't lived in Newfoundland for 400 years for nothing. They've learned to take their amusements in whatever form the good Lord sees fit to send them.

So this great upsurge in Social Consciousness has helped them stave off the boredom and listlessness engendered by welfare and seasonal unemployment. During the past few years, the rocks have been swarming with Socially Conscious writers, newspaper reporters, sociology students, TV filmers and moviemakers who know a Relevant topic when they see one.

Mowat himself is presently making a movie on the subject. They're quite used to the camera and the tape recorder by now and I wouldn't be surprised if they stick Farley for ACTRA union rates.

The last time I was out there working on that aforementioned grand finalé for the season, one horny-handed photogenic centralized toiler of the deep produced his own makeup kit and automatically put forward his best profile for the photographer.

If you like, you may get in touch with me again when the season opens in mid-June and I'll be rarin' to go. Meanwhile, I leave you with that quaint old Newfoundland saying, the social relevancy of which should not escape you: "Long may your big jib draw." ▪

There's Clark Kent and he really is Superman!

December 30, 1970   *News and Propaganda*

As I entered the Duckworth Street door of the People's Paper yesternoon, I was met in the foyer by a little old lady who said she was looking for the newsroom to see about putting in a snap of her anniversary.

"Allow me, madam," I said, proffering my arm, "the pleasure of accompanying you to the lift which will take us directly to the third floor and that nerve center of communications or Intelligence Central as we call it."

We reached the newsroom in a thrice and I summoned to the counter our Mr. Stratton, chief of communications clerks, to attend to the dear soul's wants.

Firmly but politely, as is his wont, he explained to her that engagements, marriages, birth, and deaths are the exclusive province of the advertising department on the first floor.

"Ah, I have been found out," she said to me. "Truth to tell that was but a subterfuge by which I hoped to see the newsroom of the People's Paper. I hope you don't mind and will humor an old woman's whim. After reading the report of the Senate Commission on the News Media and that column on it by Dennis Braithwaite in your paper I just had to see for myself."

"I shall be more than pleased, madam," I said, smiling graciously, "to escort you on a tour of our 'boneyard of broken dreams', as the Senate report so aptly puts it."

"How exciting," she cried, adjusting her bonnet. "Is it really true that 'squalor and journalism traditionally go together' or, as Mr. Braithwaite says, that 'within six months any city room staff can reimpose total squalor on the classiest new premises'?"

"See for yourself, ma'm," I said. "You may not believe it but these premises were originally modeled after the grand ballroom on the *Queen Mary*. For all that, the staff here seem to be rarities among newsmen.

"In fact, they're all regular little Old Dutch Cleansers and fastidious and tidy to a fault. For instance, you see here our Mr. Butler of Promotions wearing white gloves so as not to get fingerprints all over his typewriter.

"And our Mr. Finn, Chief Desker, over there, is up looking for dust specks on the piano-top finish of the news desk. I am afraid it has been left almost solely to myself to maintain the grand old traditions of squalor in the newsroom. I do my best but sometimes it seems to be a losing battle.

"It is correct, as Braithwaite points out, that the newsroom gets the short end of the stick. Never a new typewriter but the castoffs from circulation and advertising. I had that present machine for three weeks with the upper case 'A' making no impression at all. Then I discovered that the previous owner had left a used teabag tangled up in the works.

"But yet," I continued, hand to forehead, "while they may have Muzak, carpet, cold water fountain and a glamorous view of the façade of Bailey's Room and Board down there in advertising, we have something more than all that.

"We have spirit and a certain Bohemian artistic excitement. As the Senate discovered, we are 'uncomfortable in surroundings of normal decent housekeeping' and, as Braithwaite points out, we are all 'vagabonds and the most of us are shiftless and even the best of us are lazy'.

"Our Mrs. Gushue of the Socio-Economic Beat, for example. And our Mr. Stratton Sr., brother to the chief of communications clerks, is another case in point, he being attached to Court, Police and Civil Disasters.

"Were we but to engage Mr. Stratton in conversation he would doubtless echo Braithwaite to the effect that we are bored 'because we have been everywhere, seen everything and done everything'. He's seen life in all its myriad aspects. He's jaded and world-weary like the rest of us."

"After you've covered the Monday morning drunk and disorderlies at magistrate's court, looked into septic tank pollution at Manuels and burned the candle at both ends at the Press Club, is there really anything else to look forward to?

"May I quote again from Braithwaite, madam: 'A good newspaperman is first of all curious and second of all burns with a need to tell someone what he has discovered – about crooked politicians, terror and man's inhumanity to man'.

"Our Mr. Collins, associate editor and special correspondent on Homes for Wayward Girls, is a case in point. He is clearly burning at this present moment. You may think his customary lunch of sardine sandwiches and chocolate milkshakes are to blame. But no. He is burning to tell someone what he has discovered about terror and man's inhumanity to man and is knocking out another piece on the misuse of crosswalks."

"It's a delicate matter, I know," said the little old lady, "but what's this in the Senate Commission's Report about journalists earning less money than schoolteachers and most skilled tradesmen?"

"My dear woman," I said, "were you to ask our Mr. Ennis, Assistant Manager and Travel Editor, about it, he would tell you that the vows of chastity and poverty we take upon entering the profession are more than worth it.

"He would doubtless exclaim along with Braithwaite that 'a newspaperman experiences more in an average week and has more fun than a schoolteacher or welder is going to have in his whole life' and that, no, you can't have another lump of coal for the fire."

As we continued our tour, I again quoted Braithwaite to the effect that we all have a love of writing, a respect for English and our only hope is to some day construct the perfect paragraph, the unimprovable sentence.

"This is no better exemplified than in the person of our Mr. Connors, assistant to the Chief of Promotions, or Copy Butcher Connors, as he is good-naturedly named by reporters. His is a never-ending search for the unimprovable sentence which in his case many would say is 99 years at hard labor."

The little old lady expressed great interest as we continued our turn around the graveyard of broken dreams. I told her that even our Mr. Spurrell, Chief Liaison for Newsroom Composing, dreams of "following after Hemingway or Ring Lardner or Mark Twain or Harold Horwood or others like them who have made good their escape from squalor to belles-lettres."

"Our Mr. Benson here, Marine Disasters and Protocol Correspondent, will readily support Braithwaite's contention that 'newspapermen burn out early and die young'. Ah, yes, a short life but a merry one down here at the People's Paper."

Just then the little old lady spied a newsman standing on a window ledge taking off his shirt. "Oh, my goodness," she cried, "there's Clark Kent and he really is Superman!"

I hated to destroy the dear's illusions so I thought it better not to tell her it was really our Mr. Carter, Chief of Intelligence and Counter Espionage, gesturing to a cop below in the street who was giving him his second parking ticket inside of an hour.

Or that the big red 'S' on the front of Mr. Carter's underdrawers can be accounted for by the fact that he does most of his shopping at the Salvation Army's Goodwill Stores.

Still he, like us all, would not – to again quote the incisive Braithwaite – exchange any of this "for a full professorship." Truly, we must indeed "burn out early" … and that from the top down. ▉

Appendix – Biographies

Abbott, Beaton J. (1903-1992) b Musgrave Harbour. Educator, magistrate, politician. MHA (L-Gander) 1956-66; (L & Independent L-Bonavista North) 1966-71. Cabinet positions: Public Welfare 1956-57, 1959-67; Municipal Affairs and Supply 1957-59; Municipal Affairs and Housing 1967-68. In 1969 Abbott supported Liberal leadership candidate J.C. Crosbie. He later sat as an Independent Liberal in the House of Assembly until his retirement from politics in 1971.

Barbour, Ross (1901-1993) b Newtown. Businessman, politician. MHA (L-Bonavista South) 1959-72. He ran as a PC in Bonavista South in 1956, but won the seat as a Liberal in 1959.

Browne, William J. (1897-1989) b St. John's. Magistrate, politician, author. MP (PC-St. John's West) 1949-53, 1957-62. MHA (Conservative-St. John's West) 1924-28; (PC-St. John's West) 1954-57; (PC-St. John's East Extern) 1962-66. Browne served as a magistrate after Commission of Government wasvestablished. He won a federal seat in 1949 following confederation with Canada, but was defeated in 1953. Browne won a provincial seat in 1954, but returned to federal politics in 1957 and served as Solicitor General. Browne was defeated in the 1962 federal election, but later that year he again won a provincial seat. He retired prior to the 1966 general election.

Burgess, Tom (1933-) b Ireland. Trade unionist, politician. MHA (L-Labrador West) 1966-69, 1971-72; (New Labrador Party-Labrador West) 1969-71. Burgess moved to Labrador West in 1959 and became president of the United Steelworkers of America local. He was elected as a Liberal in 1966, but crossed the floor of the House of Assembly in 1969 to establish the New Labrador Party. Burgess held the balance of power following the 1971 election, which had resulted in a virtual tie between the Liberals and the PCs. He re-joined the Liberals and made an unsuccessful bid for leadership of the party. Burgess was defeated in the 1972 general election.

Callahan, William R. (1931-) b St. John's. Journalist, politician, author. MHA (L-Port au Port) 1966-71. Cabinet position: Mines, Agriculture and Resources 1968-71. Callahan was appointed managing editor of *The Western Star* in Corner Brook following the resignation of Ed Finn over the newspaper's stand against a strike by the International Woodworkers of America in 1959. Callahan was elected to the House of Assembly in 1966 and was defeated in 1971. He returned to journalism, first as publisher of the *Daily News*, then in editorial positions with the Roman Catholic *Monitor* and *The Evening Telegram*.

Canning, Patrick J. (1915-1991) b Merasheen. Teacher, businessman, politician. MHA (L-Placentia West) 1949-72; (L-Burin-Placentia West) 1975-79.

Carter, John A. (1933-   ) b St. John's. Farmer, politician. MHA (PC-St. John's North) 1971-89. Cabinet position: Education 1972. Carter produced savory at Mount Scio Farms in St. John's. He ran unsuccessfully for leadership of the PCs in 1970, and served briefly in the Moores cabinet.

Carter, Walter C. (1929-2002) b Greenspond. Businessman, politician, author. MP (PC-St. John's West) 1972-75. MHA (L-White Bay North) 1962-66; (PC-St. Mary's-the-Capes) 1975-79; (L-Twillingate) 1985-96. St. John's City Council 1961-68. Cabinet positions (provincial): Fisheries 1975-80, 1989-94. A political gadfly, Carter switched political parties and served as fisheries minister under both PC and Liberal administrations. He began his political career in St. John's where he sat on city council from 1961 to 1968. Concurrently, he held a seat in the House of Assembly as a Liberal 1962-66. He subsequently joined the PCs and in 1968 was elected as an MP by defeating Richard Cashin (L-St. John's West). He ran unsuccessfully for leadership of the provincial PCs in 1970. In 1975 he resigned to re-enter provincial politics and was appointed minister of fisheries by premiers Moores and Peckford. Carter attempted a return to federal politics, running unsuccessfully as a PC against Roger Simmons (L-Burin-St. George's). By 1984 he had re-joined the federal Liberals but failed to defeat John Crosbie (PC-St. John's West). He once again turned to provincial politics and won a seat as a Liberal in 1985. He was appointed minister of fisheries by Premier Wells in 1989. After leaving the House of Assembly, he ran unsuccessfully for mayor of St. John's in 1997.

Cashin, Richard J. (1937-   ) b St. John's. Politician, lawyer, trade unionist. MP (L-St. John's East) 1962-68. After his defeat in 1968 Cashin and Father Desmond McGrath began organizing a union for fisheries workers. From 1971 to 1994 Cashin served as president of the Newfoundland Fish, Food and Allied Workers Union.

Chalker, James R. (1912-2003) b St. John's. Businessman, politician. MHA (L-Harbour Grace)1949-56; (L-St. Barbe) 1956-62; (L-St. Barbe North) 1962-72. Cabinet positions: Public Health 1949-52; Education 1952-56; Economic Development 1956-57; Public Works 1957-71; Provincial Affairs 1971-72. Chalker was the only minister to serve continuously in cabinet throughout J.R. Smallwood's years as premier.

Clarke, George W. (1910-2000) b Carbonear. Educator, magistrate, politician. MHA (L-Carbonear-Harbour Grace) 1956-62; (L-Carbonear) 1962-71. Speaker 1963-71.

Crosbie, John C. (1931-) b St. John's. Lawyer, politician, lieutenant governor. MP (PC-St. John's West) 1967-93. MHA (L-St. John's West) 1966-69; (Independent L & L Reform) 1969-71; (PC) 1971-76. Municipal councilor St. John's 1965-66. Cabinet positions (provincial): Municipal Affairs and Housing 1966-67; Health 1967-68; Finance 1972-74; Economic Development 1972-74; Fisheries 1974-75; Intergovernmental Affairs 1974-76; Mines and Energy 1975-76. Cabinet positions (federal): Finance 1979-80; Justice 1984-86; Transport 1986-88; International Trade 1988-91; Atlantic Canada Opportunities Agency 1991-93; Fisheries 1991-93. Crosbie resigned from cabinet in 1968 over a disagreement with Smallwood over government loan guarantees for an oil refinery at Come By Chance. After losing his campaign for leadership of the Liberal Party to J.R. Smallwood in 1970, he became an Opposition member in the House of Assembly. Crosbie joined the PC Party in 1971 and served in the Moores cabinet from 1972 to 1976. Crosbie won a federal by-election in 1976 and became a high profile cabinet minister in the governments of Joseph Clark and Brian Mulroney. He was appointed Lieutenant Governor of Newfoundland and Labrador in 2008.

Curtis, Leslie R. (1895-1980) b Twillingate. Lawyer, politician. MHA (L-Twillingate) 1949-71. Cabinet positions: Justice and Attorney General 1949-66, 1969-71; President Executive Council 1966-71.

Davis, Jack (1916-1991) b British Columbia. Politician. MP (L-Coast-Capliano) 1962-74. Cabinet positions: Fisheries 1968-69; Forestry 1969-71; Environment 1971-74.

Dawe, Eric N. (1921-) b Bay Roberts. Businessman, politician. MHA (L-Port de Grave) 1962-71; (L Reform-Port de Grave) 1975-79. Mayor Bay Roberts 1956-64. Cabinet position: Municipal Affairs and Housing 1969-71. After being elected as an MHA, Dawe continued to serve as mayor of Bay Roberts for two years, and was later promoted to cabinet while acting as president of the Newfoundland Federation of Mayors and Municipalities in 1969-70. Dawe returned to his family's business, Avalon Coal and Salt Ltd., in Bay Roberts after leaving politics.

Diefenbaker, John G. (1895-1979) b Saskatchewan. Prime Minister of Canada 1957-63. Leader of PC Party 1956-67.

Doyle, John C. (1915-2000) b United States. Businessman. Established Canadian Javelin Ltd., a coal and steel company, and became an important financier for Premier Smallwood's industrialization programs. Javelin acquired timber and mineral rights in Labrador, and led the consortium that developed Wabush Mines. Although Doyle was indicted for securities violations in the US in 1963, Smallwood asked him to develop a "third mill" in Labrador. Originally to be located on Lake Melville, the Labrador Linerboard mill site was moved to Stephenville by the time construction began in 1971. In 1974 Doyle fled Canada after being charged with fraud in connection with the mill. He died in exile at his home in Panama. The Stephenville mill was acquired by the provincial government, and sold to Abitibi Price which converted it to newsprint production. The mill was closed in 2005 and the facilities dismantled.

Earle, H.R.Valence (Val) (1911-1996) b Fogo. Businessman, politician. MHA (L-Fortune) 1962-69; (PC-Fortune) 1969-71; (PC-Fortune Bay) 1972-75. Cabinet positions: Education 1964-67; Public Welfare 1967-68; Finance 1968-69, 1974-75; Economic Development 1972; Public Works and Services 1972-74; Municipal Affairs and Housing 1973-74. Earle resigned from cabinet in 1969 to support T. Alex Hickman for leadership of the Liberal party. In 1970 he crossed the floor of the House of Assembly to sit as a PC member. Earle was defeated in the 1971 general election, but returned to the House in 1972 and served in the Moores cabinet. He was again defeated in 1975.

Farrell, Mary L. (1942-) b St. John's. Singer, actress. In 1994 Farrell won the titles of Miss Newfoundland and Miss Canada, and was runner-up in the Miss World competition. The publicity launched her singing and acting career, and she performed in several Broadway musicals.

Frecker, George A. (1905-1979) b St. Pierre. Educator, civil servant, politician. MHA (L-Placentia East) 1959-71. Cabinet positions: Education 1959-64; Provincial Affairs 1970-71. Frecker left politics in 1971 to become chancellor of Memorial University.

Gardiner, Peter J. (1929-1978) b England. Accountant, businessman, trade unionist. In 1957 Gardiner became the first director of the School of Commerce at Memorial University and served as president of the Memorial University Teachers Association. He was founding chair of the Newfoundland Medicare Commission and sat on several boards of directors, including BRINCO and CFLCo.

Goff, Brian M. (1947-) b St. John's. Journalist. A broadcast journalist, Goff worked for CJON Radio and Television before serving as press attaché to J.R. Smallwood in the 1969 Liberal leadership contest. He had the same role in 1970 with F.D. Moores during his campaign for the PC leadership. Goff moved to Ontario where he ran unsuccessfully for the federal Liberals in 1974.

Granger, Charles R.M. (1912-1995) b Catalina. Trade unionist, politician. MP (L-Grand Falls-White Bay-Labrador) 1958-66; (L-Bonavista-Twillingate) 1967-68. MHA (L-Gander) 1966-67. Cabinet position (federal): Minister Without Portfolio 1967-68. Cabinet position (provincial): Labrador Affairs

1966-67. Granger worked for the Fishermen's Protective Union and was president 1948-49. From 1953 to 1957 Granger was executive assistant to J.W. Pickersgill MP (L-Bonavista-Twillingate) before being elected to the House of Commons. He resigned in 1966 to become an MHA, but returned to federal politics a year later. He was defeated in the 1968 federal election and became vice-president of Shaheen Natural Resources.

Greene, James J. (1928-   ) b St. John's. Lawyer, politician. MHA (PC-St. John's East) 1959-66. Leader of the Opposition 1960-66.

Gwyn, Richard (1934-   ) b England. Journalist, author. Gwyn moved to Newfoundland from England with his first wife, Sandra Fraser, in the mid-1950s. Shortly thereafter, he began working as a journalist in Ottawa. He became a highly successful political reporter and foreign correspondent, and an author of numerous books including *Smallwood: The Unlikely Revolutionary* (1969), *The Northern Magus: Pierre Trudeau and Canadians* (1980), and *John A: The Man Who Made Us. John A. Macdonald, 1815-1891* (2007). He started the annual Winterset Award for Newfoundland writing to commemorate the life of Sandra Fraser.

Hibbs, Henry (Harry) (1942-1989) b Bell Island. Musician. Hibbs began his career as a musician after an industrial accident in Toronto, and in 1968 began performing as a singer and accordionist. His best-selling first album, *Harry Hibbs at the Caribou Club*, led to a weekly television program in Ontario that ran until 1976. The recipient of a Maple Award (precursor of the Juno Awards) for Best Folk Artist in 1972, Hibbs produced 19 albums. In 2001 he was posthumously awarded the Dr. Helen Creighton Lifetime Achievement Award by the East Coast Music Association. Hibbs is credited with popularizing Atlantic Canadian folk music and for making a major contribution to Newfoundland music, particularly among expatriate Newfoundlanders.

Hickey, Thomas V. (1933-   ) b Outer Cove. Social worker, businessman, politician. MHA (PC-St. John's East Extern) 1966-86. Municipal councilor Placentia 1962-66. Cabinet positions: Social Services 1962, 1979-85; Provincial Affairs 1972-73; Transportation and Communications 1973-74; Tourism 1974-78; Rehabilitation and Recreation 1978-79. In 1966 Hickey was one of three PCs elected to the House of Assembly. He held several ministerial posts in both the Moores and Peckford governments. Hickey lost a federal by-election in 1987 to Jack Harris (NDP-St. John's East).

Hickman, T. Alexander (1925-) b Grand Bank. Lawyer, politician, magistrate. MHA (L- Burin) 1966-69; (PC- Burin) 1969-75. Cabinet positions: Justice 1966-69, 1972-79; Health 1968-69; Intergovernmental Affairs 1975-78; Finance 1978-79; Education 1979. In 1969 Hickman left cabinet to contest the

Liberal leadership, offering himself as an alternative to Crosbie and Smallwood. He finished third and joined the PC party. He held numerous cabinet positions in the Moores and Peckford governments until his appointment as Chief Justice (Trials Division) of the Supreme Court of Newfoundland.

Higgins, James (1913-1974) b St. John's. Lawyer, politician, magistrate. MHA (PC-St. John's East) 1941-59. Municipal councilor St. John's 1949-61; deputy mayor 1953-61. Higgins left the PC party in 1959 to form the United Newfoundland Party (UNP). He was defeated as a UNP candidate for St. John's East in the 1959 provincial election by PC J.J. Greene. After being defeated as a Liberal in the 1962 election, Higgins was appointed to the Supreme Court of Newfoundland.

Hodder, Walter H. (1909-1993) b Ireland's Eye. Educator, politician. MHA (L-LaPoile) 1962-71. A mayor of Channel-Port aux Basques, in 1962 Hodder was elected as an MHA.

Horwood, Harold A. (1923-2006) b St. John's. Trade unionist, politician, author, journalist. MHA (L-Labrador) 1949-51. In 1946, Horwood helped organize St. John's longshoremen while co-founding the literary magazine, *Protocol*. He aided the pro-Confederation campaign with Canada and was elected to the House of Assembly in 1949, but did not re-offer in 1951. Horwood turned to journalism and wrote columns critical of the Smallwood government for *The Evening Telegram*. His first novel, *Tomorrow Will Be Sunday* (1966), won a national Beta Sigma Phi award for best novel of the year. Horwood moved to Nova Scotia in 1977 and co-founded the Canadian Writers Union.

Jamieson, Donald C. (1921-1986) b St. John's. Radio broadcaster, businessman, politician. MP (L-Burin-Burgeo) 1966-79. MHA (L-Bellevue) 1979-80. Cabinet positions: Defence Production 1968-69; Supply and Services 1969; Transportation 1969-72; Regional Economic Expansion (DREE) 1972-75; Trade and Commerce 1975-76; External Affairs 1976-79. Jamieson became a popular radio personality in Newfoundland during the Second World War. He favored economic union with the US during the National Convention 1946-48. He and Geoffrey Stirling, who had also campaigned for US economic union, founded radio station CJON in 1951, which quickly expanded throughout the province. They established CJON-TV (NTV) in 1955 with Jamieson as president. He won a federal by-election in 1966 and became an influential voice for Newfoundland in Ottawa. Jamieson replaced William Rowe as provincial Liberal leader in 1979, but failed to defeat the governing PCs in the election that year.

Jones, Eric S. (1914-1982) b Fogo. Educator, magistrate, politician. MHA (L-Burin) 1956-66; (L-Fogo) 1966-71. Cabinet positions: Highways 1964-69;

Finance 1969-71. Jones replaced H.R.V. Earle as minister of finance when Earle resigned from cabinet to support T.A. Hickman for leadership of the Liberal Party.

Joy, Clifton J. (1922-1994) b Port au Port. Physician, politician. MHA (L-Harbour Main) 1962-66. Joy practiced medicine in St. John's prior to his election as an MHA in 1962. During his term in office, Joy wrote an analysis of the state of child health in the province and recommended establishing a children's hospital – the Janeway Child Health Centre. He served as acting chief of staff at the Janeway from 1966 to1968.

Keough, William J. (1913-1971) b St. John's. Journalist, cooperatives organizer, politician. National Convention delegate, St. George's, 1946-48. MHA (L-St. George's-Port au Port) 1949-56; (L-St. George's) 1956-71. Cabinet positions: Natural Resources 1949; Fisheries and Cooperatives 1949-56; Mines and Resources 1956-67; Labour 1967-71. An organizer in the cooperative movement, Keough became one of the few prominent Roman Catholics to actively support Confederation. He was honored with a state funeral upon his death in 1971.

Kitchen, Hubert W. (1927-   ) b Harbour Grace. Educator, politician. MHA (L-Harbour Grace) 1971-72; (L-St. John's West) 1977-79; (L-St. John's Centre) 1989-96. Cabinet positions: Education and Youth 1971-72; Finance 1989-92; Health 1992-96. Kitchen first became involved in politics as a PC and was elected president of the party in 1968. After losing his campaign for leadership of the PCs in 1970, Kitchen joined the Liberals and was elected as an MHA in 1971. He was defeated in the 1972 election, but was victorious in 1977. He lost in 1979, but after being elected once again in 1989 was appointed minister of finance.

Lane, C. Maxwell (1905-1992) b Salvage. Educator, magistrate, politician. MHA (L-White Bay North) 1956-62; (L-Trinity North) 1963-71. Cabinet positions: Public Welfare 1961-63; Fisheries 1963-67; Mines and Agricultural Resources 1967-68. Premier Smallwood selected Lane to lead two key government-sponsored trade unions, starting with the Newfoundland Federation of Fishermen (1951-61). After the government broke the International Woodworkers of America (IWA) strike in 1959, Lane was chosen to lead a replacement union, the Newfoundland Brotherhood of Woodworkers (1959-61). He resigned from both organizations upon being appointed to cabinet in 1961.

Lewis, Philip J. (1900-1985) b Holyrood. Lawyer, politician. MHA (L-Harbour Main) 1928-32; (United Newfoundland Party-Placentia & St. Mary's) 1932-34;

(L-Harbour Main-Bell Island) 1951-56; (L-Harbour Main) 1956-71. Cabinet positions: Minister Without Portfolio 1928-32, 1951-71. Lewis was one of the few post-Confederation MHAs with experience in government, as he had served in the administrations of Richard Squires and Frederick Alderdice. He supported a return to Responsible Government in 1948, but was elected as a Liberal in 1951.

Maloney, Aidan J. (1920-　) b King's Cove. Businessman, civil servant, politician. MHA (L-Ferryland) 1966-71. Cabinet positions: Public Welfare 1966-67; Fisheries 1967-71. Maloney worked in the Department of Fisheries prior to entering politics. He resigned from cabinet in 1971 to head the Canadian Saltfish Corporation.

McGrath, James M. (1902-1975) b St. John's. Physician, medical officer, politician. MHA (L-St. Mary's) 1956-71. Cabinet positions: Health 1956-67; Finance 1967-68. McGrath established the Avalon Health Unit at Harbour Grace, and in 1943 was appointed deputy minister of health. McGrath became minister of health after his election to the House of Assembly in 1956.

Moores, Alexander D. (1919-　) b Blackhead. Businessman, politician. MHA (L-Harbour Grace) 1966-71. Moores worked in the banking sector in Newfoundland and Montreal before becoming general manager of Northeastern Fish Industries in Bay Roberts in 1948. He also served as president of the Newfoundland Fisheries Association starting in 1961. Moores served five years in the House of Assembly, but continued working for Northereastern Fish Industries during and after his term in office.

Moores, Frank D. (1933-2005) b Carbonear. Businessman, politician. MP (PC-Bonavista-Trinity-Conception) 1968-71. MHA (PC-Humber West) 1971-79. Moores worked for Northeastern Fisheries Ltd. in Harbour Grace, and was elected as an MP in 1968. He won the leadership of the Newfoundland PC Party in 1970, which brought the Liberals to a virtual draw in the October 1971 campaign. This political stalemate resulted in another election in March 1972, in which the PCs were victorious. Moores served as premier until 1979. He became a senior organizer in the successful campaign of Brian Mulroney for leadership of the federal PCs in 1983, and relocated to Ottawa to establish a consulting firm.

Moss, William (1911-1969) b Princeton. Mariner. Moss, one of Newfoundland's best-known sealing captains, made three unsuccessful attempts at federal and provincial politics as a PC. He died at sea while commanding a sealing ship.

Mowat, Farley (1921-　) b Ontario. Author, conservationist. A biologist and writer, Mowat lived in Burgeo 1961-67. Among his best-known writings about

Newfoundland are *The Boat Who Wouldn't Float* (1969) and *A Whale for the Killing* (1972).

Murphy, Anthony J. (Ank) (1913-1996) b St. John's. Businessman, politician. MHA (PC-St. John's Centre) 1962-79. Cabinet positions: Labrador Affairs 1972-73; Provincial Affairs 1972-73, 1975-76; Social Services 1973-75; Environment 1975-79; Consumer Affairs 1976-79. Leader of the Opposition 1970.

Myrden, Gerald H. (1922-   ) b Nova Scotia. Businessman, politician, civil servant. MHA (L-St. Barbe South) 1966-69; (Independent L-St. Barbe South) 1969-71. Myrden moved to Corner Brook as a child and later owned a construction company. He was elected as a Liberal in 1966, but joined J.C. Crosbie and C.K. Wells as an Independent Liberal following the victory of J.R. Smallwood for leadership of the Liberal Party in 1969. He left politics in 1971, and, from the mid-1970s until his retirement, worked for the Federal Business Development Bank.

Neary, Stephen A. (1925-1996) b Bell Island. Miner, trade unionist, politician. MHA (L-Bell Island) 1962-75; (L-LaPoile) 1975-85. Cabinet positions: Minister Without Portfolio 1968-69; Public Welfare 1969-70; Social Services and Rehabilitation 1970-72. Leader of the Opposition 1982-84. Neary was secretary-treasurer of the Newfoundland Federation of Labour during the IWA loggers' strike in 1959, and ran unsuccessfully for the NDP that year in Bell Island. He won the district as a Liberal in 1962 and subsequently held a number of cabinet positions. He was defeated by William Rowe for leadership of the Liberals in 1977, but in 1982 he became interim leader following the defeat of Leonard Stirling in a general election. In 1987, he ran unsuccessfully in a federal by-election in St. John's East.

Noel, Nathaniel S. (1920-2006) b St. John's. Lawyer, magistrate, politician. MHA (L-St. John's North) 1966-71. Noel supported T.A. Hickman for leadership of the Liberals against J.R. Smallwood in 1969. He did not run for re-election and was appointed to the Supreme Court of Newfoundland (Trials Division) in 1973.

Nolan, John A. (1930-2004) b St. John's. Journalist, politician. MHA (L-St. John's South) 1966-71; (L-Conception Bay South) 1975-79. Cabinet positions: Supply and Services 1970-71; Economic Development 1971-72. Nolan was a popular broadcast journalist with CJON Radio and Television prior to his election to the House of Assembly in 1966. He returned to broadcasting following his defeat in 1971, but was re-elected to the House in 1975. He was appointed a citizenship judge after again losing his seat in 1979.

Ottenheimer, Gerald R. (1934-1998) b England. Educator, businessman, politician. MHA (PC-St. John's East) 1966-70; (PC-St. Mary's) 1971-75; (PC-Waterford-Kenmount) 1975-88. Cabinet positions: Intergovernmental Affairs 1972, 1985-87; Education 1972-75; Justice 1979-85; Labour 1985; Energy 1987-88. Speaker 1975-79. Leader of the Opposition 1967-70. Senator 1987-98. Ottenheimer won a provincial seat after unsuccessfully running for the federal PCs in St. John's West in the 1965 election. He became Leader of the Opposition in 1967, but in 1970 he resigned this position and his seat in the House of Assembly for undisclosed reasons. He returned to politics a year later and served as Speaker during the Moores years. Ottenheimer then served in numerous cabinet positions in the Peckford government, until his appointment to the Senate in 1987.

Pearson, Lester B. (1897-1972) b Ontario. Diplomat, Prime Minister 1963-68. Leader of the Opposition 1958-63.

Peddle, Ambrose H. (1927-　) b Corner Brook. Businessman, politician, ombudsman. MP (PC-Grand Falls-White Bay-Labrador) 1968-72. MHA (PC-Grand Falls) 1962-66. Peddle was mayor of Windsor until his election as an MHA. After his defeat in 1966, Peddle was elected as an MP for one term. He was appointed provincial ombudsman in 1975 and held the post until Premier Wells abolished the position in 1990.

Roberts, Edward M. (1940-　) b St. John's. Lawyer, politician, lieutenant governor. MHA (L-White Bay North) 1966-75; (L-Strait of Belle Isle) 1975-85; (L-Nascopie) 1992-96. Cabinet positions: Public Welfare 1968-69; Health 1969-72; Justice and Attorney General 1992-96. Leader of the Opposition 1972-77. Roberts worked for MP J.W. Pickersgill (L-Bonavista-Twillingate) and Premier Smallwood before being elected to the House of Assembly in 1966. He succeeded Smallwood as Liberal leader in 1972, and defeated the former premier in a leadership convention in 1974. Smallwood formed the Liberal Reform Party, which is credited with splitting Liberal support in the 1975 general election and allowing the re-election of the PC Party. In 1977 Roberts lost the leadership to W.N. Rowe. He retired from politics in 1985, but returned in 1992 and became a senior cabinet minister in the Wells government. He served as lieutenant governor 2002-08.

Rowe, Frederick W. (1912-1994) b Lewisporte. Educator, civil servant, politician, senator, author. MHA (L-Labrador) 1951-56; (L-White Bay South) 1956-66; (L-Grand Falls) 1966-71. Cabinet positions: Mines and Resources 1951-56; Education 1956-59, 1967-71; Highways 1959-64; Finance 1964-67, 1971; Community and Social Development 1967; Labrador Affairs 1967-79. Senator 1971-87. Rowe was deputy minister in the Department of Public Welfare prior to his election to the House of Assembly in 1951. He became one of Premier Smallwood's most trusted cabinet ministers, and served in numerous portfolios until his defeat in 1971. He subsequently published several books.

Rowe, William N. (1942-   ) b Grand Bank. Lawyer, politician, civil servant, radio host, author. MHA (L-White Bay South) 1966-74; (L-Twillingate) 1977-83. Cabinet positions: Minister Without Portfolio 1968; Housing 1968-69; Community and Social Development 1969-71. Leader of the Opposition 1977-79. Son of F.W. Rowe, W.N. Rowe was elected to the House of Assembly in 1966 and two years later became Canada's youngest cabinet minister. Rowe resigned his seat in 1974, but returned to politics in 1977 when he defeated E.M. Roberts in a Liberal leadership convention. Rowe never fought an election as leader, however, as he resigned in early 1979 following his admission that he had leaked documents to the media concerning a police investigation of PC MHA Thomas Farrell. Rowe unsuccessfully contested nominations in the 1980s as a PC at both the federal and provincial levels. He is author of several books, the best known being *Clapp's Rock* (1983). Rowe joined VOCM during the mid-1980s as a radio talk show host, and, in 2004-05, served as the provincial government's representative in Ottawa.

Shaheen, John M. (1915-1985) b United States. Businessman. Shaheen's company, Golden Eagle Refining, built oil refineries in Panama and California prior to establishing a refinery in Holyrood in 1960. Golden Eagle also opened a chain of Golden Eagle gasoline service stations that were subsequently controlled by Ultramar. Shaheen backed a proposed pulp mill and anhydrous ammonia plant at Come By Chance, projects which did not proceed. In 1967, however, his company, Shaheen Natural Resources, announced it would build an oil refinery at Come By Chance. An agreement was reached with the provincial government in 1969 to provide loan guarantees and bridge financing for the project, which was touted as being the world's largest oil refinery. The province's investment led to the resignation of two cabinet ministers, J.C. Crosbie and C.K. Wells. The refinery opened for business in 1973, but it never met initial expectations. High operating costs and a lack of cheap crude oil led to the refinery's closure in 1976, making it the largest bankruptcy in Canadian history. It began operating again in 1987 under new owners.

Shea, Hugh J. (1932-1993) b St. John's. Businessman, politician. MHA (PC-St. John's South) 1971-72. Shea ran unsuccessfully for leadership of the PCs in 1970. In 1971 he won a seat in the House of Assembly as a PC, but left the party to sit as a Liberal after being left out of Premier Moores's cabinet. He ran unsuccessfully as an Independent Liberal in 1972, and suffered two subsequent defeats as a Liberal. Shea then opened a convenience store in St. John's named Shea's Rip-Off, and a take-out restaurant, Hamburger Hell.

Smallwood, Joseph R. (1900-1991) b Gambo. Journalist, trade unionist, author, politician. MHA (L-Bonavista North) 1949-59, 1962-66, (L-St. John's West) 1959-62; (L-Humber West) 1966-71; (L-Placentia East) 1971-72; (L Reform-Twillingate) 1975-77. Premier 1949-72. Cabinet positions: Economic Development 1949-56, 1957-72; Finance 1951; Natural Resources 1952; Education 1959. Smallwood worked as a journalist in New York in the early 1920s and returned to Newfoundland in 1925 as a union organizer. He became involved with the Liberal Party and in 1932 was defeated in a general election. His career as an author began during the 1920-30s, starting with *Coaker of Newfoundland* (1927) and the first two volumes of *The Book of Newfoundland* (1937). He began a newspaper column in the *Daily News* named "The Barrelman," which was subsequently turned into a highly popular radio program. Smallwood's success led to him being elected as a delegate to the National Convention on Newfoundland's future in 1946-48. After leading confederates to victory in 1948, his Liberal Party won Newfoundland's first election as a province of Canada in 1949. Smallwood's 23 years as premier were marked by attempts at industrializing Newfoundland and diversifying its economy. Smallwood hired economist Alfred Valdmanis as director-general of Economic Development in 1950 to establish new industries, using $45 million left from the Commission of Government. The program was largely a failure; Valdmanis resigned in 1954 and was convicted of fraud. During the 1960s Smallwood attempted to build a so-called "third mill" (behind paper mills at Grand Falls and Corner Brook), first at Come By Chance and then in Labrador; these efforts failed until J.C. Doyle agreed to build a linerboard mill in Stephenville. Smallwood signed an agreement with Quebec in 1968 to sell hydroelectric power from Churchill Falls, and also oversaw development of iron ore mines in western Labrador. His hold on power began to slip in 1969 when J.C. Crosbie and C.K. Wells resigned from cabinet and joined the Opposition over government financing of the Come By Chance oil refinery. He announced that a Liberal leadership convention would be held later that year, but decided to run for the position after Crosbie announced his candidacy. Smallwood defeated Crosbie and T.A. Hickman, who both subsequently joined the PCs. Smallwood clung to power when the 1971 election ended in a virtual tie, but soon resigned as Liberal leader and was replaced by E.M. Roberts – who lost the 1972 election. After losing the 1974 Liberal leadership campaign to Roberts, Smallwood led a group of dissidents and established the Liberal Reform Party. This new party won four seats in the 1975 general election, but re-joined the Liberals in 1977. Smallwood resigned from politics that year and returned to writing. He completed the first two volumes of the *Encyclopedia of Newfoundland* during the early 1980s, but had insufficient funds to complete the project. The remaining three volumes were completed by the Joseph R. Smallwood Heritage Foundation.

Smallwood, William R. (1928-2001) b Corner Brook. Lawyer, politician. MHA (L-Green Bay) 1956-71. Son of J.R. Smallwood, W.R. Smallwood was defeated in the 1971 general election and failed in three subsequent attempts at re-election.

Stanfield, Robert (1914-2003) b Nova Scotia. PC Premier of Nova Scotia 1956-67. Leader of the Opposition 1967-76.

Starkes, Harold E.J. (1917-1996) b Nipper's Harbour. Businessman, politician. MHA (L-Lewisporte) 1962-71; (L-Green Bay) 1971-72. Cabinet position: Highways 1969-72. Starkes was mayor of Lewisporte 1958-60 and became president of the Newfoundland Federation of Mayors and Municipalities. He was elected to the House of Assembly 1962-72.

Strickland, Uriah F. (1907-1976) b Hant's Harbour. Educator, mariner, politician. MHA (L-Bonavista South) 1956-59; (L-Trinity South) 1959-71; (L-Trinity North) 1971-72. Cabinet positions: Minister Without Portfolio 1971; Municipal Affairs and Housing 1971-72.

Thoms, James R. (1929-2001) b St. Anthony. Journalist, political assistant, author. Thoms worked as a journalist with CJON Radio and Television, and from 1968 to 1971 was an information officer with the Smallwood government. He joined the *Daily News* in 1971 and remained until it closed in 1984. Thoms returned to CJON (NTV) as a television reporter. He edited numerous books, including volumes three to six of the *Book of Newfoundland*, and the third edition of *A History of Newfoundland* (1972) by D.W. Prowse.

Trudeau, Pierre E. (1919-2000) b Quebec. Prime Minister 1968-79 and 1980-84. Leader of the Opposition 1979-80.

Valdmanis, Alfred A. (1908-1970) b Latvia. Economist, civil servant. Valdmanis was Latvia's Minister of Finance 1938-39 for the country's fascist regime, and during the Second World War he worked closely with both Soviet and Nazi occupiers of the country. He worked as a refugee resettlement coordinator after the war and moved to Canada in 1948. Premier Smallwood appointed him director-general of Economic Development 1950-53 and chairman of the Newfoundland and Labrador Corporation 1951-54. Valdmanis used his Latvian and German connections – and Newfoundland government grants – to launch over a dozen business ventures, most of which either failed prior to being established or collapsed once government funding had been exhausted. These "new industries" included a tannery, a textile mill, a glove factory, a rubber plant, a battery-manufacturing facility, and a chocolate factory. Despite many spectacular failures, some initiatives did prove profitable, including United Cotton Mills and North Star Cement. In the mid-1950s Valdmanis was convicted of soliciting bribes from German businesses under the guise of Liberal Party campaign contributions.

Vardy, Oliver L. (1906-1980) b Channel. Journalist, politician, civil servant. MHA (L-St. John's West) 1949-51. Cabinet position: Minister Without Portfolio 1950-51. Vardy served a prison sentence in the US during the 1930s. He returned to Newfoundland and, after working as a journalist, was elected to St. John's City Council 1941-49. He was elected as an MHA in 1949 and became parliamentary assistant to Premier Smallwood. After retiring from politics in 1951 he was appointed director of tourist development for the province. When the PCs came to power in 1972 Vardy was charged with fraud, bribery and breach of trust for activities related to funding the Stephenville linerboard mill. He fled to Panama and successfully fought extradition to Canada.

Wells, Clyde K. (1937-   ) b Buchans Junction. Lawyer, politician, magistrate. MHA (L-Humber East) 1966-68; (Independent L-Humber East) 1968-71; (L-Windsor-Buchans) 1987-89; (L-Bay of Islands) 1989-96. Premier 1989-96. Cabinet positions: Labour 1966-68; Intergovernmental Affairs and Native Policy 1989-96. Wells was appointed to cabinet in 1966 prior to winning a seat in the House of Assembly. He resigned from the Liberal caucus and sat as an Independent Liberal 1968-71 over government financial guarantees provided to the Come By Chance oil refinery. He was elected leader of the Liberals in 1987 and won a seat in a by-election. Although he led the Liberals to power in 1989, Wells lost his bid to unseat PC Lynn Verge in Humber East. MHA Edward Joyce (L-Bay of Islands) resigned and Wells won the subsequent by-election. He resigned as premier in 1996 and in 1998 was appointed to the Newfoundland and Labrador Court of Appeal. He became Chief Justice in 1999.

Wornell, Abel, C. (1914-2004) b Greenspond. Businessman, politician, author. MHA (L-Hermitage) 1966-71. Prior to being elected, Wornell published two books of poetry, and later in life won several Newfoundland literary awards.

Wulff, Lee (1905-1991) b United States. Sports fisherman, film producer, author. A filmmaker on sports fishing, Wulff was invited by the Commission of Government to Newfoundland in the late 1930s. He operated fishing camps on the Northern Peninsula and produced numerous films on fishing and hunting in Newfoundland.

Terms of Endearment

Bonavista Boss: Ross Barbour
Croppy: Fred Rowe
Dancing Dollars: John Nolan
Me 'n Ned: Ank Murphy

Moxon Roberts: Edward Roberts
O.L.F.: Joseph R. Smallwood
Silica: William Callahan
Wabana Warbler: Stephen Neary

Index – by Topic

Great New Industries

In the House

Joey

Juvenile Outharbor Delights

Liberals and Pea Seas

News and Propaganda

Policing

Resettlement and Rural Life

Roads, Rails and Water

Schools

Spy Thriller